THE ILLUSTRATED HISTORY OF THE KINGS & QUEENS OF BRITAIN

... potens adquisita ...
ā de bello ubi triumpharat fundavit. Regnavit ānis xxi. 7 āplius

trem ei recepere ...
Aula Westm̄ cōstruxit. Tandem sagitta p'cuss' regnauit ā...

enricus vir potens 7 sapiens Juravit leges sc̄i Edwardi ...

Iste Stephanus miles strenuissim' omnib; dieb,

THE ILLUSTRATED HISTORY OF THE KINGS & QUEENS OF BRITAIN

A COMPREHENSIVE VISUAL ENCYCLOPEDIA OF EVERY KING AND QUEEN OF BRITAIN, FROM SAXON TIMES THROUGH THE TUDORS TO TODAY

CHARLES PHILLIPS

LORENZ BOOKS

CONTENTS

INTRODUCTION

On 2 June 1953, Elizabeth, eldest daughter of the late King George VI, rode in the golden coach of state through London streets, from Buckingham Palace to Westminster Abbey, to be crowned Queen Elizabeth II in a ceremony of the utmost gravity and splendour.

The young queen made a solemn series of vows, among other things, 'To govern the Peoples of the United Kingdom of Great Britain and Northern Ireland, Canada, Australia, New Zealand, the Union of South Africa, Pakistan and Ceylon, and of [her] Possessions and other Territories to any of them belonging or pertaining, according to their respective laws and customs', to 'Cause Law and Justice, in Mercy, to be executed in all [her] judgements', and to 'Maintain and preserve inviolably the settlement of the Church of England, and the doctrine, worship, discipline and government thereof, by law established in England'. Then, dressed in a simple linen dress, having removed her ermine-trimmed crimson velvet robes, she was anointed with holy oil on the palms of both hands, on the breast and on the crown of the head in commemoration of the coronation of the Biblical King Solomon of Israel. 'As Solomon was anointed king by Zadok the priest and Nathan the prophet, so be thou anointed, blessed, and consecrated Queen over the Peoples, whom the Lord thy God hath given thee to rule and govern.'

Below: William the Conqueror began building the White Tower in 1066. It became a part of the Tower of London.

Above: Edward the Confessor's body is carried to Westminster Abbey, in a detail from the Bayeux Tapestry (1082).

The pomp and splendour of the coronation celebrated the queen's pre-eminence and her elevation far above her subjects; throughout the order of service she was referred to as 'Her Majesty'. At the same time, the resonant liturgical language emphasized that the queen's status as God's chosen ruler laid upon her a sacred duty to be the faithful servant of her subjects.

NINE CENTURIES OF HISTORY

Elizabeth II's coronation was rich in royal history and tradition. Performed in the abbey church established at Westminster by King Edward the Confessor (1042–66), it closely followed the order for coronation in the 14th-century *Liber regalis*, which was itself derived from the rite of ordination and coronation devised by St Dunstan, Archbishop of Canterbury, for the elevation to the throne of King Edgar at Bath on 11 May 973. At Edgar's ceremony a choir sang the anthem 'Zadok the Priest'. The anthem has been used at every subsequent coronation, and since the crowning of George II, in 1727, in the celebrated setting by German-born court composer George Frideric Handel.

At the moment of her anointment, Elizabeth sat in 'King Edward's Chair', the throne built *c.*1300 by Edward I to contain the ancient Pictish-Scottish royal 'Stone of Scone', which was supposedly used for the anointing of Scottish rulers from the time of Fergus Mor (AD498-501). (In 1953 the coronation chair still contained the 'Stone of Scone', but the stone was subsequently removed. It was returned to Scotland on 15 November 1996.) By receiving the blessing of God and the acclamation of her people in the abbey, Elizabeth II took her place in a line of monarchs stretching right back to King Harold II (1066). Every king and queen since Harold has been crowned in Westminster Abbey except Edward V and Edward VIII, neither of whom found time to be crowned at all in their brief reigns.

Above: Dunstan of Canterbury (AD924–88) was a monastic reformer as well as the creator of royal ordination–coronation rites.

Above: The legitimate son of Henry I (1100–35) died in 1120. Henry's nephew and daughter disputed the succession.

DEFENDERS OF THE FAITH

Major changes intervened in the long years from 1066 to 1953, not least the introduction of the royal oath to preserve the Church of England. From the time of King Henry VIII, who established the Church of England in 1534, the English sovereign was 'Defender of the Faith'. Then, beginning in 1688 when the English Parliament replaced the Catholic Stuart king, James II, with James's eldest daughter, Mary, and her husband, the Protestant William of Orange, kings and queens crowned in Westminster Abbey had to vow to 'Maintain in the United Kingdom the Protestant Reformed Religion established by law'.

William and Mary came to the throne at the invitation of parliament, which interfered in the dynastic succession to remove a Catholic king and so safeguard the Protestant faith in England. At their coronation, they swore therefore to 'Rule in line with the statutes of Parliament'. William and Mary were king and queen in a 'constitutional monarchy' wherein the real power lay with elected MPs rather than with leading members of an hereditary royal family. In the 300-odd years since William and Mary took these vows, kings and queens have adapted to being subject to parliament, to being figureheads for the state, to reigning rather than ruling. Yet in the same period, and particularly from around 1850 onwards as Britain created the greatest empire known to history, the prestige of the monarchy, and the public pomp and ceremony associated with the crown, rose ever higher.

Below: Built by Edward IV in 1475, St George's Chapel, within Windsor Castle, has been the burial place of many kings.

By 1953 the empire was being dismantled but its successor, the Commonwealth of Nations, was thriving; Elizabeth's coronation procession included state vehicles bearing heads of government from many Commonwealth countries. Subsequently, Elizabeth II had to adapt the monarchy to fast-changing times, with unprecedented levels of television and press scrutiny. As Britain's longest-reigning and longest-lived monarch, she has wisely maintained the ceremony associated with earlier times, as seen in four meticulously planned and highly successful royal occasions of the 21st century: the celebrations for the wedding of Prince William and Kate Middleton (2011), the Diamond Jubilee (2012), the Queen's 90th birthday (2016) and the Platinum Jubilee (2022).

THE RIGHT TO RULE

The English word 'king' derives from the Germanic *cyning/kuning*, which was imported by Anglo-Saxon raiders who sailed across the North Sea to invade Britain in the 5th and 6th centuries AD. In modern usage, the word usually means a supreme ruler, with sovereign authority over an independent state.

Britain certainly had 'kings' in the sense of supreme rulers before Anglo-Saxon times. The first known by name are those who faced the Roman invasions of 55–54BC and then AD43, tribal leaders such as Cassivellaunus and Caratacus, rulers of the Catuvellauni of southern England.

In this period and throughout the era of the early Anglo-Saxons, kings were warrior leaders who held power primarily on the basis of force. When a warrior-king died, his kingdom often died with him, as there was little, if any, belief in a hereditary right to rule.

However, very slowly the idea of an inherited right to rule began to develop: not necessarily through a dynasty of blood relations, but at least by means of a king's designation of his chosen successor. This introduced the idea of a ruler's legitimacy, so that force of arms alone was no longer all.

Below: Mary Queen of Scots was queen at the age of seven days in 1542, but was forced to abdicate, aged 24, in 1567.

By the 7th century, Christianity was taking root in Britain. As the religion spread after the conversion in *c.* AD600 of King Aethelbert of Kent, the first Anglo-Saxon monarch to become Christian, so the idea developed of divine election. Kings were presented to their subjects as God's chosen instruments, with a special capacity to bring God's blessing to the kingdom and its people. As the Christian God was King of Heaven, bringing justice and showering blessings on the needy, so the king on earth brought similar if less glorious benefits to his people. Kings were, like priests, servants of the Lord: the ordination-coronation in 973 of King Edgar, in which he was anointed with holy oil, brought out this point explicitly.

Centuries later, it was still a key part of Elizabeth II's ordination ceremony in 1953. 'O Lord and heavenly Father, the exalter of the humble and the strength of thy chosen, who by anointing with Oil didst of old make and consecrate kings, priests, and prophets, to teach and govern thy people Israel: Bless and sanctify thy chosen servant Elizabeth, who by our office and ministry is now to be anointed with this Oil and consecrated Queen.'

THE FAERIE QUEENE

On 30 November 1601 Elizabeth II's revered predecessor and namesake Elizabeth I made a celebrated speech to a representative group of MPs. She was 68 years old, and had been on the throne for 43 years.

As Elizabeth drew towards the end of a reign of magnificent achievements for her country, a reign that would give its name to the 'Elizabethan age', she was popularly and officially revered as the 'Virgin Queen', 'married' to her country and tied to her people by bonds of love and gratitude. Her words that day celebrated these bonds and came to be known as her 'golden speech'. She declared, 'There is no jewel, be it of never so rich a price, which I set before this jewel: I mean your love. For I do esteem it more than any treasure or riches ... I have cause to wish nothing more than to content the subject and that is a duty which I owe.

Above: Henry VIII (1509–47) ruled through council and other instruments of government, but his will was not to be crossed.

Below: Mother to her people. Elizabeth I (1558–1603), who never married, was promoted as a Protestant 'Madonna'.

Neither do I desire to live longer days than I may see your prosperity and that is my only desire.'

The relationship between queen and subjects celebrated in these memorable words was like that of a mother and her loyal offspring: a connection sustained by deep feelings of love and duty. The queen loved and was loved: her behaviour was bound by her sense of duty to her subjects and to God, whose chosen instrument of government she was.

The speech was, of course, propaganda: it represented an idealized image of Elizabeth's interaction with her subjects and government through parliament. Nonetheless, it captured the romance of the Elizabethan age, of years in which men such as Sir Francis Drake carried the name of England and her queen to far-flung corners of the world, and in which the poet Edmund Spenser immortalized the queen in Gloriana, heroine of his epic *The Faerie Queene*.

If the relationship of the monarch with MPs and the people could be seen as a chaste love affair at the close of Elizabeth's reign, it was one that soured quickly under the strain of attempts by Elizabeth's Stuart successors – James I and his son Charles I – to rule with absolute authority.

Above: Divine right. In 1598 James VI of Scots (later James I of England) declared that kings were instruments of God's will.

Below: Return of the House of Stuart. Eleven years after Charles I's execution, Charles II regained the crown in 1660.

THE AGE OF THE BARONS

From the time of England's Anglo-Saxon kingdoms, monarchs sought to establish and extend their authority through the rule of the king's law. To this end the Anglo-Saxon kings relied on the support of the king's council or Witan. This body, which consisted of leading nobles and churchmen, was summoned by the king to advise him, to approve new laws, to attest royal grants of land and to back him when confronting rebels.

The Witan legitimized the king's actions, his rule and even his accession: in theory, members of the Witan were responsible for electing the king, although in practice this was a matter of approving a *fait accompli*. Even though the role and person of Anglo-Saxon monarchs remained to a large extent in the Germanic tradition of king as warrior-leader, the king's power was stabilized by the role of the Witan.

From the 11th century onwards, the Witan's successor, the *commune concilium* of Anglo-Norman kings, performed the same role: the king ruled with full authority, given the consent of his barons. These men, the principal landowners in England, were formally bound to the monarch in a subordinate position through the ties of the feudal system.

Above: *James Thornhill's painting at Greenwich of George I glorifies the triumph of the Protestant succession.*

A CHARTER OF LIBERTIES

In the 13th century, the barons asserted their power in the face of abuses of royal authority, forcing the agreement of King John to the Magna Carta, a charter guaranteeing the 'liberties' of leading subjects, in 1215. Henry I, King Stephen and Henry II had all issued charters, but these had been granted by royal will. The Magna Carta was the first charter imposed upon the king by barons threatening civil war. It contained a clause empowering a baronial council of 25 men to take up arms against the king, should he fail to abide by the agreed terms.

In the reign of King John's son, Henry III, the barons were increasingly angered by the king's reliance on French advisers, following his marriage to Eleanor of Provence, and imposed significant limits on royal power by forcing Henry to agree to the Provisions of Oxford in 1258. Under this agreement, a privy council of 15 members, appointed by the barons, was established to control government.

Henry later renounced the Provisions, leading to a civil war in which he was briefly deposed and power passed into the hands of the nobleman Simon de Montfort. While in power, in 1263-5, de Montfort called a widely representative governmental council, which in addition to clerics and barons included two knights from each shire and two burgesses from each borough. Henry III's son, Prince Edward, defeated de Montfort in 1265 at Evesham and subsequently ruled with great authority as King Edward I. Yet even he was reliant on the support of a council of advisers, principally to approve taxation to fund his ferocious military campaigns against the Scots and Welsh.

Below: Venetian master Antonio Canaletto (1697–1768) celebrates Westminster Abbey, scene of coronations since 1066.

THE RISE OF PARLIAMENT

At around this time the council began to be called 'parliament' (from the Old French *parlement*, 'a talk'). Edward I summoned combined meetings of the *Magnum Concilium* ('Major Council'), which was made up mainly of churchmen and magnates and the *Curia Regis* ('Royal Court') of lay advisers. Some meetings of the *Curia Regis* began to be known as the *Concilium Regis in Parliamento* ('Royal Council in Parliament'). To some meetings – around one in every seven – Edward called knights and burgesses. The meeting in 1295 is generally labelled the 'Model Parliament' and identified as the first representative English parliament. In addition to magnates and leading churchmen, it included representatives of lesser clergy, pairs of knights from each county, two burgesses from every borough and two citizens from every city.

Thereafter, for some 400 years, the king of England ruled through parliament. He could call it and dismiss it at will. Members of parliament were by no means independent of royal power – and individuals might be imprisoned or put to death if they overstepped the mark.

Only in the reign of Charles I, the second successive ruler of the House of Stuart to seek to rule with absolute

Above: George IV acted as Prince Regent during the illness of his father George III who reigned for nearly 60 years.

power, did parliament present itself as an equal player in its relationship with the king. A 'Grand Remonstrance' passed by MPs on 22 November 1641, presented a long list of the King's failings in government – and for the first time made it clear that parliament could remove a king who was guilty of abuses of power. The scene was set for the civil war, Charles's execution, the abolition of the monarchy and England's brief experiment with republicanism.

Within 50 years came the establishment, in 1688, of the constitutional monarchy, in which the king and queen were subject to the will of MPs.

THE ROYAL COURT

From at least the time of Henry I, when the oldest surviving account of a king's household was written, the royal court was at the centre of government. The chamberlain and the treasurer were key officials who took responsibility for the king's living chambers and finances. The chancellor was in charge of the king's chapel, his scribes and the royal seal, which was used as a mark of authority on proclamations and other documents. Royal household positions included the butler, cooks, grooms and the bearer of the king's bed. A standing army, consisting of household cavalry and infantry, accompanied the court. In the medieval period the court was often on the move as the king maintained his visibility throughout his territories, although from as early as Henry I's reign, Westminster began to be increasingly established as the centre of government. It was only from the late 17th century, with the gradual establishment of a constitutional monarchy, that the court began to be eclipsed by parliament as the centre of self-advancement and political intrigue.

This process has continued and the court in the 21st century has a ceremonial rather than a political importance. The celebrations for Queen Victoria's Diamond Jubilee on 20 June 1897, marking 60 years of her reign, attracted attention from all over the British Empire. Similarly, since Elizabeth II is Head of the Commonwealth, the events surrounding the Diamond and Platinum Jubilees of her reign in June 2012 and 2022 were planned as international celebrations. Even today the royal court retains a significant role in national life, not least as a setting for state receptions and formal dinners for visiting politicians and dignitaries, and in the honours system as the arena in which knighthoods, MBEs, OBEs and other rewards for national service are bestowed.

Above: Victoria, the first royal to celebrate her Diamond Jubilee, with Edward VII, George V and Edward VIII as a baby.

Below: The Queen and other members of the royal family at the wedding of Prince Charles and Camilla Parker-Bowles.

THE MONARCHS

This list of monarchs names the kings and queens of Britain from the time of the ancient rulers of England and Scotland to the present day.

Much of the monarchy's authority and prestige derives from its ancient roots, from the centuries of historical continuity celebrated in genealogical and dynastic tables. Yet there are countless examples of force of arms and political manoeuvring intervening in dynastic or designated succession. In 1066, Duke William of Normandy famously had to enforce his claim that he was the designated successor of King Edward the Confessor in the face of several rival claims, including that of Harold Godwine, Earl of Wessex, who had himself declared King Harold II and was crowned on the very day after Edward the Confessor's death. William's claim triumphed at the Battle of Hastings.

The great Scottish national hero Robert the Bruce killed his chief rival to the succession, John Comyn, before having himself crowned King Robert I of Scots. Richard III of England occupied the throne at the expense of his uncrowned nephew, the 12-year-old King Edward V, whom Richard almost certainly had murdered in the Tower of London. King Henry VII won the English crown in battle against King Richard III.

Throughout these and many other upheavals, the theory of dynastic succession with God's blessing was maintained and all these kings – usurpers or murderers as they might be – laid claim to a dynastic link and were anointed as God's chosen servants on the throne. Henry IV, a usurper, brought an innovation to the coronation in an attempt to legitimize his rule. His ordination was the first to use holy oil reputedly given to Saint Thomas à Becket by the Virgin Mary.

KINGS AND QUEENS OF SCOTLAND (TO 1603)

THE HOUSE OF MACALPINE

Kenneth I mac Alpin 841–859
Donald I 859–863
Constantine I 863–877
Aed Whitefoot 877–878
Eochaid 878–889 (joint)
Giric 878–889
Donald II Dasachtach 889–900
Constantine II 900–943
Malcolm I 943–954
Indulf 954–962
Dubh 962–967
Culen 967–971
Kenneth II 971–995
Constantine III 995–997
Kenneth III 997–1005
Malcolm II 1005–1034

THE HOUSE OF DUNKELD

Duncan I 1034–1040
Macbeth 1040–1057
Lulach 1057–1058
Malcolm III Canmore 1058–1093
Donald III 1093–1094
Duncan II 1094
Donald III 1094–1097 (joint)

Below: King David II of Scotland (left) makes peace with King Edward III of England, in 1357.

Above: James IV of Scotland presenting arms to his wife Queen Margaret, daughter of King Henry VII of England.

Edmund 1094–1097 (joint)
Edgar 1097–1107
Alexander I 1107–1124
David I 1124–1153
Malcolm IV the Maiden 1153–1165
William I the Lion 1165–1214
Alexander II 1214–1249
Alexander III 1249–1286
Margaret, Maid of Norway 1286–1290

THE HOUSE OF BALLIOL

John Balliol 1292–1296

THE HOUSE OF BRUCE

Robert I the Bruce 1306–1329
David II 1329–1332, 1338–1371

THE HOUSE OF BALLIOL

Edward Balliol 1332–1336

THE HOUSE OF STEWART

Robert II 1371–1390
Robert III 1390–1406
James I 1406–1437
James II 1437–1460
James III 1460–1488
James IV 1488–1513
James V 1513–1542
Mary, Queen of Scots 1542–1567
James VI 1567–1603

KINGS AND QUEENS OF ENGLAND

THE HOUSE OF WESSEX
Egbert (802–839)
Aethelwulf (839–858)
Aethelbald (858–860)
Aethelbert (860–865/6)
Aethelred I (865/6–871)
Alfred the Great (871–899)
Edward the Elder (899–924/5)
Athelstan (924/5–939)
Edmund I (939–946)
Eadred (946–955)
Eadwig (955–959)
Edgar (959–975)
Edward the Martyr (975–978)
Aethelred II the Unready (978–1013, 1014–1016)
Edmund Ironside (1016)

THE DANISH LINE
Cnut (1016–1035)
Harold I Harefoot (1035–1040)
Harthacnut (1040–1042)

THE HOUSE OF WESSEX, RESTORED
Edward the Confessor (1042–1066)
Harold II (1066)

THE NORMANS
William I the Conqueror (1066–1087)
William II Rufus (1087–1100)
Henry I (1100–1135)
Stephen (1135–1154)

Above: King John goes riding. Hunting was the sport of kings from William I.

THE PLANTAGENETS
Henry II (1154–1189)
Richard I the Lionheart (1189–1199)
John (1199–1216)
Henry III (1216–1272)
Edward I (1272–1307)
Edward II (1307–1327)
Edward III (1327–1377)
Richard II (1377–1399)

THE HOUSE OF LANCASTER
Henry IV (1399–1413)
Henry V (1413–1422)
Henry VI (1422–1461, 1470–1471)

THE HOUSE OF YORK
Edward IV (1461–1470, 1471–1483)
Edward V (1483)
Richard III (1483–1485)

THE HOUSE OF TUDOR
Henry VII (1485–1509)
Henry VIII (1509–1547)
Edward VI (1547–1553)
Lady Jane Grey (1553)
Mary I (1553–1558)
Elizabeth I (1558–1603)

Left: The heraldic badges of Kings Edward III, Richard II and Henry IV from Writhe's Garter Book.

KINGS AND QUEENS OF GREAT BRITAIN

THE HOUSE OF STUART
James I (1603-1625)
Charles I (1625-1649)
Charles II (1660-1685)
James II (1685-1688)
William III and Mary II (1689-1694)
William III (1689-1702)
Anne (1702-1714)

THE HOUSE OF HANOVER
George I (1714-1727)
George II (1727-1760)
George III (1760-1820)
George IV (1820-1830)
William IV (1830-1837)
Victoria (1837-1901)

THE HOUSE OF SAXE-COBURG-GOTHA
Edward VII (1901-1910)

THE HOUSE OF WINDSOR
George V (1910-1936)
Edward VIII (1936)
George VI (1936-1952)
Elizabeth II (1952-)

Below: The Archbishop of Canterbury reverently places the crown on George V's head at the coronation in 1911.

reg
Primus reg

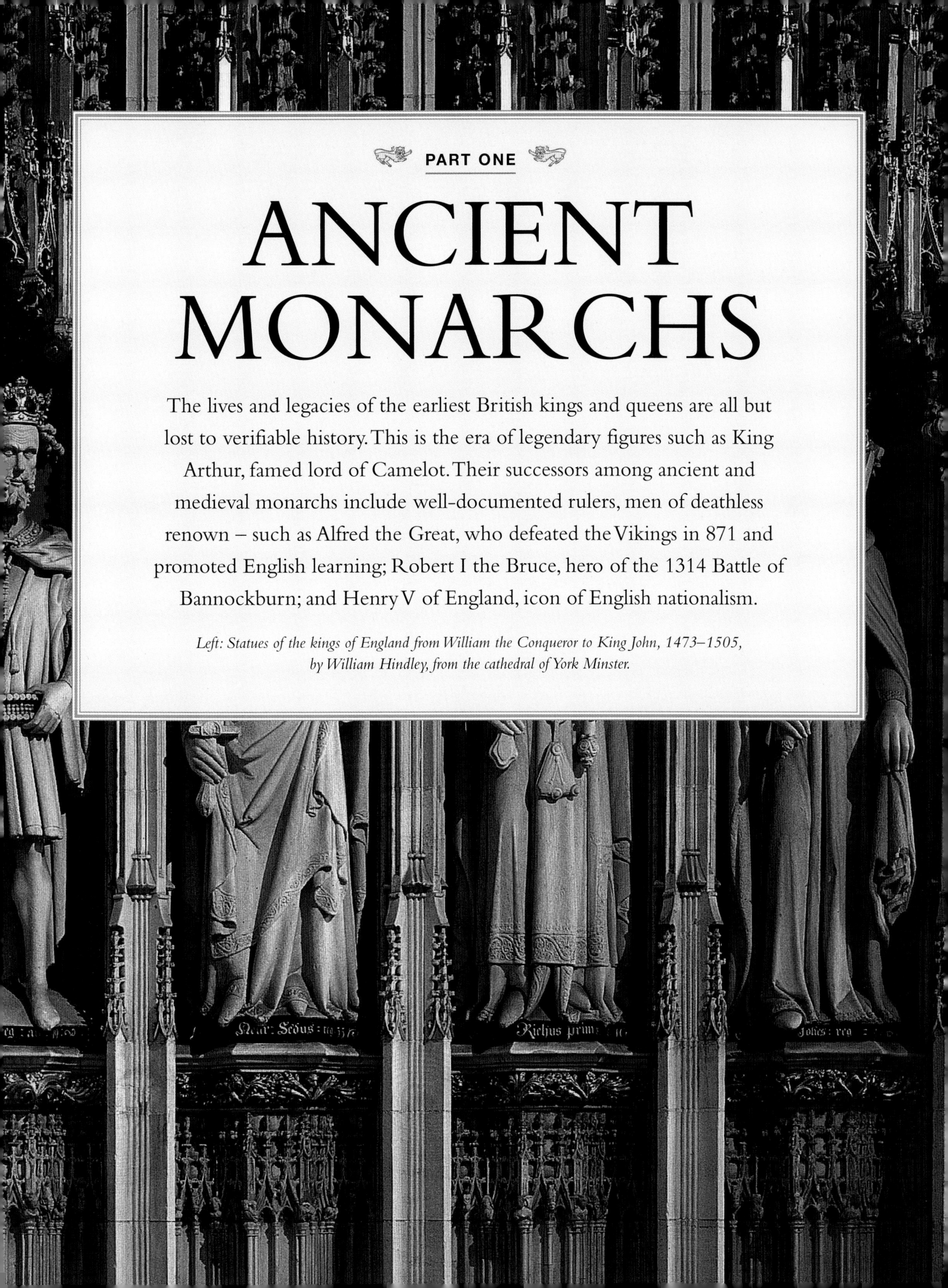

PART ONE

ANCIENT MONARCHS

The lives and legacies of the earliest British kings and queens are all but lost to verifiable history. This is the era of legendary figures such as King Arthur, famed lord of Camelot. Their successors among ancient and medieval monarchs include well-documented rulers, men of deathless renown – such as Alfred the Great, who defeated the Vikings in 871 and promoted English learning; Robert I the Bruce, hero of the 1314 Battle of Bannockburn; and Henry V of England, icon of English nationalism.

Left: Statues of the kings of England from William the Conqueror to King John, 1473–1505, by William Hindley, from the cathedral of York Minster.

HIC RESIDET: HAROL
REX: ANGLORUM:
STIGAN
ARCHI

CHAPTER ONE

BOUDICCA TO STEPHEN

TO 1154

The origins of the British monarchy are shrouded in legend. The 12th-century Welsh churchman and chronicler Geoffrey of Monmouth produced, in his *Historia regum Britanniae* ('History of the Kings of Britain', *c.*1135–9), a chronology of 76 kings of Britain descended from the island's supposed first settlers: Brutus, great-grandson of Aeneas of Troy and his fellow-Trojan Corineus, who gave his name to Cornwall. Geoffrey claimed that he translated his chronicle from 'a very old book in the British tongue', but in truth the *Historia* was a combination of oral history, folklore, legend and the writer's invention.

Monmouth's chronology contains many romantic tales of famous kings, such as King Leir (the original of Shakespeare's *King Lear*), King Coel ('Old King Cole', supposedly the King of the Britons in the 3rd century and the grandfather of the Roman emperor Constantine the Great), and King Lud (said to have given his name to London). Lud's tale brings us to the beginning of true royal history for, according to Geoffrey, Lud was the brother of Cassivellaunus, an historical figure who fought against Julius Caesar's invaders in 54BC. Because of their encounters with the literate Romans, who wrote about them, the kings of this time in south-east England are the first British rulers whose names we know. Among the contemporaries or near-contemporaries of Cassivellaunus were Commius, king of the Atrebates tribe of Hampshire, and Togidubnus (formerly Cogidubnus), king of the Regnenses tribe (Sussex), who built himself the splendid Roman palace at Fishbourne, near Chichester.

Left: In a scene from the Norman Bayeux Tapestry (1082), Harold Godwine is crowned King of England by Archbishop Stigand.

TRIBAL AND ROMAN RULE
TO AD449

When Roman general and dictator Julius Caesar invaded Britain from Gaul in 54BC, he encountered organized resistance under the command of Cassivellaunus, king of the Catuvellauni tribe, which occupied the territory of modern Hertfordshire. Cassivellaunus was probably the most powerful man in Celtic Britain at that time, but he was not the chosen leader of a united country. His tribal state was one of several in fierce competition: rivals in what would become south-east England included the tribes of the Regnenses (occupying Sussex), the Cantiaci (Kent), the Atrebates (Hampshire) and the Trinovantes (Essex).

Above: One of the coins issued in the name of Tasciovanus. His principal mint was at St Albans, the Catuvellauni capital.

Caesar, who famously declared, '*Veni, vidi, vici*' ('I came, I saw, I conquered'), in fact had mixed success on his two invasion raids of Britain in 55BC and 54BC. But, on the second raid, Cassivellunus was unable to prevent his opponent from returning to Gaul with alliance agreements and hostages.

Almost everything we know about British rulers of this period comes from Roman written sources. Cassivellaunus is the first British native whose name is recorded, because Caesar wrote it down. However, coinage also provides some evidence. For example, Cassivellaunus's successor as ruler of the Catuvellauni, Tasciovanus, is the first British ruler whose face and name can be seen on a coin, which was minted *c.*10BC.

The next king of the Catuvellauni, Cunobelinus (ruled AD10–41) was described as *Rex Britannorum* ('King of the Britons') by the Roman historian Suetonius, but like his predecessor Cassivellaunus he was by no means the ruler of a united land, merely the most important and powerful of several rival kings. Nevertheless, he called himself *rex* and after conquering the Essex territories of the Trinovantes ruled almost the whole of south-east England from his capital at Colchester.

Above: Julius Caesar led two seaborne invasions of Britain in 55–54BC. Both times he landed on Deal Beach in Kent.

KING LEAR

One of the legendary British kings recorded by Geoffrey of Monmouth is King Leir, whose story, known from British and Irish folklore, was used by William Shakespeare as the basis for his great tragedy *King Lear.*

Geoffrey of Monmouth recounted that Leir ruled for 60 years and that, in the course of his reign, he founded the city of Leicester. Monmouth's narrative was reworked by 16th-century chronicler Raphael Holinshed, who wrote that Lear governed Britain for around 40 years *c.*800BC. Holinshed was one of William Shakespeare's key sources for *King Lear.*

The tale of Lear was also told by Edmund Spenser in his allegorical epic *The Faerie Queene.* According to the legend, the king in his old age unwisely divided his country between his daughters on the basis of their professions of love for him. The most devoted daughter, Cordelia, refused to make profession of her love on demand, so the king cut her off from her inheritance and split the kingdom between his harsh elder daughters Goneril and Regan. They mistreated him and he lost his wits.

In the version told by Monmouth, Leir is reunited with Cordelia and comes back to the throne, but in Shakespeare's better-known version, Cordelia dies and Lear grieves for her with words of devastating simplicity.

INVASIONS FROM ROME

Roman emperor Claudius launched a new invasion of Britain in AD43, landing an army of 40,000–50,000 well-organized troops on the coast of Kent. Many tribes, mindful of the benefits of Roman trading links as well as the might of the invading army, accepted rule from Rome under a consular governor of Britain. The first was Aulus Plautius, who governed until AD47.

Some Britons put up resistance. Cunobelinus died in AD40, to be replaced by his sons Caratacus and Togodumnus, who both chose to fight the Romans. Togodumnus was slain in combat and Caratacus was driven to the west until AD50 when, after a defeat at the hands of Plautius's successor as Roman governor, Ostorius Scapula, he fled to Yorkshire. There Cartimandua, queen of the Brigantes and an ally of Rome, handed Caratacus over to the invaders. Caratacus and his family were transported to Italy. He famously made such a dignified appeal for mercy that Emperor Claudius allowed the British king and his family to live on in Rome.

Above: Warrior queen. This 1902 statue celebrates Boudicca's heroic resistance against Roman tyranny. It stands by the Houses of Parliament in central London.

ANGER OF A ROYAL WIDOW

The year AD60 saw the death of Prasutagus, king of the Iceni tribe of Norfolk. As a client king under Roman rule, he left half his estate to the Emperor Nero and half to his two daughters, but imperial officials disregarded these instructions and attempted to seize the entire inheritance, while Roman soldiers ran amok, flogging Prasutagus's widow, Boudicca and raping her daughters.

Boudicca and the Iceni rose in revolt, slaughtering as many as 70,000 Romans and their allies. However, at Mancetter (Warwickshire) her 100,000-strong army was humiliated by a Roman force barely one-tenth its size. Boudicca took poison rather than be captured.

Below: Togidubnus, king of the Regnenses tribe of Sussex, accepted Roman rule. He built a splendid palace at Fishbourne.

The occupying Roman army made steady progress in stamping out pockets of Celtic-British resistance. In the years AD77–84, Roman governor Julius Agricola won major victories in southern Scotland, northern England and Wales, more or less completing the process, although parts of Wales and northern England remained resistant and a large portion of Scotland was never incorporated into the empire. The conquest initiated over 300 years of Roman rule in Britain, when the kings of rival British states were subject to a consular governor appointed by Rome. However, in about AD410 the Britons effectively declared independence, expelling the Roman administration. Initially the patterns of Roman life in Britain carried on. As time passed and the Romans did not return, there was increasing competition between Celtic rulers and Romanized Britons, as well as waves of invasion by Germanic peoples from the east, Irish from the west and Picts from the north.

A British ruler named Vortigern ('Great king') was pre-eminent by *c.*AD430. To bolster defences against the northern Picts, he hired Germanic mercenaries and rewarded them by allowing them to settle along the eastern coast of Britain.

In AD449, however, settlers led by Horsa ('Horse') and Hengest ('Stallion') began to seize land and operate independently. The scene was set for centuries of struggle between Germanic incomers and British natives, whom the incomers tended to call 'Welsh' (meaning, in this instance, 'foreigners').

ARTHUR
KING OF CAMELOT

In folklore, legend and literature, King Arthur of Camelot, lord of the Knights of the Round Table, is revered above all other kings and queens. Narratives of the golden age of chivalry in his court at Camelot are tinged with knowledge of its inevitable decay and self-destruction, an elegiac sadness rooted in the knowledge that all things – youth, physical perfection, political achievement, life itself – must pass.

THE HISTORICAL ARTHUR

Stirring legends of King Arthur grew up around the life of a relatively minor 5th- or 6th-century British or Welsh prince who fought against the advancing Saxons and who was perhaps the British leader at a famous victory over the Saxons at 'Mount Badon' *c.*AD500. Arthur was first mentioned by name in the *Historia Brittonum* ('History of the Britons') by the Welsh cleric Nennius *c.*AD830, some 300-odd years after his probable death. Nennius lists 12 battles in which Arthur took on the Saxons, including the great triumph at Mons Badonicus (Mount Badon). In the slightly later *Annales Cambriae* ('Annals of Wales', *c.*AD960) the anonymous chronicler records that Arthur led his people to victory at Mount Badon in AD516 but was killed in battle at 'Camlann' in AD539.

An earlier reference by the British priest Gildas in his *De excidio et conquestu Britanniae* ('The Ruin and Conquest of Britain', *c.*AD550) describes an unnamed British war leader who triumphed at the Battle of Mount Badon (here dated to *c.*AD500) and who was probably Ambrosius Aurelianus, the historical prototype for Arthur. One theory contends that the name Arthur, which means 'bear man', was a nickname given to Ambrosius by his men because he was big and hairy like a bear or because he wore the bearskin cloak of late Roman officers.

Many historians locate Mount Badon near Bath in southern England, perhaps at the vast hillfort of Little Solsbury Hill, which archaeologists have shown was used by the British at the end of the 4th century. They suggest that Arthur's victory there drove back West Saxons advancing from the Thames Valley. However, other clues point to the north of England and some believe that 'Camlann' might refer to Birdoswald (Cumbria), which was known as Camboglanna in the Roman era.

Above: Arthur and his queen Guinevere leave a banquet, from a manuscript by French poet Chrétien de Troyes (d. 1183).

Left: Brothers in arms. An image from a late 15th-century manuscript shows the knights gathered around the Round Table.

If Arthur was active in that region in the early 6th century, then he cannot have been combating Saxons, for their advance had not reached this area.

But the search for the historical Arthur is probably beside the point: the King of Camelot is mainly a figure of legend, whose enduring importance lies in his use by successive ages as a symbol of a past golden age of knightly virtue, right government and peace.

KING ARTHUR'S INFLUENCE AND LEGACY

The romance of Arthur's court at Camelot and of the company of the Knights of the Round Table, together with the popularity of the Continental tradition of courtly love, inspired the enduring cult of chivalry at the royal courts of England in the 14th–16th centuries. King Edward III and his leading barons were devoted to the practice of jousting and in 1348 Edward founded the knightly Order of the Garter based on that of Arthur and the Knights of the Round Table, whom he regarded as historical figures. At the Tudor courts of King Henry VIII and Queen Elizabeth I, the Arthurian chivalric tradition was still in full flower: Edmund Spenser used Malory's *Le Morte d'Arthur* as a key source for his poem in praise of Elizabeth, *The Faerie Queene* (*c.*1590).

The Arthurian tradition became very popular once more in the Victorian period, when the Pre-Raphaelite artistic movement used Arthurian themes in painting, stained glass and other forms, while English poet Alfred, Lord Tennyson wrote *The Idylls of the King* (1842) using elements of the legend.

In the 20th century, the narrative of King Arthur was the inspiration for the English novelist T.H. White's series of books *The Once and Future King*, which in turn inspired the Broadway musical *Camelot* (1960). In the English language, the word Camelot has come to be used to describe any golden age doomed to end before its time, such as the administration of US President John F. Kennedy, which was cut short by his assassination in Dallas, Texas, in 1963.

THE LEGEND GROWS

In Welsh folklore and early literature King Arthur began to be associated with tales of wonder and magic. The 12th-century Welsh prose romance *Kulhwch and Olwen* identified Arthur with a band of heroes, an idea that would develop into the Arthurian court and the Knights of the Round Table. The legend was given life by Geoffrey of Monmouth in his *Historia regum Britanniae* ('History of the Kings of Britain', *c.*1135–9). His version contains many familiar elements: the magician Merlin changes Uther Pendragon, King of Britain, into the likeness of Gorloise, Duke of Cornwall, so Uther can sleep with Gorloise's ravishing wife, Ygerna. Arthur is born as a result of this union, and crowned king at a time when the country is threatened by marauding Saxons. He trounces the Saxons, then defeats the Irish and Picts, marries Guinevere and inaugurates a golden age of chivalry. When he travels to France to defeat a Roman army, he leaves England in the care of his nephew Mordred, who seduces Guinevere and usurps the throne. Upon his return, Arthur is defeated and killed in Cornwall.

Geoffrey of Monmouth's work was translated into French in the *Roman de Brut* (1155) of the Anglo-Norman author Wace. The *Roman* was the first book to mention the round table used at Arthur's court. A group of 13th-century French romances known to scholars as the 'Vulgate' and 'post-Vulgate' cycles then developed the elements of the legend: an illicit romance between Arthur's queen, Guinevere, and his knight, Lancelot; the quest for the Holy Grail and the identification of Lancelot's son, Sir Galahad, as the only knight pure enough to succeed in the Grail quest. Another strand of the Vulgate cycle developed the theme of Arthur's childhood and the narrative of how he proved his royal standing by drawing the magic sword Excalibur from stone. The legend of King Arthur had a new flowering in England in the 15th and 16th centuries, with Monmouth's *Historia* and Sir Thomas Malory's English prose romance, *Le Morte d'Arthur* (*c.*1470).

Below: The 'Arthurian' round table in the Great Hall of Winchester Castle was made in the 1270s, in Edward I's reign.

Below: The Arthurian legend developed in a series of French romances. This image is from a 15th-century Grail manuscript.

ANGLO-SAXON KINGDOMS

AD500–871

Waves of Germanic invaders swept into Britain in the 5th and 6th centuries AD. There were three main groups: the Angles, from the region of Angulus (modern Angeln district) in northern Germany on the Baltic coast; the Saxons, from the North Sea Coast between the Jutland peninsula and the River Weser; and the Jutes, probably from Jutland in Scandinavia. The Angles settled mainly in East Anglia and to the north of the river Humber, and gave their name both to England and the English language; the Saxons settled largely in southern England; and the Jutes made their home in Kent.

They spread out across south-east England, meeting only the occasional setback. Among the most notable of these was at Mount Badon, the heroic British victory *c.* AD500 celebrated in the mythology of King Arthur. By *c.*AD600, seven main Anglo-Saxon kingdoms were established: Mercia, Northumbria, East Anglia, Kent, Wessex, Sussex and Essex. The British Celts held only Wales and the south-western kingdom of Dumnonia, part of today's Somerset, Devon and Cornwall.

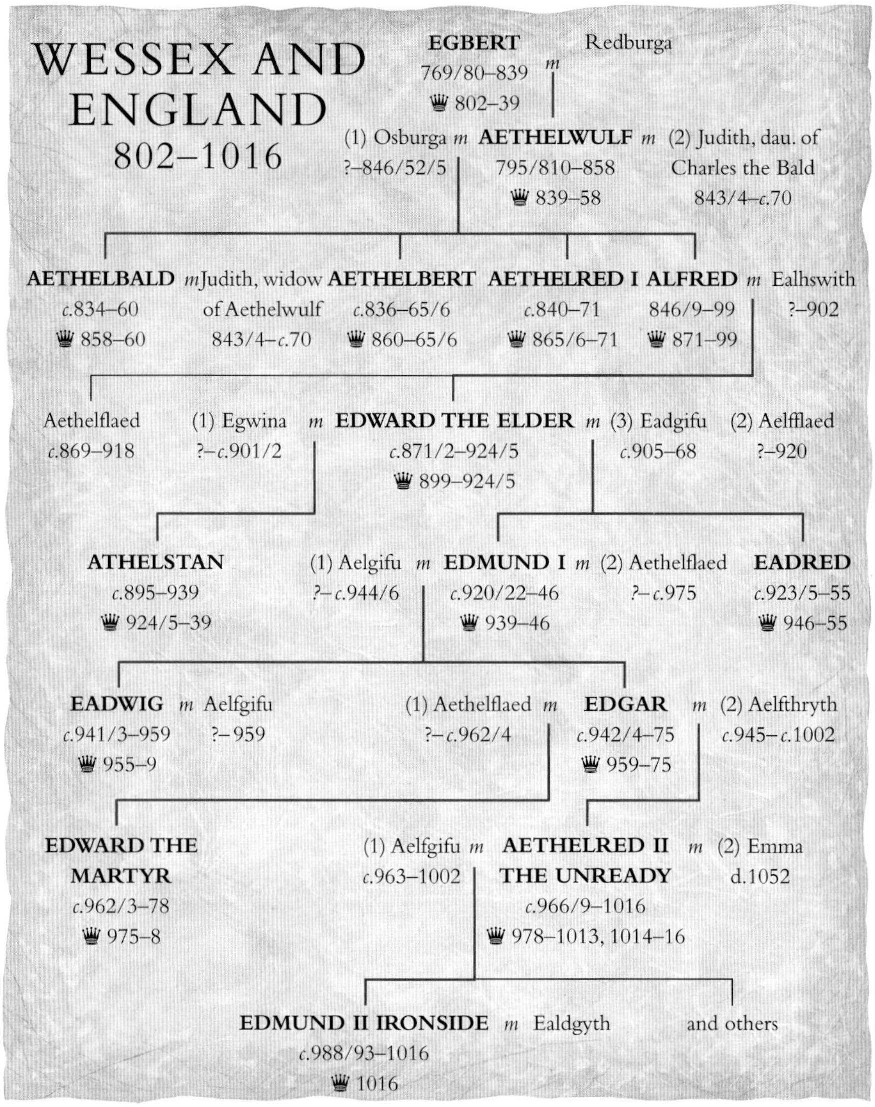

Below: This helmet was among the treasure buried with a king – probably Raedwald of East Anglia – at Sutton Hoo c.*AD625.*

KINGDOMS IN COMPETITION

The rival Anglo-Saxon realms were drawn into competition, seeking territory and wider control. Northumbria and Mercia were the dominant forces in the 7th century. Northumbria began the century as two kingdoms, those of Bernicia and Deira. These were combined by AD616.

Under Edwin (AD616–33), Oswy (AD642–70) and Ecgfrith (AD670–85), Northumbria became a power to be reckoned with, especially after Oswy defeated and killed his rival warrior-king, Penda, ruler of Mercia in AD655. Northumbria's importance began to

Below: An illuminated manuscript of the first words of Saint Luke's Gospel, from the Lindisfarne Gospels, written c.*AD694.*

Right: Kings of Kent. Aethelbert (left) was the first Christian Anglo-Saxon king and Eadbald (right) was his successor.

decline after Ecgfrith was killed fighting the Picts at Nechtansmere near modern Forfar on 20 May AD685.

In Mercia, King Wulfhere (AD657–70) expanded southwards as far as the River Thames. The Mercian ruler Aethelbald (AD716–57) called himself 'King of Britain' and seized London and the whole of modern Middlesex from Essex, as well taking control of large parts of Wessex and even conquering territories in Wales. However, he was assassinated by his bodyguard in AD757. His successor was the renowned Offa, who declared himself 'King of the English' and ruled most of Wessex, and all of Sussex, Kent and East Anglia as well as his Mercian heartland. His fame spread far and wide and he was addressed as 'brother' by great Charlemagne, King of the Franks, when negotiating trade terms. Offa also embarked upon the building of a vast – but not continuous – earth barrier along Mercia's border with Wales – Long sections of 'Offa's Dyke', a vast construction, 149 miles (240km) long, 11ft (3.3m) tall and 22 yards (20m) in width, still stand today.

After Offa's death in AD796, Wessex rose to become the pre-eminent Anglo-Saxon kingdom under the rule of King Egbert. Egbert annexed Sussex, Kent and Essex and also campaigned to the west, taking control of former Celtic lands in modern Devon and Cornwall. To the north, he defeated the Mercians in AD825 at the Battle of Ellendun.

From the late 8th century, all Anglo-Saxon kings faced a common foe, the marauding Vikings, whose first raid on England was at Portland in Wessex *c.*AD786. Egbert of Wessex defeated a Cornish and Viking army in AD838 at Hingston Down, Cornwall, but the raiders remained a major problem for Anglo-Saxon England until the reign of Egbert's grandson, Alfred the Great.

THE RISE OF CHRISTIANITY

Aethelbert, the long-lived King of Kent (r. AD560–616), was the first Anglo-Saxon monarch to adopt Christianity. Under the influence of his Frankish queen, who had already been baptized in the religion, Aethelbert allowed a Christian missionary from Rome, Augustine, to settle and begin preaching at Canterbury. Augustine, who was hugely influential and who won many converts, was made the first Archbishop of Canterbury. In AD600 King Aethelbert himself converted to Christianity.

Further north, Christian missionaries spreading south from Scotland were disseminating a distinct form of Christianity that followed Irish instead of Roman customs. Christianity had been established in Ireland since as early as *c.*AD400–450. The Irish monk Saint Colomba founded a monastery on the island of Iona off the west coasts of Scotland in *c.*AD563 and Saint Aidan came from Iona to found the celebrated monastery of Lindisfarne, off the coast of Northumberland in northern England, in AD634. It was here that the beautifully illuminated Lindisfarne Gospels were made in about the year AD694.

By this date, the Roman Christian tradition had won an important victory over its Irish counterpart on the mainland. This was decided at the Synod of Whitby called by King Oswy of Northumbria in AD663–4.

KINGS OF IRELAND

From time immemorial, according to the songs of the Celtic bards, Ireland was governed by a high king, who ruled from Tara (north of modern Dublin). In the bardic tradition, the first high king was Niall Noígiallachi ('Niall, Taker of Nine Hostages'), who led military campaigns into Britain.

In fact, the Ireland they described consisted of more than 100 clan groupings (*tuatha*), each with an elected king. *Tuatha* were clustered in larger regional groups, each under one king acting as overlord. The main groups were the Cuig Cuigi ('Five Fifths'), Connacht (Connaught), Laighin (Leinster), Midhe (Meath), Mumhain (Munster) and Ulaidh (Ulster). The historical Niall was a king of Midhe (d. early 5th century). His descendants, ruling from Tara, were claiming to be kings of all Ireland by the 6th century. From AD795, all the Irish kingdoms faced an onslaught from the invading Norse Vikings, who founded the settlement that would become Dublin in AD841. The kings of Mumhain, ruling from Cashel, grew powerful enough to sack the Norse settlements at Limerick and Dublin. The acclaimed Brian Boru, ruler of Mumhain, became the first true high king of all Ireland in 1002.

ALFRED THE GREAT

AD871–899

As Alfred came to the throne of Wessex, aged 22 in AD871, his kingdom and, indeed, the whole of Anglo-Saxon England, was seemingly at the mercy of Viking invaders. Nonetheless, he managed to contain and then drive back the Viking threat and to rule with wisdom and energy for almost three decades. In his reign, learning was revived in England and the incomparable *Anglo-Saxon Chronicle* begun. He is the only monarch in English history to have been awarded the epithet 'Great'.

THE VIKING ONSLAUGHT

After the landing of a Danish Viking 'Great Army' in East Anglia in AD865, the Vikings had taken York, captured Northumbria in AD867 and taken control of East Anglia in AD869. However, in the spring of AD871, Alfred and his brother King Aethelred of Wessex led the men of Wessex in a morale-boosting victory over the Vikings on the Ridgeway at Ashdown in Berkshire, killing thousands of invaders, including five earls and a king.

A few weeks later, on 23 April AD871, Alfred came to the throne on Aethelred's death, but the Ridgeway victory brought little lasting benefit to the new king. Almost at once Alfred's army was scattered far and wide by a renewed Viking assault that hit when he was attending Aethelred's funeral at Wimborne. One of Alfred's first acts as king, therefore, was to 'buy peace' by bribing the Vikings. This brought respite for a few years, while the Vikings were occupied in conquering Mercia, but in AD877 a Viking force led by Guthrum renewed the attack and captured Exeter. The following January, when a surprise attack on Chippenham resulted in another Viking victory, Guthrum won control of most of Wessex.

Alfred was forced to retreat deep into the Somerset countryside and, from a base at Athelney in the Somerset marshes, he began to conduct a guerrilla war against the invaders. In May AD878, he led an army of men from Wiltshire, Somerset and Hampshire in a famous victory over the Vikings at Edington, at the northern limit of Salisbury Plain, and drove the remnants of the enemy all the way back to their base at Chippenham, a distance of over 15 miles (24km).

Under the peace treaty that followed, the Vikings agreed to withdraw entirely from Wessex and Guthrum accepted baptism as a Christian. Alfred showed great generosity to his former adversary, recognizing him as an adoptive son.

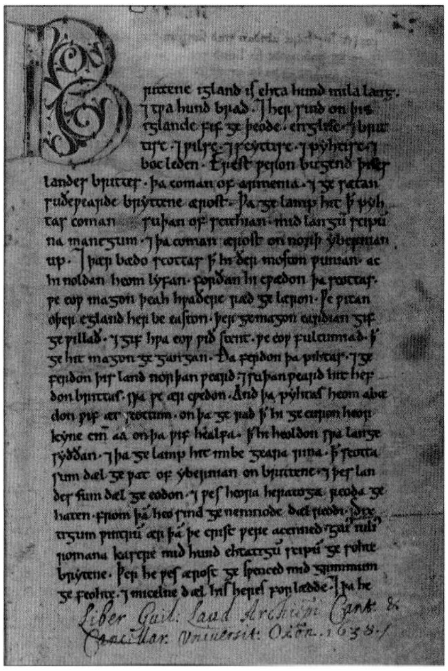

Above: The Anglo-Saxon Chronicle *was unusual for the period in being written entirely in Anglo-Saxon rather than Latin.*

Below: The Great King Alfred. Hamo Thorneycroft's statue of Alfred was unveiled in Winchester in 1901.

KING ALFRED THE GREAT, AD871–899

Born: *c.*AD849, Wantage
Father: King Aethelwulf of Wessex
Mother: Queen Osburga
Accession: 23 April AD871, Dorset
Queen: Ealhswith (m. AD868; d. AD905)
Succeeded by: His son, Edward 'the Elder'
Greatest achievement: Containing the Viking threat
AD871: Leads English army to victory over Vikings at Ashdown
May AD878: Defeats Vikings at Battle of Edington
***c.*AD886:** Captures formerly Mercian city of London
***c.*AD887:** Learns Latin and begins translation of Pope Gregory the Great's *Cura Pastoralis* ('Pastoral Care or Rule')
Death: 26 Oct AD899, Winchester

THE KING WHO BURNT THE CAKES

At the lowest ebb of his reign, while King Alfred was forced to live incognito in deepest Somerset, he was scolded by a swineherd's wife. The story goes that Alfred was seated by the fireside in the swineherd's hut, lost in thought as he tried to plot a way of defeating the seemingly invincible Vikings. Perhaps he did not hear the woman of the house, who was leaving for a few moments, ask him to mind the cakes that she was baking, or perhaps he forgot to do as he was asked. When she returned and found that the cakes were burnt she was furious and battered the king about the head with her stick. This apocryphal story can be traced as far back as a *Life of St Neot*, written in the 10th century, and was mistakenly included in the edition of Bishop Asser's *Life of King Alfred* (AD893) which was published by Archbishop Matthew Parker in 1574. Thereafter it appeared in many modern accounts of Alfred's life and the story continues to be told into the 21st century.

Right: Sir David Wilkie painted King Alfred burning the cakes in 1806.

THE DANELAW

Guthrum and the Vikings pledged not to attack Wessex, but they remained in strength in other English kingdoms, establishing themselves in East Anglia and the lands to the north and east of Watling Street, the Roman road running from London in the south-east to Chester in the north-west. Here, in the 'Danelaw' (roughly modern Yorkshire, east Midlands and East Anglia), they flourished, establishing several prosperous settlements.

Alfred meanwhile set about strengthening the military defences of Wessex. He built several *burhs*, or fortified towns, reorganized the army so that half could be rested while the other half was on campaign and created an English navy, consisting of manoeuvrable warships of his own design, each with 60 oars. The navy proved its worth in AD896 by defeating a powerful Danish Viking raiding party off the Isle of Wight.

THE REVIVAL OF LEARNING

Alfred was able to provide stability for the people of Wessex and, in a previously lawless era, his kingdom came to be known for its just royal laws and honest administration. He collected laws from diverse sources and published an English law code. His coins recognized him as *Rex Anglorum* ('King of all the English') and he was increasingly accepted as king of all Englishmen and women not subject to the Danes.

As a young child, Alfred had visited the learned Frankish court, which had been established early in the 9th century by the great Charlemagne. This experience may have inspired him to initiate and oversee the revival of education and learning that occurred at his court in Winchester and throughout his kingdom.

Alfred himself was illiterate until his later teens but he determined that free-born English boys should have the chance to learn through reading, and established schools to this end. He also saw that those books in his words 'most necessary for all men to know' should be made available to his people in their own tongue and provided for their translation.

King Alfred learned Latin at the age of 38 in order to translate the *Cura Pastoralis* ('Pastoral Care or Rule') by Pope Gregory the Great, and he subsequently sent a copy of his translation with an exquisite aestel (bookmark) to every bishop in the kingdom. A key part of his commitment to knowledge was his sponsorship of the vast *Anglo-Saxon Chronicle,* an historical record of England which went as far back as the Roman invasion.

A TEMPLATE FOR KINGSHIP

Alfred was plagued throughout his life by illness. Some scholars suggest he was an epileptic, others that he suffered from haemorrhoids or from venereal disease contracted in his bachelor days before his AD868 marriage to Ealhswith of Mercia. Yet despite the debilitating effect of his illness, the king brought energy, intelligence, and courage to all his endeavours. He was, in the words of his devoted and perspicacious biographer Bishop Asser of Sherborne, an 'immovable pillar of the people of the west, a just man, an energetic warrior, full of learning in speech, above all instructed in divine knowledge'.

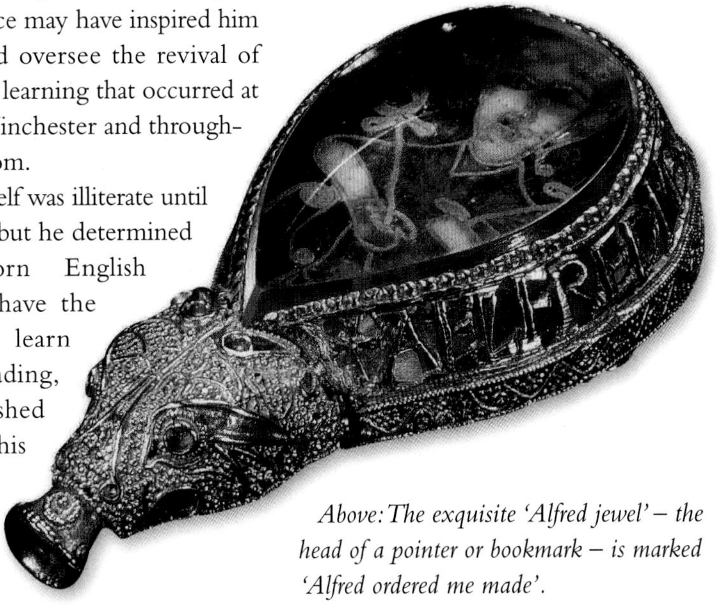

Above: The exquisite 'Alfred jewel' – the head of a pointer or bookmark – is marked 'Alfred ordered me made'.

THE HOUSE OF WESSEX

AD899–978

The great King Alfred was succeeded in AD899 by his son, Edward, who performed wonders in consolidating and extending his father's achievements. Where Alfred had concentrated on defence against the Viking threat, Edward took an aggressive approach. In a series of stunning victories in AD917, he captured Essex and the East Midlands and forced the Vikings of East Anglia to submit to the rule of Wessex. Then, in AD918, he further expanded the kingdom by taking control of western (English) Mercia from its female ruler, his niece Aelfwynn, and conquered Danish Mercia (the region known as 'the Five Boroughs') and the Danish-ruled kingdom of East Anglia. Before his death, on 17 July AD924, he had also received the submission of the rulers of the Welsh kingdoms of Dyfed and Gwynnedd, while the kings of the northern Danish territory of York and the independent Anglo-Saxon earldom of Northumbria, Strathclyde and Alba (Scotland) had accepted him as 'lord'. His dominance extended across the entire island.

Below: King Edgar, one of the first kings to be anointed with holy oil, with St Dunstan, creator of the coronation ceremony.

LINE OF SUCCESSION

Edward, usually known as 'the Elder', was briefly succeeded by his son Aelfweard, (who ruled for just 16 days and may have been assassinated) and then by another son, Athelstan, who won further victories for Wessex and was the first king to rule all of England.

Athelstan was succeeded by another of Edward's sons, Edmund I (AD939–46), who suffered a major setback when Olaf Gothfrithson, King of the Dublin Norse, captured York and parts of Mercia in AD940. Edmund won back most of the land for Wessex in AD942, then died an untimely death four years later, aged just 25, when he was killed in a skirmish while attempting to defend his steward from a thief named Leofa.

Yet another son of Edward the Elder, Eadred (AD946–55), defeated Erik Bloodaxe, the last Viking king of York, in AD954 and consolidated the Wessex dynasty's control of all England. His natural death at around the age of 30 created something of a succession crisis, as his two sons were just 15 and 14.

ATHELSTAN, KING OF ENGLAND, AD924–939

Birth: *c.*AD895
Father: Edward the Elder
Mother: Egwina
Accession: 17 July AD924
Coronation: 4 Sept AD924
Succeeded by: His half-brother, Edmund I
Death: 27 Oct AD939, Gloucester

ROYAL SEX SCANDAL

The accession of Edmund's elder son Eadwig threatened all that Alfred's heirs had achieved, for Eadwig, while a good-looking young boy, lacked the seriousness his position demanded.

His reign began in scandal when he left his coronation feast and was discovered by the venerable Abbot Dunstan *in flagrante* with both a maiden named Aelfgifu and her mother.

Within two years the kingdom split when Mercia and Northumbria rejected the young king's dubious authority and chose his 14-year-old brother Edgar in his place. Fortunately for the future of England, the dissolute Eadwig died before his 20th birthday, on 1 October AD959, and the energetic, pious and astute Edgar came to the throne in his place.

Right: The lands ruled by Athelstan, King of Wessex. His power reached as far north as York and as far west as Cornwall.

THE LORD'S ANOINTED

Edgar brought to England an era of peace and reform of the kind attributed to his great predecessor Alfred. With his Archbishop of Canterbury, the renowned Dunstan, he introduced church and monastic reforms and developed the idea of the king as God's representative on Earth.

On Whit Sunday, 11 May AD973, Edgar was crowned king of England in a splendid ceremony in Bath that included an anointing: a deliberate reference to the ordination of a priest. The coronation-anointing took place 14 years into the reign because by AD973 Edgar was 30, the minimum age for a priest. Later the same year, in a celebration at Chester, Edgar was recognized as overlord by no fewer than eight kings – including King Kenneth II of Scots, King Malcolm of Strathclyde and King Iago of Gwynnedd.

Edgar was a great reformer. He oversaw a realignment of county boundaries that would endure for more then 1000 years (until 1974), and also reformed weights and measures and the coinage, introducing a new currency in AD973.

Below: Athelstan's coins were inscribed 'King of all Britain', indicating that the Scots and Welsh accepted his authority.

ATHELSTAN: KING OF ALL ENGLAND

Edward the Elder's son Athelstan (AD934–9) was the first king to rule all of England. In AD927 he pushed Wessex's borders further north by conquering the Viking kingdom of York. He received vows of submission from the Britons of Cornwall and five kings in Wales *c.*AD930. The *Anglo-Saxon Chronicle* praised him in ringing tones: 'Royal Athelstan, lord of warriors, giver of rings to men, with his kingly brother Edmund, won glory beyond compare with their sharp swords.'

Athelstan was the king who first sent Englishmen into military action on the European Continent. In AD939 he despatched a fleet to Flanders to back his nephew, Louis of France. He commissioned an illuminated edition of Bede's *Life of St Cuthbert* that contains a portrait of the king. This is the first contemporary image in English history of a ruling monarch.

Left: Athelstan's portrait is contained by a capital G in an illuminated edition of Bede's Life of St Cuthbert.

FROM AETHELRED II TO HARTHACNUT

AD978–1042

The rule of Aethelred II (AD978–1016) began in treachery. He came to the throne at the age of just 10, when his half-brother King Edward was stabbed to death by Aethelred's retainers.

King Edward was the son of King Edgar by his beautiful first wife, Aethelflaed, while Aethelred was Edgar's son by his second wife, Aelfthryth. Naturally, Aelfthryth was opposed to Edward's accession and when the king was killed during a visit to Aelfthryth's house, suspicion inevitably fell upon her. Although no proof was ever found of the involvement of Aethelred or of Aelfthryth in the murder, the deed cast a shadow over the king's rule.

AN INHERITANCE LOST

Aethelred's reign ended with the king sidelined and his son Edmund 'Ironside' facing defeat in the struggle against Cnut's Danish forces. In just 38 years, Aethelred lost a stable and prosperous kingdom, which had been built up over 100 years by Alfred the Great and his heirs.

The king is often known as 'King Aethelred the Unready'. This derives from 'Aethelred unraed', which is a pun on his name and means 'Noble advice, evil advice'. In fact, Aethelred's reign was not a failure because he was 'unready' or unprepared, or because he took poor advice – although he did make a number of costly mistakes that had profound long-term effects. The principal reason Aethelred lost a kingdom was the sudden surge of Danish power under King Harold Bluetooth and his son Sweyn in the years after AD980.

It certainly did not help that Aethelred was an unconvincing general. He lost much of the support of his leading subjects in a series of defeats by the Danish invaders. After the Battle of Maldon, in Essex, in AD991, Aethelred initiated a doomed policy of bribing the Danes to stay away with vast sums of gold and silver. Over a period of 20 years, these bribes, known as *Danegeld*, cost England a fortune. Aethelred made another decision with damaging long-term consequences when, in 1001, he married Emma, daughter of the Duke of Normandy, as part of an Anglo-Norman alliance designed to outmanoeuvre the Danes.

Aethelred then made plans for a massacre of all the Danes in England on St Brice's Day, 13 November 1002, However, this was only partially carried out and served to provoke the Danes into fiercer military action. In 1013 King Aethelred fled to Normandy, and the Danish king, Sweyn, claimed the English throne. However, Aethelred returned the following year and succeeded in ousting Sweyn's son, Cnut. To win the support of his leading nobles he was forced to pledge reforms and surer government in future in the first such agreement between monarch and subjects in English history.

In 1015 Aethelred's son Edmund – known as 'Ironside' for his strength and courage – revolted against his father's rule and took control of the army. Aethelred died, powerless, in April 1016 and after a bruising series of battles Edmund Ironside and Cnut agreed to share power, with Edmund taking Wessex and Cnut ruling all the land to the north of the River Thames.

Above: Aethelred, Rex Anglorum ('King of the English'). In his reign, a few of these pennies would have bought a sheep.

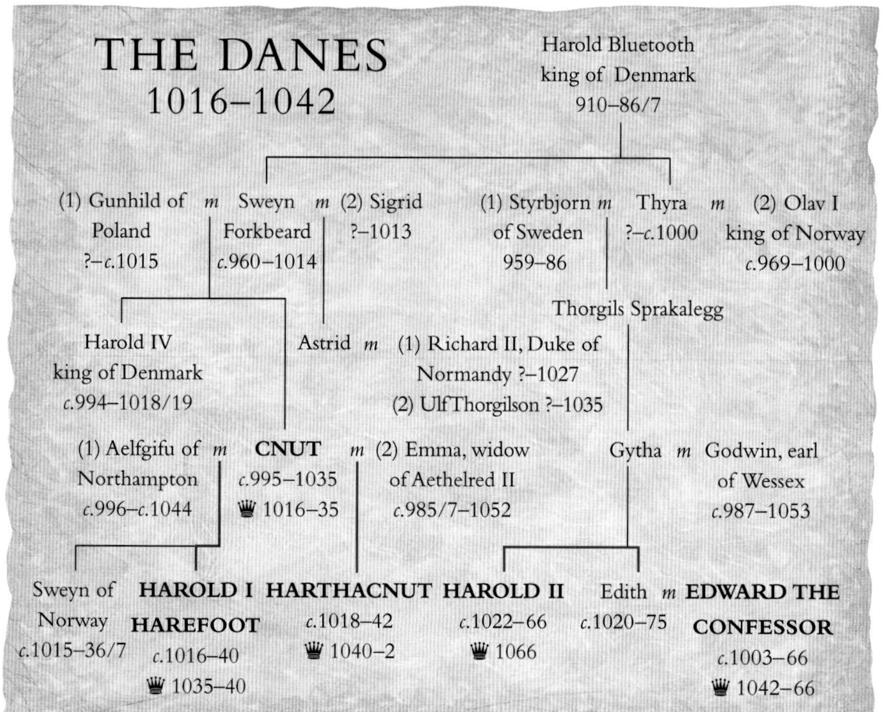

Above: The scandal that dogged Aethelred. A 15th-century manuscript depicts events surrounding the murder of King Edward.

THE KING WHO COULD NOT TAME THE WAVES

The best-known story about King Cnut is the legend – of doubtful authenticity – that he taught his flattering courtiers a lesson by pretending he thought he could tell the waves to go back. With an empire including land on both sides of the North Sea, Cnut was the most powerful ruler in Europe in the early 11th century.

As an increasingly devout Christian Cnut was ever mindful of the divine power from which his own claim to rule was derived. Impatient with courtiers who flattered and praised him too much, he played along with the idea that he thought he was important enough to command the waves. He had a throne placed on the edge of the beach and ordered the waves to retreat. When they did not, and indeed rushed over his feet and drenched his robes, he pretended to be angry and ordered them back once more. When he finally dropped the game, he told his courtiers never again to forget the extent to which his own mortal power was limited and bade them to remember how little consequence it had beside the power of God, who could command the oceans.

Right: Cnut and his queen, Emma, present a cross to the New Minster, Winchester, in an image of c.1030.

CNUT RULES ALONE

When King Edmund Ironside also died, on 30 November 1016, his subjects in Wessex were left to the mercy of King Cnut. The new king acted swiftly to secure his position: he had Edmund Ironside's brother, Eadwig, killed; he executed the powerful earls of East Anglia and Mercia; and he married King Aethelred's widow, Emma of Normandy, hoping to consolidate his standing in the country by marrying its queen.

Cnut already had two sons by his existing English wife, Aelfgifu, but under the terms of the new marriage agreement, only his children by Emma would have a claim to the throne. In 1019 Cnut became King of Denmark and at a stroke England became part of a Scandinavian empire. Cnut was increasingly committed to imperial expansion in Norway and wanted to maintain England as a secure, untroublesome source of wealth. Cnut was a Christian and made pilgrimages to Rome in 1027 and 1031. According to a chronicler of the 12th century, Cnut changed from a wild warrior to 'a most Christian king'.

A TROUBLED SUCCESSION

Cnut had proved himself a very effective ruler. However, after his death in 1035, his dynasty was destroyed by infighting in just seven years. Cnut's designated successor was Harthacnut, but because he was in Norway at the time of Cnut's death, Harthacnut appointed his half-brother Harold regent. Harold then claimed the throne but he was soon dead, probably having been assassinated. Harthacnut returned to England to occupy the throne, but he died on 8 June 1042, apparently from overindulging in drink at a wedding.

Left: The Danes are coming. Aethelred's nemesis, King Sweyn, disembarks with his army and invades England.

EDWARD THE CONFESSOR AND HAROLD II

1042–1066

On the death of Harthacnut, the throne passed to Edward, son of Queen Emma by her first husband, Aethelred. His accession was manoeuvred by the ruthless Earl Harold Godwine. In 1045 Edward married Godwine's daughter, Edith. Then, in 1051, Edward attempted to assert his independence by exiling Godwine and by naming his cousin, Duke William of Normandy, as his successor – if William's later account is to be believed. Nevertheless, the following year Godwine returned stronger than ever to win the full support of the king's ruling council, the Witan. Godwine died in 1053 but his sons, Tostig, Gyrth and Harold, occupied powerful positions as the earls of Northumbria, East Anglia and Wessex.

EDWARD THE CONFESSOR, KING OF ENGLAND, 1042–1066

Birth: *c.*1003, Islip
Father: Aethelred II
Mother: Emma of Normandy
Accession: 8 June 1042
Coronation: 3 April 1043, Winchester Cathedral
Succeeded by: Harold II
Death: 5 Jan 1066, Westminster

HAROLD II, KING OF ENGLAND, 1066

Birth: *c.*1022
Father: Godwine, Earl of Wessex
Accession: 5 Jan 1066
Coronation: 6 Jan 1066, Westminster Abbey
Succeeded by: William I
Greatest achievement: Securing the throne, Battle of Stamford Bridge
Jan 1066: Marries Ealdgyth, sister of Earls of Mercia and Northumbria
25 Sept 1066: Defeats Harald Hardrada and Earl Tostig at the Battle of Stamford Bridge
14 Oct 1066: Defeated by Duke William of Normandy at the Battle of Hastings; dies during battle

STRUGGLE FOR SUCCESSION

In his final years, Edward was much occupied with rebuilding the abbey church of St Peter at Westminster. By the time it was consecrated, in December 1065, however, he was too ill to attend, and on 5 January 1066 he died. Harold Godwineson, Earl of Wessex, was crowned King of England the very next day, claiming to have been designated by Edward as his successor.

William of Normandy was enraged. He claimed both that Edward had chosen him as successor in 1051 and that Harold Godwine had pledged to support William's claim on a mission to Normandy in 1064. William also had a hereditary claim to the throne, albeit a tenuous one: he was the great-nephew of King Cnut's second wife, Emma of Normandy. In addition to William, King Harold faced two other rivals for his throne: King Harald Hardrada of Norway and Edgar the Atheling (or 'prince'). Harald's claim to the throne was inherited from his nephew King Magnus the Good of Norway who had acquired the claim by treaty from Harthacnut in 1036. Edgar the Atheling had the most convincing hereditary claim as Aethelred II's great-grandson, but he was fatally handicapped by being just 14 years old and having no proof that he was a man of war or fit for power.

King Harold had the throne by virtue of acting swiftly. His two rivals prepared to invade. In addition, Harold had made an enemy of his brother, Earl Tostig, by depriving him of power in Northumbria because of his incompetence, and replacing him with the earl of Mercia's brother, Morcar.

In the summer of 1066 Harold waited for the twin invasions – but nothing happened. In September he

Below: Edward the Confessor celebrates Easter at a banquet in 1053. Godwine's death is depicted in the foregound.

allowed his soldiers to return home, but then had hastily to gather an army and march north to York when news reached him that Earl Tostig and King Harald Hardrada had mounted a joint invasion. He routed their combined force at the Battle of Stamford Bridge, near York, on 25 September.

Harold now heard that William had landed a fleet 250 miles (400km) to the south. He gathered his 7000-odd troops and marched south in 11 days. He could have chosen to hold back and engage the Norman army in the course of the winter, but instead staked everything on a quick victory in battle at Hastings.

Right: The Norman cavalry take on Anglo-Saxon foot soldiers in a Bayeux Tapestry scene from the Battle of Hastings.

THE BATTLE OF HASTINGS

The battle near Hastings on 14 October 1066 lasted all day. King Harold's army of 7000, including many untrained peasants, occupied a strong position on high ground, with Duke William's smaller force of around 4000 – consisting of archers, foot soldiers and cavalry – arranged on the slope beneath them.

The Normans opened the assault with their archers and the Anglo-Saxons fought back with spears and slings. When the Norman cavalry attacked, its men and horses were cut to pieces by Harold's soldiers with their double-handed axes. Twice the Norman cavalry pretended to retreat, drawing groups of Anglo-Saxons from the high ground, and then turned to destroy them.

At one point, scholars believe, William's horse was cut from under him and the word went among his men that he was dead. However, he claimed another horse and, once in the saddle, raised his helmet to rally his troops by showing them his face, declaring, 'Look, I am alive – and by God's grace will still win the victory!'

The decisive moment in the battle came when King Harold was killed. From the evidence of the Bayeux Tapestry (made about 1077) he was either shot in the eye with an arrow or had his legs hacked from under him by a Norman foot soldier. The Anglo-Saxons fought on without a leader, but at dusk they broke and fled, leaving the field to Duke William of Normandy. Some historians believe that King Harold's corpse was chopped into many pieces by victors maddened by battle.

Left: A 13th-century manuscript depicts the moment of Harold's death.

After his triumph over Harold at Hastings, William marched his Norman army across south-east England in a show of military might. Canterbury and Winchester surrendered almost immediately and by December resistance was over and the throne was secured.

Below: Feudal power. An enthroned William I grants lands to Alain de Brittany, who swears loyalty in return.

WILLIAM I THE CONQUEROR

1066–1087

The illegitimate Norman known in his homeland as Guillaume le Bâtard was crowned King William I of England in Edward the Confessor's abbey church at Westminster by Ealdred, Archbishop of York, on Christmas Day, 1066.

His initial victory had been won by military might and it was consolidated with great ruthlessness in the ensuing six years in the face of a series of revolts. William and his army put down rebellions in Cornwall in 1068 and then repeated uprisings in the north in 1068–9, during which Norman earl Robert de Comines was burnt alive with 900 men in Durham. King Sweyn II of Denmark and Edgar the Atheling captured York briefly during this period, burning the Minster. William's brutal reprisals laid waste the countryside so that thousands of people died of starvation and disease. In 1070, Anglo-Saxon rebels in East Anglia led by Hereward the Wake joined up with Danish sailors to plunder Peterborough Abbey. William made peace with King Sweyn II in June 1070 and the Danes departed, but Hereward became a focus for Anglo-Saxon rebels who gathered to him in his hideout on the Isle of Ely. William defeated them in April 1071, but Hereward escaped to carry on the fight as an outlaw.

INVASION CONSOLIDATED

Across the country the Normans raised imposing castles to keep their peace. In 1067–8 alone, William built castles in Exeter, Warwick, Nottingham, York, Lincoln, Huntingdon and Cambridge. In the course of his reign, William raised 78 castles, including the White Tower, now the heart of the Tower of London, and the New Castle near the mouth of the river Tyne that gave its name to Newcastle. In the Welsh Marches, on the English border with Wales, William settled powerful Norman nobles who were allowed free rein so long as they kept the Welsh and English under control.

Above: A scene from the Bayeux Tapestry depicts William the Conqueror with Bishop Odo and Robert de Mortain.

The Normans now 'invaded' the land-owning aristocracy and the Church, replacing Anglo-Saxons in a host of key positions. In 1066 there were 4,000 landowning *thegns* in King Harold's country, but by 1087 (the year of William's death) this territory had been appropriated and shared out among 200 French aristocrats; only two Anglo-Saxon landowners remained.

William made his intentions towards the Church clear in 1070, when he replaced the native Archbishop of Canterbury, Stigand, with his own man, Lanfranc, previously Abbot of St Stephen's in Caen, Normandy. Most of the country's bishops and abbots were replaced by Norman clerics.

By about 1072, England was securely conquered. William spent most of the remainder of his reign in France, campaigning against the French king, Philip I, the Counts of Flanders and Anjou and, from time to time, against his own eldest son, Robert Curthose.

THE DANES AND DOMESDAY

William returned to England in 1085, to face a threatened Danish invasion under King Cnut IV. To raise finance for an army he declared a land tax on all, but then – realizing the need for more accurate records of landholdings – he commissioned a land survey, 'The Description of All England', dubbed *The Domesday Book* by his subjects because there was no escaping it, just like the Day of Judgement. This remarkable survey was completed in less than a year and presented to William on 1 August 1086. In the end, King Cnut died and the invasion did not come.

William then returned to France, where he died in 1087 after being seriously injured in a fall from his horse during an attack on Nantes as part of a campaign against Philip I. He was buried on 12 September in St Stephen's Abbey, Caen. His unfortunate mourners left the building gagging after the king's fat and decomposing body burst its sarcophagus, emitting a stench of rotting flesh.

Before he died, William was ill for some weeks and had time to repent. He reputedly confessed his brutality with some remorse, saying, 'I am stained with the rivers of blood that I have spilled'.

WILLIAM I THE CONQUEROR, KING OF ENGLAND, 1066–1087

Birth: *c.*1027, Falaise, Normandy
Father: Robert, Duke of Normandy
Mother: Herleva
Accession: 14 Oct 1066
Coronation: 25 Dec 1066, Westminster Abbey
Queen: Matilda, daughter of Baldwin V (m. *c.* 1050–2; d. 2 Nov 1083)
Succeeded by: His son William II Rufus
Death: 9 Sept 1087, Priory of St Gervais, Rouen

WILLIAM II RUFUS

1087–1100

On his deathbed, William I is supposed to have left the English crown to his second son, William, while giving Normandy to his eldest son, Robert Curthose, and giving his third son, Henry, no land but the compensation of £5,000. William secured the crown for himself before Robert could act. Travelling swiftly to England from Normandy, he was crowned king in Westminster Abbey on 26 September 1087.

Before a year was out, William faced rebellion. His uncle, Bishop Odo, Earl of Kent, led an uprising with the aim of replacing William with Robert. Although the rebels captured several towns, the rebellion collapsed, Odo and his supporters were exiled and William seized their land.

William spent some years fighting on and off in Normandy to seize his brother's lands and reunite their father's inheritance. In 1096 Robert Curthose joined the First Crusade and, to finance his part in the expedition, pawned his duchy to William for 10,000 marks. Before Robert returned from the Crusade, William was dead – perhaps assassinated – after what was officially a hunting accident in the New Forest.

WILLIAM II RUFUS, KING OF ENGLAND, 1087–1100

Birth: *c.*1056/60, Normandy
Father: William I
Mother: Matilda of Flanders
Accession: 9 Sept 1087
Coronation: 26 Sept 1087, Westminster Abbey
Succeeded by: His brother, Henry I
Death: 2 Aug 1100, New Forest, Hampshire

ROYAL WHODUNIT

King William II died in suspicious circumstances while out hunting in August 1100. The official story is that the king and his friends were taking their pleasure in the New Forest, Hampshire, the vast 95,000-acre hunting preserve created by William I, when the fateful arrow was loosed by William's friend, Walter Tirel. The arrow struck William in the chest and he died at once. However, suspicion is inevitable that William's brother Henry, who was in the party and who subsequently became king, was somehow involved in the 'accident'. Henry rode at once to Winchester, where he secured the royal treasury, then proceeded to London to have himself elected king by the ruling council.

Crucially, the 'accident' happened while the rightful heir, Duke Robert Curthose of Normandy, was away on the First Crusade and Tirel himself was never punished.

Left: William II's red hair, which won him the nickname 'Rufus' (from the Latin for 'red'), is not visible in this later portrait.

THE NORMANS
1066–1154

WILLIAM THE CONQUEROR *c.*1027–87, ♛ 1066–1087 *m* Matilda of Flanders *c.*1032–83

- Robert Duke of Normandy *c.*1052/4–1134/5
- Richard ?–1075
- **WILLIAM II** *c.*1056/60–1100, ♛ 1087–1100
- Adela *c.*1062–1137/38 *m* Stephen Count of Blois ?–1102
  - **STEPHEN** *c.*1096/7–1154, ♛ 1135–1154 *m* Matilda of Boulogne ?–1152
- **HENRY I** 1068–1135, ♛ 1100–1135 *m* Edith (Matilda) dau of Malcolm III of Scotland 1080–1118
  - William *c.*1103–20
  - (1) Henry V Emperor of Germany ?–1125 *m* Matilda 1102–67 *m* (2) Geoffrey Count of Anjou 1113–51

HENRY I

1100–1135

The first years of King Henry I's reign were clouded by doubt over his succession and by revolts led by barons seeking to put Duke Robert Curthose of Normandy, William the Conqueror's eldest son, on the throne. These were effectively ended by Henry's defeat of Robert at Tinchebrai, Normandy, in September 1106.

The new king also bolstered his position by recalling and making peace with Anselm, the Archbishop of Canterbury, with whom William II had quarrelled bitterly. Anselm had been in exile overseas since 1097, but returned early in the new reign, at Henry's invitation, in October 1100.

A NEW MORALITY

One of the main points of disagreement between William II and Archbishop Anselm had been the Archbishop's disapproval of what he saw as decadence at William's court. In a Lenten sermon in 1094, Anselm had attacked effeminacy and the practice of homosexuality at the court, denouncing the men of the court for growing beards, wearing their hair long and sporting extravagant shoes.

Life at Henry's court was far more sober and clean-shaven, and Henry was a loyal patron of the church. For example, he sponsored the rebuilding of Canterbury Cathedral choir, a project that was completed in 1130.

Henry's marriage to Edith, the great-granddaughter of Edmund II 'Ironside' (who was briefly king in 1016) and sister of King Edgar of Scots, cemented a valuable alliance with the Scots and allowed Henry to reinforce his claim to the throne by marrying into the royal line of the Anglo-Saxons. After the wedding, Edith took the Norman name Matilda, perhaps in honour of Henry's mother.

LOSS OF THE WHITE SHIP

In 1120, Henry I won a diplomatic triumph by agreeing a peace treaty with King Louis VI of France, under which the long-disputed duchy of Normandy was to pass to Henry's only legitimate male heir, his son Prince William the Atheling, on Henry's death. However, as the royal court returned to England from Normandy, a ship transporting Prince William, sank in the Channel. Apparently the pilot was drunk and he had allowed the vessel, the *White Ship*, to run on to a rock off Barfleur. Everyone on board died, apart from one Rouen butcher.

NO MALE HEIR

Although Henry had fathered 21 children, only two of them were legitimate. The White Ship tragedy killed William the Atheling, his only legitimate male heir, leaving only a daughter, Matilda, who in 1114 had married Holy Roman Emperor Henry V. On 1 January 1127 Henry prevailed over his reluctant barons, persuading them to accept Matilda, by now a widow, as his heir. But baronial opposition to her succession only grew stronger when, the following year, she married Count Geoffrey of Anjou, who was nicknamed 'Plantagenet' because he used the broom plant (Latin: *planta genista*) as his family emblem.

Left: A detail from a manuscript image of the loss of the White Ship *shows Henry mourning the death of his sons.*

Above: Henry's jester, Rahere, founded the priory church of St Bartholomew the Great in Smithfield, London, in 1123.

King Henry I died in December 1135 after overindulging in eating lampreys. Although his daughter Matilda was his official heir, many barons instead supported the claim of Henry's nephew Count Stephen of Blois.

HENRY I, KING OF ENGLAND, 1100–1135

Birth: Sept 1068, Selby, Yorkshire
Father: William I
Mother: Matilda of Flanders
Accession 3 Aug 1100
Coronation: 5/6 Aug 1100, Westminster Abbey
Queens: (1) Matilda, daughter of Malcolm III of Scotland (m. 11 Nov 1100; d. 1 May 1118); (2) Adeliza, daughter of Geoffrey VII, Count of Louvain (m. 1121; d. 1151)
Succeeded by: His nephew, Stephen of Blois, although Henry had named his daughter Matilda as his successor
Death: 1/2 Dec 1135, near Rouen, Normandy

STEPHEN

1135–1154

On learning of his uncle King Henry I's death, Count Stephen sailed to England and was crowned in Westminster Abbey on 26 December 1135. His accession, in direct contravention of the oath he and leading English barons had sworn to King Henry I to support the Empress Matilda as Queen, plunged the country into a bitter civil war.

YEARS OF CIVIL TURMOIL

In 1139, the Empress Matilda and her husband Geoffrey of Anjou, in alliance with her half-brother, the illegitimate Robert, Earl of Gloucester, landed an army in south-west England to claim the throne and set up their own royal court in Bristol. In 1140 Earl Ranulf of Chester rose in revolt and captured Lincoln. In 1141, King Stephen was defeated by Robert, Earl of Gloucester, at the battle of Lincoln, on 2 February.

Right: The coronation of King Stephen, a miniature from the Flores Historiarum *by the Benedictine monk and chronicler Matthew Paris (d.1259).*

STEPHEN, 1135–1154

Birth: *c.*1096/7 (before 1100), Blois, France
Father: Stephen Henry, Count Palatine of Blois, Brie, Chartres and Meaux
Mother: Adela of Normandy
Accession: Usurps the throne 22 December 1135
Coronation: 26 Dec 1135, Westminster Abbey
Queen: Matilda (m. before 1125; d. 2/3 May 1152)
Succeeded by: His second cousin, Henry II
Death: 25 Oct 1154, Dover, Kent

He was imprisoned in chains in Gloucester's castle. The Empress Matilda was elected Queen at Winchester on 8 April. Stephen's wife – another Matilda – arrived with an army of mercenaries from Flanders.

When the armies of the two Matildas met at Winchester, the troops of the Empress were defeated and her key ally Gloucester was taken prisoner. The Empress Matilda's brief ascendancy was over; she was forced to exchange Stephen for Gloucester, and Stephen was crowned King of England for a second time, at Canterbury on Christmas Day 1141.

The civil war ran on for another decade or more. The key years were 1147–8, when the Earl of Gloucester died, and 1153 when Stephen lost his only heir with the death of his beloved son Eustace. However, the bruising conflict could not truly be said to be over until, on 6 November 1153, in the Treaty of Wallingford, King Stephen agreed that the Empress Matilda's son Henry Plantagenet was to be his heir and would inherit the throne. The following year, on 25 October 1154, King Stephen died and Henry inherited the throne of England as King Henry II.

CHAPTER TWO

THE PLANTAGENETS

1154–1399

When Henry, Duke of Normandy, Count of Anjou, Touraine and Maine and Duke of Aquitaine was crowned King Henry II of England in 1154, he founded England's longest-reigning dynasty, that of the Plantagenets. The House of Plantagenet ruled for 331 years, until 1485, supplying 14 English kings.

The name 'Plantagenet' came from a nickname for Henry II's father, Geoffrey, Count of Anjou. The nickname derived from *planta genista*, the Latin name for the broom plant, and was applied to Geoffrey either because he used the plant as his emblem, because he wore broom sprigs in his hat or because he planted broom on his land to provide cover when hunting. Although historians use the name Plantagenet, Count Geoffrey's descendants went without any form of surname for 250-odd years.

Some historians identify the first kings of the Plantagenet line – Henry II, Richard I and John – as 'Angevins', from their title as Count of Anjou, and reserve the title 'Plantagenet' for the succeeding kings, Edward I, Edward II and Edward III. The three Plantagenet kings who were descendants of the Duke of Lancaster are identified as the House of Lancaster (Henry IV, Henry V and Henry VI), and the final three, descendants of the Duke of York, as the House of York (Edward IV, Edward V and Richard III). Nonetheless, all were Plantagenets.

Left: In 1382, Richard II married Anne of Bohemia at Westminster. Both were aged 15. The illustration is from the Chronicles of Jean Froissart *(c. 1333–1400).*

HENRY II

1154–1189

At Christmas 1154 the newly crowned Henry II celebrated the first undisputed accession to the English throne since that of Harold II in 1066. Henry's claim to the throne was not beyond dispute: it was as the son of Empress Matilda, who had plagued Stephen I's reign with repeated assertions of her own royal pedigree as the daughter of King Henry I. However, he acceded peacefully under the terms of an 1153 agreement between Stephen and Matilda that guaranteed the crown for Matilda's son. After years of civil war in Stephen's reign, there was no appetite for a struggle against the king among the nobles and people of England.

HENRY II, KING OF ENGLAND, 1154–1189

Birth: 5 March 1133, Le Mans
Father: Geoffrey Plantagenet, Count of Anjou
Mother: Empress Matilda, daughter of King Henry I of England
Accession: 25 Oct 1154
Coronation: 19 Dec 1154, Westminster Abbey
Queen: Eleanor of Aquitaine (m. 1152; d. 1204)
Succeeded by: His son, Richard I
Greatest achievement: Founding Royal House of Plantagenet
June 1162: Thomas à Becket appointed Archbishop of Canterbury
1163: Overlord of Wales
1166: Assize of Clarendon establishes trial by jury
29 Dec 1170: Becket killed, Canterbury
1174: Overlord of Scotland under Treaty of Falaise
12 July 1174: Henry does penance in Canterbury Cathedral
1175: Overlord of Ireland under Treaty of Windsor
Death: 6 July 1189, Chinon, France

FIRST PLANTAGENET KING

In England, Henry acted swiftly and decisively to quell opposition among the barons, destroying a number of castles that had been used as bases for tyrannical local rule. He also made a series of legal reforms that created the foundation of the English 'common law' that has endured for centuries. To replace the existing local courts presided over by the barons, he established royal courts with the king's officials travelling on a circuit to bring impartial justice to all parts of the realm. The law was codified in works such as the *Treatise on the Laws and Customs of England*, written by the king's justiciar, or legal officer, Ranulph Glanville. Trial by a 12-man jury was introduced in 1166.

Above: King and Archbishop in dispute. A manuscript of 1300 depicts Henry and Becket engaged in an intense debate.

Henry, the first Plantagenet king and ruler over western Europe's largest 'empire', was king of England by sovereign right. He held all of his French titles and lands – as Duke of Normandy, Count of Anjou, Touraine and Maine and Duke of Aquitaine – as a vassal of the king of France, and herein lies one of the causes of the Hundred Years' War.

HENRY AND BECKET

For the first ten years of the reign, Henry and Thomas à Becket, England's leading prelate, were close allies: Henry appointed Becket Chancellor in one of his first acts as king in January 1155, and in June 1162 named Becket Archbishop of Canterbury. However, in 1164 the pair argued after Becket rejected the Constitutions of Clarendon, which attempted to establish royal authority over churchmen and prevent clerics appealing on legal matters to the Pope in Rome.

Becket fled to a Cistercian monastery in France and Henry confiscated the Archbishop's English possessions. By 1170 Henry and Becket had moved towards reconciliation and, at the king's invitation, Becket returned to England. Once there, however, he defied Henry once more by suspending or excommunicating bishops who had opposed him. In a moment of exasperated rage, Henry is reported to have cried out, 'Will no one rid me of this turbulent priest?' This was the trigger for the attack that led to Becket's death. Four knights, led by Sir Reginald FitzUrse, confronted Becket in Canterbury Cathedral and violated its sanctuary by killing him with their swords.

Within 18 months and amid outrage, the Pope declared Becket a saint. Papal legates found that Henry was not responsible for the murder, and the king made a public act of penance at Becket's tomb in Canterbury Cathedral in July 1174.

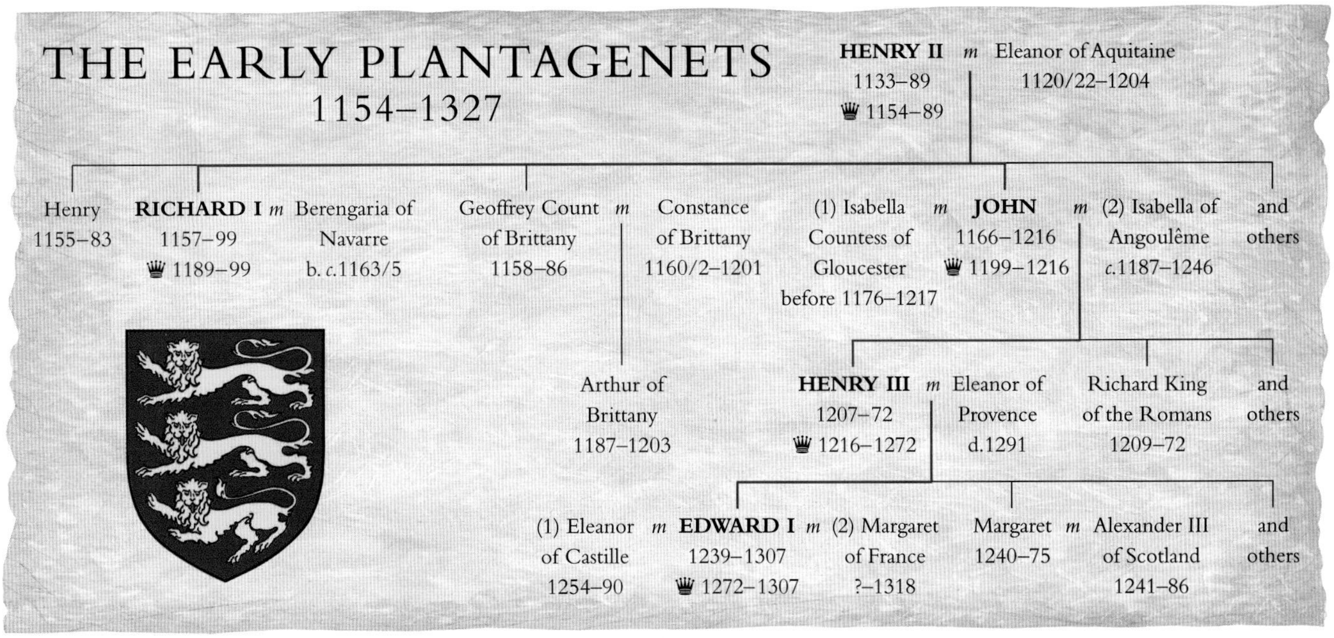

A FORBIDDING QUEEN: ELEANOR OF AQUITAINE

Henry's queen, Eleanor of Aquitaine, was the most powerful woman of her age, who married two kings and was the mother of two more. She encouraged her sons to revolt against their father and, according to tradition, arranged the slaughter of King Henry's beloved mistress, Rosamund Clifford.

Eleanor was the wife of King Louis VII of France before she married Henry. Just eight weeks before Eleanor wed Henry, in the summer of 1152, Louis had had their marriage annulled by mutual consent. Although she was 12 years older than the 18-year-old Henry and was capricious in character, she was a great beauty and became a patron of the arts, especially of courtly literature. She brought with her the vast territories of Aquitaine in central-southern France, which she had inherited from her father and which, under feudal law, reverted to her on her divorce.

Henry and Eleanor had seven children, including two future kings of England: Richard I and King John. However, king and queen grew apart and an ageing Eleanor was increasingly jealous of King Henry's many younger mistresses. In 1173 she encouraged a rebellion by his sons and even tried to join the campaign, disguised as a man, but was captured by King Henry's troops. Henry survived this revolt but a second family rebellion in 1189 sent him to his deathbed.

After 1173 Henry and Eleanor were publicly estranged and the king lived with his favourite mistress, Rosamund Clifford. According to legend, Eleanor killed 'Fair Rosamund' – in one account, confronting her with a dagger and a cup of poison and forcing her to choose which way to die. She outlasted her husband and lived to see two of her sons on the throne. She died, aged 82, in 1204.

Left: After the failed rebellion of 1173, Eleanor was captured by her husband; a fresco of c.1200 from Chinon, France.

Without shirt or shoes, he walked to the cathedral and flung himself before the tomb of his former enemy and friend before submitting to a penitential flogging at the hands of monks.

ROYAL OVERLORD

In a series of treaties, Henry won recognition as feudal overlord from rulers at home and abroad. In 1163 Owain Gwynedd, king of Gwynedd, reaffirmed Henry's overlordship. Henry had power over Scotland under the Treaty of Falaise signed in 1174 with King William of Scots, and he was overlord of Ireland under the 1175 Treaty of Windsor.

FAMILY BETRAYAL

Although Henry crushed a revolt by his sons and estranged queen in 1173, he was outmanoeuvred and defeated 16 years later by his son Prince Richard in alliance with King Philip II of France. Henry was forced to pay homage to Philip for all England's territories in France and to pass England and his Plantagenet holdings to Richard. It is said that when the ageing king discovered that his favourite youngest son, John, had joined the alliance against him, it broke his heart and two days later he died. His final words were, 'Shame, shame on a vanquished king'.

RICHARD I THE LIONHEART

1189–1199

King Richard I is celebrated as the English warrior-king above all others, dubbed *Coeur de Lion* ('Lion Heart') for his chivalrous achievements on the Third Crusade (1190–92) and on the battlefields of Europe. In fact, he had limited connection to his English territories and only spent six months of his 10-year reign in England.

Above: Crusader king. The English Luttrell psalter (1340s) depicts Richard fighting his great foe, Saladin, on crusade.

KNIGHTLY AMBITION

Born in 1157 in Oxford, Richard was raised in France where his French mother, Queen Eleanor of Aquitaine, held court at Poitiers. He was schooled in the arts of knighthood and grew up with a passionate desire to prove himself a chivalric prince in the Holy Land, perhaps inspired by tales of his fearless mother's travels there during the Second Crusade (1147–49) when she was still married to her first husband Louis VII of France. Encouraged by Eleanor, Richard joined a revolt against his father King Henry II in 1173, when he was only 15 years old. In 1179 he proved himself in battle, capturing the castle of Taillebourg during a campaign in Aquitaine to put down rebel lords. At his coronation on 3 September 1189 he cut a dashing figure. Tall, blue-eyed, he was the perfect knight.

IN THE MIDDLE EAST

Richard's main interest at the start of his reign was to raise money for a new crusade. To this end, in December 1189, he cancelled the Treaty of Falaise, under which the Scots recognized English overlordship, in return for a payment from King William of Scots of 10,000 marks. He departed for the Holy Land with Philip of France in the following year. However, the venture got off to a bad start because the kings quarreled before they even reached the Holy

Below: In an image from the Chronicles of England *(c.1470) of Jean de Wavrin, Richard processes to his coronation.*

RICHARD I, KING OF ENGLAND, 1189–1199

Birth: 8 Sept 1157, Oxford
Father: King Henry II of England
Mother: Queen Eleanor of Aquitaine
Accession: 6 July 1189
Coronation: 3 Sept 1189, Westminster Abbey; recrowned 17 April 1194, Winchester
Queen: Berengaria of Navarre (m. 1191; d. 1230)
Succeeded by: His brother, John
Greatest achievement: Military victories on Third Crusade
Dec 1189: Cancels Treaty of Falaise
1191: Captures Arsuf in Holy Land
1192: Imprisoned by Holy Roman Emperor Henry VI
1193: Freed on payment of ransom of 150,000 marks
Death: 6 April 1199, Châlus, France

Above: Richard is shown imprisoned in Vienna (left) and in the moment before being shot by a crossbowman at Châlus.

Land. At a stop in Sicily, Philip and Richard argued over Richard's refusal to keep his promise to make a dynastic marriage with Philip's sister, Alice.

Philip travelled ahead. Richard captured Cyprus after a quarrel with its Greek king and there, on 12 May 1191, he married Berengaria of Navarre, who was crowned Queen of England. In the Holy Land, Richard and Philip patched up their quarrel and together captured Acre. Here Richard quarrelled bitterly with Duke Leopold of Austria over the sharing out of the gains and also alienated Philip once more.

Philip left for home in August 1191, while Richard proceeded to capture Arsuf and to march on Jerusalem. He twice came within view of the holy city but was forced to retreat because of the strength of Saladin's defending army. The crusade ended in a truce, under which Saladin remained in control of Jerusalem, but Christian pilgrims were permitted to visit the city. Richard set sail for home in September 1192. Although he had not achieved all his goals, his victories re-established a viable Crusader kingdom in the Holy Land.

TROUBLE AT HOME

Richard had laid plans to protect his English realm while he was away. He entrusted William Longchamps, Bishop of Ely, with the position of Chief Justiciar and the power to rule the country, while making his brother Prince John promise not to travel to England from France or attempt to take control there. The plan failed. John did not keep his word and set up his own government, driving Longchamps into exile in France and plotting with Philip of France to prevent Richard returning.

CAPTURED IN AUSTRIA

Hearing of this plot while returning from the Holy Land, Richard attempted to evade capture. After he was shipwrecked he disguised himself but he was recognized in Vienna and imprisoned, first by his enemy Duke Leopold of Austria and then by the Holy Roman Emperor Henry VI. His release was made subject to payment of a king's ransom of 150,000 marks, the equivalent of 35 tonnes of gold.

In England, the new Chief Justiciar Hubert Walter somehow managed to raise this vast sum. Freed in 1193, Richard returned to England the following year and was crowned for a second time by Walter, now Archbishop of Canterbury, at Winchester on 17 April 1194. The king forgave his brother for his part in the plot against him. Then, after spending a mere two months in England he returned to France to seek revenge against Philip and to fight for the return of lost territories. He died there on 6 April 1199 after the wound made in his shoulder by a crossbow bolt at Châlus became gangrenous. He was buried alongside his father – and later joined by his mother, Eleanor of Aquitaine – at Fontevrault Abbey in Normandy.

Below: Coeur de lion. *Richard's image as the crusading king* par excellence *has inspired artists of many eras.*

JOHN
1199–1216

An unprincipled opportunist, King John made a series of bad decisions in pursuit of short-term advantage. By the end of his reign he had not only lost the vast French empire created by his father, Henry II, but had also alienated the crown's leading English supporters as well as the pope and the Church establishment.

Right: John's favourite hunting lands were said to be Clipstone in Sherwood Forest, home of legendary outlaw Robin Hood.

'LACKLAND' AND LOYALTY

John was the youngest of King Henry's sons, and because his older brothers received large territorial inheritances and he was given nothing, he was nicknamed 'Lackland'. In 1189 John joined Richard in revolt against their father. This betrayal is said to have left Henry a broken man, for John was his father's favourite. Then when Richard I was on the Third Crusade in 1190–2, John reneged on a promise not to interfere in England. He declared himself King of England when Richard was captured and imprisoned in Austria on his way home from the Holy Land in 1192. Richard nonetheless forgave John and the pair fought in tandem to regain Richard's French lands.

On Richard's death in April 1199, John was invested Duke of Normandy in Rouen and then crowned King of England in Westminster Abbey. When John dropped the banner bearing his ducal insignia at the Rouen ceremony, many saw it as a bad omen.

John came to the throne at the age of 32. As he did so, his attention was focused on safeguarding his French lands in the face of a challenge from his nephew, Arthur of Brittany, who claimed Anjou and Touraine.

JOHN, KING OF ENGLAND, 1199–1216

Born: 24 Dec 1167, Oxford
Father: King Henry II of England
Mother: Queen Eleanor of Aquitaine
Accession: 6 April 1199
Coronation: 27 May 1199, Westminster Abbey
Queens: (1) Isabella of Gloucester (m. 1176; divorced 1200; d. 1217); (2) Isabella of Angoulême (m. 1200; d. 1246)
Succeeded by: His son, Henry III
Greatest achievement: Defeat of Irish revolt, 1210
Nov 1209: Excommunicated by Pope Innocent III
1215: Magna Carta
Death: 18 Oct 1216, Newark

THE PRINCE OF ALL WALES

Welsh overlord Llewelyn ab Iorwerth, prince of Gwynedd, established himself as ruler without equal in Wales at the end of King John's reign, earning himself the epithet 'the Great'. Hearing of plans for a joint attack on Gwynedd by King John and Gwenwynwyn, lord of the rival Welsh kingdom of Powys, Llewelyn declared Gwenwynwyn guilty of treachery and marched into his lands to annex them. Gwenwynwyn returned from England to defend Powys, but failed, was injured and forced to retreat to Cheshire. Llewelyn's queen was Joan, an illegitimate daughter of King John. After Llewelyn's death, on 11 April 1240 at Aberconway in Gwynedd, a chronicler called him 'Prince of Wales'.

Above: A 1957 memorial marks the spot at Runnymede near Windsor at which John signed the Magna Carta.

FRENCH LOSSES

In the first year of his reign, after divorcing his first wife, Isabella of Gloucester, John married the 12-year-old Isabella of Angoulême, making an enemy of the French baron Hugh de Lusignan, who had been betrothed to Isabella. The de Lusignans owed John allegiance in his role as Count of Aquitaine but they appealed to his feudal overlord, King Philip of France, for justice in the case of the marriage. John refused to appear before the French king to answer the charges, and Philip dispossessed John of all the lands he held in France, on the grounds that John was a 'contumacious vassal' (since he had failed to fulfil his feudal obligation).

The dispute with the de Lusignans and other French nobles led to war in 1202. John was initially successful, capturing Arthur and the de Lusignans at Mirebeau, but when word got out that he had murdered Arthur, Brittany rose against him and John lost the support of the barons in Anjou and Normandy. He retreated to England in 1203 and by 1206 had lost all his French holdings save Aquitaine.

DISPUTE WITH ROME

When the Archbishop of Canterbury, Hubert Walter, died in 1206, John refused to accept Stephen Langton, the man nominated by the pope, as Walter's successor. The dispute led to John's excommunication by Pope Innocent III in 1209. In theory the pope had the power to order John's subjects to depose him and replace their king with a more godly man, but John backed down. He accepted Langton as archbishop in 1213 and then agreed that Ireland and England were fiefs of Rome. At Winchester on 20 July 1213, Archbishop Langton formally absolved John of his excommunication.

JOHN AND MAGNA CARTA

In 1214 John launched an ill-fated attempt to regain his French possessions that ended with the defeat of his German ally, the emperor Otto of Brunswick, at Bouvines. His campaigns had been extremely expensive and John's English subjects were restless under the weight of taxation that he imposed to finance them. In 1215 a revolt by leading barons forced John to agree to a charter of liberties, *Magna Carta* ('Great Charter') at Runnymede to the west of London.

The charter, which was reissued in 1216, 1217, 1225 and 1297, guaranteed the reform of royal abuses of power and turned out to be the first step in establishing constitutional government in England. It stated that the law had force independently of the will of the king. The following year, when John renounced it, the barons rebelled, imported Louis, the son of King Philip II of France, and prepared to depose John. Before this could happen John died of dysentery at Newark on 18 October 1216. The final event of his reign was a characteristically bungled manoeuvre in which he lost the crown jewels in quicksand while crossing the Wash, a tidal estuary in eastern England.

THREE LIONS

John adopted three gold lions *passant*, or striding, on a red background as his coat of arms. He based the device on the emblem used by his father and brother, of two striding lions. Heraldic devices were worn by knights jousting at chivalric tournaments and in battle as an identifying mark. John's three lions were incorporated into the royal seal.

Below: John's tomb (1232) in Worcester Cathedral is carved with an effigy of the king flanked by St Wulfstan and St Oswald.

HENRY III

1216–1272

Above: In this miniature of his coronation ceremony, Henry holds a model of Westminster Abbey, rebuilt in his reign.

Following King John's sudden death and with London in the hands of rebel barons preparing to elevate France's Prince Louis to the English throne, nine-year-old Prince Henry was crowned in great haste at Gloucester Abbey on 28 October 1216. A bracelet belonging to his mother, Queen Isabella, was used in place of the crown because King John had lost the crown jewels. With the Archbishop of Canterbury away in Rome, the ceremony was performed by the French-born Bishop of Winchester.

John's disastrous reign had brought England to its knees and the future of the Angevin dynasty looked grim. However, thanks to an effective regency by William Marshal, Earl of Pembroke, the knight chosen on his deathbed by King John, the country and the dynasty were stabilized. Marshal defeated the rebels in 1217, bringing the civil war to an end, and on his death in 1219 was succeeded by Hubert de Burgh. Henry III took the reins of power in January 1227, aged 20.

ROYAL WEDDING

Henry married the beautiful 19-year-old Eleanor of Provence in Canterbury Cathedral on 14 January 1236. To house his new queen in suitable splendour he renovated the royal palace at Westminster, installing glass in the windows and plumbing, fitting large fireplaces and commissioning fine wall-paintings for private chambers. Later the same month, on 30 January 1236, Eleanor was crowned Queen of England, in Westminster Abbey.

The marriage brought trouble, for the influx of the new queen's relatives seeking wealth and power made the English barons resentful. Trouble broke out in the mid-1250s after Henry agreed to provide financial support for Pope Innocent IV's proposed military campaign in Sicily. In June 1258 he was forced to agree to the Provisions of

HENRY III, KING OF ENGLAND, 1216–1272

Birth: 1 Oct 1207, Winchester
Father: King John of England
Mother: Queen Isabella of Angoulême
Accession: 18 Oct 1216
Coronations: (1) 28 Oct 1216 Gloucester; (2) 17 May 1220, Westminster Abbey
Queen: Eleanor of Provence (m. 14 Jan 1236; d. 1291)
Succeeded by: His son, Edward I
Jan 1227: Henry takes power at the end of his minority
May 1240: Crowns Dafydd of Gwynedd 'paramount prince in Wales'
June 1258: Provisions of Oxford
1264: Civil war
14 May 1264: Captured by Simon de Montfort
4 Aug 1265: Defeat of Simon de Montfort at Battle of Evesham
Death: 16 Nov 1272, London

KING OF ANIMALS

In London Henry built a menagerie at the Tower of London, partly as a home for the first elephant ever to be brought to England. The beast was a gift to Henry from France's King Louis IX in 1255. It was carried as far as Tilbury Docks by water and then walked the remainder of the way while gaping crowds marvelled at the sight. Earlier, in 1237, Henry had built a leopard house at the Tower, and he was given a polar bear as a gift from the King of Norway in 1252. In keeping a zoo, Henry was following the example of his great grandfather, Henry I, who had kept a collection of camels, lions and leopards at Woodstock in Oxfordshire. Richard I, it is said, even brought a crocodile to England from his travels, but the creature escaped into the Thames.

Oxford, by which a council of 15 barons was created to govern jointly with the king.

DE MONTFORT'S RISE AND FALL

Simon de Montfort, Earl of Leicester, was the driving force behind this challenge to royal authority. Born in France, he had arrived in England in 1229 and set about building a power base. In January 1238 he married the king's sister, Eleanor, thus provoking the anger of Henry's brother Richard, Earl of Cornwall, and that of leading barons. Exiled as a result in 1239, he won great honour on crusade (1240–2) and during King Henry's unsuccessful invasion of France in 1242. He subsequently became convinced that Henry was unfit to govern, largely because of the king's poor decision-making after sending him to put down a baronial revolt in Gascony in 1248.

In 1264 de Montfort led an open rebellion to reinstate the Provisions of Oxford after they had been repudiated by Henry in 1262 and then annulled at an agreed arbitration by King Louis IX of France. De Montfort defeated the king's army at Lewes in 1264, captured Henry III and his son Edward, and for a year became the effective ruler of England. At this time he called a Parliament that, in addition to barons and clerics, held two burgesses from each borough and two knights from each shire. However, in the summer of 1265, Prince Edward escaped and, joining up with allies, turned on de Montfort and won a crushing victory at the Battle of Evesham in Worcestershire. In death, de Montfort was horribly mutilated by royalist soldiers. His head, hands and feet were cut off and his genitals thrown on to his face.

The king's authority had been restored – by his son. However, de Montfort had achieved a lasting legacy, because England's king would ever afterwards have to be mindful of the will of Parliament.

A PRINCE FOR WALES

In May 1240, amid great ceremony at Gloucester, Henry III crowned Dafydd of Gwynedd the 'paramount prince in Wales'. Dafydd was the younger son of Llywelyn the Great of Gwynedd and his wife Joan, an illegitimate daughter of King John, and was therefore Henry's nephew. Towards the end of Henry's reign, in 1267, the English king recognised Dafydd's nephew Llywelyn ap Gruffudd as Prince of Wales.

Left: Salisbury Cathedral was begun in 1220 and dedicated in 1258. The 404ft (123m) spire was added in 1330.

Above: 14th-century chroniclers stressed Henry's piety. He supported orphans and provided food for paupers. He is even said to have washed and kissed lepers' feet.

ROYAL PATRON

Henry was a pious and highly cultured man, whose 56-year reign was a golden age of learning, architecture and the arts. In addition to his large-scale renovation of Westminster Palace, Henry oversaw a major rebuilding of Westminster Abbey to house a shrine to the church's original royal founder, Edward the Confessor. The French-trained architect Master Henry de Reyns pulled down all of Edward's church except the nave and rebuilt it in the Gothic style on a French cathedral plan. The work took 36 years and cost £46,000. Henry's reign also saw major work on the magnificent cathedrals at St Alban's, Salisbury, Lincoln and Wells in Somerset. Learning thrived under this cultured king, and the first colleges in Oxford University – Merton, University and Balliol – were founded in the years between 1249 and 1264.

EDWARD I

1272–1307

Edward I came to the throne, aged 33, a proven warrior. He had already fought with distinction in Henry III's campaigns against Welsh prince Llywelyn ap Gruffudd in 1259 and in 1265 had restored royal power by crushing Simon de Montfort's rebellion at the Battle of Evesham. He was in Sicily, returning from fighting on the Eighth Crusade (1270–2) when he was declared king on 17 November 1272.

'LONGSHANKS'

Edward brought a ferocious martial vigour to his reign, forcefully imposing his authority on his realm, ending Welsh independence and waging a series of brutal wars in the north that later earned him the nickname 'Hammer of the Scots'. Standing imperiously 6ft 2in (1.9m) tall – an astonishing height for the 13th century – he cut a commanding and regal figure and was admiringly known as 'Longshanks'.

At home he carried out much needed legal reforms, improved the efficiency of administration and is remembered as the king in whose reign Parliament's role in government was consolidated. The changes he oversaw in government strengthened rather than diluted royal authority, clarifying Parliament's role as an instrument of the king's rule – used in particular to levy

EDWARD I, KING OF ENGLAND, 1272–1307

Birth: 17 June 1239, Westminster
Father: Henry III of England
Mother: Eleanor of Provence
Accession: 16 Nov 1272
Coronation: 19 Aug 1274, Westminster Abbey
Queens: (1) Eleanor of Castile (m. Oct 1254; d. 1290); (2) Margaret of France (m. 10 Sept 1299; d. 1318)
Succeeded by: His son, Edward II
March 1284: Statute of Rhuddlan
1290: Royal edict expelling Jews from England
1296: Invades Scotland, Battle of Dunbar
1301: Edward's son Edward created first English 'Prince of Wales'
1305: Captures and executes Scottish rebel William Wallace
Death: 7 July 1307 of dysentery at Burgh by Sands, near Carlisle

Above: Realm of fortresses. The map shows the network of castles built between 1066 and the end of Edward I's reign in 1307.

Above: One of Edward's forbidding Welsh castles, Harlech was built in 1283–90 by his engineer, Master James of St George.

taxes to pay for military campaigns. The legal reforms codified English law, providing a legal basis for inheritance of land and improving public order laws.

VICTORY IN WALES

Llywelyn ap Gruffydd was the first sole ruler of a united Wales. However, he grew overconfident of his position and, when he refused to pay homage to Edward I, provoked a savage 1276 invasion that within a year reduced his realm to a small region in Snowdonia. An uprising led by Llywelyn's brother Dafydd in 1282 provoked a second English invasion in which Llywelyn was killed at Builth and then Dafydd was hung, drawn and quartered as a traitor at Shrewsbury.

Under the Statute of Rhuddlan of March 1284, English officials were brought in to govern the new English-style shires that were to replace the existing Welsh kingdoms. Edward built a series of forbidding castles across Wales at Flint, Rhuddlan, Builth, Conway, Caernarfon, Criccieth, Harlech, Denbigh and Beaumaris to impose his will on what was now a subject country. In Caernarfon castle, in 1284 the king's son Edward was born. Some 17 years later this boy, now heir to the throne, was created the first English Prince of Wales. This was the first time an English royal ruler officially took the title of 'prince'.

THE HAMMER OF THE SCOTS

When John Balliol was named King of Scots in 1292 after a two-year interregnum following the death of the infant Queen Margaret, he paid homage to Edward as his feudal overlord. However, in October 1295 the Scots made an alliance with France rather than join Edward in a French military campaign, and the following spring John Balliol refused to pay homage to Edward.

Edward invaded Scotland with a 25,000-strong army and overran Berwick, killing 7,000 of its population, before defeating a Scottish army at Dunbar. King John Balliol abdicated and, in a humiliating public ceremony, was stripped of his crown and royal finery.

Edward unleashed the force of the English army and its powerful longbowmen on the Scots again in 1298 and 1300. That year he made a calculated insult to Scottish pride by removing the Scots' ancient coronation stone from its place at Scone and installing it at Westminster as part of a new coronation throne.

Edward invaded Scotland again in 1301–2 and in 1303–5. When he finally captured the outlawed Scottish leader William Wallace, he was taken to London and executed by having his head and limbs severed from his body.

When Edward died near Carlisle, on 7 July 1307, he was travelling north in preparation for yet another of his Scottish campaigns.

A LOYAL HUSBAND

Edward was devoted to his first wife, Eleanor of Castile. Their marriage in 1254 was a diplomatic one, made when the future king was 15 and his wife just 9, but grew to be a love match. An elegant, dark-haired woman, Eleanor travelled with her husband to Wales, Gascony and even to the Holy Land on crusade. Perhaps their bond was strengthened by a brush with death in 1287, when a lightning strike in Gascony killed two people in the very room in which the royal couple were sitting.

Queen Eleanor bore Edward 11 daughters and 4 sons, including the future Edward II. When she herself died, aged 54, on 28 November 1290, her desolate spouse wrote 'in life I dearly loved her and I will not stop loving her in death'. In her honour he erected 12 Memorial Crosses to mark the places where her funeral cortège stopped on its journey from Harby, in Nottinghamshire, where the queen died, to Westminster Abbey, where she was buried. Three of these crosses survive today – at Geddington and Hardingstone in Nottinghamshire and Waltham Cross in Essex; a memorial at Charing Cross in London is a 19th-century replica of the original cross that stood there.

Edward married for a second time, on 10 September 1299, again making a diplomatic match when he wed Margaret, the sister of France's King Philip IV. Despite a 40-year age differential between the 60-year-old king and his 20-year-old bride, this marriage too turned out well.

Below: Eleanor's memory was celebrated by this monument at Hardingstone.

Below: Liberties confirmed. The 14th-century manuscript, Statutes of England, *shows Edward reissuing Magna Carta.*

EDWARD II

1307–1327

Edward II was blessed with intelligence, bravery and good looks and inherited the throne of a secure and well-governed country. However, he exhibited a self-indulgence and lack of judgement in public and private life that made a bitter enemy of his formidable queen and of prominent barons and that led inexorably to the loss of his crown and a gruesome end in a prison cell.

Above: Gravity and majesty. Edward II stands between Edwards I and III in a group of statues at York Cathedral.

A ROYAL FAVOURITE

Before he became king, Edward's close friendship – and probably homosexual relationship – with Piers Gaveston, the son of a Gascon knight, caused scandal at court. Edward I is said to have been outraged when his son asked for a gift of territory for his friend. The king exiled Gaveston and reportedly tore at his son's hair, shouting, 'You base-born whoreson! Do you want to give lands away now, you who have never gained any?' However, there was nothing to stand in Edward's way when he became king and within a month of acceding to the throne he recalled Gaveston and made him Earl of Cornwall, a position normally reserved for the son of the reigning king. Shortly afterwards Edward gave his niece in marriage to Gaveston, then made his friend regent while he, Edward, travelled to France to make a diplomatic wedding match with the French king's daughter, Isabella.

Leading barons led by Thomas, Earl of Lancaster turned against the king, who in 1311 was forced to accede to a series of demands that placed limits on his power and in particular required him to strip Gaveston of his title and send him into exile. Edward did as he was required to do, but Gaveston returned the following year. The angry barons seized the royal favourite and, at Blacklow Hill in Warwickshire, they

EDWARD II, KING OF ENGLAND, 1307–1327

Birth: 25 April 1284, Caernarfon
Father: Edward I of England
Mother: Eleanor of Castile
Accession: 8 July 1307
Coronation: 25 Feb 1308, Westminster Abbey
Queen: Isabella of France (m. 25 Jan 1308; d. 1358)
Succeeded by: His son, Edward III
Greatest achievement: English economic boom fuelled by exports to continental Europe of English wool
Sept 1311: Ordinances strengthen power of Parliament
24 June 1314: Defeated by Scots in Battle of Bannockburn
1326: Civil war
24 Jan 1327: abdicated
Death: 22 Sept 1327 murdered Berkeley Castle, Gloucestershire

Below: Edward II founded Oriel College, Oxford, in 1326 as 'The House of the Blessed Mary the Virgin in Oxford'.

beheaded him. Gaveston's death greatly upset Edward, but had the effect of repairing his relationship with Queen Isabella. The couple's son, who was named Edward after his father, was born on 13 November 1312.

DEFEAT AND HUMILIATION

In 1314, Edward led an English army into Scotland to relieve Stirling Castle, which was besieged by Scottish forces under King Robert I 'the Bruce'. Although they outnumbered the Scots, Edward's army was humiliated in the two-day Battle of Bannockburn, afterwards celebrated as the event that cemented Scottish independence. Edward was forced to flee for his life. In England, Thomas, Earl of Lancaster sidelined the king and established himself as the country's effective ruler.

CIVIL WAR

Edward did not change his ways. He found new favourites in two lords from the Welsh Marches, Hugh le Despenser and his father, also Hugh, to whom he gave an abundance of titles and territories in Wales. Lancaster banished the Despensers in August 1321, and the king went to war on their behalf, defeating the Earl in the Battle of Boroughbridge, in Yorkshire, in March 1322. Edward then had Lancaster executed, recalled the Despensers and for a short while governed as he pleased. However, trouble was brewing.

Queen Isabella, angered at her husband's relationship with the younger Hugh le Despenser, abandoned him. She began to live openly in France with Roger Mortimer, Earl of March, an exiled opponent of the Despensers, and to plot the king's downfall. Such was the ferocity of her newfound hatred of her husband that at court in England they nicknamed her the 'she-wolf of France'. Crucially for their planned revolt, Mortimer and Isabella had the king's heir, Edward, living with them.

Backed by a mercenary army from Flanders, Isabella and Mortimer invaded in October 1326. Edward fled to Wales, while the queen's forces set themselves up at Gloucester. The following month the queen had her revenge on the younger Despenser. At Hereford, on 24 November 1326, he was cruelly executed. His genitals were sliced off because, contemporary accounts said, 'he was held to be guilty of unnatural practices with the king'. His entrails were cut from him and burned. Finally, he was decapitated and his body quartered. His head was sent to London and the pieces of his body sent to the corners of the kingdom.

Isabella and Mortimer imprisoned Edward II in Kenilworth Castle, and forced him to abdicate his throne. They declared the 14-year-old Prince Edward king. After the coronation, they kept the former King Edward II imprisoned in Berkeley Castle, Gloucestershire, where he met a death matching that of his former lover le Despenser for atrocity.

Below: Gothic masterpiece. Edward III honoured his father by building this superb marble tomb in Gloucester Cathedral.

THE DEATH OF KING EDWARD II

After installing Edward III on the throne, Queen Isabella and Roger Mortimer ordered that Edward II be jailed at Berkeley Castle in Gloucestershire and starved to death. But the king, whose spirit must have remained strong, lingered painfully on. The king's minders devised a sadistic means of killing their prisoner that would leave no mark on his body: after a metal funnel was inserted into the king's anus, a red-hot soldering iron was thrust into his bowels. His screams of agony filled the air.

The king's colourful reign and brutal end inspired 16th-century English dramatist Christopher Marlowe to write *Edward II* (*c.*1592), one of the first historical plays of the Elizabethan era. This play in turn inspired the 20th-century filmmaker Derek Jarman to make the acclaimed movie *Edward II* (1991).

Below: Berkeley Castle was built by Roger de Berkeley in the 11th century.

EDWARD III
1327–1377

When Edward III became king at the age of only 14, he was little more than a pawn of his power-hungry mother, Queen Isabella, and her lover Roger Mortimer, Earl of March, who had used the boy-king to depose his father Edward II. However, he grew quickly to manhood and shortly before his 18th birthday took power into his own hands. He led a night raid in Nottingham Castle that surprised Isabella and Mortimer as they prepared for bed, sent Mortimer to the Tower and exiled his mother from power and the royal court by despatching her to Castle Rising in Norfolk.

CHAUCER'S KING

Edward proved to be a forceful king, the Christian world's most celebrated warrior of the day. At home he repaired the civil ructions of his father's years and presided over a court in which chivalry, fashion and the finest literature were all celebrated, knights jousted in single combat, courtiers wore extravagant gowns and robes, and the first great English poet, Geoffrey Chaucer, found employment as a civil servant and trusted diplomat.

AT WAR WITH FRANCE

Early in Edward's reign Charles IV of France died without issue and Queen Isabella pressed Edward's claim to the French throne on the basis that Edward was Charles's nephew. The French *parlement* chose Charles's cousin to rule as Philip VI. Initially Edward paid homage to Philip for his French lands, but in 1340 he declared himself King of France. He destroyed the French fleet in July 1340, beginning a prolonged military campaign in France that would later be identified as the first phase of the Hundred Years War (1337–1453).

In 1346 Edward led an invasion of France that climaxed in a famous victory at Crécy on 26 August, when an army of professional English soldiers and Welsh longbowmen trounced a much larger French force under King Philip VI. Some 10,000 Frenchmen were killed in an encounter that led to just 42 English dead and a few dozen Welsh infantry.

Above: The Black Prince captured King Jean II of France in the course of the English triumph at Poitiers in 1356.

A major figure in Edward's French campaigns was his son Edward, the Prince of Wales, known as the Black Prince because of his black armour. Knighted by his father at the age of 16 in France in 1346, the Black Prince fought bravely that year at Crécy, where he killed the King of Bohemia and took as his own the king's emblem of three feathers and the motto *Ich Dien* ('I serve'). He led the English to another proud victory, in 1356, at the Battle of Poitiers, where an English army of no more than 8,000 defeated a French force of 50,000, killing 13 counts and 66 barons and capturing the French king, Jean II.

From this high point, English fortunes in France declined, for King Edward and his commanders were unable to translate military victories into more lasting power.

EDWARD III, KING OF ENGLAND, 1327–1377

Birth: 13 Nov 1312, Windsor Castle
Father: Edward II of England
Mother: Queen Isabella
Accession: 24 Jan 1327
Coronation: 1 Feb 1327, Westminster Abbey
Queen: Philippa of Hainault (m. 24 Jan 1328; d. 1369)
Succeeded by: His grandson, Richard II
Greatest achievement: Victories over French in Battles of Crécy and Poitiers
26 Aug 1346: Battle of Crécy
17 Oct 1346: Battle of Neville's Cross, Durham
1348: Black Death strikes England
24 June 1348: founds the Most Noble Order of the Garter
19 Sept 1356: Battle of Poitiers
Death: 21 June 1377, Sheen Palace

Above: Regal warrior. This anonymous portrait of the king is at Hampton Court.

THE LATER PLANTAGENETS 1127–1413

EDWARD II *m* Isabella of France
1284–1327 | 1292/5–1358
♛ 1307–1327

EDWARD III *m* Philippa of Hainault
1312–77 | c.1313/14–69
♛ 1327–77

Joan *m* David II of Scotland
1321–62 | 1324–71

and others

Edward The Black Prince *m* Joan of Kent
1330–76 | 1328–85

Lionel Duke of Clarence
1338–68

John of Gaunt Duke of Lancaster *m* (1) Blanche of Lancaster (1345–69) (2) Constance of Castile (1354–94) (3) Katherine Swynford (c.1350–1403)
1340–99

Edmund Duke of York
1341–1402

Thomas Duke of Gloucester
1355–97

and others

RICHARD II *m* (1) Anne of Bohemia (1366–94) (2) Isabella of France (1389–1409)
1367–1400
♛ 1377–1399

HENRY IV
1367–1413
♛ 1399–1413

In September 1360 under the Treaty of Brétigny, Jean II was returned to his countrymen – after four years in English captivity – for a ransom of three million gold crowns. Edward renounced his claim to the French throne, while the French recognized English rights in Calais, Poitou and Gascony.

In the following 20-odd years, the French won back many of these lands. Thus, despite heroic victories on French soil, the great warrior king Edward III had fewer French holdings at his death than he had had at his accession.

SCOTTISH KING IN CUSTODY

King Edward also held Scotland's King David II in captivity for almost exactly 11 years after David was captured at the battle of Neville's Cross in 1346.

Earlier in his reign, Edward had provided military backing for the claim of John Balliol's son Edward to the Scottish throne, and in 1334 King David, then just nine years old, was forced to flee to France. In 1341, David had returned to Scotland and then attempted an ill-fated invasion of northern England intended to regain land ceded to Edward III by Edward Balliol.

David was released under the Treaty of Berwick, signed on 6 November 1357, under which the Scots promised to pay a ransom of 100,000 marks for their king and a ten-year Anglo-Scottish truce was agreed. For a short while in 1356–7, Edward had the strange distinction of holding the kings of both France and Scotland in captivity.

POWER FOR PARLIAMENT

Edward's military campaigns in France and Scotland proved extremely expensive and he needed regular levies of taxation to pay for them. Parliament was in a strong bargaining position and won a number of new powers. These included agreements in 1340 that no new taxes could be imposed without the approval of the Commons in Parliament and, the following year, that the king's ministers would be required to pledge acceptance of Magna Carta and the law in Parliament.

THE BLACK DEATH

The Black Death – a Europe-wide pandemic of bubonic and pneumonic plague – hit England in 1348. It killed the king's favourite daughter, Princess Joan, two archbishops of Canterbury and around one third to one half of the population of the country. As a result of the drastic loss of labour this entailed, the survivors were able to charge more for their labours, leading to severe wage inflation. The 1351 Statute of Labourers once more set wages at pre-1348 levels.

THE ORDER OF THE GARTER

In 1344, Edward III held a round-table tournament at Windsor and took a solemn vow to form an order of Arthurian knights. The Most Noble Order of the Garter, consisting of 26 knights – the king and the Prince of Wales, each with 12 companions – was formed at Windsor on 24 June 1348.

Legend has it that the Order's name and motto derived from a racy incident at a ball in 1347, when a lady – in some accounts Joan of Kent, future wife of Edward the Black Prince – dropped her garter and the king picked it neatly up and tied it around his knee, saying gallantly, *Honi soit qui mal y pense* ('may evil come to the one who has impure thoughts'). St George was the Order's patron saint.

RICHARD II
1377–1399

Richard of Bordeaux, son of Edward, the Black Prince, acceded to the crown of England at the age of 10 in 1377. He had become heir to the throne only the previous year, on the death from dysentery of his warrior father. Richard was crowned amid great pageantry and solemn ceremony on 16 July 1377, watched by his uncle John of Gaunt, Duke of Lancaster, oldest surviving son of the late King Edward III. Until Richard came of age, power was in the hands of a ruling council.

THE PEASANTS' REVOLT

The young king proved that he had inherited his father's courage when he faced down a crowd of angry country labourers at Smithfield on 15 June 1381. The men of Kent and Essex had risen in the 'Peasants' Revolt' to protest against the inequitable poll tax that demanded one shilling from every person, whether rich or poor.

The peasants had arrived in London on 13 June and run riot, demolishing John of Gaunt's palace and the following day storming the Tower of London and executing the Chancellor, Archbishop Simon of Sudbury.

Returning from attending Mass at Westminster on the morning of 15 June, Richard met the rebels in person. When the rebel leader Wat Tyler rode forward to press their demands upon their ruler, he was stabbed to death by the Mayor of London, William Walworth. Tyler's men were about to attack when Richard silenced them with the words, 'Sirs, would you kill your king? I am your king, I am your captain and your leader.' The moment of crisis passed thanks to his bravery and he proceeded to promise sufficient concessions to make the men disperse. Subsequently he would go back on his promises, making the celebrated declaration, 'Villeins ye are, and villeins ye shall remain'.

Richard's early success may have encouraged the traits of arrogance and unwillingness to compromise that led eventually to his downfall. He clashed repeatedly with Parliament and his leading barons, notably over his favourite Robert de Vere, whom he made Duke of Ireland in 1386. Leading barons led by Richard, Duke of Gloucester took up arms in 1387 and issued an appeal to the king to rid himself of de Vere and the Earl of Suffolk, whom they accused of treason. Richard was always unwilling to compromise and called on de Vere to defend the royal cause. At the Battle of Radcot Bridge near Oxford, rebel forces under Gloucester and his nephew Henry Bolingbroke defeated de Vere and forced him to flee. The following year, Gloucester and the leading barons – known as the 'Lords Appellant' because they had issued the 1387 appeal to the king – forced Richard to renew his coronation oaths and at the 'Merciless Parliament' purged the court of Richard's intimates and favourites.

RICHARD II, KING OF ENGLAND 1377–1399

Birth: 6 Jan 1367, Bordeaux
Father: Edward, Prince of Wales ('the Black Prince')
Mother: Countess Joan ('the Fair Maid of Kent')
Accession: 21 June 1377
Coronation: 16 July 1377, Westminster Abbey
Queens: (1) Anne of Bohemia (m. 1382; d. 1394); (2) Isabella of France (m. 1397; d. 1409)
Succeeded by: His cousin, Henry Bolingbroke, Duke of Lancaster
Greatest achievement: Facing down Peasants' Revolt 1381; receiving lords' submission in Ireland 1395
1381: Peasants' Revolt
1387: Uprising of 'Lords Appellant'
1397: Murder and execution of the Lords Appellant Gloucester and Arundel
1398: Exile of Henry Bolingbroke
30 Sept 1399: Deposed in Parliament
14 Feb 1400: Dies in captivity, Pontefract Castle

Left: A late 15th-century Flemish chronicle represents the teenage Richard surrounded by his ruling council.

The Lords condemned the exiled de Vere and Suffolk for treason and executed Sir Nichols Bembre, former London mayor, and Sir Robert Tresilian, former chief justice.

Richard waited nine years to have his revenge. In July 1397 the king arrested Gloucester and the Earl of Arundel. He sent Gloucester to Calais, where he was murdered. In September Parliament condemned all the Lords Appellant for plotting against the monarch: Arundel was executed and Warwick exiled. The following year Richard also exiled Henry Bolingbroke for ten years. However, the repercussions of this conflict would bring the king down, for in 1399 Henry Bolingbroke returned to seize the crown and Richard – now deposed – met his end in captivity, possibly at the hands of a murderer in 1400.

DIPLOMATIC SUCCESS

Before the drama of the Lords Appellant had been fully played out, Richard achieved one of the triumphs of his reign. In 1394–5 he led an army to triumph in Ireland and, after spending Christmas in Dublin, received the submission of 80 Irish chiefs, who as a result were confirmed as rulers in their inherited lands. Under the agreement, all land east of a line from Dundalk to Waterford was considered English territory and later called the 'English Pale'. In 1396, moreover, Richard negotiated a 28-year truce with France. At a meeting with Charles VI near Calais, he pledged friendship, promising to support French policy while nevertheless maintaining his claim to the throne.

RICHARD'S MARRIAGES

Richard had two queens. His first was Anne of Bohemia, married in 1382 when both were 15 years old. Although initially a diplomatic match – Anne's father was Holy Roman Emperor Charles IV – this became a close and loving relationship. When Anne died aged just 28 on 7 June 1394, Richard commissioned a truly magnificent Westminster Abbey tomb with twin effigies of himself and his queen. At her funeral in the Abbey, on 3 August, he was enraged when the Earl of Arundel rudely arrived late, and felled him with his sceptre. In 1397 he made a second diplomatic marriage. As part of the treaty signed with France he took Charles VI's eldest daughter Isabella, aged just seven, as his wife.

Above: In the exquisite Wilton Diptych, Richard kneels beside St Edward the Confessor, St Edmund and a pilgrim, before the Virgin Mary and Christ.

Richard was a major artistic patron. He supported poet Geoffrey Chaucer, who had been a diplomat in Edward III's reign and who wrote his poem 'The Parliament of Fowls' in 1382 to celebrate Richard's marriage to Anne of Bohemia. In the 1380s Chaucer was much troubled by debt, and in 1389 he was appointed Clerk of the King's Works, a well-salaried position that brought responsibility for maintaining royal buildings. In 1391 the poet was given work as a forester on the king's lands at North Petherton, in Somerset.

To mark his coming of age Richard commissioned a royal portrait by Andre Beauneveu of Valenciennes to be placed in Westminster Abbey. This image, which represents the king crowned and splendidly robed while holding the royal sceptre, is the first royal portrait painted from life. Richard also rebuilt Westminster Hall from 1393 onwards, adding a porch and an oak hammer-beam roof that had the broadest unsupported span in the country. In the 1390s he commissioned a beautiful but anonymous painting, the Wilton Diptych, which he may have used as a portable altarpiece when travelling from palace to palace.

Below: The great poet of Richard's age, Geoffrey Chaucer, was saved from financial troubles by royal patronage.

ACOBVS.QVINTVS.SCOTTORVM REX
ANNO.ÆTATIS.SVE.

CHAPTER THREE

RULERS OF SCOTLAND

TO 1603

In 1306, Robert the Bruce, newly established as King of Scots, was in miserable exile in the Western Isles following defeats to English forces at Methven, near Perth, and at Dalry, close to Tyndrum in Perthshire. The old enemy, England, appeared unbeatable, and its vigorous martial ruler King Edward I seemed determined to destroy Scotland as an independent nation and bring its beautiful lands within his own realm.

According to legend, at this low ebb Robert drew comfort from watching a spider as it attempted again and again, undaunted by failure, to spin its web – and finally succeeded. Robert was inspired to fight back, and eight years later he led a Scots army to a famous victory over the English at the Battle of Bannockburn, in 1314. In 1323 he forced Edward I's successor, Edward II of England, to sue for peace. Of course the peace did not last, but Robert is remembered as probably Scotland's greatest king and national hero, 'the Bruce'.

Among the Bruce's lords at Bannockburn was Walter Stewart, scion of a famous family whose name came from their hereditary position as High Steward of Scotland. Walter married the Bruce's daughter Marjorie, and their son, who ruled as Robert II (r.1371–90), founded the great royal house of Stewart (or Stuart, in the French spelling), which was later established by his descendant Mary, Queen of Scots.

In 1603, Mary's son James Charles Stuart united the crowns of Scotland and England when he travelled south to London as King James VI of Scots (r.1567–1603). There he was finally crowned as King James I of England (r.1603–25).

Left: James V took Frenchwoman Mary of Guise as his second queen in 1538. Their daughter was Mary, Queen of Scots.

THE CREATION OF SCOTLAND
TO 1040

The lands now known as Scotland were a military battleground until the 9th century, when King Kenneth mac Alpin forged the first recognizable ancestor of the modern country of the Scots.

ANCIENT FOREBEARS

Four rival groups played an important part in the creation of this country. The first and most venerable were the Picts, present from c.AD300. Little is known about them because their culture was apparently entirely oral; and most of the evidence was destroyed when they were defeated by their rivals in the 9th century. By the 3rd century AD the dozen or so British tribes north of the Forth-Clyde isthmus had merged to form the Caledonians and the Maetae, and it was from these two tribal coalitions the Picts emerged as a recognizable ethnic group.

Celtic Britons made inroads into the south-west of what would become Scotland. The partially Romanized but still independent Britons who lived between the Forth-Clyde isthmus and Hadrian's Wall established a number of kingdoms around the time of the end of Roman rule, most notably Rheged and Gododdin. By *c.*AD700 they were forced back to the small kingdom of Strathclyde in south-western Scotland.

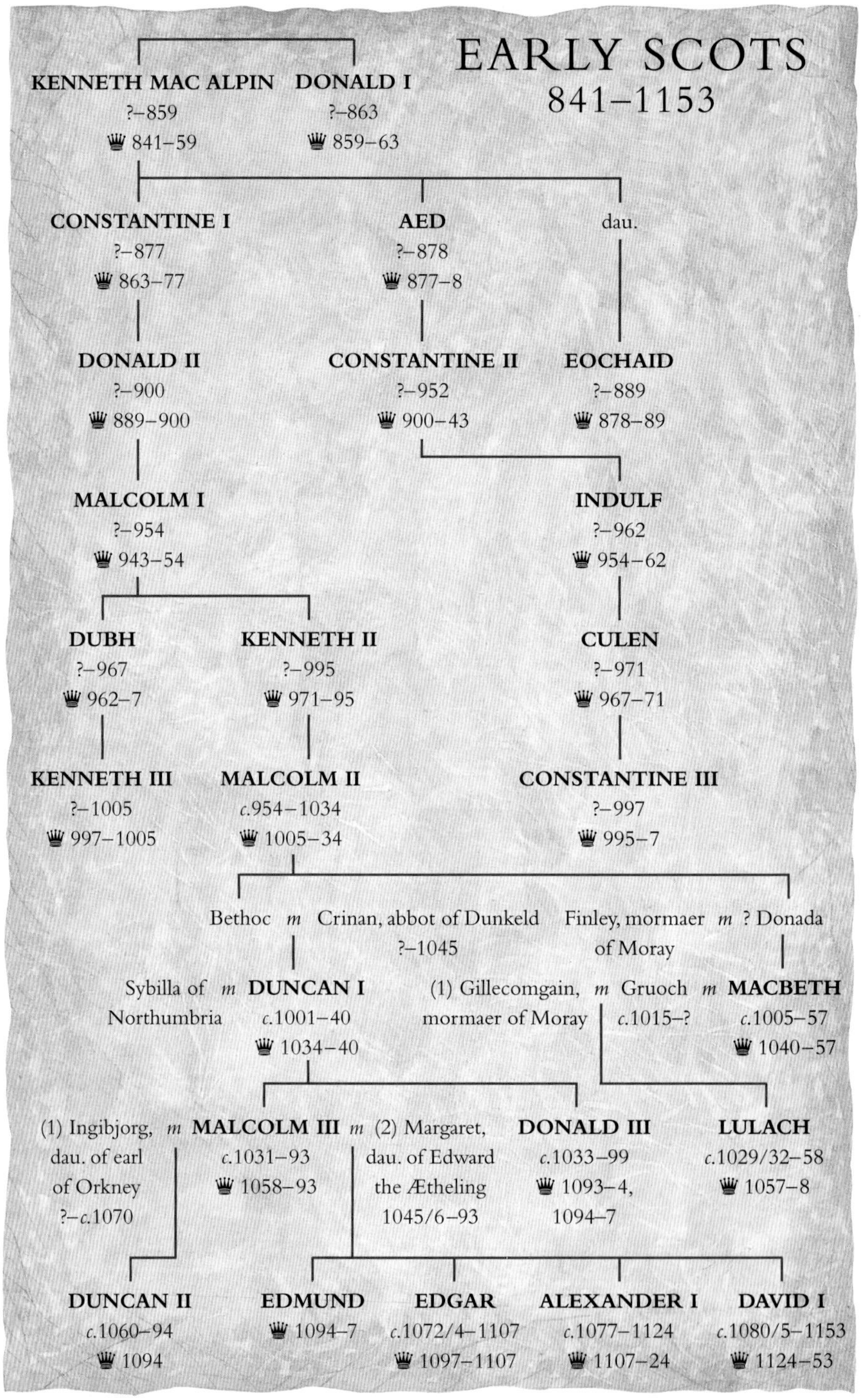

Above: Scandinavian horseman. This Viking warrior is from a tapestry in Baldishol Church, Norway (1180).

Both Picts and Britons faced incursions into western Scotland from Irish tribes. The Irish established the kingdom of Dal Riada, traditionally under their founding king Fergus Mor (AD498–501), in the area now called Argyll. These people were later called the Scotti (Latin for 'Irish').

The fourth group were the Angles from northern Germany, who arrived as part of the influx of Germanic tribes into Britain in the 5th and 6th centuries AD. They founded the kingdom of Bernicia, which later became part of the northern Anglo-Saxon realm of Northumbria.

Left: Scotland in c.AD850, at the time when Kenneth mac Alpin took advantage of Pictish defeats by the Vikings to forge the Scottish–Pictish kingdom of Alba.

FOUNDING FATHER

Scholars often compare the Scottish founding monarch Kenneth mac Alpin to Alfred the Great. Like Alfred, Kenneth forged a united kingdom under persistent threat from Viking invaders, which was consolidated over several reigns. Kenneth's kingdom of Alba was ruled by his brother Donald I (AD859–63), by Kenneth's sons Constantine (AD863–77) and Aed (AD877–8), by their cousin Giric who ruled jointly with Eochaid (AD878–89), by Constantine's son, Donald II (AD889–900), and then by Donald II's nephew and Kenneth's grandson, Constantine II (AD900–43).

In the 9th century the Vikings created kingdoms in Shetland, the western isles and Orkney. The Scots tried to contain the expansionism of Wessex and other 'English' kingdoms in the 10th century. The beginning of English kings' claims to be overlord of Scotland began in AD918 with Edward the Elder of Wessex, who made Constantine II submit to his rule.

Above: Seaborne invaders in the north. This whalebone plaque was found in the boat burial of a Viking chieftain on Sanday, Orkney.

THE STONE OF DESTINY

In AD843 King Kenneth mac Alpin held a sacred investment ceremony on Moot Hill at Scone, ancient royal site of the Picts, using the venerable Irish-Dal Riadan royal stone, the Stone of Destiny. Traditionally the Stone was brought to Scotland from Ireland by King Fergus Mor. According to legend, it originated in the Holy Land and came to Ireland by way of Egypt and Spain. The stone was used for the investment of all Scottish kings until King Edward I of England (1272–1307) removed it from Scone and placed it in Westminster Abbey, where it remained until 1996, when it was finally brought back to Scotland.

Above: The stone was incorporated into Edward I's Coronation Chair.

MACBETH

1040–1057

King Duncan I of Scots, grandson of Malcolm II and son of Crinan, the Abbot of Dunkeld, came to the throne in 1034. Six years later he was slain and his crown taken by Macbeth Macfinlay, the ruler of Moray. Shakespeare's tragedy *Macbeth* (probably first performed in 1606) made these royal names among the most resonant in British history, with King Duncan celebrated as the archetype of the wise, noble and divinely ordained ruler and Macbeth as the usurper maddened first by ambition and superstitious belief in prophecy, then by guilt.

MACBETH, KING OF SCOTLAND, 1040–1057
Birth: *c.*1005
Accession: 14 Aug 1040
Queen: Gruoch (m. after 1032)
Succeeded by: His stepson, Lulach
Death: 15 Aug 1057 at the Battle of Lumphanan

Above: Engraver John Boydell (1719–1804) had a romantic vision of Macbeth's encounter with the Three Witches.

FROM FACT TO FOLKLORE

In Shakespeare's play, Macbeth is a brave and well-respected general in King Duncan's army who encounters three witches on a heath and hears their prophecy that he will be made Thane of Cawdor and become king. When Duncan makes him Thane of Cawdor, the prophecy begins to work at him and, encouraged by his wife, Lady Macbeth, he murders Duncan in his bed during the king's visit to his castle.

Below: Haunted by his misdeeds, Macbeth shies away from the ghost of his fellow general Banquo, whom he murdered.

In fact, as *mormaer* ('ruler' in Gaelic, or high steward) of Moray, the region of northern Scotland around Inverness, Macbeth Macfinlay was a natural rival of Duncan's for power. The Moray *mormaers* were long-term opponents of the kings of Scotland. Moreover, although Macbeth probably had no hereditary claim to Duncan's throne, Macbeth's wife Gruoch and Duncan were third-generation rivals for the throne of Scotland, for Gruoch was granddaughter of King Kenneth III, who had been killed in battle at Monzievaird in 1005 by Duncan's grandfather, Malcolm II. The historical Duncan does not seem to have been an effective king, for he led several unsuccessful raids into Northumbria, including a failed attack on Durham in 1039. His authority was doubtless weakened by these events.

Duncan's campaign against Macbeth ended in his own death at the Battle of Pitgaveny, near Elgin, on 14 August 1040. Duncan's son Malcolm escaped into exile and stayed first with his mother's relatives at the northern court of Siward, Earl of Northumberland, and then at the court of Edward the Confessor, King of England.

DRAMATIC LICENCE

In Shakespeare's play, Macbeth is unhinged by guilt and fear. He gets drawn further and further into bloodshed as, maddened by new prophecies, he slaughters his fellow general Banquo and the wife and children of Macduff, Thane of Cawdor, against whom he has been warned. Then, in alliance with Duncan's son Malcolm, Macduff invades and kills Macbeth at Dunsinane and Malcolm is proclaimed king.

In fact, Macbeth Macfinlay enjoyed a relatively long and stable rule. He fought several campaigns against the

TANISTRY'S LEGACY OF FAMILY VIOLENCE

For the century prior to the reigns of Duncan and Macbeth, Scots followed a form of succession known as tanistry, under which two branches of Kenneth mac Alpin's family shared the succession. The Scottish throne passed successively from one branch to the other, cousin to cousin or uncle to nephew. The system had the unfortunate effect of fostering violence.

AD943: Constantine II retires to St Andrew's monastery, Fife. He is succeeded by his cousin Malcolm I, who subjugates Moray

AD954: King Malcolm I is killed in Moray uprising and is succeeded by his cousin Indulf

AD962: Indulf is killed by Danes and succeeded by Malcolm's son Dubh

AD967: Dubh is murdered on the orders of his cousin Culen, who succeeds to the crown

AD971: Culen in assassinated in a revenge attack by Dubh's brother; Kenneth II succeeds

AD995: Kenneth II is killed by noblewoman Finvela; his cousin Constantine III succeeds

AD997: Constantine III is killed; Dubh's son Kenneth III succeeds

1005: Kenneth II's son Malcolm kills Kenneth III and takes the throne as Malcolm II

***c.*1018:** Malcolm II acquires Strathclyde and Lothian for Scotland

1034: After a 28-year reign Malcolm II rejects the tanistry tradition and leaves the country to his grandson Duncan.

Norse in Caithness and Sutherland, defeated a rebel force near Dunkeld (modern Tayside) in 1045, killing Malcolm's grandfather Crinan, Abbot of Dunkeld, and in 1046 was victorious over Siward, Earl of Northumbria, who was seeking to elevate Duncan's son Malcolm to the kingship.

On 27 July 1054, however, he was defeated at Dunsinane, near Scone, by Siward and Malcolm and forced to cede Lothian and Strathclyde in southern Scotland to Malcolm. The invasion was supported by the English troops of Edward the Confessor, who had provided hospitality to Malcolm at his court and who envisaged him as a puppet ruler on the Scottish throne. In 1057 Macbeth was killed in battle at Lumphanan, west of Aberdeen, by Malcolm himself. Macbeth's 25-year-old stepson Lulach briefly inherited the crown, but was killed by Malcolm in an ambush in 1058. Macbeth himself was clearly not regarded as a usurper, for he was laid to rest on Iona, which was the burial ground only of lawful monarchs.

Below: Far from being the paragon of noble kingship celebrated by Shakespeare, Duncan was a rather ineffectual ruler.

Below: The historical Macbeth was mormaer *of Moray from c.1031 and ruled all of Scotland for 17 years.*

Above: Cawdor Castle, the supposed site of Macbeth's murder of Duncan, was actually built in the late 14th century.

THE DEADLY APPLE

Contrary to Shakespeare's account, Duncan was not in truth a victim of treachery in Macbeth's household, but one of his royal predecessors did fall foul of deadly hospitality.

In AD995 King Kenneth II was murdered by or at the instigation of Scots noblewoman Finvela, who blamed him for the death of her only son. According to legend, she invited him to her house and treated him to a great banquet with wine. When her royal guest was drunk, Finvela led him into another chamber, where she had prepared a bizarre contraption: a statue bearing a golden apple connected to a number of hidden crossbows, which were set to fire when the apple was lifted. She invited Kenneth to take the apple as a symbol of their reconciliation and, when he lifted the golden fruit, he was shot.

FROM MALCOLM III TO MALCOLM IV

1058–1165

Malcolm III Canmore ('big head' or 'great leader') regained the throne lost 18 years earlier by his father King Duncan, in 1058, with English backing. The 18-year rule of the lords of Moray – Macbeth Macfinlay (1040–57) and his stepson Lulach (1057–8) – was over. Malcolm had spent the first 14 of those 18 years in exile in England and after returning to Scotland remained involved in the upheavals south of the border.

ENGLISH ALLIANCES

In 1066, when Harold Godwineson became King Harold II of England, Malcolm III Canmore joined the northern invasion raised by Earl Tostig and King Harald Hardrada of Norway. Then, in 1068, following Duke William of Normandy's occupation of the English throne as King William I, Malcolm gave sanctuary in Scotland to another of William's rivals, Edgar the Atheling and his mother and sisters. The next year he took one of the sisters, the pious and later sainted Margaret, as his wife. Malcolm raided Northumbria in 1070, and in 1072 William I invaded eastern Scotland with naval backup to punish him. Malcolm made peace rather than engage the formidable Norman army. In a treaty signed at Abernethy, near Perth, on 15 August 1072, Malcolm acknowledged William I's overlordship. He was also forced to send his son Duncan into exile as an English hostage and to expel his brother-in-law Edgar the Atheling from Scotland.

Despite having acknowledged English overlordship, Malcolm again raided Northumbria in 1079, 1090 and 1093. The last attack ended in Malcolm's death in an ambush. Malcolm's son and heir Edward was also killed and a succession crisis was sparked.

Four years of dynastic disputes were ended by the victory in 1097 of Edgar, one of Malcolm's sons with Queen Margaret. During his ten-year reign, Edgar restored stability. His pious character and patronage of the Church won him the nickname 'Gentle King Edgar' and one contemporary, St Aelred of Rievaulx, declared that he equalled Edward the Confessor in holiness.

Left: Edinburgh Castle stands high on a rock above the city. It contains a Norman chapel to St Margaret, wife of Malcolm III.

Above: Might and right. A manuscript of 1588 depicts King Malcolm III of Scots and his pious second wife, Margaret.

Two key events of Edgar's reign were the recognition in 1098 of Norwegian rule in the Hebrides by King Magnus III 'Barefoot' of Norway and the diplomatic marriage in 1100 between England's new king, Henry I, and Edgar's sister Edith (who later took the Norman name Matilda). Edgar himself remained unmarried. At his death, aged 33, on 8 January 1107 he was succeeded by his brother, Alexander.

RISE OF KING DAVID

Alexander I followed his elder brother Edgar's instructions in allowing his younger brother, David, to govern southern Scotland while he himself controlled the north. Alexander maintained good relations with his brother-in-law King Henry I of

ROYAL INFANTICIDE

King David paid a high price for offering hospitality in 1114, when he was governing southern Scotland in his brother Alexander I's reign. David gave houseroom to a Scandinavian priest who had been blinded and had had his feet and hands amputated as a punishment for the brutal sacrifice of a colleague on a church altar in Norway. Sadly the priest proved to be insane: he used the metal hook he wore in place of a hand to cut open and kill David's infant son Malcolm. Wild with a father's grief, David ordered the priest to be tied to horses so that he would be torn apart when they were whipped and sent galloping in different directions.

England, accepted the status of Henry's feudal vassal and entered a diplomatic marriage to Sibylla, Henry's illegitimate daughter. Alexander also fought alongside the English king, leading a Scottish troop during Henry's campaigns in Wales in 1114.

On Alexander's death aged 47, on 23 April 1124, David took power over all of Scotland and ruled as King David I. He had many connections with England. He was brother-in-law to King Henry I through the late Queen Matilda (formerly 'Edith') and was himself married to Maud, daughter of Earl Waltheof of Northumbria. Furthermore, he had lived as an exile at the English court in the 1090s during the succession crisis that followed the death of his father Malcolm III.

In David's reign, Scotland and its monarchy gained a new strength and prestige. He established a central government administration, introduced royal coinage and imported an Anglo-Norman feudal system. Many notable Anglo-Norman lords settled in Scotland, receiving grants of land in return for royal service and intermarrying with the local aristocracy. Celebrated Scottish families including Bruce, Stewart and Comyn were among the influx of Anglo-Normans that occurred during King David's reign.

David was a great church patron, founding many Cistercian and Augustinian monastic establishments. Several castles and burghs, or fortified settlements, were also raised or rebuilt under his rule, including Edinburgh, Berwick, Roxburgh and Stirling.

Under David, the country grew to its largest extent. After 1130, he succeeded in subjugating the always troublesome earldom of Moray, possession of the descendants of Macbeth Macfinlay (1040–57). In the course of the civil war in England in King Stephen's reign (1135–54), David initially backed Henry I's daughter, the Empress Matilda, but twice made peace with Stephen. He gained Cumberland, Northumberland, Durham, Westmorland and, for a time, Lancaster for Scotland, a state of affairs recognized by Henry Plantagenet (the future Henry II) in 1149.

SWIFT DECLINE

David's territorial gains in northern England were short-lived, however. He died in Carlisle on 24 May 1153 and, because both his sons were already dead, was succeeded by his 12-year-old grandson Malcolm IV. The youthful king did succeed in subduing Galloway in 1160, and in 1164 put down a rebellion led by Somerled, 'Lord of the Western Isles', at Renfrew, but aside from that, his reign was short and largely uneventful and he died aged only 23.

Below: Growing territory. By the end of King David's reign in 1153, Scotland stretched as far south as the River Tees.

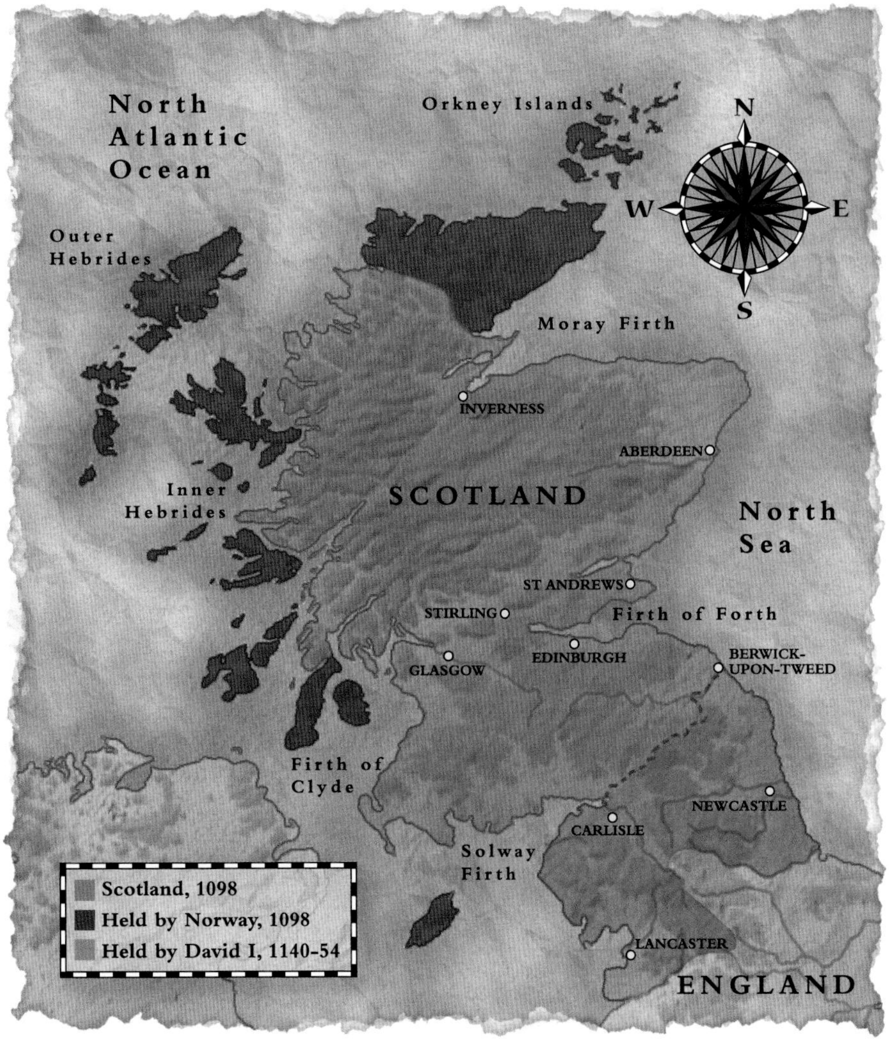

WILLIAM I THE LION

1165–1214

On the unexpected death of the quiet, pious and chaste King Malcolm IV in December 1165, his energetic, red-haired brother William came to the throne. Invested at Scone on Christmas Eve 1165, William would remain on the throne for 49 years, the longest reign of any Scots king in the medieval period. His posthumous nickname, 'the Lion', may derive from his fearlessness and strength in battle, but is more likely to have been a reference to the heraldic device he adopted, of a red lion rampant against a yellow background.

Above: In the 14th century, John of Fordun named William leo justitiae *('lion of justice') – a possible source of his nickname 'the Lion'.*

WILLIAM I 'THE LION', KING OF SCOTLAND, 1165–1214

Birth: 1142/3
Father: Henry, Earl of Northumberland
Mother: Ada de Warenne
Accession: 9 Dec 1165
Investiture: 24 Dec, 1165, Scone
Queen: Ermengarde (m. 5 Sept 1186; d. 1233)
Succeeded by: His son Alexander
Greatest achievement: Stability of a 49-year reign
1168: Alliance with France
1174: Captured at Alnwick and imprisoned by Henry II
Dec 1174: Treaty of Falaise: William swears allegiance to Henry II
1178: Founds Arbroath Abbey
1189: Treaty of Falaise cancelled by King Richard I
Death: 4 Dec 1214, Stirling

NORTHUMBERLAND CONTROL

The vexed question of Scottish control over Northumberland, gained by William's grandfather David I but lost by Malcolm IV, troubled much of William's reign. Early on, in 1174, William saw an opportunity. Henry II's sons Henry the Young King, Richard and Geoffrey were in open revolt against their father in Normandy, so William invaded Northumberland. However, the Scots king was caught unawares in mist when besieging Alnwick Castle. Unable to see clearly, he mistook a group of English cavalry for his own knights. He was surprised and, although he fought valiantly, had his horse killed beneath him and was ultimately overpowered. The humiliation of being captured alive was made worse when he was thrown in jail and kept as a prisoner of King Henry II for five months, powerless to prevent the gleeful English troops from plundering southern Scotland.

ARBROATH ABBEY

King William the Lion established the Abbey of Arbroath in 1178 to honour the memory of St Thomas à Becket. Becket had been murdered eight years earlier at Canterbury by knights who were probably acting on behalf of Henry I, and he was canonized only 15 months later in 1172. The Abbey housed monks of the Tironensian order, which originated in Tiron, France, and had Kelso Abbey – founded by King David I – as its main Scottish base. However, the monks of Arbroath were independent of the 'mother house'.

Arbroath Abbey became one of the wealthiest in Scotland. William made the monks many grants of income and also allowed them to establish a fortified settlement, hold a market and construct a harbour. Following his death in 1214, King William was buried at the Abbey. A little over a century later, in 1320, Scotland's resounding statement of independence from England, the Declaration of Arbroath, was signed at the Abbey.

Left: The impressive south transept still stands among the ruins of Arbroath Abbey.

Below: Stirling Castle. William created a royal hunting ground at Stirling and died in the castle on 4 December 1214.

Above: Alnwick Castle, Northumberland, was the site of William the Lion's catastrophic capture by English knights.

Worse still was to follow. The price of William's release was the punitive Treaty of Falaise, signed in December 1174, under which William had to pledge allegiance to Henry as his vassal, to accept that the English Church was supreme over the Scottish Church and to pay for the establishment of English garrisons in Scottish territory. Scotland had become a feudal possession of the English king.

FREEDOM FOR SALE

This state of affairs improved 15 years later when, following the death of Henry II, King Richard I 'the Lionheart' was raising money to fund his departure for the Holy Land on the Third Crusade. Richard I agreed to accept that the Treaty of Falaise had been obtained by force and reversed its terms in return for a cash payment of 10,000 marks.

A little later, the clause of the treaty that had established the supremacy of the English Church was undermined by Pope Celestine III who, in 1192, declared that the Church in Scotland owed allegiance to Rome alone and could not be forced to submit to the English Church.

Following the accession of King John in 1199, William plotted a further invasion to reassert Scotland's claim over Northumberland. According to tradition, the king – who was a pious man – received a divine warning that a major campaign in northern England would have dire consequences for Scotland. He limited himself to minor raiding, which in itself brought disastrous results. A show of English military strength forced a treaty signed at Norham, Northumberland, on 7 September 1209, in which William again had to recognize the English king as his feudal overlord and allow John to arrange marriages for his daughters.

FRENCH CONNECTION

In 1168 William made an alliance with Louis VII of France that some scholars identify as the beginning of the 'Auld Alliance', the centuries-long diplomatic 'friendship' between French and Scottish monarchs eager to strengthen their position against the English.

At home William built on David's legacy, founding burghs and consolidating a local law system of sheriffs and justices.

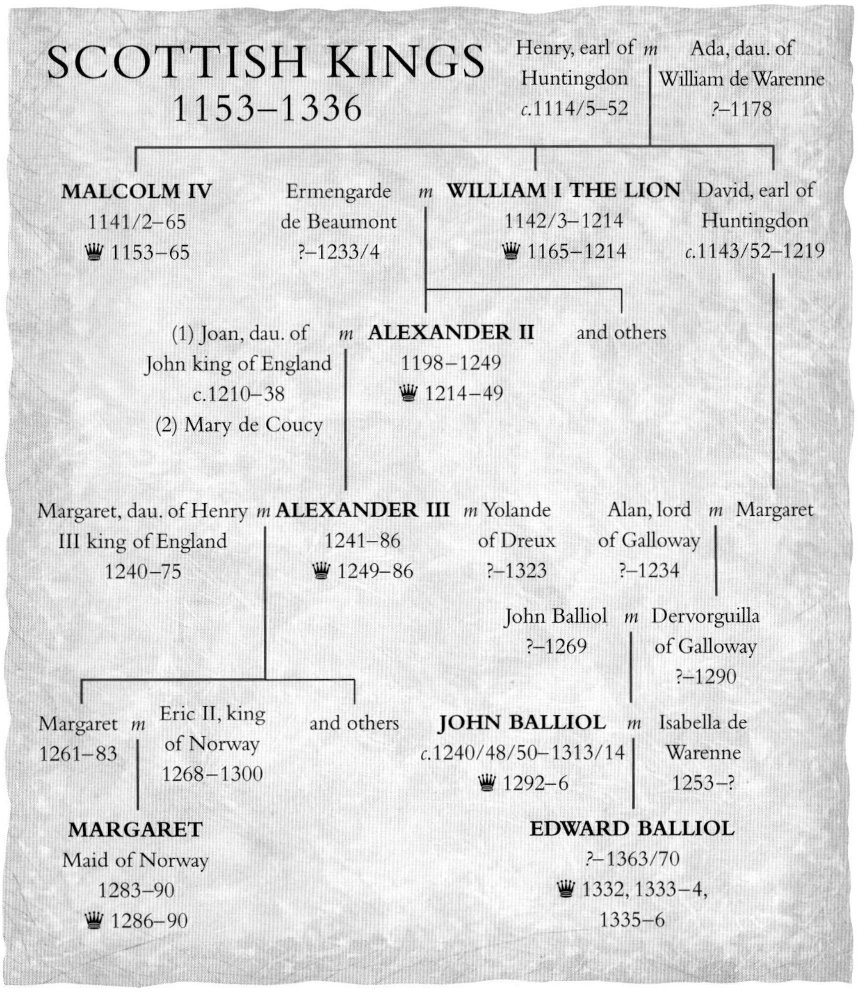

ALEXANDER II

1214–1249

Following the stability of William the Lion's 49-year reign, William's 16-year-old son Alexander came to the throne in 1214. The next year, sensing an opportunity to make progress towards his father's long-held dream of regaining former Scottish territory in Northumberland, Alexander sided with the barons of England when they rose up and imposed the Magna Carta on King John.

THE PEACE OF YORK

Alexander paid homage to Prince Louis, heir to the French crown, who had been offered the English throne. However, John had his revenge, launching a savage attack on Lothian designed, he declared, to 'hunt the red foxcub from his lairs', a reference to the red hair that Alexander had inherited from his father. Following the death of King John in 1216 and the collapse of the baronial rebellion in 1217, Alexander made peace with England's new king, Henry III, paying homage to him for his lands in England at Christmas 1217. Then on 19 June 1221, at York, he married Henry's sister, Joan.

Above: Alexander allied himself to the English barons who in the Magna Carta set limits on his father-in-law King John's authority.

The new harmonious Anglo-Scottish atmosphere resulted in the 1237 Peace of York, under which Alexander renounced his claim to the disputed northern territories, including Northumberland, and the border between the two countries was agreed as running north-east from the Solway to the Tweed – roughly the border that has survived to this day. The peace treaty rewarded Alexander's accommodating approach by giving him rights to a number of English estates.

PEACE AND STABILITY

Alexander II maintained peace for Scotland and his byname became 'the Peaceful'. However, he had to be tough and pragmatic. Like his predecessors, he had his work cut out to impose his authority in the west and north-west of his realm. He put down revolts in Galloway in 1234–5 and 1247 and brutally punished rebels in Caithness, in the far north, by ordering that each captured rebel have one hand and one foot cut off. He caught a fever whilst on campaign and died aged 50 in 1249.

Left: Alexander II was warned in a dream not to try to recapture the Hebrides from Norway. He disregarded the advice – and died of a fever while on campaign.

ALEXANDER II, KING OF SCOTLAND, 1214–1249

Birth: 24 Aug 1198, Haddington, East Lothian
Father: William I the Lion
Mother: Ermengarde de Beaumont
Accession: 4 Dec 1214
Coronation: 6 Dec 1214, Scone Abbey
Queens: (1) Joan, daughter of King John of England (m. June 1221; d.1238); (2) Mary de Coucy (m. 15 May 1239)
Succeeded by: His son Alexander III
Death: 6 July 1249, on the Isle of Kerrara in the Bay of Oban

ALEXANDER III

1249–1286

Alexander II had reigned for a very respectable 34 years, but his unexpected end was not well timed, for his son and heir, who came to the throne as King Alexander III, was just eight years old.

JUNIOR ROYAL WEDDING

Within three years, at the age of just ten, Alexander III made a major diplomatic match when he was married to King Henry III's 21-year-old daughter Margaret. The ceremony took place on 26 December 1251 in York Abbey and was long remembered, not least for Henry's attempt to take advantage of Alexander's tender years and make him pay homage to the English king for all his Scottish lands. Alexander, canny and well prepared, replied that he was present to be married and 'not to answer about so difficult a matter'.

A DEAL WITH NORWAY

At peace with England, Alexander pressed on with his father's project of regaining control of the Western Isles. In 1263 he offered to buy Kintyre and the Western Isles from King Haakon IV of Norway. Haakon refused and, acting on reports that the Scots had attacked Skye, led a punitive raid along the west coast. His fleet anchored off Largs, near Ayr, but was wrecked in a storm and an invading party was driven back by Scottish troops in a beach battle at Largs on 2 October. On his return from this bungled expedition, Haakon became ill and died in Orkney.

Haakon's successor on the Norwegian throne, King Magnus V, agreed the Treaty of Perth in 1266 under which Scotland regained the Western Isles.

In August 1274 King Alexander and Queen Margaret were guests at the coronation of Margaret's brother Edward as King Edward I of England. Alexander was pleased to maintain friendly relations with England, but he would not allow Scotland's independence to be undermined. Visiting Westminster in October 1278, he willingly paid homage for his lands in England to Edward I, but made a proud declaration of Scotland's independence when it was suggested by the Bishop of Norwich that a Scottish king should pay homage to his English counterpart for all his territories. Alexander replied in ringing tones, 'To homage for my kingdom of Scotland no one has right except God alone. Nor do I hold it except of God alone'.

Alexander's Scotland was prosperous, stable and secure, but his sudden death in March 1286 plunged the country into a succession crisis. Riding from Edinburgh to Dunfermline on 19 March 1286, Alexander and his horse fell over a cliff during a storm. With his three children already dead, his only heir was his granddaughter Margaret, the daughter of King Eric II of Norway, and Alexander III's daughter, another Margaret. This infant girl, born only the previous year and known as the 'Maid of Norway', was therefore declared Queen of Scotland.

ALEXANDER III, KING OF SCOTLAND, 1249–1286
Birth: 4 Sept 1241, Roxburgh
Father: Alexander II
Mother: Mary de Coucy
Accession: 8 July 1249
Coronation: 13 July 1249, Scone Abbey
Queens: (1) Margaret, daughter of Henry III of England (m. 26 Dec 1251); (2) Yolande or Joletta, daughter of Robert IV, Count of Dreux (m. 1 Nov 1285; d. 1323)
Succeeded by: Margaret
Death: 19 March 1286

Right: Tradition has it that Colin Fitzgerald, first chief of Clan Mackenzie, saved Alexander III from a stag. Benjamin West imagined the scene in 1786.

JOHN BALLIOL AND ROBERT I 'THE BRUCE'

1286–1329

Scotland's child-queen, Margaret the 'Maid of Norway', ruled for four years without setting foot in her realm. She died in the Orkney Islands in 1290, aged just seven, as she was travelling to Scotland for the first time. She left a power vacuum in which there were 13 rival claimants for the throne. The strongest of these were John Balliol and Robert Bruce (the grandfather of Robert I Bruce), both descendants of King David I's daughters.

AN EMPTY THRONE

Edward I of England was determined to force the Scots to recognize him as their overlord and sensed a magnificent opportunity in this succession crisis.

At Norham, near Berwick, he acted as mediator between the rivals and chose Balliol, who had the stronger legal claim and who also promised to pay homage to Edward. However, Balliol later defied Edward by choosing to ally with France in the 1295 Treaty of Paris rather than fight alongside Edward in a proposed war against the French. Edward's army invaded Scotland in 1296, sacked Berwick and then crushed Balliol's Scottish army at Dunbar. On 10 July, Balliol was stripped of his knightly arms, crown, sword and sceptre and then despatched to London, where he was cast into the Tower. The event won John the mocking nickname 'Toom Tabard' (vacant coat'), a reference to the removal of his heraldic arms.

Below: King John Balliol is pictured with the heraldic arms that he had stripped from him by a merciless Edward I of England.

JOHN BALLIOL, KING OF SCOTLAND, 1292–1296

Birth: *c.*1240/48/50, Barnard Castle
Father: John Balliol
Mother: Devorguilla of Galloway
Accession: 17 Nov 1292
Coronation: 30 Nov 1292, Scone Abbey
Queen: Isabella, daughter of John de Warenne, 6th Earl of Surrey (m. before 7 Feb 1281)
10/11 July 1296: Abdicates at Brechin
Death: 1313/14, Normandy

For ten years the Scottish throne remained empty. In 1300 Edward I rubbed in his victory by removing the Stone of Destiny from Scotland and using it as part of a newly constructed coronation chair in Westminster Abbey.

Scottish pride was in the hands of rebel leader Sir William Wallace, who defied Edward for eight years, crushing an English army at Stirling in 1297 and later the same year taunting the English king by raiding Northumberland and Cumberland. Wallace was captured in Scotland in 1305, taken to London, condemned as a traitor and brutally executed. His name lived on, however, as an inspiration to those fighting for Scottish independence.

BRUCE TAKES POWER

Meanwhile the Scottish families of Bruce and Comyn (Cumming) were the principal claimants to the vacant Scottish throne. Robert the Bruce (grandson of the Robert Bruce who had lost the crown to Balliol in 1292) seized the initiative. On 10 February 1306 he or his followers murdered his chief rival, John Comyn, in the Franciscan Church at Dumfries. Bruce then had himself crowned King Robert I of Scots, at Scone, on 27 March. He immediately set about eliminating resistance to his rule. However, he received two major and near-immediate setbacks in the form of military defeats by English troops at Methven on 19 June and Dalry, close to Tyndrum, on 11 August. He fled into exile.

VICTORY AT BANNOCKBURN

In 1307 Robert I's prospects improved when his principal adversary, the great warrior-king Edward I, died of dysentery as he was travelling north to invade Scotland once more. Edward I's successor, the hot-headed Edward II, was far less of a threat. In Scotland, Robert I established his own rule over all of the

Above: 'We fight…for freedom alone'. Scotland's independence was declared at Arbroath by Robert I's nobles in 1320.

Right: The Holkham Bible *of 1327 has a near-contemporary representation of the Scots' 1314 victory at Bannockburn.*

country save the south-east corner and routed Edward II's army at the battle of Bannockburn, in June 1314.

Edward had led his large army into Scotland to relieve the English garrison in Stirling Castle, which was besieged by Robert I. Greatly outnumbered, the Scots were rallied by King Robert, who told them, 'Fight for your nation's honour'. First with cavalry and then with spearmen, the Scots took the battle to the English. The invading army panicked and broke when King Edward II fled for his life. Thousands of Englishmen were slain.

This remarkable victory over the Plantagenet English army made Robert the Bruce a hero in Scotland, established his claim to the throne beyond doubt, united the Scots and ended the Bruce–Comyn war.

ROBERT I THE BRUCE, KING OF SCOTLAND, 1306–1329

Birth: 11 July 1274, Turnberry Castle, Ayrshire
Father: Robert (VI) de Brus (d. 1304)
Mother: Marjory, Countess of Carrick
Accession: 10 Feb 1306
Investiture: 27 March 1306, Scone
Queen: Elizabeth (m. 1302; d. 1327)
Succeeded by: His son David
Greatest achievement: Safeguarding Scottish independence
10 Feb 1306: Murders rival John Comyn and seizes power
June-August 1306: Military defeats drive him into hiding
24 June 1314: Battle of Bannockburn
1320: Declaration of Arbroath
1328: Treaty of Edinburgh
Death: 7 June 1329, Cardross, Dumbartonshire

DECLARATION OF ARBROATH

In 1320, Robert encouraged his leading nobles to make the resonant statement of Scotland's independence known as the Declaration of Arbroath. The document, drawn up on 6 April 1320, probably by Bernard de Linton, Abbot of Arbroath Abbey and Chancellor of Scotland, was addressed to Pope John XXII at Avignon, who had excommunicated Robert I following the murder of John Comyn and who so far refused to accept Scottish independence. The Declaration stated that the Scots were bound to their King Robert, 'By law and by his strengths, so that we may continue free, and we will continue to stand by him, come what may', but it added that they would drive their king out, 'As an enemy' if he consented to make Scotland subject to England once more. The Declaration also stated that the Scots were fighting not for wealth or glory or worldy status, 'But for freedom – and for freedom only, which no honourable man will give up but with his life'.

Robert's dream was realized in 1328, following the deposition of Edward II and the accession of the youthful Edward III, in the Treaty of Edinburgh and Northampton. England recognized Scotland's independence.

Robert I, great hero of Scottish independence, suffered from illness in his later years and died, probably of leprosy, in 1329. In 1328 the Pope had lifted the writ of excommunication that he had imposed ten years earlier. On his deathbed, Robert arranged to have his heart excized after his death and made Sir James Douglas pledge to take the heart with him on crusade to the Holy Land. The king's body was buried at Dunfermline Abbey and the heart – returned to Scotland after Douglas was killed in Spain en route for the Holy Land – was interred at Melrose Abbey.

Below: Robert I is shown with his first wife, Isabel. Their grandson was Robert II, the founder of the House of Stewart.

DAVID II

1329–1371

Robert I's death in June 1329 plunged newly independent Scotland back into rivalry between Balliol and Bruce as dynastic feuding erupted. John Balliol's son Edward claimed the throne, invaded Scotland, defeated David II's guardian Donald of Mar on Dupplin Moor and was made king in September. In December, barons loyal to Bruce drove Balliol out and reinstated David II. In March 1333 Balliol invaded again and, with Edward III, defeated the Scots at Halidon Hill on 19 July to regain the throne. David II fled into exile.

Balliol was little more than Edward III's puppet, to whom he paid homage as feudal overlord and ceded large parts of southern Scotland in June 1334. Balliol proved unable to impose his authority on the country. He was deposed once more in 1334, ruled again in 1335–6 but was deposed yet again in 1336, after which he effectively abandoned his pretensions to the Scottish crown.

DAVID II, KING OF SCOTLAND, 1329–1371

Birth: 5 March 1324, Dunfermline
Father: Robert I the Bruce
Mother: Elizabeth de Burgh
Accession: 7 June 1329
Coronation: 24 Nov 1331, Scone Abbey
Queens: (1) Joan of England (m. 17 July 1328; d. 7 Sept 1362); (2) Margaret Drummond (m. 1363/4; d. 31 Jan 1375)
Succeeded by: His nephew Robert II
Death: 22 Feb 1371, Edinburgh Castle

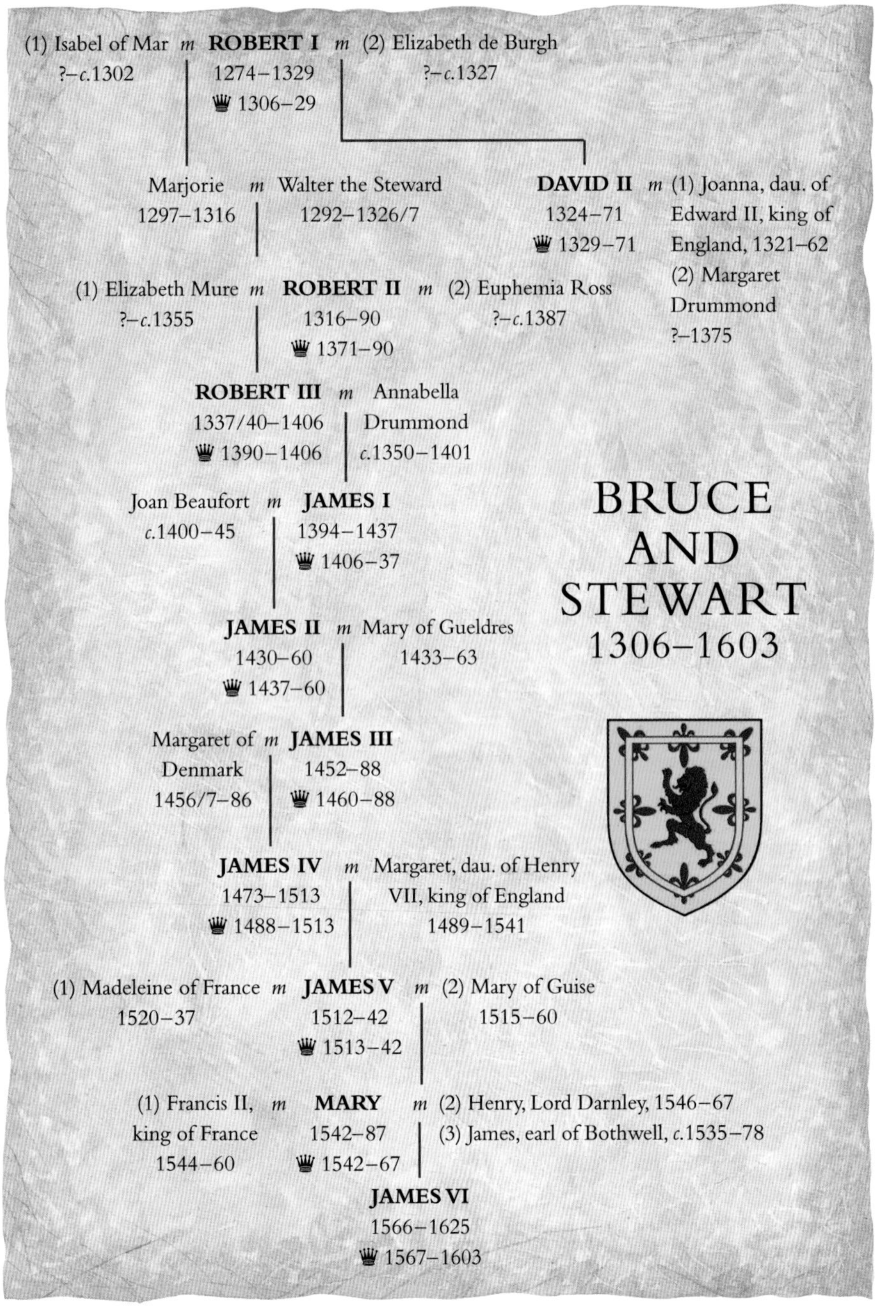

KING DAVID'S RETURN

After seven years' exile in France, David returned to reclaim the throne in 1341. The Scots army was crushed in 1346 by an English force at the Battle of Neville's Cross, and David took an arrow in the face before being captured and thrown in jail. He remained in English captivity until 1357.

Below: Peace reigns. In the 1357 Treaty of Berwick David II of Scots agreed terms with the powerful Edward III of England.

ROBERT II AND ROBERT III

1371–1406

David's ill-starred reign ended in February 1371. He died without offspring and was succeeded by his nephew Robert Stewart.

THE HOUSE OF STEWART

The new king inaugurating a new and subsequently celebrated dynasty was the grandson of the great Robert I through his daughter Marjorie Bruce. Marjorie married the wealthy and powerful Walter Stewart in 1315. His surname derived from the fact that his family had held the hereditary post of Great Steward of Scotland since the reign of David I.

On accession, Robert was a mature man of 55 years, who had been the king's heir apparent for 45 years. During David II's exile and imprisonment Robert had been variously joint-regent and sole regent. In the course of his reign the Scots regained many English-held territories in southern Scotland in 1384 and then launched several raids in northern England, in 1388 winning a long-celebrated victory over an English army led by Henry Percy at the Battle of Otterburn. However, Robert took no part in these heroics and, indeed, left affairs of government to his eldest son John, Earl of Carrick.

ROBERT II, KING OF SCOTLAND, 1371–1390
Birth: 2 March 1316, Paisley
Father: Walter the Steward
Mother: Marjorie, daughter of Robert I
Accession: 22 Feb 1371
Coronation: 22 Feb or 26 March 1371, Scone Abbey
Queens: Elizabeth Mure (m. 1336; d. before 1355); (2) Euphemia, Countess of Moray (m. after 2 May 1355; d. 1387)
Succeeded by: His son John, who took the name Robert on his accession to the throne
Death: 19 April 1390, Dundonald Castle

Above: On accession, Robert II was a mature man of 55, who had been David II's heir apparent for 45 years.

THE INEFFECTUAL ROBERT III

Robert II died in April 1390 and was succeeded by Carrick who, on his accession, took the name Robert III because after the years of John Balliol, the name 'John' was considered to be unlucky for a king. However, following an accident in 1388, in which he was badly kicked by a horse, Carrick became an invalid no longer fully capable of public life. When he became king, government was largely in the hands of his brother Robert, Earl of Fife and from 1398 Duke of Albany.

Below: The circular Rothesay Castle, on the Isle of Bute, was a favoured dwelling of Robert II and his Stewart successors.

ROBERT III, KING OF SCOTLAND, 1390–1406
Birth: c.1337/40
Father: Robert II
Mother: Elizabeth Mure
Accession: 19 April 1390
Coronation: 14 Aug 1390, Scone Abbey
Queen: Annabella Drummond (m. c.1366/7; d. c.Oct 1401)
Succeeded by: His son James I
Death: 4 April 1406, Dundonald Castle

Under Albany's venal rule Scotland became a lawless and corrupt place. He tried to refashion the succession, in 1401 arresting and imprisoning his nephew David, Duke of Rothesay, who was heir to the throne. Rothesay died in Albany's castle, according to some accounts from starvation – although an enquiry in 1402 found that he had 'departed this life by divine providence'.

In 1406, to prevent a similar fate befalling the next in succession to the throne, Robert III sent his remaining son, the 11-year-old James Stewart, to safety in France, but James was captured by English pirates, taken to King Henry IV and cast into the Tower of London.

Robert III died later in 1406. He had become a depressive in his later years and famously declared that he could fittingly be buried in a refuse heap beneath the epitaph, 'Here lies the worst among kings and the most wretched of men in the entire country'.

JAMES I
1406–1437

On the death of King Robert III in 1406, his son James Stewart became James I of Scots at the age of 11. James had been captured that very year while travelling to France to escape potential harm at the hands of his corrupt uncle the Duke of Albany and on accession was in prison in the Tower of London. He became king in exile, but power in Scotland remained in the hands of Albany.

Above: Scots king and English rose. While forcibly exiled in England, James I married the beautiful Lady Joan Beaufort.

DEATH OF ALBANY

Secure in his position, Albany had little incentive to ransom James; by contrast he did succeed in negotiating the release of his own son, Murdoch Stewart, who was freed by King Henry V of England in 1416. Albany had been the power behind the throne since *c.*1388–90, but his long 'rule' came to an end on 3 September 1420, when he died aged 80 in Stirling Castle. Murdoch became regent in his stead.

In April 1424, James was freed to return to Scotland, following agreement of a £40,000 ransom to be paid in instalments. Once home, he moved swiftly to impose his authority. On the very day of his return, he is said to have declared, 'If God spares me...I shall see to it throughout the whole of my kingdom that the key keeps the castle and the thorn bush the cow', meaning that property would once again be safe. Within a year he had arrested several rebellious lords and had Murdoch, Duke of Albany executed at Stirling Castle, with two corrupt Stewart kinsmen.

THE POET-KING IN EXILE

James was a man of intelligence, bravery and great ability, and while in England he certainly did not merely rot in prison. He fought in the famous campaigns of King Henry V in France, and he must have won that great monarch's admiration, for in April 1421, Henry invested James as a Knight of the Garter, the prestigious order founded by King Edward III. In addition, James learned about England's developing systems of administration, taxation and government. In 1423 he fell deeply in love with one of Henry's relatives, Lady Joan Beaufort, whom he married in February 1424. Inspired by his love for Joan, James wrote the intense and complex 379-line poem *The Kingis Quair* ('The King's Book'), a work of the highest quality in the tradition of the great Geoffrey Chaucer.

A REFORMING KING

James moved to remodel the Scottish Parliament by increasing the role for lesser nobility (probably in imitation of the House of Commons in Westminster). He greatly improved local justice and instigated reforms of taxation and royal finances. He also had some success in suppressing the independent power of Highland clan leaders. However, on 21 February 1437 he was stabbed to death at Blackfriars Priory in Perth in an attack by several of his leading nobles. They were angered by the king's decision to default on his ransom payments, which had left noble hostages to die in England. James's reputation had also been damaged by his humiliating failure to recapture Roxburgh Castle from the English in a campaign the previous year. The murdered king was succeeded by his 6-year-old son, who ruled as James II.

JAMES I, KING OF SCOTLAND, 1406–1437

Birth: probably late July 1394, Dunfermline Palace
Father: Robert III
Mother: Annabella Drummond
Accession: 4 April 1406 (proclaimed in June 1406)
Coronation: 2 or 21 May 1424
Queen: Joan Beaufort (m. February 1424; d. 1445)
Succeeded by: His son James II
Death: Assassinated in the monastery of Friars Preachers, 21 Feb 1437

Left: James I was a man of many accomplishments – archer, wrestler, athlete, horserider, musician and poet.

JAMES II AND JAMES III

1437–1488

James II came to the throne at the age of just six. The violent feuding of Scotland's lawless nobility continued throughout his minority, as three leading families – Douglas, Crichton and Livingston – competed for the prince and the crown.

A HOT-HEADED KING

James began to rule as king in 1449, (when he also married Mary of Gueldres) and he dealt severely with his foes, seizing the Livingstone lands. James was a hot-headed young man and in 1452 he murdered William, eighth Earl of Douglas, in a quarrel at Stirling Castle by stabbing him in the neck. He then took on the full might of that powerful family, winning a decisive victory at the Battle of Arkinholm in 1455 and greatly enriching the crown by confiscating the vast Douglas estates.

After 1457, largely secure at home, James turned his attention to the persistent problem of the border with England and led a number of successful military raids against English garrisons. He was killed at Roxburgh Castle, in 1460, when a cannon exploded next to him and blew him to pieces.

JAMES II, KING OF SCOTLAND, 1437–1460

Birth: 16 Oct 1430, Holyrood Palace, Edinburgh
Father: James I
Mother: Joan Beaufort
Accession: 21 Feb 1437
Coronation: 25 March 1437, Holyrood Abbey, Edinburgh
Queen: Mary of Gueldres (m. 3 July 1449; d. 1463)
Succeeded by: His son James III
Death: 3 Aug 1460, killed in cannon explosion at the siege of Roxburgh

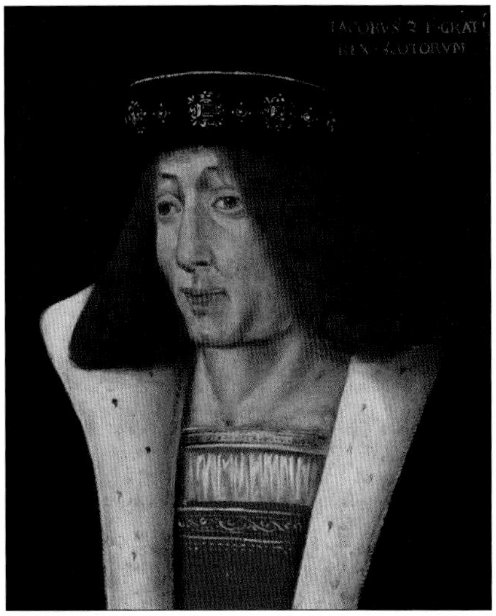

Above: James II of Scots had a vermilion birthmark on the left-hand side of his face, not shown in this 16th-century portrait.

Above: This formal 18th-century portrait of James III of Scots transformed him into a posed, bewigged figure of that later age.

JAMES III

Scotland was plunged into another minority with the accession of the eight-year-old James III on 3 August 1460. Keen to avoid further feuding, the Scottish parliament awarded custody of the boy-king to his mother, the queen dowager Mary of Gueldres, a strong and devout woman. When she died in 1463, James was under the protection of James Kennedy, Bishop of St Andrews. In 1466 he was seized by Sir Alexander Boyd, Keeper of Edinburgh Castle, who declared himself Guardian of Scotland.

In 1469, James broke free of the Boyds and began to rule in his own right. The same year he wed Margaret of Denmark. A major benefit accrued to Scotland under the marriage treaty, when Denmark agreed to cede the Shetlands and Orkney Islands to Scotland as dowry.

Trouble broke out in the 1470s, when James arrested his brothers Alexander, Duke of Albany, and John, Earl of Mar, accusing them of plotting against him. Mar was killed, while Albany escaped and then returned with an English army, claiming the throne as Alexander IV. Berwick was captured, Edinburgh sacked and Albany restored to his landholdings, but James continued to reign.

James was killed during another uprising in 1488, by rebels promoting his son the Duke of Rothesay as King James IV. The throne thus passed to yet another youthful Scots king, the 15-year-old James IV.

JAMES III, KING OF SCOTLAND, 1460–1488

Birth: May 1452
Father: James II
Mother: Mary of Gueldres
Accession: 3 Aug 1460
Coronation: 10 Aug 1460, Kelso Abbey
Queen: Margaret of Denmark (m. July 1469; d. 1486)
Succeeded by: His son James IV
Death: 11 June 1488, near Bannockburn

JAMES IV
1488–1513

James IV of Scots became involved in government from his accession, aged 15, in 1488. His efforts to extend the power of the crown into the north and west of the country met with success. In 1493 he humbled the fiercely independent John MacDonald, fourth and last Lord of the Isles, and could boast that his rule extended throughout the Northern and Western Isles.

A RENAISSANCE MAN

James lived up to the ideal of the 'Renaissance prince'. He was a firm and effective ruler who presided over a largely peaceful Scotland and greatly strengthened royal finances: in the course of the reign the king's revenue rose threefold. He was also a renowned patron of the arts and architecture: he built a royal chapel at Stirling Castle and a palace at Falkland and began work on the magnificent Holyrood Palace in Edinburgh. His court became famous throughout Europe as a centre for the arts and the most up-to-date sciences. The king himself was dedicated to medicine and education: he founded King's College, Aberdeen, in 1495, the first British university to have a chair of medicine, and a surgeons' college in Edinburgh. James was also keen on arcane subjects such as alchemy and the possibility of man-powered flight and financed the researches of an Italian scholar, John Damien, in these areas. He was a keen student of literature and devoured the works of the Scottish poets William Dunbar and Robert Henryson. He also granted a charter in 1507 to Scotland's first printing press.

JAMES IV, KING OF SCOTLAND, 1488–1513

Birth: 17 March 1473
Father: James III
Mother: Margaret of Denmark
Accession: 11 June 1488
Coronation: 26 June 1488, Scone Abbey
Queen: Margaret Tudor (m. 8 Aug 1503; d. 1541)
Succeeded by: His son James V
Death: 9 Sept 1513 at the Battle of Flodden

Above: James IV, Scotland's first authenticated golfer. Royal accounts in the early 1500s include a record of payment for the king's 'golf clubbis and ballis'.

RELATIONS WITH ENGLAND

In the 1490s James was drawn into the dynastic unrest in England that followed Henry Tudor's seizure of the crown as King Henry VII in 1485.

In 1495 the Scottish court at Stirling welcomed the Pretender to the English throne, Perkin Warbeck, who claimed to be Richard, Duke of York. James became friendly with the imposter, whom he addressed as 'Prince Richard', and even prepared to invade England in support of Warbeck.

In the event, the 'war' was no more than a few raids, and in late 1497 England and Scotland agreed a seven-year truce. Subsequently Warbeck was captured, confessed that his claim was false and was executed on 24 November 1499. The English truce, though, was transformed into a perpetual peace agreement in a treaty signed in London on 24 January 1502, which also provided for James's marriage to Margaret Tudor, daughter of King Henry VII.

Left: Stewart wed Tudor when James IV of Scots married Henry VII of England's daughter, Margaret, in August 1503.

James and Margaret's wedding on 8 August 1503, was celebrated with pageants, tournaments and a poem, 'The Thistle and the Rose', by William Dunbar. Although none can have known this at the time, it paved the way for the union of the crowns of Scotland and England in 1603, when James and Margaret's great-grandson, James Stuart, James VI of Scots, would accede as King James I of England.

The 'perpetual peace' was short-lived. By 1513 Scotland was once more at war with England. When England's King Henry VIII invaded France in 1513, James sent his fleet to Normandy to help Louis XII of France and himself invaded northern England with the Scottish army. The move was a disaster. At the battle of Flodden Field on 9 September 1513, James's army was routed. Around 10,000 Scots were killed, including the king himself.

JAMES V
1513–1542

Once again Scotland's heir was an infant: James's 17-month-old son, another James, who was crowned King James V at Stirling Castle on 21 September 1513.

FRANCE OR ENGLAND?

In his minority, pro-French and pro-English factions competed for control of king and country. Initially the boy's mother, Queen Margaret, was his guardian but after her marriage to the pro-English Archibald Douglas, 6th Earl of Angus, the pro-French John Stewart, Duke of Albany, was named regent in her place in July 1515.

In 1522, Albany left for France, hoping to raise military backing for an attack on England, and there he remained after a 1524 coup brought the queen's pro-English party back to power. In 1526, Angus captured James and for the following two years kept him captive, but in 1528 James escaped, raised an army of supporters and drove Angus into exile in England.

As king, James set about enforcing his authority. A Catholic at the time of King Henry VIII's break with Rome, he pursued a strongly pro-French policy and, in 1537, married Madeleine, the 16-year-old daughter of King Francis I of France. She was a frail creature who died only seven months into their marriage, but her vast dowry of 100,000 livres must have been some comfort to James, especially as he was able to negotiate a second prestigious marriage in as many years when he wed the prominent French noblewoman Mary of Guise in 1538.

War erupted with England in 1542 and initial minor successes encouraged King James to invade. At Solway Moss, near Carlisle, on 24 November 1542 the Scots army suffered another catastrophic defeat. Before the year was out the king was dead, aged only 30, devastated by the defeat and the loss the previous year of his two young sons.

JAMES V, KING OF SCOTLAND, 1513–1542

Birth: 10 April 1512, Linlithgow Palace
Father: James IV
Mother: Margaret Tudor
Accession: 9 Sept 1513
Coronation: 21 Sept 1513
Queens: (1) Madeleine de Valois (m. 1 Jan 1537; d. 7 July 1537); (2) Mary of Guise (m. 12 June 1538; d. 11 June 1560)
Succeeded by: His daughter Mary
Death: 14 Dec 1542, Falkland Palace

THE 'AULD ALLIANCE'

The alliance between Scotland and France that played such an important part in the reigns of Kings James IV and V of Scots was more than two centuries old. Historians usually date the alliance from the 1295 Treaty of Paris, agreed in the reign of John Balliol by leading Scots nobles with King Philip IV of France.

However, some trace the long-standing and intermittently renewed alliance right back to the 1168 treaty between King William I 'the Lion' of Scotland and King Louis VII of France.

The alliance survived the 14th and 15th centuries, but might have been expected to die following the 1502 Treaty of Perpetual Peace with England. Yet James IV renewed the alliance in 1512 in the face of Henry VIII's aggression towards both France and Scotland, and the French alliance was important in the reign of his successor, King James V.

The Auld Alliance had two important side effects. Scots soldiers fought in the French army, particularly after Agincourt (1415). Scottish merchants had a preferential deal on French claret, and so the nobles of Scotland enjoyed finer wine.

Left: James V. In his reign, the Treaty of Rouen renewed the Auld Alliance between Scotland and France.

Below: According to tradition, James V liked to travel his country in disguise, identified as 'The tenant of Ballengiech'.

MARY, QUEEN OF SCOTS

1542–1567

When King James V of Scots died in despair at Falkland Palace on 14 December 1542, he had only one heir, his seven-day-old daughter, Mary. She became the first Queen of Scots and the country's youngest-ever monarch. The regency was secured for the tiny queen's French-born mother, Mary of Guise.

A GLORIOUS DESTINY

Mary, Queen of Scots was sent to France at the age of five and there enjoyed a royal education and gilded youth. She grew up a staunch Catholic, speaking French while also learning Latin, Greek, Spanish and Italian, and she became a renowned dancer. As a result of her French upbringing, she changed the spelling of her family name from 'Stewart' to the French form, 'Stuart'.

At the age of 15, in 1558, she married the French heir to the throne, the Dauphin Francis, and with the accession of Queen Elizabeth I of England in November that year, Mary became next in line for the English throne too. For Catholics (who did not accept Henry VIII's divorce of Catherine of Aragon and 1533 marriage to Elizabeth's mother, Queen Anne Boleyn), she was the rightful Queen of England. Finally, with the death in July 1559 of Henry II of France from the effects of a hunting wound, her husband Francis became king of France. The young queen's destiny appeared to be glorious.

Above: This 19th-century French portrait represents Mary mourning the death of her first husband, Francis II of France.

MARY, QUEEN OF SCOTS, 1542–1567

Birth: 8 Dec 1542, Linlithgow Palace
Father: James V
Mother: Mary of Guise
Accession: 14 Dec 1542
Coronation: 9 Sept 1543
Husbands: (1) Francis II of France (m. 24 April 1558; d. 5 Dec 1560); (2) Henry Stuart, Lord Darnley (m. 29 July 1565; d. 10 Feb 1567); (3) James Hepburn, fourth Earl of Bothwell (m 15 May 1567; d. 14 April 1578)
Abdicates: 24 July 1567
Succeeded by: Her son James I and VI
Death: Executed 8 Feb 1587

MISSED OPPORTUNITY

Somehow it all went wrong. Mary loved her young husband, but he died aged only 16 in 1560. She bravely returned home to Scotland and tried without success to find a middle way acceptable to competing Protestant and Catholic camps. She was unable to tame the violent power struggle among competing barons.

Four years after her return, Mary married her handsome but unpopular Tudor cousin Henry Stuart, Lord Darnley, a fellow Catholic who also had a claim to the English throne.

The events of 1566–7 sealed her fate. First her husband Darnley led a group of nobles in butchering Mary's Italian secretary David Rizzio. Next Mary gave birth to a son, James Stuart: while the 'Virgin Queen' Elizabeth I of England remained childless, this boy would be heir to the English throne as well as that of Scotland. Then Darnley was murdered in 1567, perhaps with Mary's involvement, by a group led by the Earl of Bothwell. Mary's marriage to Bothwell in May convinced Scots that she had been involved in Darnley's murder. Rebel nobles triumphed over Mary and Bothwell, and in July 1567 the queen was forced to abdicate in favour of her 13-month-old son.

In 1568 Mary fled to England, seeking sanctuary with her cousin Elizabeth. She was several times the focus of Catholic plots to oust Queen Elizabeth. Mary remained in Elizabeth's custody until her conviction for plotting against Elizabeth's life and was executed on 1 February 1587. After her flight from Scotland she never again set eyes on her only son.

Above: Mary's ill-advised third marriage to James Hepburn, the Earl of Bothwell, forced events that led to her abdication.

JAMES VI OF SCOTS
1567–1603

James VI of Scots was crowned aged one year on 29 July 1567 in a church by the gates of Stirling Castle, where he was being kept. In Scotland a succession of four regents – the earls of Moray, Lennox, Mar and Morton – took power. Meanwhile, James received a thorough classical and Protestant religious education, studying Latin, Greek and French under the guidance of his tutor, the learned scholar George Buchanan.

At the age of 16, in August 1582, James was kidnapped by Protestant nobles led by the first Earl of Gowrie, to prevent him falling further under the spell of his Catholic friend Esmé Stuart, the French-born Duke of Lennox and specifically to avert a rumoured plot in which Lennox would force James to convert to Catholicism and then mount an invasion of England. However, James escaped after ten months confinement, and thereafter ruled in his own name.

THE ANGLO-SCOTTISH PACT

As King of Scots, James VI set about cultivating a good relationship with England and in particular with Queen Elizabeth I, with a view to bolstering his chances of succession to the English throne after her death. In May 1585 the two monarchs agreed a defensive peace treaty under which James received £4,000 annually. Even Elizabeth's execution of James's mother, Mary, Queen of Scots two years later in 1587 did not seriously disturb the new Anglo-Scottish pact. Although James made a formal complaint about the execution, he knew that his mother's death made him next in line for the English throne.

In Scotland James maintained a strong rule, successfully managing rival Protestant and Catholic sections of the nobility, and establishing his authority as head of the Presbyterian Church.

When, as he had long planned, James acceded to the throne of England on the death of Queen Elizabeth I in 1603, he had been on the throne for 36 years; quite an achievement in the wildly unstable environment of late 16th-century Scotland; and as he told the English Parliament, he was already, 'An old and experienced king'.

THE DIVINE RIGHT OF KINGS

James VI was a highly educated intellectual as well as a largely effective, practical king. In September 1598 he published a theory of kingship in his *The Trew Law of Free Monarchies: Or the Reciprock and Mutuall Dutie Betwixt a Free King and his Naturall Subjects*. He argued that kings rule by divine right and are responsible to the Almighty for their actions: 'Kings are called gods by the prophetical King David (the Biblical Psalmist David) because they sit upon God's throne on Earth and have the account of their administration to give unto him'. Their duty is to 'minister justice', 'advance the good and punish the evil', 'establish good lawes' and 'procure the peace of the people'. It follows that subjects have no right to rebel. James urged his people to 'arme your selves with patience and humilitie', adding that since God 'hath the only power to make [a king]' he also 'hath the onely power to unmake him' and subjects' duty was 'onely to obey'. This assertion was to cause a lot of trouble for James' successors.

JAMES VI, KING OF SCOTLAND, 1567–1603; KING OF ENGLAND AND SCOTLAND 1603–1625

Birth: 19 June 1566, Edinburgh Castle
Father: Henry Stuart, Lord Darnley
Mother: Mary, Queen of Scots
Accession: 24 July 1567
Coronation: 29 July 1567
Queen: Anne of Denmark (m. 23 Nov 1589; d. 2 March 1619)
Succeeded by: His son Charles I
Death: 27 March 1625, Theobalds Park, Herts

Above: The two sides of the Jacobus 6 Dei Gratia Rex Scotorum, a gold 'hat piece', worth £4, minted in Edinburgh in 1591.

Right: This portrait of James VI was sent to the Danish court during negotiations for his marriage to Anne of Denmark.

CHAPTER FOUR

LANCASTER AND YORK

1399–1485

A leading baron and a warrior, Henry Bolingbroke elevated martial vigour above the right of hereditary succession to the throne in the summer and autumn of 1399. Having returned from the exile into which King Richard II had cast him, Bolingbroke led a rebel army to London and forced the king to abdicate in Parliament before claiming the throne himself. When Bolingbroke was crowned King Henry IV in Westminster Abbey on 13 October 1399, he founded the House of Lancaster, a cadet or junior line of the House of Plantagenet. Henry IV's claim to the throne was as the son of John of Gaunt, fourth son of King Edward III. John of Gaunt had married Blanche, the heiress to the duchy of Lancaster, so his son Bolingbroke was Duke of Lancaster. The king he deposed, Richard II, was his cousin.

The usurper king's dynasty lasted for the reigns of three monarchs – Henry IV himself, his son Henry V, the battle-winning hero of Agincourt, and his ineffective grandson Henry VI who ascended the English throne at the age of just nine months.

The decline of Henry VI into madness led to the elevation of the ambitious Richard, Duke of York, to the role of Protector and Defender of the Kingdom in March 1454. Richard himself had a viable claim to the throne as the great-grandson of King Edward III through the male line via Edmund of Langley, 1st Duke of York (1341–1402). The bitter Wars of the Roses in the second half of the 15th century were fought between the supporters of the rival 'Yorkist' and 'Lancastrian' claims to the throne.

Left: Henry IV was a usurper, but he made sure that his magnificent coronation stressed his majesty and divine appointment to the throne.

HENRY IV
1399–1413

HENRY IV, KING OF ENGLAND, 1399–1413

Birth: 3 April 1367, Bolingbroke Castle
Father: John of Gaunt, Duke of Lancaster
Mother: Blanche of Lancaster
Accession: 30 Sept 1399
Coronation: 13 Oct 1399, Westminster Abbey
Queens: (1) Mary de Bohun (m. 5 Feb 1381; d. 1394); (2) Joan of Navarre (m. 7 Feb 1403; d. 1437)
Succeeded by: His son Henry V
Greatest achievement: Founding the House of Lancaster
30 Sept 1399: Richard II deposed
21 July 1403: Defeats rebels at Battle of Shrewsbury
1406: Develops mystery illness – leprosy?
1409: Captures Harlech Castle to end long-running Welsh revolt
Death: 20 March 1413, Westminster

Henry IV claimed the throne of England on the basis of his descent from King Edward III, but the claim was distant. Henry was the son of King Edward's fourth son, John of Gaunt, and Blanche, daughter of the Duke of Lancaster. His claim thus came through the male line. However, if a claim through the female line were allowed, as it had been before, then Edmund Mortimer, Earl of March, had a stronger claim, as the great-grandson of King Edward III's second son, Lionel Duke of Clarence through Lionel's daughter Philippa, Countess of Ulster. Also in his favour was the fact that Richard had recognized him as his heir presumptive. In fact, Henry's most compelling claim to the throne lay in his person; in 1399 he was an accomplished soldier and a man of drive, wealth and education while Edmund Mortimer was a boy of less than ten.

STRUGGLE FOR SUCCESSION

Henry could also claim to have been wronged by Richard II. Henry was one of the Lords Appellant, who had challenged Richard's rule in 1387 and forced the king to restate his coronation oath the following year. He suffered when the king revenged himself in the late 1390s. Richard exiled Henry for ten years in 1398, and in the following year seized Henry's inheritance on the death of John of Gaunt.

On 4 July 1399, while King Richard was campaigning in Ireland, Henry landed from France near Spurn Head with a force of 300 men. Initially he claimed he wanted only to regain his rightful inheritance but as he marched southwards and his army swelled with supporters his demands rose. By then Richard was in hiding in Wales, following his return from Ireland; when the king finally arrived in London, Henry cast him into the Tower.

On 30 September 1399, Richard II was deposed in parliament and the following month Henry was crowned King Henry IV in Westminster Abbey. Richard was imprisoned in Pontefract Castle. The deposed king – no longer Richard II, but merely Richard of Bordeaux – died in jail early the following year, apparently brutally put to death on the orders of Henry IV.

Below: The English gold noble coin was inscribed with a king standing on a ship. First issued by Edward III in 1344, this one was minted for Henry IV in 1412.

REBEL CHALLENGES

Henry defeated two major uprisings in his reign. His principal opponents were the Welsh prince Owain Glyndwr and the Percy family of Northumberland. Early in the reign, Glyndwr, Lord of Glyndyfrydwy, declared himself Prince of Wales and gathered support for an uprising against English rule. Despite a largely successful attack on Wales in autumn 1403 and a series of raids led by the English Prince of Wales, the 16-year-old heir to the throne, Prince Henry, the rebellion remained a thorn in Henry's side until 1409.

The Percys were Henry's former allies. They rose in revolt because they believed that the king had failed to reward them sufficiently for their past

Below: Princely patriarch. John of Gaunt, son of Edward III, founded the House of Lancaster through his son, Henry IV.

Above: Froissart's Chronicles *depicts Henry riding into London, the English crown within his grasp.*

support, so they rallied around the claim to the throne of Edmund Mortimer, Earl of March. However, in July 1403 the king defeated a rebel army led by Henry Percy ('Hotspur'), warrior son of the Earl of Northumberland, in the Battle of Shrewsbury.

The rebellion continued. In 1405, conspirators Thomas Mowbray and Richard Scrope, Archbishop of York, were captured and put to death. Then in 1406 Glyndwr, Sir Edmund Mortimer, the younger Edmund's uncle, and the Percys agreed to split England between them in the event that they defeated Henry. The rebels, however, suffered a decisive defeat at the Battle of Bramham Moor in February 1408, after which Hotspur's father, the Earl of Northumberland, was executed. In 1409 the king's capture of Harlech Castle effectively ended the Welsh revolt, reducing the proud prince Glyndwr to a landless rebel who had no choice but to hide in caves. His place and date of death are unknown.

TROUBLED IN OLD AGE

Victory did not bring Henry peace of mind or body. Beginning in 1406, he suffered an agonizing illness that may have been leprosy and was identified by some as the judgement of God, perhaps for the murder of Archbishop Scrope of York. Henry was also increasingly at odds with his son, Prince Henry, partly because of rumours in 1411–12 that the prince was plotting to take the throne from his father.

In these later years, the formerly ruthless and ambitious Henry Bolingbroke became careworn and tormented by guilt. As early as 1409, in his will, he declared, 'I Henry, sinful wretch, ask my lords and true people forgiveness if I have misentreated them in any wise'. He died on 20 March 1413 after fainting before the Westminster Abbey shrine to his saintly predecessor on the English throne, Edward the Confessor. He was given the last rites and died in the 'Jerusalem Chamber' in the abbot's house at Westminster. His death thus fulfilled a prophecy that the king would die 'in Jerusalem'.

Above: The young man who seized the crown spoke French, Latin and English. He holds the red rose of Lancaster.

LANCASTER AND YORK 1399–1485

HENRY IV 1367–1413 ♛ 1399–1413 *m* (1) Mary de Bohun 1369/70–94 (2) Joan of Navarre *c.*1370–1437

Anne Mortimer *m* Richard Earl of Cambridge 1385–1415

HENRY V 1387–1422 ♛ 1413–22 *m* Catherine of France 1401–38

Thomas Duke of Clarence 1388–1421

John Duke of Bedford 1389–1435

Humphrey Duke of Gloucester 1390–1447

and others

Richard Duke of York 1411/12–60 *m* Cecily Neville 1415–95

HENRY VI 1421–1471 ♛ 1422–1461, 1470–1 *m* Margaret of Anjou 1429–82

Elizabeth Woodville *c.*1437–92 *m* **EDWARD IV** 1442–83 ♛ 1461–70 ♛ 1471–83

Richard Neville Earl of Warwick "The Kingmaker" 1428–71

Edward Prince of Wales 1453–71 *m* Anne Neville 1456–85

EDWARD V 1470–83 ♛ 1483

Richard Duke of York 1473–83

George Duke of Clarence 1449–78 *m* Isabella 1451–76

Anne 1456–85 *m* **RICHARD III** 1452–85 ♛ 1483–5

and others

HENRY V

1413–1422

Henry V led a bedraggled 6,000-strong army in one of the greatest and most celebrated military exploits in English history – the defeat of a French force more than three times larger, at the Battle of Agincourt, on 25 October 1415. His victories during a whirlwind, four-month campaign in France that autumn won him an enduring place in English history and also set the scene for the remarkable treaty signed at Troyes on 21 May 1420, under which Henry was made French regent and recognized as heir to the throne of France.

Before he was king, Henry had made declaration of his martial vigour. He took the fight to Welsh rebel Owain Glyndwr in 1400, when in his early teens, and in 1409 aged 21, he won decisive victories at Aberystwyth and Harlech. When Henry IV lay dying, young Henry took the crown from his father's head, but his father, rallying, asked him what right he had to the crown since it had been won in blood and not received through a divinely blessed hereditary line. The future Henry V told the ailing king, 'As you have kept the crown by the sword, so will I keep it while my life lasts'.

A REFORMED CHARACTER

Henry was crowned King Henry V in Westminster Abbey on Passion Sunday, 9 April 1413. A blizzard enveloped the

Above: Henry married Catherine, daughter of Charles VI of France, on 2 June 1420. James I of Scots was a wedding guest.

Right: Henry V's campaigns in France yielded memorable victories that led to the triumph of the Treaty of Troyes.

HENRY V, KING OF ENGLAND, 1413–1422

Birth: 16 Sept 1387
Father: King Henry IV of England
Mother: Mary de Bohun
Accession: 20 March 1413
Coronation: 9 April 1413, Westminster Abbey
Queen: Catherine of France (m. 2 June 1420; d. 1438)
Succeeded by: His son Henry of Windsor
Greatest achievement: Battle of Agincourt 1415, Treaty of Troyes 1420
25 Oct 1415: Wins Battle of Agincourt
c.1416: Death of Owain Glyndwr
21 May 1420: Becomes regent of France and heir to the French king Charles VI
Death: 31 Aug 1422, Castle of Bois-de-Vincennes, France

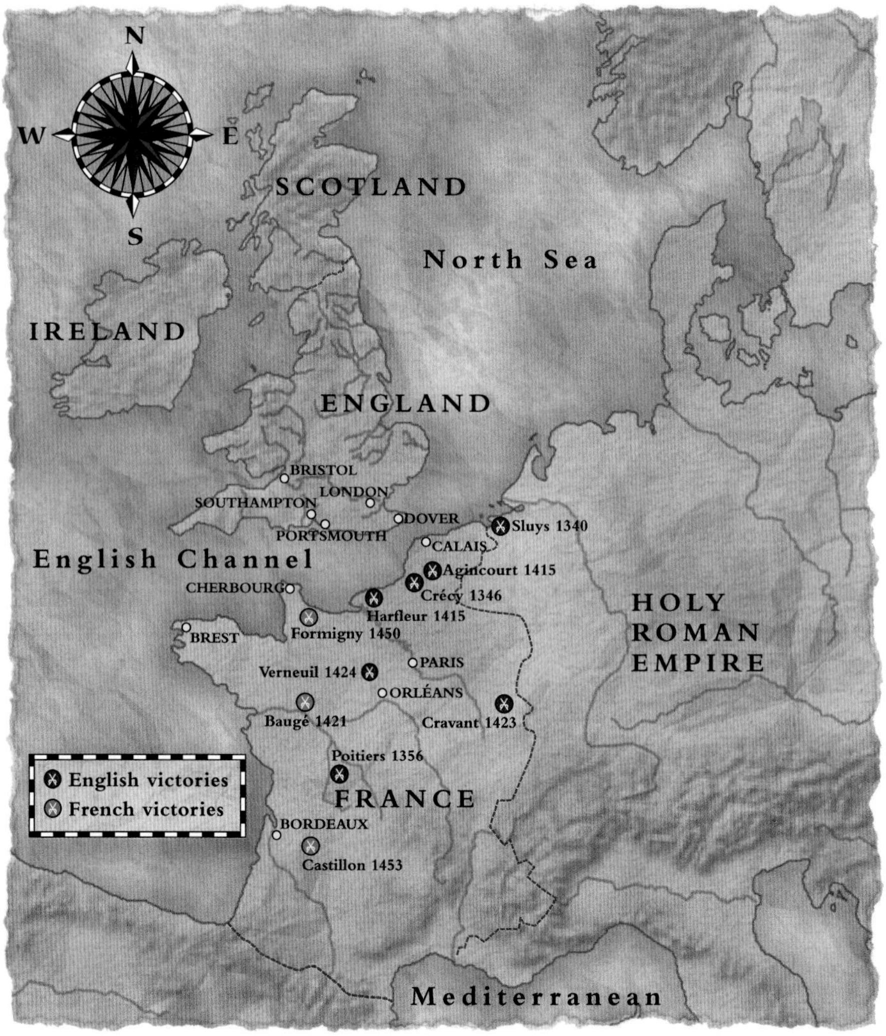

THE KING'S FRIEND EXECUTED FOR HERESY

Sir John Oldcastle became a friend of the Prince of Wales during the campaigns against Owain Glyndwr in Wales in Henry IV's reign. However, this did not save him from a heretic's death in 1417.

Oldcastle was executed under Henry IV's 1401 statute 'On the burning of heretics'. He was condemned as a 'Lollard', a member of a group of religious reformers inspired by John Wyclif (d. 1384). Wyclif rejected the doctrine of transubstantiation and argued that the Church and its priests should reject wealth and power and adopt material poverty. Lollards got their name, which derived from a Dutch word meaning 'mumbler', because many of them prayed aloud. Some were a direct political threat to the monarchy, since they proclaimed the rightful king, Richard II, was still alive and living in Scotland. Oldcastle was condemned as a heretic in 1413, but escaped from the Tower of London and remained at large until his capture and execution in 1417.

William Shakespeare transformed Oldcastle into the character of Sir John Falstaff in the *Henry IV* plays. Falstaff is referred to as 'my old lad of the castle', but has none of Oldcastle's controversial religious beliefs.

Above: Warrior king. Henry sported a soldier's haircut; such was his athleticism, he was said to be able to outrun a deer.

Abbey, and during the new king's coronation feast onlookers noted that he looked serious and severe and did not indulge in the splendid feast laid out on the banqueting tables before him. As Prince of Wales, Henry had been celebrated for the raucous company he kept and for their wild escapades. Famously, he was involved in a midnight brawl in an Eastcheap tavern, and he also laid ambushes for members of the royal household. Upon his coronation he decisively put his wild years behind him however, declaring that none of his former companions were permitted to come within 10 miles (16km) of him.

WAR IN FRANCE

Henry declared his intention of fighting for the throne of France in early July 1415. He laid claim to the French crown as great-grandson of Edward III, whose mother was the daughter of French king Philip IV. He saw an opportunity to be grasped in France, where the king, Charles VI, was intermittently subject to bouts of madness. Henry set sail in August, besieged and captured Harfleur, then marched for Calais. He defeated the French at Agincourt, then returned to great acclaim from his countrymen, who shouted, 'Welcome, Henry V, King of England and France' as he rode through the city of London. In a second campaign in 1417–19, Henry captured Caen and Rouen, capital of Normandy. Under the Treaty of Troyes he then married Catherine, daughter of the French King Charles VI, and was thereby recognized as heir to the French throne and installed as regent for the French king's periods of madness. But Henry had to fight on to counter the threat presented by King Charles's son, the Dauphin Charles, who was disinherited by this treaty.

Henry's queen, Catherine of France, gave birth to a son, Henry, on 6 December 1421 at Windsor. As Henry lay dying the following year of dysentery contracted during the siege of Meaux, near Paris, he appointed his brothers as regents of his domains. Humphrey, Duke of Gloucester, was appointed regent of England, and John, Duke of Bedford, became regent of France. Henry died at the age of just 35.

Below: On 25 October 1415, at the Battle of Agincourt, Henry V's army of 6,000 defeated a French force of 20,000. The victory entered English folklore.

HENRY VI

1422–1461, 1470–1471

The unexpected death of Henry V thrust greatness on his infant son. Coming to the throne at the age of just nine months, Henry VI set a record (which stands to this day) as the youngest ever king of England.

At first government was in the hands of the young king's uncle, Duke Humphrey of Gloucester, who had been appointed regent by Henry V. Gloucester was soon in open conflict with Henry Beaufort, Bishop of Winchester and Chancellor of England, for control of the boy-king and of the country. Henry was unable to provide the strong rule needed to safeguard the achievements of his illustrious warrior father. Even when he came to adulthood, his character prevented him from becoming master of events and establishing authority over the squabbling barons who surrounded him. For the king was simple, pious, easily swayed and, like his maternal grandfather, King Charles VI of France, subject to bouts of madness. Henry VI's reign was a long, slow decline from the position of considerable strength he inherited. A decline in which England lost its holdings in France and slid into the violent dynastic conflicts that came to be known as the 'Wars of the Roses'.

Above: Boy among men. Even as an adult, Henry VI was never equal to the task of ruling 15th-century England.

DISASTERS IN FRANCE

In the spring and early summer of 1429, a French peasant girl known as Joan of Arc led the French army in a string of remarkable triumphs against the English. Then in July, the Dauphin, Charles, son of the French King Charles VI, was crowned King Charles VII of France. This coronation was in direct

Below: Joan of Arc said she was guided by Saints Michael, Catherine and Margaret in her campaign against the English in France.

HENRY VI, KING OF ENGLAND, 1422–1461, 1470–1471

Birth: 6 Dec 1421, Windsor Castle
Father: King Henry V of England
Mother: Queen Catherine of Valois
Accession: 31 Aug 1422
Coronation: 6 Nov 1429, Westminster Abbey; 16 Dec 1431 (as King of France), Notre Dame de Paris
Queen: Margaret of Anjou (m. 22 April 1445; d. 1482)
Succeeded by: Edward IV
Greatest achievement: Founding King's College, Cambridge, and Eton College
1450: Jack Cade's rebellion
17 July 1453: English defeated at Battle of Castillon
22 May 1455: Battle of St Albans
4 March 1461: Deposed by Edward IV
3 Oct 1470: Restored to throne
11 April 1471: Deposed once more
Death: 21 May 1471, probably murdered, Tower of London

Above: In 1450, Jack Cade's rebels called for the recall of Richard, Duke of York and the dismissal of several ministers.

contravention of the 1420 Treaty of Troyes, which guaranteed the French crown to King Henry V's son and his descendants. In order to counter this, the 10-year-old Henry VI was taken to Paris and crowned as Henri II, King of France, in December 1431. By this time Joan of Arc had been captured, tried for heresy and burnt at the stake in Rouen. Despite her personal fate, Joan had done much to restore French pride.

In 1435 English hopes in France suffered a double blow. The Duke of Burgundy, previously a key ally of England, made peace with the Dauphin. Then Henry VI's uncle, the Duke of Bedford and regent of France, died in Rouen. The Dauphin's army captured Paris from the English in 1436.

In August 1443, Henry – by now 21 years old and ruling in his own right – despatched an English army to France under the command of John Beaufort, Duke of Somerset. The following year, the two countries negotiated a five-year peace and Henry VI married Margaret, daughter of the Duke of Anjou. However, England's French possessions continued to dwindle. Within six months of the wedding, at the urging of his forceful new queen, Henry agreed to hand over the duchy of Maine to Margaret's father, René of Anjou. War resumed in 1448–9 and the English lost Normandy in 1450 and Bordeaux and Gascony in 1451. The English sent a force to recover Gascony but the French won a decisive victory at Castillon in July 1453, finally bringing to a close the conflict of the Hundred Years War and leaving Calais England's only remaining French possession.

A PATRON OF EDUCATION

Henry's authority dwindled at home. In 1450 Jack Cade, a former soldier going under the name of 'John Mortimer', led a rebel force of labourers towards the royal court. As Henry fled to the north, the rebels ran riot in London. They were only dispersed when the intrepid Queen Margaret, who had remained in London, offered them pardons.

Henry's mild and pious character may have ill fitted him to be an effective king in late medieval England, but his devoutness inspired him to be a great educational patron, the founder of two major English institutions. In 1440, he established the King's College of Our Lady of Eton, later known as Eton College, and in 1441 he laid the foundation stone for King's College, Cambridge. Generous royal funding provided free education for the 25 poor scholars and 25 paupers at Eton; they were expected to proceed to King's College to complete their education.

A SECRET WEDDING

King Henry V's widow, Catherine of Valois, kept her marriage to a Welsh squire secret for six years before it was discovered in 1436. After mourning Henry's untimely death, Catherine settled at Baynard's Castle, at Blackfriars in London. Here, despite a 1428 law declaring that the dowager queen could marry only with the king's consent, in 1430 she secretly wed a Welsh squire named Owain ap Maredudd ap Tudor, better known as Owen Tudor. The couple had a daughter and three sons before their union was discovered. To escape public shame Queen Catherine retired to the nunnery at Bermondsey; meanwhile Owain was cast into Newgate Prison, but escaped in 1438 and returned home to Wales.

Below: 101 years' work. The magnificent chapel in King's College, Cambridge, was begun in 1446 and completed in 1547.

THE WARS OF THE ROSES

ENGLAND AT WAR, 1455–1485

The weak rule of King Henry VI made England vulnerable to power struggles and civil conflict. The king was unable to stamp his authority on the feuding barons around him, who included the ambitious Duke of York, his backer Richard Neville, the Earl of Warwick (later known as 'Warwick the kingmaker') and royal favourites the dukes of Suffolk and Somerset. The barons came into increasingly open competition. Following Suffolk's death in 1450, the struggle was between York and Somerset. The king's susceptibility to periods of madness tipped the balance and a tense standoff eventually erupted into open conflict.

Below: After a defeat for the Yorkist cause at Ludford Bridge in October 1459, the future Edward IV fled to Calais.

Above: The Wars of the Roses are named from the badges of the opposing sides: a red rose for Lancaster and a white rose for York.

THE SLIDE TO CIVIL WAR

King Henry's first attack of insanity in 1453 followed hard on the loss of England's possessions in France. Henry became incapable of making decisions or holding reasoned debate. Richard, Duke of York, was named Protector and Defender of the Kingdom in March 1454 and at once imprisoned Somerset. However, in 1455, after regaining his clarity and sense of purpose, Henry resumed royal rule and released Somerset from the Tower of London.

York rebelled against the king in an attempt to recover his lost authority. On 22 May 1455, York defeated the 'Lancastrian' forces of the king and Somerset at St Albans. As fighting raged in the town, Somerset was trapped in the Castle Inn and put to the sword by Yorkist soldiers. King Henry was shot in the neck with an arrow but managed to escape to safety in the home of a local tanner. York found him there and swore loyalty to his monarch before escorting him from the battlefield to St Albans Abbey and then to London.

The battle was no more than a skirmish, but it marked the beginning of the 33 years of dynastic and political instability and occasional civil war that would be remembered as the Wars of the Roses. In these wars, Lancastrians loyal to King Henry VI and the royal House of Lancaster fought with Yorkist supporters of Richard, Duke of York. The Duke of York had a valid claim to the throne, for he was the nephew of Edmund Mortimer, Earl of March, who had been excluded from the succession when Henry IV seized the throne.

At first the Yorkists had the upper hand. The Duke of York became Constable of England in May, following the St Albans battle, and in November was made Protector for the second time. However, the following year he was deprived of the Protectorship once more as Queen Margaret and her Lancastrian allies manoeuvred against him. In 1458 Henry enforced a reconciliation between the warring parties.

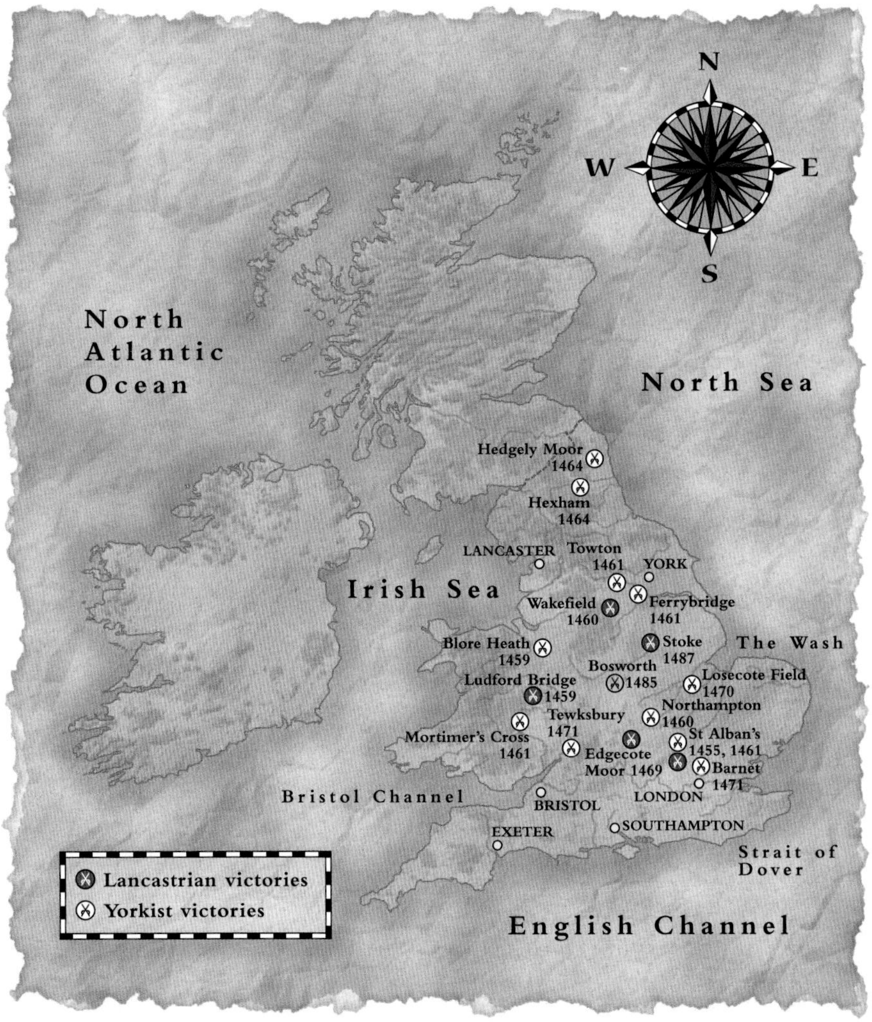

Above: King Henry VI is captured by the forces of Richard, Earl of Warwick, after the Battle of Northampton, in 1460.

Right: Major battle sites of the Wars of the Roses. The conflict was fought out over 30 years and virtually the whole of England.

On 25 March – remembered as 'Loveday' – Yorkists and Lancastrians were made to walk in procession, hand in hand, to St Paul's Cathedral in London, and the Yorkists were forced to agree to compensate the descendants of those harmed at St Albans. However, the king was not strong enough to impose peace for long and the following year battle recommenced. After an initial victory at Blore Heath on 23 September, the Yorkists suffered a devastating defeat in the Battle of Ludford Bridge on 12 October. The Duke of York fled to Ireland and in November was condemned as a traitor by Parliament.

A YEAR OF MIXED FORTUNES

In 1460 the Yorkists experienced both triumph and despair. On 10 July, at Northampton, a Yorkist army led by Richard Neville, Earl of Warwick, and the Duke of York's son, Edward, Earl of March, trounced the Lancastrian-royalist forces and captured Henry VI. This appeared to be a decisive victory: York returned from Ireland and in the Act of Accord of 24 October, was named as the heir to Henry VI. However, the ever-resourceful Queen Margaret orchestrated a Lancastrian response and the pendulum swung in her favour before the year was out.

The queen's army, led by Somerset, defeated the Yorkists at Wakefield in December and killed Richard, Duke of York. The Lancastrians, on Margaret's orders, cut off his head and displayed it in a paper crown on the gates of York. On 17 February 1461, back at St Albans, her army defeated Warwick and rescued Henry VI from captivity. Just two weeks later, the Yorkists gained the upper hand. Warwick and Edward of York entered London and on 4 March Edward declared himself King Edward IV.

YEARS OF CONFLICT

Edward IV ruled with a firm hand for 22 years, establishing the new dynasty of the House of York. However, the country endured two further bouts of bloody dynastic conflict as the Wars of the Roses re-ignited. In 1470–1, Edward was forced into exile and Henry VI was briefly declared king once more, before Edward returned to defeat and kill Warwick. The triumph of the House of York seemed complete.

But 12 years later in 1483, following Edward's death, his brother Richard seized the throne as Richard III, apparently having had Edward's sons Edward V and Richard killed. Richard III's reign lasted no more than two years: the Lancastrians returned to win a final victory – in the form of Henry Tudor, the grandson of Henry V's widow, Catherine of Valois, and great-grandson of John of Gaunt, Duke of Lancaster (1340–99).

EDWARD IV

1461–1470, 1471–1483

In the eyes of his subjects, Edward proved the justice of his claim to the throne and his fitness to govern by defeating a Lancastrian army under the Duke of Somerset at the Battle of Towton, in March 1461. With the Lancastrian cause in disarray and Queen Margaret having fled to Scotland, Edward was crowned with great ceremony on 28 June in Westminster Abbey.

AN UNDIPLOMATIC MARRIAGE

A proven warrior, Edward had little of his predecessor Henry VI's profound piety, instead exhibiting a strong liking for the pleasures of the flesh. Early in his reign he won himself a reputation as a

Above: Physical authority. Powerfully built and 6ft 4in (1.93m) tall, Edward IV was both approachable and charismatic.

EDWARD IV, KING OF ENGLAND, 1461–1470, 1471–1483
Birth: 28 April 1442, Rouen, Normandy
Father: Richard, Duke of York
Mother: Cecily, Duchess of York
Accession: 4 March 1461
Coronation: 28 June 1461, Westminster Abbey
Queen: Elizabeth Woodville (m. 1 May 1464; d. 1492)
Succeeded by: His son Edward V
Greatest achievement: Establishment of House of York
29 March 1461: Battle of Towton
1470: Flees into exile
14 April 1471: Defeats Warwick the Kingmaker at Battle of Barnet
21 May 1471: Reclaims throne
Death: 9 April 1483, Windsor

Below: King Edward had a taste for lavish clothes, made from the finest animal furs, velvet and cloth of gold.

womanizer. Indeed, Edward's weakness for beautiful women led to one of the major misjudgements of his reign: his secret marriage to Elizabeth Woodville, the widow of a Lancastrian nobleman who had been killed in the 1461 Battle of St Albans. The story goes that Edward met Elizabeth when he visited a castle during a hunting trip and was at once deeply taken with her looks. She resisted all his advances and declared that he would have to marry her in order to have what he wanted. Unable to resist her charms, Edward married Elizabeth in utmost secrecy in May 1464.

Edward's subjects felt that Elizabeth did not have the social status necessary to be queen. More importantly, the marriage angered Edward's great noble ally Warwick the Kingmaker, for Elizabeth imported her five brothers and seven sisters to the royal court and insisted that Edward shower them with favours that Warwick resented. In addition, Warwick was secretly in negotiations with King Louis of France, in which he had promised the king's hand in marriage to a French princess and these talks now came to nothing.

FORCED INTO EXILE

In 1469 Warwick inspired a revolt in Yorkshire against Edward. The rebels, fronted by 'Robin of Redesdale' (in reality close Warwick ally Sir John Conyers), defeated the king in battle. Edward was briefly imprisoned by Warwick before he was released and returned to the throne in London.

Then, in 1470, Edward was betrayed and forced into exile. Journeying to France, Warwick had allied himself with his former enemy Queen Margaret and with the king's brother, the Duke of Clarence. When Edward marched north to deal with further Warwick-inspired rebellions, Warwick and Clarence landed an army on the south coast with the intention of restoring Henry VI to the throne. Even then, Edward remained confident of his ability to see off his former mentor, but he was betrayed by the Marquis of Montagu who allied himself with Warwick and left the king so heavily outnumbered that he was forced to flee to exile in Burgundy. Warwick and Clarence took control, freed Henry VI from the Tower of London, where he had been kept, and crowned him once more as King of England.

The revival of Henry's reign lasted no more than six months. Edward returned to England, made peace with Clarence, then defeated and killed Warwick and Montagu in battle at Barnet on 14 April 1471. Afterwards he returned Henry to imprisonment in the Tower.

In May he trounced the forces of Queen Margaret at Tewkesbury, capturing Margaret herself and beheading her prominent supporters, including the Duke of Somerset. Margaret's son Edward, the Prince of Wales, was killed as he tried to escape and shortly thereafter Henry VI died in mysterious circumstances. It is likely that he was killed, perhaps by Edward's brother Richard of Gloucester. The new king's victory seemed complete and the crown secure with the new House of York.

APPETITE FOR PLEASURE

Edward was a man of urgent appetites, who was rumoured to make himself vomit during banquets so he could continue to gorge on rich foods and who boasted that he had three mistresses, 'One the merriest, the other the wiliest, the third the holiest harlot in the realm'. They included Elizabeth Shore, a London grocer's wife, and Elizabeth Lucy, daughter of a Hampshire nobleman and mother of a notable illegitmate son, Arthur Plantagenet.

Edward's overindulgence probably contributed to his sudden death, aged 40. In his later years he grew corpulent, and in March 1483 he was struck down by a mystery illness variously said to have been malaria, pneumonia or a stroke. He died on 9 April, 1483.

ENGLAND'S FIRST PRINTED BOOK

King Edward was a man of culture and taste as well as a warrior and political schemer. He financed the printing of the first dated book in English, which was also the first book printed in England.

The Dictes and Sayenges of the Phylosophers was printed by William Caxton in 1477. Caxton was a Kent-born merchant who flourished in Flanders and Holland and learned printing in Cologne in the early 1470s. He translated *The Recuyell of the Historyes of Troye* into English and printed it, but without a date, in Bruges, in 1475. The following year Caxton returned to London and set up his printing press in Westminster. He presented *The Dictes and Sayenges of the Phylosophers* to Edward in the year of its publication.

Left: This woodcut of a knight was used to illustrate Caxton's Game of the Chesse.

Below: Beguiled by beauty, Edward recklessly plunged into a secret marriage to Elizabeth Woodville in May 1464.

Below: Edward asserted his authority at Barnet in April 1471, killing the Marquis of Montagu and Earl of Warwick.

THE PRINCES IN THE TOWER

ROYAL MURDER, 1483

As Protector of the Kingdom in summer 1483, Richard Duke of Gloucester had the 12-year-old King Edward V and the king's brother Richard housed in the Tower Of London, which at that time was a palace as well as a jail. Shortly after Gloucester engineered his elevation to the throne, the princes disappeared and many assumed, then and since, that they had been murdered on Richard's orders. The question of what happened to the princes in the Tower is one of the most enduringly fascinating mysteries of English royal history.

THE PRINCES DISAPPEAR

Around the time of Gloucester's coronation as King Richard III on 6 July 1483, Edward and Richard were moved within the Tower of London complex from the royal apartments to the Garden Tower. They were seen playing with bows and arrows in the constable's garden close by. They were then moved again, to the White Tower, where many prison cells were situated. After this, they simply disappeared.

In the 16th century, Richard III was generally assumed to have been behind the princes' disappearance. Within weeks of their disappearance, the Venetian ambassador wrote home to say that the princes had been murdered on Richard's orders. It is certain that Richard had plenty to gain from their deaths. When he claimed the throne he justified it by declaring that the young King Edward V and his brother were illegitimate, since their father Edward IV's marriage to Queen Elizabeth Woodville had been invalid. He knew that if Edward lived

Below: Many romantic visions of the brothers were painted in the 19th century, including this one by Paul Delaroche.

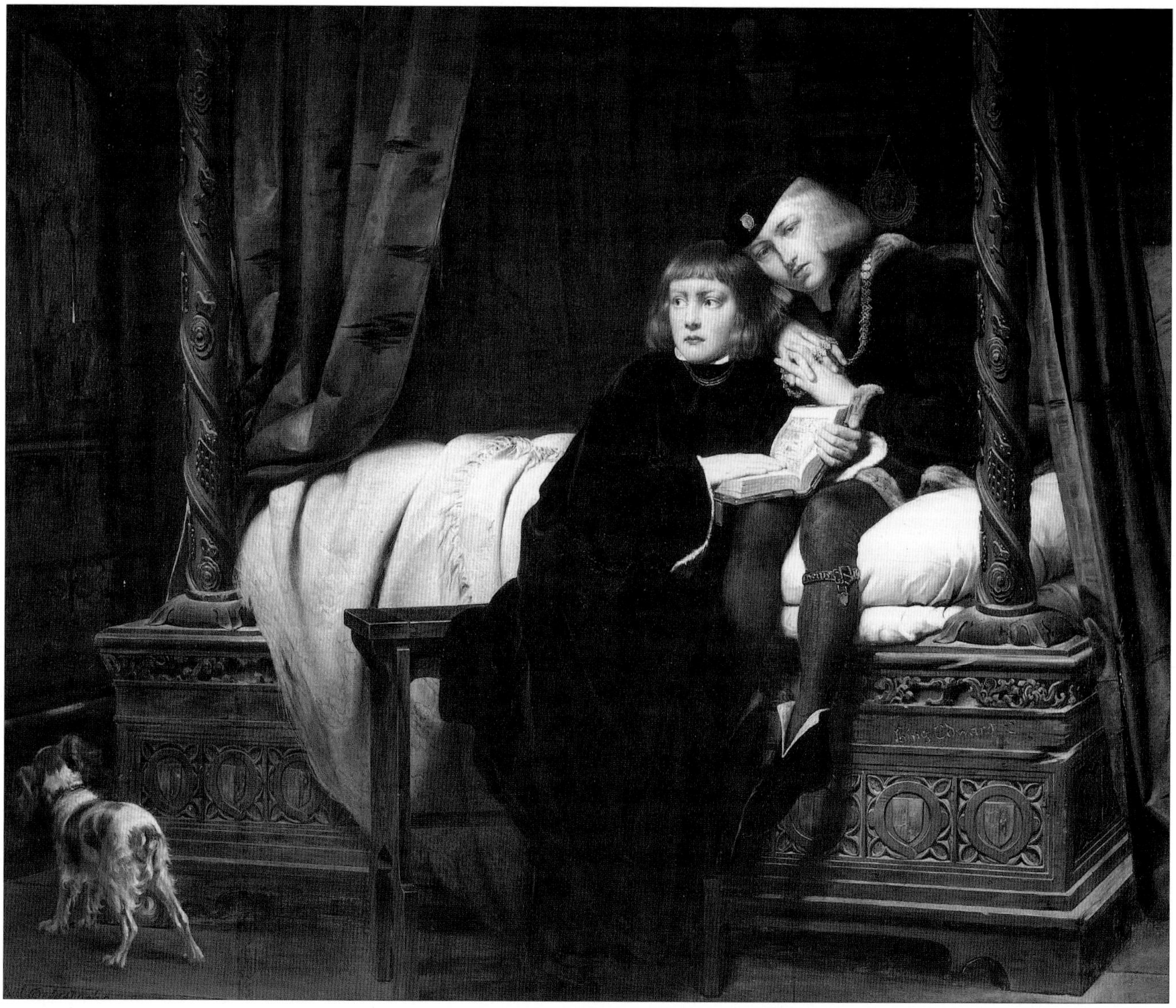

Above: In 1878, Sir John Everett Millais pictured the princes caught like innocent animals with nowhere to run.

he would be a figurehead for rebellions. It was a common occurrence in the political-dynastic manoeuvrings of 14th- and 15th-century royal history for a deposed monarch to die, usually in captivity and in mysterious circumstances, shortly after losing power. This fate had befallen Edward II, and the case of Henry VI would have cautioned Richard against allowing the princes to live. Henry had remained a figurehead for rebel discontent long after his deposition by Edward IV in 1461 and was even released from imprisonment to reoccupy the throne briefly in 1470. After that event, Henry VI himself met a mysterious death in May 1471, according to some reports at the hand of the future Richard III, at the time the brother of the ruling king, Edward IV.

THE BONES OF THE PRINCES?

In 1674, in the reign of King Charles II, two skeletons were discovered buried at the Tower of London. Judged to be the bones of the young princes, they were reinterred at Westminster Abbey. In 1993, scientists examined the bones and determined that they were the remains of males who had died in boyhood, consistent with the possibility that the skeletons were those of the young princes. However, the scientists were unable to find definitive proof that the skeletons were those of the ousted King Edward V and his brother.

CHARACTER ASSASSINATION?

Traditionally, Richard III has been seen as a cruel, treacherous and ruthlessly ambitious man, easily capable of dark deeds such as the murder of the boys, his life blighted by the success of his brother Edward IV and his own hunchbacked physique. However, this popular conception of the king's build and character derives from propaganda issued by the Tudors after Henry Tudor had taken Richard's crown at Bosworth in August 1485. Historians know, for example, that the idea of Richard being a hunchback – so familiar from Shakespeare's play *King Richard III* – was entirely an invention, and that he was broad-shouldered and 5 ft 8in (1.72m) in height, taller than most of his contemporaries.

Henry Tudor had as much, if not more, to gain from the death of young Edward V, for his own claim to the throne did not stand if Edward lived. It was squarely in his interests for the boys to disappear and for the blame to be cast on their uncle Richard. Henry was able to rally support for his attack on Richard by casting him as a scheming usurper, a murderer of the rightful king, young Edward.

THEORIES ASSESSED

According to one theory, the princes were still alive when Richard was defeated by Henry Tudor at Bosworth Field and lived on in captivity for around two years into the reign of Henry VII. At that time Henry decided they were a threat to his own position, and they were murdered. Another theory is that Henry, Duke of Buckingham was responsible for the deed. Buckingham, a former ally of Richard III, himself had a viable claim to the throne as a descendant of King Edward III; he was also a supporter of the cause of Henry Tudor. In killing the boys he could have been seeking to open the way to the throne either for himself or for Tudor.

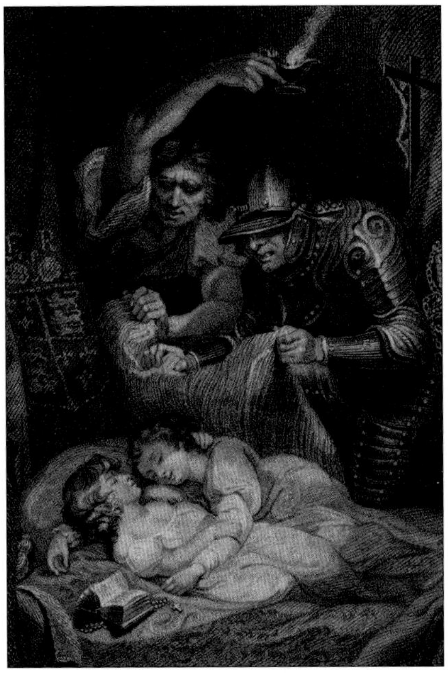

Above: Innocence betrayed. Another 19th-century view imagines the dark hour of the boys' murder by Richard III's henchmen.

On balance, however, it seems most likely that King Richard was responsible for the boys' deaths. Few people would claim that he killed them with his own hands. Sixteenth-century accounts indicated that Sir James Tyrell, carrying out the king's orders, hired two of the boys' keepers, Miles Forest and John Dighton, as assassins. They smothered the princes as they slept in their beds and afterwards buried their lifeless bodies in the grounds of the Tower.

According to the doctor who attended the boys in the Tower before their disappearance, Edward was living in fear that he might die at any time. The doctor relates that the doomed boy declared poignantly, 'I would my uncle would let me have my life though I lose my kingdom'.

EDWARD V AND RICHARD III

1483–1485

Edward V's reign is the shortest in English history. Coming to the throne aged 12, he was king for a mere two months and 17 days, from the death of his father Edward IV, on 9 April 1483, to the fateful day of 25 June, on which the boy-king's uncle Richard Duke of Gloucester accepted Parliament's request that he accede to the throne himself as King Richard III.

EDWARD V, KING OF ENGLAND, 1483

Birth: 2 Nov 1470, the Sanctuary, Westminster Abbey
Father: Edward IV
Mother: Elizabeth Woodville
Accession: 9 April 1483
Deposed: 25 June 1483
Succeeded by: His uncle Richard III
Death: 3 Sept 1483. Probably murdered with his brother Richard, Duke of York, in the Tower

A ROYAL COUP

Gloucester engineered a coup. On his deathbed, Edward IV named Gloucester Protector of the Kingdom and guardian of young Prince Edward. The late king's widow, Queen Elizabeth Woodville, had other plans, however. She was determined to exclude Gloucester from power, to have her son crowned without delay and to surround him with members of the Woodville family, who were highly unpopular at court. She asked young Edward's guardian, Anthony Woodville, Earl Rivers, to escort the prince from Ludlow Castle in Shropshire, where they were staying, to London for a coronation ceremony planned for 4 May. Gloucester, who was in Yorkshire at the time of Edward IV's death, travelled south to intervene.

Near Northampton on 30 April, Gloucester and his close ally Henry, Duke of Buckingham, arrested Rivers and the escort and took Prince Edward into their own care. Hearing the news, Queen Elizabeth took sanctuary in Westminster Abbey with her younger son, Richard, Duke of York.

In London, Gloucester became Protector on 6 May and rescheduled Edward's coronation for 22 June. He put Edward in the Tower of London. On 13 June he accused his former ally Lord Hastings of plotting against him and had him executed. Then he took the nine-year-old Duke of York from sanctuary in the Abbey and put him with his brother in the Tower. On 22 June he declared that the late king's secret marriage to Elizabeth Woodville was not valid and that the heir to the throne and his brother were illegitimate. On these grounds he declared himself the rightful inheritor of the crown. On 25 June Parliament backed Gloucester's claims and asked him to be king. He was crowned Richard III on 6 July.

Below: The general image of King Richard is that of an ogre tormented by his sins, as presented in Shakespeare's Richard III.

Above: Edward V seemed destined for greatness on the throne. He was known for his charm, intelligence and good looks.

POLITICAL FALLOUT

The young princes officially remained in the Tower, but they were not seen after Richard III's coronation day. People were increasingly convinced the princes were dead, probably murdered. When Richard's former ally Henry Stafford, Duke of Buckingham, rose in revolt in October, he assumed the boys were dead and proposed that Richard be replaced on the throne by Henry Tudor, a descendant

THE SAINTED MEMORY OF HENRY VI

In August 1484 King Richard III had the body of his predecessor Henry VI moved from Chertsey Abbey, where it was buried in 1471 after his unexplained death in the Tower of London, to a tomb in the choir of St George's Chapel, Windsor. There it lies, directly opposite the tomb of Richard's brother King Edward IV, who was Henry's rival in life. Henry VI was increasingly revered as a saintly figure, capable of working miracles for his supporters.

Above: This 16th-century portrait follows chronicle accounts, which represent Richard III as thin-lipped, haggard and nervous.

RICHARD III, KING OF ENGLAND, 1483–1485
Birth: 2 Oct 1452, Fotheringhay Castle, Northamptonshire
Father: Richard Plantagenet, Duke of York
Mother: Cecily Neville
Accession: 26 June 1483
Coronation: 6 July 1483
Queen: Anne Neville (m. 12 July 1472; d. 16 March 1485)
Succeeded by: Henry VII
Death: 22 Aug 1485 at the Battle of Bosworth Field, Lincs

of Henry V's queen, Catherine of Valois and also a representative of the Lancastrian claim to the throne as the son of Margaret Beaufort, granddaughter of John of Gaunt. Henry prepared to invade England from exile in Brittany, but Buckingham was captured and executed on 2 November, and Henry retreated.

PERSONAL COSTS

The following year King Richard's 11-year-old son and only child, Edward, Prince of Wales, died. Richard and his queen, Anne, were maddened with grief. The prospect of a Yorkist inheritance, so dear to Richard's heart, began to look extremely vulnerable and when, in March 1485, Queen Anne died after a prolonged illness, rumours circulated that Richard had had her killed so that he could bolster his position by marrying his niece, Elizabeth of York.

In the event, Yorkist rule only lasted a further five months. Henry Tudor won the backing of Charles VIII of France as well as of Queen Elizabeth and the Woodville camp for his claim to the throne.

BOSWORTH FIELD

Henry encountered Richard's army at Market Bosworth on 22 August. The battle was decided by the king's desperate attempt to try and bring the fighting to a quick conclusion, a manoeuvre that threw away a position of strength. As Richard watched the vanguard of his army take on the vanguard of Henry's, he had plenty of strength in reserve. However, in the distance he saw Henry Tudor's standard defended by only a few score troops and decided to attack, in the hope of bringing the clash to an early end by killing Henry.

At first the onslaught was successful and Richard killed several of Henry's bodyguards. When his horse was slain, he fought on, on foot. At this point Sir William Stanley threw his men into an attack on the king. Richard was killed, his body stripped and slung naked across a horse. Henry Tudor left Bosworth Field wearing the crown he had won.

Richard III's body was lost for more than five centuries, but in 2012 an archaeological excavation on the site of the church of Greyfriars, Leicester, unearthed a male skeleton affected by scoliosis. In February 2013, the University of Leicester confirmed that beyond reasonable doubt this was the skeleton of Richard III.

Below: In August 1485, the succession was decided at Bosworth. Richard III fought bravely, if recklessly, in his final battle.

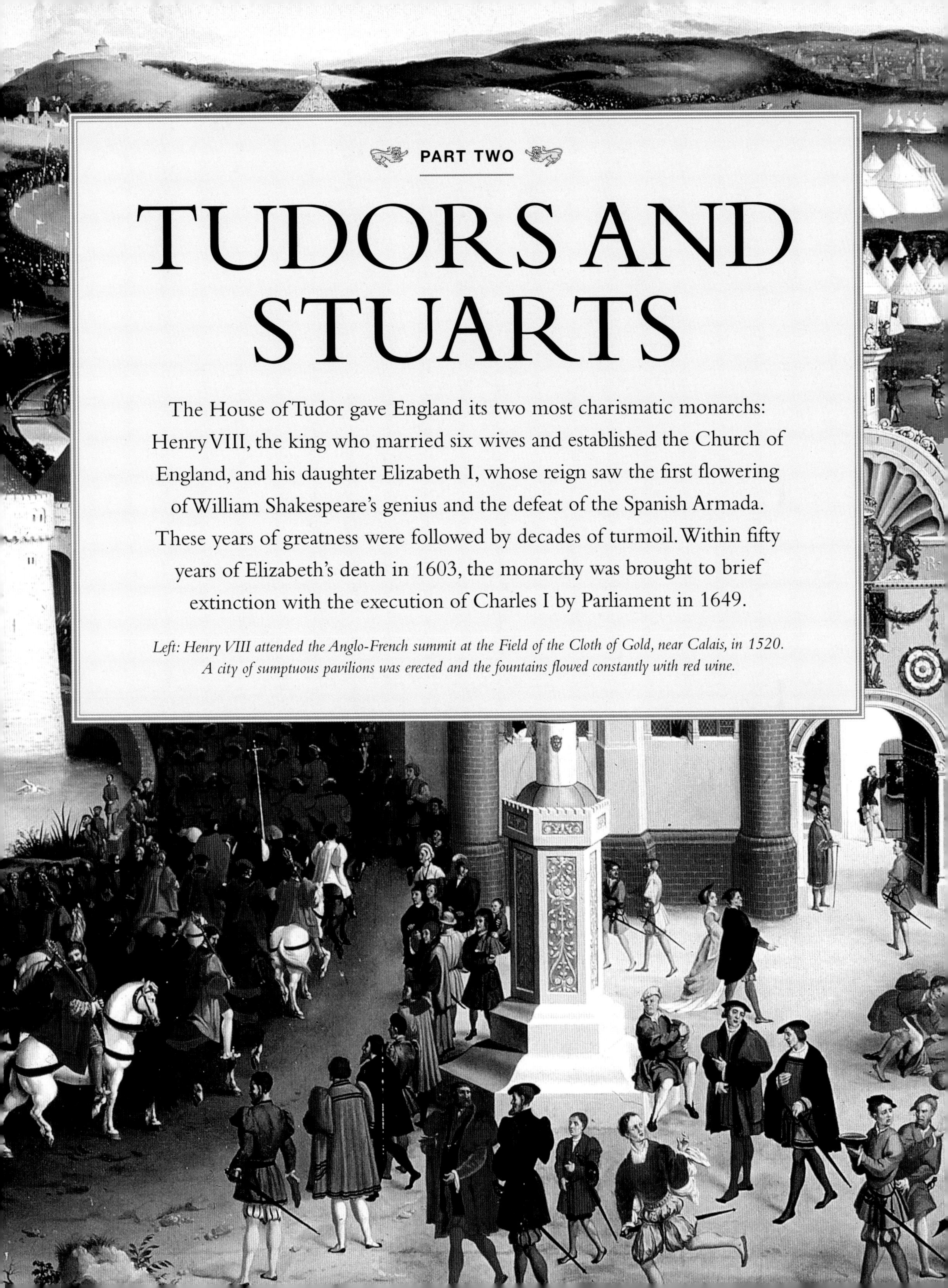

PART TWO

TUDORS AND STUARTS

The House of Tudor gave England its two most charismatic monarchs: Henry VIII, the king who married six wives and established the Church of England, and his daughter Elizabeth I, whose reign saw the first flowering of William Shakespeare's genius and the defeat of the Spanish Armada. These years of greatness were followed by decades of turmoil. Within fifty years of Elizabeth's death in 1603, the monarchy was brought to brief extinction with the execution of Charles I by Parliament in 1649.

Left: Henry VIII attended the Anglo-French summit at the Field of the Cloth of Gold, near Calais, in 1520. A city of sumptuous pavilions was erected and the fountains flowed constantly with red wine.

CHAPTER FIVE

THE HOUSE OF TUDOR

1485–1558

In defeating Richard III and claiming the crown at Bosworth Field, Henry VII not only founded the Tudor dynasty but also won final victory for the Lancastrians in their decades-long struggle against the House of York for the English crown.

The House of Tudor encompassed the reigns of five monarchs – Henry VII, Henry VIII, Edward VI, Mary I and Elizabeth I – across 118 years, 1485–1603. The Tudors reigned during a time of religious turmoil, when the European Reformation created the new cultural and intellectual force of Protestantism. In England, Catholics and Protestants struggled for control of the country's future and hundreds of men and women were executed for holding true to new or traditional religious beliefs. These were years, too, of magnificent cultural achievement and enduring fame: when Christopher Marlowe and William Shakespeare were at work and England was beginning to look abroad to the 'New World' of North America.

In these years, the monarchy exercised a more concentrated, centralized authority than ever before, and came to be far less dependent on the support of leading nobles. Arising from the ashes of the Wars of the Roses, the Tudors claimed to give the country a secure and lasting foundation for prosperity: providing an heir and a stable succession became a Tudor obsession. Ultimately, however, the House of Tudor was undone by the lack of an heir. The crown passed out of the Tudor line on the death of Queen Elizabeth, to the first Stuart monarch: King James VI of Scots and I of England.

Left: The Tudor Succession. Henry VIII seated, with Edward VI kneeling on his left, Mary I (left, with her husband, Philip of Spain) and (right) his daughter, Elizabeth I.

HENRY VII

1485–1509

Henry Tudor's defeat of Richard III at Bosworth Field was decisive. The battle ushered in the new Tudor dynasty and brought to an end 30 years of dynastic feuding in the Wars of the Roses. Over the ensuing 12 months, Henry proved himself an astute and resourceful king in consolidating a somewhat tenuous grip on the crown. For although he had invaded Richard III's kingdom as representative of the Lancastrian cause, his claim to the throne was relatively weak (he was descended through the female line from Edward III's fourth son John of Gaunt, first Duke of Lancaster).

CONSOLIDATING POWER

The new king's position had been strengthened by the death of the principal Yorkist figureheads, the 'princes in the Tower' Edward V and Richard, Duke of York. To be on the safe side, however, the day after Bosworth, Henry seized and imprisoned in the Tower the next in the Yorkist line to the throne, Edward, Earl of Warwick, 15-year-old son of Edward IV's brother George, Duke of Clarence. It was also an advantage that many of Richard III's most important supporters had been killed with him at Bosworth Field.

Henry now determined to bolster his position by attempting to bring an end to Yorkist and Lancastrian rivalries, initially through marriage. During his exile in Brittany, he had pledged to marry Elizabeth, daughter of Edward IV and heiress of the Yorkist cause. Following his coronation as Henry VII in October 1485, he married Elizabeth in Westminster Abbey in January 1486. In March, Henry received papal dispensation for the match, which was against strict church law because the couple were distant cousins. The document sent by Pope Innocent stated further that any who rebelled against Henry and his heirs would be excommunicated. As a symbol of the newfound spirit of reconciliation, Henry's personal device, the Tudor Rose, combined the white rose of York and the red rose of Lancaster.

Above: A watchful eye. Philosopher Sir Francis Bacon wrote of Henry, 'He was a prince sad, serious and full of thoughts.'

YORKIST PRETENDERS

Henry still faced two Yorkist challenges in the first decade of his reign. The first arose in 1487, when an Oxford joiner's son named Lambert Simnel was promoted by Yorkists as Edward, Earl of Warwick, despite the fact that the real Earl of Warwick was in the Tower of London. Simnel was crowned Edward VI in Dublin, in May 1487, then landed with a Yorkist army in Lancashire on 4 June. Henry and his army marched to

Below: The imposter Perkin Warbeck who was adopted by Henry VII's Yorkist foes. He was coached in aristocratic manners by Margaret, sister of Edward IV.

HENRY VII, KING OF ENGLAND, 1485–1509

Birth: 28 Jan 1457, Pembroke Castle
Father: Edmund Tudor, 1st earl of Richmond
Mother: Margaret Beaufort
Accession: 22 Aug 1485
Coronation: 30 Oct 1485, Westminster Abbey
Queen: Elizabeth of York (m. 18 Jan 1486; d. 1503)
Succeeded by: His son Henry VIII
Greatest achievement: Establishing the House of Tudor
16 June 1487: Defeats and captures Pretender Lambert Simnel
Oct 1497: Captures Pretender Perkin Warbeck
1497: Cornishmen revolt over taxes and march on London
14 Nov 1501: Prince Arthur marries Catherine of Aragon
8 Aug 1503: King James IV of Scots weds Henry's daughter Margaret Tudor
Death: 21 April 1509, Richmond Palace, Surrey

QUEST FOR A 'NEW WORLD'

In 1492, Genoese adventurer Christopher Colombus made landfall in the 'New World' of the Caribbean islands with the backing of King Ferdinand of Aragon and Queen Isabella of Castile. Just a few years later, in 1497, another Italian sailor, John Cabot, captained an English voyage of exploration backed by King Henry VII. Cabot, known as Giovanni Caboto in his native land, sailed from Bristol in the *Matthew* in May 1497, made landfall on 24 June on the far side of the Atlantic Ocean and returned to Bristol on 6 August. The place where Cabot landed has never been definitively identified. Possible sites are Cape Breton Island, Newfoundland and southern Labrador. Cabot himself thought it was the north-east of Asia, which he claimed for England. Cabot reported to King Henry, who was delighted and made him a gift of £10. The explorer embarked on a second voyage, with five ships, in 1498. The fleet was lost at sea, though it is not known whether this was before or after he reached north America.

Below: Global view. Henry stands with Venetian sailor John Cabot, in a portrait from the Doge's Palace, Venice.

Above: White rose entwined with red when Elizabeth of York married the Lancastrian Henry Tudor (Henry VII) in 1486.

meet them, and at Stoke on 16 June the royalists defeated the rebel force and captured Simnel. Rebel leader John de la Pole, Earl of Lincoln, was killed. Backing for this uprising was never wholehearted among Yorkists. When Lincoln tried to raise support in Yorkshire he met with little success, and the gates of York were shut against him. King Henry felt that he could afford to be magnanimous and, rather than have Simnel executed, he gave him a job in the palace kitchens.

A second Pretender to the throne made more of an impact and proved a greater threat. Arriving in Ireland in 1491, an elegant and well-built young man from Flanders named Perkin Warbeck claimed to be Richard, Duke of York, the younger of the two princes in the Tower.

He won the support of various European rulers, including Charles VIII of France, Holy Roman Emperor Maximilian I and James IV, King of Scots, who awarded Warbeck a £1200 annual allowance and the hand of James's cousin, Lady Catherine Gordon. In 1497, Warbeck led an invasion of England, landing in Cornwall with a small force and proclaiming himself King Richard IV. Marching inland, he did manage to gather some support but the revolt melted away in the face of an approaching royal army. Warbeck was captured and confessed himself to be an imposter. Henry cast him in the Tower alongside Edward, Earl of Warwick, but in 1499 had both men executed for plotting against the king.

Below: In Westminster Abbey a bronze tomb of 1518 by Italian Pietro Torrigiano commemorates Henry and Elizabeth.

THE TUDOR SUCCESSION

THE NEW DYNASTY, 1485–1509

QUEEN ELIZABETH'S CHILDREN

Queen Elizabeth gave birth to seven (or perhaps eight) children, but four died an untimely death, as did the queen herself. She died giving birth to her fourth daughter Katherine, on 2 Feb 1503. Her children were:

Arthur: Born 19 Sept 1486, died 2 April 1502
Margaret: Born 28 Nov 1489, died 18 Oct 1541
Henry: (the future King Henry VIII) Born 28 June 1491, died 28 Jan 1547
Elizabeth: Born 2 July 1492, died 14 Sept 1495
Mary: Born 18 March 1496, died 25 June 1533
Edmund: Born 21 Feb 1499, died 19 June 1500
Katherine: Born and died 2 Feb 1503

In some accounts another son named Edward was born, but most historians believe this name to be a mistaken form of Edmund.

Below: Three siblings. Arthur, Prince of Wales, with Prince Henry and Princess Margaret, aged 10, 5 and 7 in 1496.

The future for the Tudor dynasty began to look brighter when, after nine months of marriage to King Henry, Elizabeth of York gave birth to a son at Winchester on 19 September 1486. Henry was keen to stress his Welsh-British rather than French-Plantagenet roots and named the boy Arthur after the legendary British king of the 5th century AD. At the age of three, Arthur was created Prince of Wales at Ludlow Castle on 29 November 1489. In the ceremony his father was praised as a restorer of Welsh pride, a King of all the Britons capable of bringing order after years of chaos.

A LOST PRINCE

Arthur was raised for kingship. He had the best education in literature and philosophy under the guidance of poet and chronicler Bernard André. At the age of 15 in 1501 he took control in his capacity as Prince of Wales of the council governing Wales. He made a significant diplomatic marriage to Princess Catherine, the daughter of King Ferdinand of Aragon, on 14 November 1501, but the following year, on 2 April 1502, the prince died of consumption, leaving Catherine a widow at the age of 18 and leaving his brother Henry, Duke of York, heir to the throne.

Below: The great Dutch New Testament scholar Erasmus, a friend of Thomas More, was a visitor at the court of Henry VII.

DIPLOMATIC MARRIAGES

Henry VII had used the promise of Arthur's hand in marriage as a bargaining tool in diplomatic talks. Arthur and Catherine of Aragon had been promised to one another as early as 1488, when Arthur was 18 months old and Catherine was three. The plans for the wedding had then been reconfirmed in the Treaty of Medina del Campo, signed on 27 March 1489.

The importance of the Spanish alliance was reconfirmed when, just over a year after Arthur's death, it was agreed that Prince Henry, now aged 12, would marry Catherine of Aragon. In the event the wedding was postponed when part of Catherine's agreed dowry was late to arrive. Prince Henry did not marry Catherine until after the death of his father Henry VII had made him King Henry VIII.

A second major diplomatic marriage was arranged with Scotland in a treaty of perpetual peace signed by English and Scottish diplomats in London, in 1502. At Holyrood House palace, Edinburgh, on 8 August 1503, King James IV of Scots married Henry VII's daughter Margaret Tudor. Scots poet William Dunbar produced a poem, 'The Thistle and the Rose', to celebrate the rapprochement between the ruling houses of Scotland and England.

A PALACE IN RICHMOND

The royal palace at Sheen in Surrey was Henry VII's favourite residence, and princes Arthur and Henry were raised there. At Christmas in 1497, however, Sheen Palace burned to the ground after a conflagration began in the king's quarters. Henry ordered the construction of a magnificent new dwelling and renamed the site Richmond after his family's earldom in Yorkshire.

Completed in 1501, Henry called the new palace, 'this earthly paradise of our realm of England'. It had four towers and a great timber-roofed hall 100ft (70m) in length.

Henry's court was a place of great culture, where leading names of European learning such as the humanists Polydore Vergil and Desiderius Erasmus were welcomed. Vergil arrived in England in 1502 and served as Archdeacon of Wells; his *Anglicae Historiae Libri XXVI* (1534–55) is a valued resource for historians studying Henry VII's reign. Erasmus was a friend and frequent guest of Thomas More – a great name of Henry VIII's reign – who was already active at court in Henry VII's time, serving as a royal envoy to Flanders. Henry rewarded acclaimed Scots poet William Dunbar for his poem in praise of London in 1501. He also began work on a magnificent new chapel at Westminster Abbey, which he hoped to dedicate to Henry VI.

Above: Richmond Palace, built by Henry VII to replace Sheen, burnt down in 1497.

A REIGN OF MANY ADVANCES

Henry died at Richmond, aged 52, after a reign of 23 years. His reign must be judged a significant success. He created stability after decades of civil dissension, thereby establishing the Tudor dynasty while, through astute diplomacy, he boosted England's standing in Europe and stabilized the country's finances.

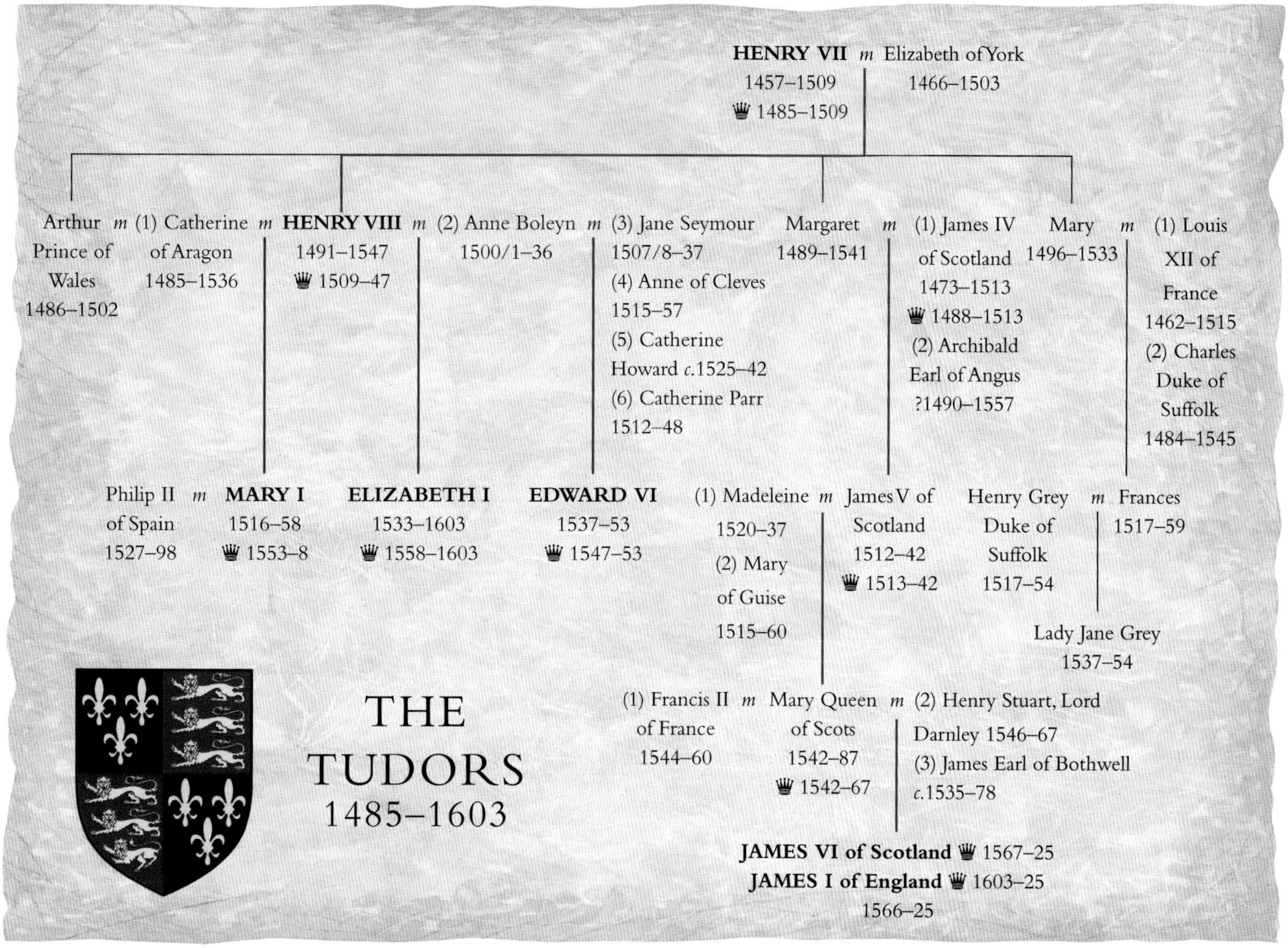

HENRY VIII
1509–1547

Henry VIII acceded to the throne aged 17, a young man of imposing build and looks, 6ft 3in (1.9m) tall, with red hair and a florid complexion, full of youthful exuberance and with a love of display and extravagant pleasures. In character and appearance, the new king presented a marked contrast to his cautious and sober-faced father, who in the last years of his reign had been stricken with tuberculosis.

HONOURING THE FATHER

In the first month of his reign, Henry honoured the memory of Henry VII, presiding over a long and splendid funeral procession and memorial service as the late king's body was carried to Westminster from Richmond, where he had died, and interred in the Abbey. Henry VII was buried there on 11 May 1509. The magnificent chapel that the late king had begun in 1503 and hoped to dedicate to Henry VI became his own final resting place and a monument to the glories of the Tudor dynasty. A magnificent marble and gilt bronze tomb effigy of Henry VII and his beloved queen, Elizabeth, by the Florentine sculptor Pietro Torrigiano, was completed in 1518.

Within two months of his accession, Henry married his brother Arthur's widow, Catherine of Aragon, in accordance with a diplomatic agreement of 1503 and, so the young king said, in honour of his father's dying wish. The marriage in the Church of the Franciscans, at Greenwich on 11 June, was followed by a joint coronation in Westminster Abbey on 24 June. A huge

Above: Cardinal Wolsey dominated Henry VIII's government, 1515–29. He had great self-belief and enormous reserves of energy.

HENRY VIII, KING OF ENGLAND, 1509–1547

Birth: 28 June 1491, Greenwich Palace
Father: Henry VII
Mother: Elizabeth of York
Accession: 21 April 1509
Coronation: 24 June 1509, Westminster Abbey
Queens: Catherine of Aragon (m. 11 June 1509; d. 1536); Anne Boleyn (m. 24 Jan 1533; executed 19 May 1536); Jane Seymour (m. 30 May 1536; d. 24 Oct 1537); Anne of Cleves (m. 6 Jan 1540; d. 17 July 1557); Catherine Howard (m. 28 July 1540; executed 13 Feb 1542); Catherine Parr (m. 12 Jul 1543; d. 7 Sept 1548).
Succeeded by: His son, Edward VI, aged 9
Greatest achievement: Introducing the Protestant Reformation to England
16 Aug 1513: Defeats French at the Battle of the Spurs
20 Feb 1516: Birth of the future Queen Mary I

Above: With a small mouth and wide face, Henry resembled Edward IV.

1518: Treaty of London: mutual defence pact between England, Spain, France and the Holy Roman Empire
7–24 June 1520: Summit with Francis I of France at 'Field of the Cloth of Gold'
23 May 1533: Marriage to Catherine of Aragon annulled
1 June 1533: Anne Boleyn crowned Queen
7 Sept 1533: Birth of the future Queen Elizabeth I
30 Apr 1534: Act of Succession declares Princess Mary illegitimate and make Princess Elizabeth heir to throne
28 Nov 1534: Act of Supremacy makes Henry 'Supreme Head' of the Church of England
19 May 1536: Anne Boleyn executed
12 Oct 1537: Queen Jane Seymour gives birth to future Edward VI
1539: Publication of the 'Great Bible' in English
1541: Henry declares himself 'King of Ireland'
13 Feb 1542: Catherine Howard executed
Death: 28 Jan 1547, Whitehall Palace

banquet in Westminster Hall was capped by a week of ceremonial jousting to mark the occasion.

'GREAT HARRY'

At more than 1000 tons in weight, with five masts and five tiers of guns, the *Henri Grace à Dieu* – or 'Great Harry', as she was more popularly known – was the world's largest battleship when she was launched at Erith on 13 June 1514. Henry was a great believer in the need for English sea power to protect merchant vessels and back up land armies in European conflicts. Unfortunately, the 'Great Harry' only just survived its namesake: six years after Henry VIII's death in 1547, the warship was accidentally destroyed in a fire in 1553.

Above: 'Great Harry' *was among the first ships to carry guns fired through side-ports.*

INTERNATIONAL DIPLOMACY

Henry VII had won England a significant place in Europe through marriage and diplomatic alliance and, in the first years of his reign, King Henry VIII determined to cement this international standing. His marriage to his brother's widow, Catherine, in 1509 cemented the alliance with the Spanish kingdom of Aragon against France. In 1511 the Holy Roman Emperor, Maximilian, made Henry a gift of a suit of the best armour in Europe, from Germany, in honour of the young king's prowess in jousting at tournaments.

In 1512 Henry set out to emulate his great predecessor Henry V by reconquering France. He won the support of Pope Julius II and, after forming an alliance with his father-in-law Ferdinand of Aragon and the Holy Roman Emperor Maximilian, declared war in April 1512 and sent an English army to Gascony. This expedition ended in mutiny and failure. The next year led to a more successful invasion of France from Calais. On 16 August 1513 Henry won the Battle of the Spurs, so called because the French fled without joining battle and suffered the indignity of the capture of several standards and important prisoners. The allied army also captured the towns of Thérouanne and Tournai. At home, meanwhile, an attempted invasion by King James IV of Scots met with disaster. His army was annihilated by an English force under the 70-year-old Earl of Surrey at Flodden, Northumberland, and James IV himself was killed.

Below: Cardinal Wolsey began the building of Hampton Court Palace in 1515. Henry took it over when Wolsey fell from favour.

Henry's chief adviser Thomas Wolsey pressed for peace with France, for the war there was achieving little but costing a great deal. A treaty was agreed on 6 August 1514 under which Henry VIII's 17-year-old sister, Mary Tudor, married France's 52-year-old king, Louis XII. This was the first marriage between French and English royals since Henry V's match with Catharine of Valois a century earlier. An unexpected alliance with France was complemented by the four-way Treaty of London of 1518 under which Spain, France, England and the Holy Roman Empire agreed a mutual defence pact.

Such was Henry's European standing that in 1519, with papal encouragement, he even manoeuvred to try to win election as Holy Roman Emperor following Maximilian's death. However, the electors in Frankfurt preferred the claim of King Charles of Spain.

The most extraordinary statement of England's new international standing in the early 16th century was the sumptuous three-week summit with France held near Calais in June 1520. Stage-managed by Thomas Wolsey and known as the 'Field of the Cloth of Gold', the event comprised a series of meetings between Henry and King Francis I of France accompanied by banquets, jousting, hunting and courtly entertainments.

THE SIX WIVES OF HENRY VIII

ROYAL MARRIAGES, 1509–1547

Within two months of his accession to the throne, Henry married his brother Arthur's widow, Catherine of Aragon. Catherine was certainly a suitable bride for the young prince. Although she had been married to his brother, she was only five years older than the 18-year-old Henry and was widely considered a beauty. She was the daughter of King Ferdinand of Aragon and Queen Isabella of Castile and the aunt of Europe's most powerful royal, Charles, Duke of Burgundy, King of Spain and future Holy Roman Emperor. Catherine was very well educated; she was fluent in Latin, French and her native Spanish, although she found it less easy to speak in English.

Above: Anne Boleyn. Although she failed to provide a male heir, she did give birth to the baby destined for glory as Elizabeth I.

Above: Jane Seymour. She was lady in waiting to both Catherine of Aragon and Anne Boleyn before marrying the king.

DESPERATE FOR AN HEIR

Catherine was, however, unable to provide what Henry, determined to safeguard the Tudor dynasty, was desperate to have: a healthy baby boy as his heir. She gave birth to a stillborn daughter in 1510, then in 1511 to a son, christened Henry, who tragically died aged two months. Another son, born in November 1513, died after only a few hours' life and a third son was stillborn in December 1514. Finally on 18 February 1516 a healthy baby daughter, later christened Mary, was born. The next child, born in November 1518, was a stillborn daughter.

Below: Catherine of Aragon. Highly intelligent, she was an effective regent when Henry fought in France 1512–14.

Henry meanwhile maintained an active sexual life with his mistresses, one of whom, Elizabeth Blount, gave birth to a healthy boy, named Henry Fitzroy, in 1519. This served to convince the king of his reproductive virility and focused his mind on the need for a legitimate male heir. Matters came to a head in 1527 when Henry, infatuated with court beauty Anne Boleyn, declared that his marriage to Catherine of Aragon had never been legitimate since she was his brother Arthur's wife before she became Henry's bride.

'ANNE OF A THOUSAND DAYS'

The daughter of Sir Thomas Boleyn, Anne was dark-haired, with beautiful features, a long graceful neck and lively manners. She was sister of one of Henry's mistresses, Mary, but despite lavish gifts of jewellery from the king, she refused to become his mistress and held out for becoming his queen. At court she was unpopular and gossip suggested she must be a witch to have driven the king to such desperation.

Henry began proceedings to have his marriage to Catherine declared invalid, but Pope Clement VII – who was under pressure from Catherine's nephew, Charles V of Spain – would not grant the annulment. After almost six years, Henry finally had his way when he secretly married Anne Boleyn on 24 January 1533.

On 23 May Thomas Cranmer, the Archbishop of Canterbury, declared the king's first marriage invalid. Anne was crowned queen on 1 June, and the following month Catherine of Aragon, who refused to renounce her own regal title, was placed under house arrest at Buckden, Cambridgeshire. On 7 September 1533, at Greenwich, Anne gave birth to a daughter, the future Queen Elizabeth I.

Above: Anne of Cleves. After accepting an annulment of her marriage to Henry, she lived on for 17 years until 1557.

Anne's elevation was short-lived. She, too, failed to provide a healthy male heir and the king's interest turned to one of Anne's ladies in waiting, Jane Seymour. After Anne had a miscarriage and then gave birth to a stillborn baby boy, Henry accused her – probably falsely – of adultery and on 2 May 1536 cast her into the Tower of London.

Anne was unanimously convicted by a court of peers under her uncle the Duke of Norfolk and beheaded on 19 May 1536. She kept her wits to the last, declaring, 'The king has been good to me. He promoted me from a simple maid to a marchioness. Then he raised me to be a queen. Now he will raise me to be a martyr'.

NO LONGER A LADY-IN-WAITING

The very next day, Henry proposed to Jane Seymour and the couple were married before the month was out, on 30 May in Whitehall Palace.

A modest woman with a child-like face, Jane was well-liked at court and finally delivered what the king and the country longed for: a legitimate male heir. Prince Edward was born on 12 October 1537 at Hampton Court Palace. However, twelve days later Jane died suddenly, perhaps from post-natal fever, causing her royal husband apparently genuine grief.

THE 'FLANDERS MARE'

Henry's fourth wedding was a diplomatic match with Princess Anne of Cleves, sister of William, Duke of Cleves in Germany, made to cement an alliance with Protestant German princes against the Holy Roman Emperor Charles V.

Henry was not pleased when he set eyes on his rather plain-looking bride, and declared to Thomas Cromwell, 'My lord, if it were not to satisfy the world and my realm, I would not do that I must this day for none earthly thing'.

Nevertheless, the wedding went ahead at Greenwich Palace on 6 January 1540. By all accounts Henry's marriage to the woman he called his 'Flanders mare' was never consummated, and Henry was apparently humiliated and angered by his impotence.

In summer 1540 the queen agreed happily to a divorce that freed Henry to marry the woman who had become the object of his latest infatuation, the ill-fated Catherine Howard.

Below: Catherine Parr. Well educated and religious, she wrote A Lamentacion or Complaynt of a Sinner *in 1548.*

Above: Catherine Howard. A cousin of Anne Boleyn, she served as a maid of honour to Anne of Cleves.

A WOMAN OF EXPERIENCE

Beautiful, buxom and with healthy appetites, Catherine was one of ten children of the impoverished Lord Edmund Howard. She married Henry on 28 July 1540, less than three weeks after the king's fourth marriage to Anne of Cleves had been annulled on 9 July. Catherine's downfall came when Henry discovered that she had had premarital affairs and may even had been unfaithful after her marriage to the king. With the backing of a parliamentary bill declaring it treason for an 'unchaste' woman to wed a king, Catherine was beheaded at the Tower of London on 13 February 1542.

A COMPANION IN OLD AGE

Henry wed his sixth wife, Catherine Parr, at Hampton Court on 12 July 1543. She had already been twice married and twice widowed. An intelligent and well-balanced woman, she was a helpful companion for Henry in his last years. She was a good stepmother to the three surviving children of his previous marriages and oversaw their education. She survived the king and took a fourth husband, Lord Thomas Seymour.

HENRY AND THE CHURCH OF ENGLAND

DEFENDER OF THE FAITH, 1529–1547

Henry VIII's momentous religious reforms were driven by self-interest: the king's increasingly desperate desire to rid himself of Catherine of Aragon so that he could wed Anne Boleyn.

Henry instructed Thomas Wolsey, the dominant statesman of the first part of the reign, to use his influence as papal legate to persuade Pope Clement VII to grant an annulment of the marriage. Wolsey failed: a legatine court in London examining the validity of King Henry's case for divorce and presided over by Wolsey and Cardinal Campeggio in May-July 1529 adjourned without reaching a decision, and on 13 July the same year Pope Clement VII ordered that the case must be heard in Rome.

Above: Cranmer, the first Protestant Archbishop of Canterbury, freed Henry to wed Anne Boleyn when he declared the marriage to Catherine of Aragon invalid.

Below: Royal palaces, major towns and the spread of monasteries in the early years of Henry VIII's reign. The Dissolution of the Monasteries began in 1536.

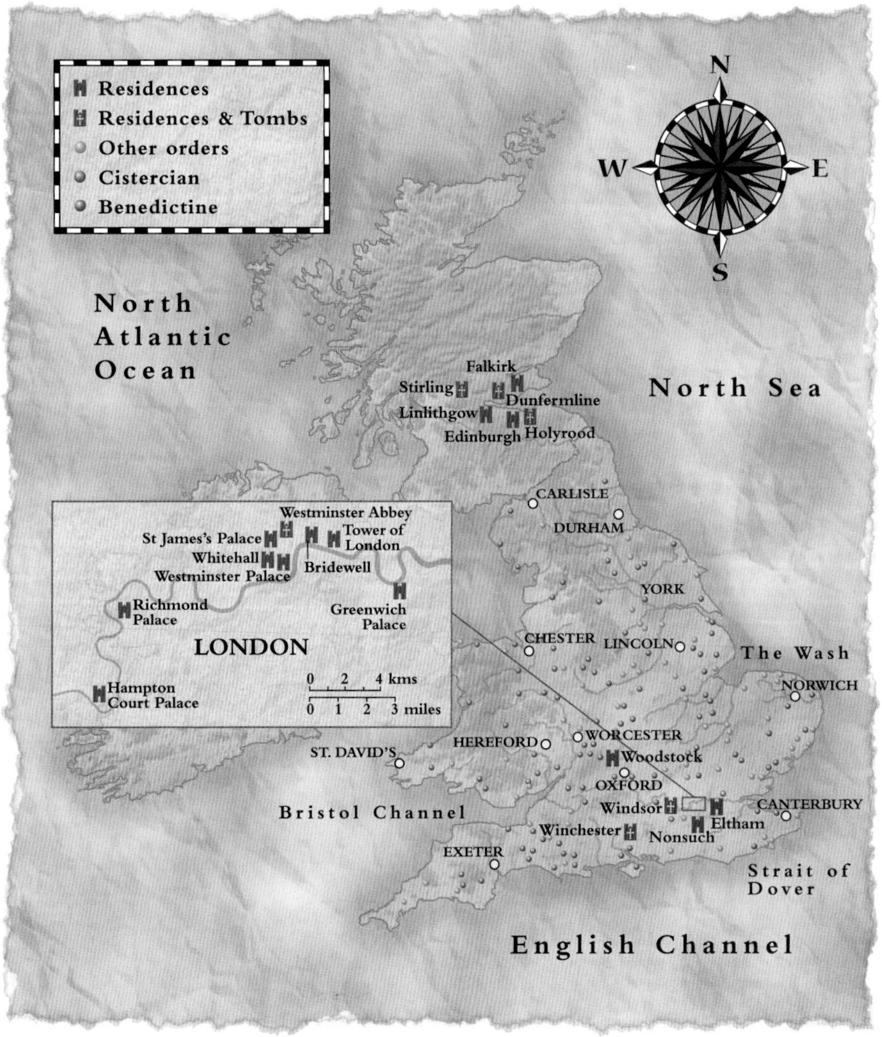

HEAD OF THE CHURCH

Henry turned on Wolsey. A broken man, the king's former adviser died before he could be thrown in the Tower. Henry forced the Convocations of the English clergy at York and Canterbury to submit to him on two issues. In February 1531 they recognized him as 'Supreme Head of the Church of England' and in May 1532 they accepted that all their legislation was subject to royal approval. The king rather than the pope was the final authority on church matters.

Henry, while remaining a Catholic, was convinced of the rightness of his case, so much so that he travelled to a diplomatic summit with the King of France in October–November 1532 with Anne Boleyn as his consort.

Thomas Cranmer, appointed Archbishop of Canterbury on 30 March 1533, won the backing of the Convocation of English clergy to the twin propositions that, first, the Bible outlawed a man's marriage to his brother's widow and, second, that the pope had no authority to allow such a union. Archbishop Cranmer declared the marriage to Catherine invalid on 23 May 1533 and Henry had Anne Boleyn crowned as Queen on 1 June. By this time Anne was already six months pregnant.

TIDE OF CHANGE

Both Cranmer and Henry's Chancellor, Thomas Cromwell, were sympathetic to what contemporaries called the 'new learning' of the Reformed (Protestant) Church, and they were happy to engineer Henry's extinction of papal authority in England.

The Act of Succession, passed by Parliament on 30 April 1534, provided legal backing to Cranmer's May 1533 declaration. Under the Act, the marriage to Catherine of Aragon was annulled, making Catherine's daughter, Mary, illegitimate, while every adult male was required to take a succession oath of allegiance to Queen Anne that recognized her daughter Elizabeth and any other possible children of the marriage as heirs to the throne.

A DEBATE FOR SCHOLARS

The debate over whether King Henry had Biblical justification for divorcing Queen Catherine exercised scholars across Europe for a decade.

The two key Biblical texts were Leviticus Chapter 20 Verse 21: 'If a man shall take his brother's wife, it is an impurity; he hath uncovered his brother's nakedness; they shall be childless' and Deuteronomy Chapter 25 Verse 5: 'When brethren dwell together and one of them dieth without children, the wife of the deceased shall not marry to another: but his brother shall take her, and raise up seed for his brother'.

While Henry could claim, citing Leviticus, that his marriage was accursed under Biblical law and that this was the reason for the trouble Catherine had had in bearing a healthy son, Catherine's defenders could argue, with the backing of Deuteronomy, that it had been Henry's duty to marry her. Moreover, Catherine argued that her marriage to Arthur had never been consummated and so the issue did not even arise.

Above: The medieval Glastonbury Abbey was one of those broken up in the Dissolution of the Monasteries.

Above: The frontispiece to the 1539 Great Bible *in English shows Henry giving the 'Word of God' to Cranmer and Cromwell.*

Under the Act of Supremacy, passed by Parliament on 28 November 1534, Henry VIII was declared, 'The only supreme head in earth of the Church of England'. Further legislation made it treasonable to deny his supremacy. Under this law the former Chancellor Thomas More and Bishop John Fisher of Rochester were executed in 1535.

SQUANDERED WEALTH

As the head of the Church in England, Henry now had access to its vast landholdings. The Dissolution of the Monasteries, which was implemented by Cromwell in 1536–40, brought immense wealth to the crown, most of which Henry squandered. The last monastery to be dissolved was Waltham Abbey in March 1540.

Throughout the years to 1540, Cromwell and Cranmer moved on the religious revolution in England – with a 1538 campaign in which the country's major shrines were closed down, and injunctions in 1536 and 1538 making use of the English-language Bible compulsory in all English parishes.

Below: Victim of the Reformation. This dramatic vision of Thomas More's fall is by French artist Antoine Caron (1521–99).

THE LAST YEARS OF HENRY VIII

DEATH OF A MONARCH, 1536–1547

The religious changes of the mid-1530s was to provoke the worst rebellion faced by any Tudor ruler and the most serious civil unrest since the Peasants' Revolt of 1381. A major Catholic uprising across the north of England in 1536 called on the king to make peace with the pope, to reopen the monasteries that had been closed, to restore Princess Mary as heir to the throne and to exclude low-born councillors from his inner circle; a reference to the widely unpopular Thomas Cromwell, Thomas Cranmer and Hugh Latimer. The rebels, who gathered under the badge of the 'Five Wounds of Christ' and who called themselves the 'Pilgrimage of Grace for the Commonweal', even reopened some of the monasteries that had been closed. Their leader was a Yorkshire lawyer named Robert Aske.

The crisis was averted. Henry's representative, Thomas Howard, the Duke of Norfolk, managed to disperse the uprising by promising a general amnesty and a Parliament in York within twelve months. That might have been that, but in January 1537, Yorkshire landowner Sir Francis Bigod tried to start a separate and entirely different revolt. The leaders of the Pilgrimage of Grace, including Aske, were arrested, given an arbitrary trial and executed in a brutal show of royal authority in June 1537.

Above: Unique glory. Henry VIII's Nonsuch Palace in Surrey was so called because there was 'none such' (none like it). He died before the palace was complete.

Left: Thomas Cromwell. He died in great agony on Tower Hill on 28 July 1540 because the executioner's axe was blunt.

AN ENGLISH 'EMPIRE'

The year 1536 saw the first of two major Acts of Parliament under which Wales became part of the kingdom of England and Wales. The 1536 Act stated, 'Wales is and ever has been incorporated, annexed, united and subject to and under the imperial Crown of the Realm as a member of the same'. In this and a second Act of 1543, Wales was organized into 13 counties, each represented by MPs at the Westminster Parliament, and the Welsh language was banned for official use. Those who spoke only Welsh were barred from public office.

In 1541 the Irish Parliament accepted Henry as King of Ireland and Head of the Irish Church. Under the Crown of Ireland Act, the king of England became automatically the king of Ireland. Henry was the first to hold this title; previous Irish rulers had been 'high kings' or 'Lord of Ireland', a title which was bestowed on Henry II by the pope. Henry VIII had no desire to rule Ireland by right of a title granted by the papacy before the Reformation.

Henry's attempt to bring Scotland into the English kingdom met with less success. The Treaty of Greenwich, in 1543, proposed a dynastic alliance in which Henry's seven-year-old heir, Prince Edward, would marry Mary, Queen of Scots, then less than one year old. However, a change of heart by Scots governor the Earl of Arran provoked Henry to unleash a military raid commanded by Edward Seymour, Earl of Hertford in 1544.

The Earl of Hertford captured Leith and Edinburgh, where he started fires that reportedly burned for four days, in a campaign dubbed 'rough wooing' because of the earlier marriage negotiations. However, the invasion had no lasting impact. In February the following year the English force was defeated by Scottish troops at the battle of Ancrum Moor.

The latter years of the reign saw England at war with Scotland, France and Ireland, These were ruinously expensive campaigns and in order to pay for them Henry was forced to sell on into private ownership the greater part of the lands he had seized from the Church in the Dissolution of the Monasteries.

Above: His Majesty. The words, associated with the Roman emperor, were first used of the king in 1534 as he sought to establish his authority to challenge the pope.

THE FALL OF CROMWELL

Henry's chief minister Thomas Cromwell fell abruptly from power in the summer of 1540, when his opponents at court, notably Thomas Howard, third Duke of Norfolk and Bishop Stephen Gardiner, persuaded the king that Cromwell was guilty of heresy and of plotting treason.

Historians generally agree that Cromwell's fall from the king's grace was mainly due to the disaster of Henry's marriage to Anne of Cleves, which Cromwell had negotiated as a diplomatic match in the autumn of 1539. The wedding took place in January 1540, but the match was apparently never consummated and, although Cromwell was elevated to the earldom of Essex as late as April 1540, he never recovered the king's favour. As a result of Norfolk's machinations, Cromwell was arrested in the king's council chamber on 10 June 1540, convicted without trial and beheaded.

CORRUPTION OF THE BODY

In the mid-1540s Henry became grossly corpulent and prematurely aged. Unable to exercise after a sporting injury to his leg, he continued to indulge his vast appetite and his waistline grew to 66in (1.68m). He could no longer walk, but had to be carried by four courtiers; he began to lose his hair and was feared at court for the ease with which he lost his temper. But his sixth wife, Catherine Parr, was attentive to his needs and brought him some peace.

Nevertheless the king fell into a long illness and the end of his reign was obviously drawing near. The Conservative-Catholic faction led by the Duke of Norfolk manoeuvred against supporters of the reformed religion for influence over the country's future direction. The matter was decided by the downfall of the Duke of Norfolk's family. Norfolk's son Henry Howard, Earl of Surrey, bragged of his family's Plantagenet ancestry – as descendants of Edward III – and added the royal arms to his heraldic device. Surrey was found guilty of treason and beheaded on 19 January 1547. His father was condemned without trial as a traitor and was scheduled to be executed on the very day that the king happened to die.

Henry's reign – which had seen such momentous changes in State and Church – ended early in the morning of 28 January 1547. Despite six marriages and all the desperate manoeuvring to ensure a succession, the king was survived by only three legitimate children, including his sole male heir, the nine-year-old Prince Edward.

EDWARD VI

1547–1553

Edward was a small, pale, precocious boy aged nine when he acceded to the throne previously occupied by his giant of a father. The boy-king was already highly educated, having learned Latin and Greek from the age of five, and well versed in Protestant ideas after studying northern Europe's religious 'reformation'. He was serious and rather withdrawn, for he had little experience of family life until the kindness of Queen Catherine Parr brought Henry's three children together after 1544. His pastimes were solitary: viewing the night sky and playing the lute.

THE LORD PROTECTOR

On 18 February, King Edward processed from the Tower of London to Westminster Abbey. He wore a magnificent outfit of cloth of silver and white velvet and rode beneath a crimson canopy on a white charger. Much to his delight, street entertainments were laid on along the route, including a high-wire act at St Paul's, an 'angel' at Cheapside, a children's choir at Cornhill and a 'giant' at London Bridge. The following day he was crowned in the Abbey, amid solemn ceremonial.

His country was in the hands of his uncle Edward Seymour, Earl of Hertford. King Henry had stipulated in

Above: Prince precocious. Edward was known throughout Europe for his learning and intelligence, and also for his saintly piety.

his will the creation of a ruling regency council. However, Seymour had been able to delay public announcement of King Henry's death for three days until 31 January, while he manoeuvred behind the scenes to have himself declared Lord Protector. Subsequently he broke up the council of regents and assumed sole power. On 16 February he was named Duke of Somerset.

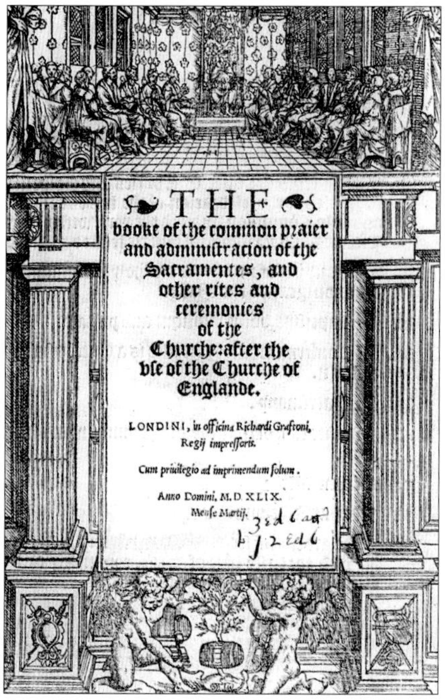

THE booke of the common praier and administracion of the Sacramentes, and other rites and ceremonies of the Churche: after the vse of the Churche of Englande.

LONDINI, in officina Richardi Graftoni, Regij impressoris.

Cum privilegio ad imprimendum solum.

Anno Domini, M.D.XLIX. Mense Martij.

Above: The frontispiece of the 1549 Book of Common Prayer *shows the young King Edward (top) sitting in council.*

The Protector maintained Henry's wars against France and Scotland. After initial difficulties he won a significant victory at the Battle of Pinkie near Musselburgh, Scotland, on 10 September 1547 but was unable to build on it. The Scots aligned themselves with the French, who besieged Boulogne, which England had taken under a 1546 treaty.

Somerset was committed to the Protestant cause and under his Protectorate strict religious reforms were put in place. The 1549 Act of Uniformity outlawed the traditional Catholic Mass and made the use of the *Book of Common Prayer* compulsory.

ROYAL LOVE TRIANGLE

Early in 1549 one of the king's uncles, Lord Thomas Seymour, was executed after an extraordinary royal love scandal. Seymour, brother of Henry VIII's favourite wife, Jane Seymour, secretly

EDWARD VI, KING OF ENGLAND, 1547–1553

Birth: 12 Oct 1537, Hampton Court
Father: Henry VIII
Mother: Jane Seymour
Accession: 28 Jan 1547
Coronation: 20 Feb 1547, Westminster Abbey
Succeeded by: His cousin Lady Jane Grey, for nine days; afterwards by his sister, Mary I
Greatest achievement: Foundation of grammar schools in several towns
10 Sept 1547: Battle of Pinkie
1549: First *Book of Common Prayer.* Popular protests against the new prayer book and land enclosures
Oct 1549: John Dudley, Earl of Warwick, replaces Edward Seymour, Duke of Somerset, as Lord Protector
1552: Second *Book of Common Prayer*
Death: 6 July 1553, London

married Henry's widow Catherine Parr in the very year of the king's death. Then reports circulated that he had been caught trying to seduce Henry's daughter, the red-haired Princess Elizabeth. Some versions indicated that a love triangle had developed involving Catherine, Thomas and Elizabeth and that he had even fathered a child with Elizabeth. Lord Thomas was charged with high treason and the fact that his brother, Edward, was Lord Protector did not save him. He was executed on 20 March 1549.

By the summer of 1549 the Duke of Somerset's hold on power was looking insecure. Catholics in the West Country rose up against the imposition of the Book of Common Prayer, while peasants in Norfolk, the Midlands and Yorkshire protested against land enclosures by local gentry. John Dudley, Earl of Warwick, led troops against the rebels at Dussindale in Norfolk on 26 August, and in the ensuing massacre at least 3,500 people were killed.

Among aristocrats at court and in London, Somerset came under concerted attack for his stated sympathy with the peasant opponents of land enclosure. Warwick saw his chance to seize power and in October had Somerset arrested and thrown in the Tower of London, while he himself was declared Lord Protector in his place.

THE KING'S SICKNESS

Warwick, created the Earl of Northumberland in 1551, oversaw the imposition of a stricter form of Protestant worship in 1552 with a second *Book of Common Prayer* and a new measure outlawing Catholic dress and forms of worship, including priestly vestments and prayers for the dead.

By the autumn and winter of that year it was clear that the young king was sickening unto death and the most pressing matter for Protestants such as Northumberland became finding a way of preventing a Catholic succession to the throne.

King Edward had fallen ill in summer 1552 and was diagnosed with smallpox and measles, but he did not recover and apparently developed pulmonary tuberculosis in the very cold winter that followed. He was also losing

Above: Sir Edward Seymour, Duke of Somerset and Lord Protector, was also a great military commander, victor both at Pinkie (1544) and Boulogne (1545).

his hair and, according to some accounts had inherited congenital syphilis from his father. Henry VIII's will stated that if Edward died childless, the throne would pass to Edward's sisters, first Mary then Elizabeth. Mary, next in line, was a Catholic and would not only undo hard-won Protestant reforms but also move against Northumberland himself.

As Edward VI neared death, he and Northumberland drew up a 'device' – a kind of will – that shut Mary and Elizabeth out from the succession, and named Lady Jane Grey as his heir.

Lady Jane, the 16-year-old daughter of the Duke of Suffolk, was Henry VIII's great-niece, for her mother Frances was the daughter of Henry VIII's sister Mary. Most importantly for those planning her succession, she was a devout Protestant.

The king's council and Parliament accepted the device. Edward VI died in London on 6 July 1553 and four days later Lady Jane Grey was declared Queen by the King's Council.

Left: The English painting An Allegory of the Reformation *(c. 1570) shows the pope and his cronies undone by Edward.*

MARY I
1553–1558

The Earl of Northumberland's attempt to engineer the succession in favour of his niece, Lady Jane Grey, was nothing more than a total failure. Henry VIII's eldest daughter and his rightful heir, Mary Tudor, proclaimed herself queen on 19 July 1553 and was welcomed to the capital by cheering crowds on 3 August.

RETURN TO CATHOLICISM

Mary was an intelligent and independent-minded woman with a fierce devotion to the Roman Catholic faith, which her father Henry VIII had sought to undermine. Now, as queen, she set about eradicating Protestantism.

By mid-September she had arrested the most important Protestant clerics, including the Archbishop of Canterbury Thomas Cranmer, principal author of the Books of Common Prayer published in 1549 and 1552 and architect of many of Edward VI's reforms.

Acts of Parliament rapidly repealed the anti-Catholic legislation introduced under Edward. On 16 November, moreover, she declared her intention of marrying the Roman Catholic Prince Philip of Spain, son of Charles V, Holy Roman Emperor and King of Spain. It was increasingly clear that Mary intended to sweep away the Church of England and return her country to full-blown European Catholicism. The proposed marriage, meanwhile, raised the unwelcome possibility that England would become no more than a satellite

Below: The Tudor Princess. This portrait, by 'Master John', shows the future queen as a young woman of 28, in 1544.

MARY I, QUEEN OF ENGLAND, 1553–1558

Birth: 18 Feb 1516, Greenwich Palace
Father: Henry VIII
Mother: Catherine of Aragon
Accession: 19 July 1553
Coronation: 1 Oct 1553, Westminster Abbey
Husband: Philip II of Spain, son of Charles V, King of Spain and Holy Roman Emperor (m. 25 July 1554; d. 1598)
Succeeded by: Her sister Elizabeth I
Greatest achievement: England's first reigning queen
25 Jan 1554: Kentish rebels attack London
30 Nov 1554: Cardinal Reginald Pole absolves England following dispute with papacy
Aug 1555: King Philip abandons Mary and leaves for Netherlands
16 Oct 1555: Bishops Hugh Latimer and Nicholas Ridley martyred
21 March 1556: Archbishop of Canterbury, Thomas Cranmer, martyred
7 Jan 1558: French retake Calais
Death: 17 Nov 1558, London

QUEEN FOR NINE DAYS

The beautiful, learned, sensitive and intelligent 15-year-old Lady Jane Grey is said to have fainted when the idea was first put to her that she should become queen. In the end she reluctantly permitted Edward and her uncle, Northumberland, to elevate her to the English crown. She married Northumberland's son, Lord Guildford Dudley, on 21 May 1553. Northumberland proclaimed her queen on 10 July and urged her to name his son king, but she steadfastly refused. In the event, she ruled for just nine days before she was deposed by the rightful heir, Mary.

Lady Jane and her husband were thrown in the Tower of London in July 1553 and executed on 12 February 1554.

Right: In 1833 Paul Delaroche painted Lady Jane Grey as an innocent victim.

Above: A Protestant cartoon celebrates the martyrdom of Hugh Latimer, Nicholas Ridley and Thomas Cranmer.

territory of Spain. Rebellion erupted: on 25 January, Sir Thomas Wyatt marched to London at the head of a troop of Kentish rebels to protest against the planned Spanish marriage.

As 7,000-odd rebels prepared to attack the City of London, Queen Mary made a passionate appeal to an assembly of Londoners declaring, 'I love you as a mother loves her child'. She won their loyalty and the rebels were crushed.

Wyatt was executed on 11 April and Mary's sister Princess Elizabeth, who was suspected of involvement in the plot, was cast into the Tower of London and only freed after a period of two months' imprisonment.

Opposition to the marriage remained strong, and broadsheets and ballads opposing the match were all the rage in London. The wedding went ahead, however. Mary, 38, married Philip – at 27, eleven years her junior – on 25 July 1554 in Winchester Cathedral. Philip was proclaimed King of England, but only in the role of king-consort. He would not succeed to the throne if the marriage were childless.

BLOODY MARY

On 20 November 1554 papal legate Cardinal Reginald Pole, exiled since 1532 in protest at Henry VIII's religious reforms, returned to England. Ten days later, Pole pronounced absolution marking England's formal peace with the pope. The following year began the execution of Protestants that earned the queen her reputation in English history as 'Bloody Mary'. In all, 287 Protestants were slain at her command.

On 16 October 1555, Bishops Hugh Latimer and Nicholas Ridley were burned at the stake while Thomas Cranmer watched from his prison cell; Latimer sounded a resounding note as he comforted his fellow victim. 'We shall this day light such a candle by God's grace in England as I trust shall never be put out'.

Mary's marriage, meanwhile, proved unhappy. The queen was deeply in love with her husband, but he did not reciprocate her feelings. In 1555 Mary suffered a phantom pregnancy, which raised and then dashed hopes that an heir might be born. The same month she was abandoned by her consort, as Philip left for the Netherlands. He did not return until July 1557, despite much anguished pleading from Mary. Even then, Philip's main motive in returning was to persuade Mary to ally England with Spain in a war against France.

Within a few months he departed once again for the Netherlands. The war with France into which he had drawn her was a disaster, resulting in the loss to French troops of Calais, England's last French possession. This deeply affected Mary, who declared, 'When I have died and am opened up, you will find Calais lying in my heart'.

On 17 November 1558 Mary died at St James's Palace, tortured by the knowledge that she had been unable to produce an heir to guarantee a Catholic succession and that her Protestant sister Elizabeth was to inherit the crown.

Below: 'Bloody Mary'. England's first reigning queen was a woman of strong convictions, iron will and ruthlessness.

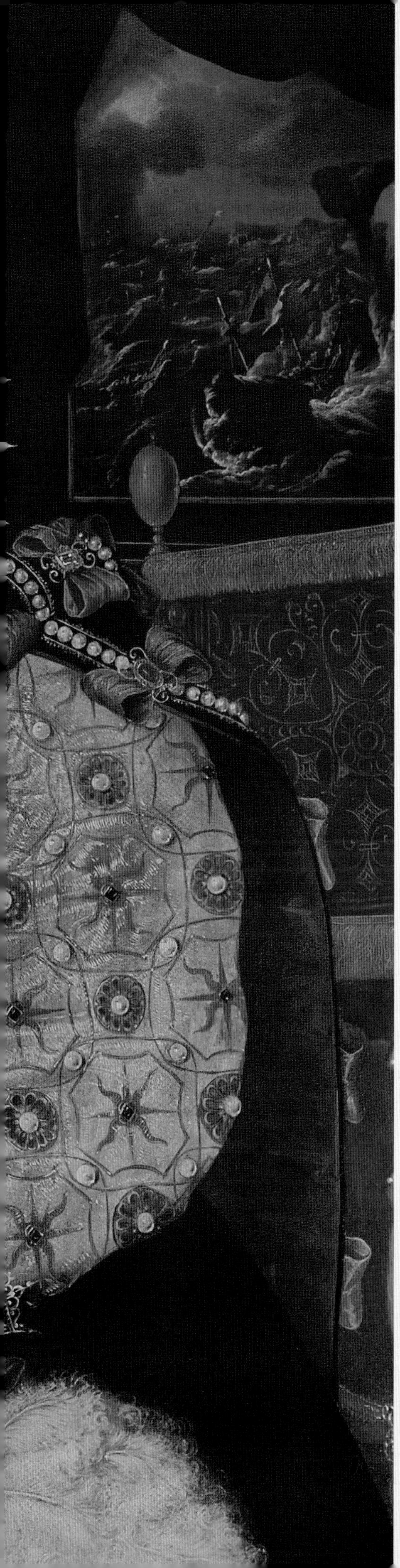

CHAPTER SIX

THE AGE OF ELIZABETH

1558–1603

The 45–year reign of the last of the Tudors, Queen Elizabeth I, was a time of triumphant English achievement. The might of the Spanish Armada was repelled, adventurers such as Sir Walter Raleigh set foot fearlessly in the New World, naval heroes such as Sir Francis Drake proved England's daring and might on the high seas, and such geniuses as dramatist William Shakespeare, artist Nicholas Hilliard and composer William Byrd hit unprecedented artistic heights. In these proud years Elizabeth kept peace at home and established England as a major player on the world stage: her people recovered from the bloody religious conflict of the reigns of King Edward VI and Queen Mary and became confident in their own abilities, her country a vibrant success.

In these years, too, the English people came to love and revere their monarch as never before or, arguably, since – in the state-proclaimed mythology of the 'Virgin Queen', Elizabeth was married not to some foreign prince but to her own realm. In her final speech to Parliament, this great queen declared herself a happy instrument of God in serving and loving her people: 'For myself I was never so much enticed with the glorious name … or royal authority of a Queen as delighted that God hath made me his instrument to maintain his truth and glory and to defend his kingdom ... There will never Queen sit in my seat with more zeal to my country, care to my subjects and that will sooner with willingness venture her life for your good and safety than myself.' And she declared in unforgettable terms: 'Though God has raised me high, yet this I count the glory of my crown, that I have reigned with your loves'.

Left: In the celebrated 'Armada Portrait', Elizabeth remains regally composed while English ships see off the Spanish invasion.

ELIZABETH I

1558–1603

When Elizabeth came to the throne in November 1558 the country was in crisis, virtually bankrupt and recently deprived of its last French possession in Calais. England was demoralized and conquest by a foreign power was all too likely: both France and Spain, whose king had been married to the last Queen Mary, eyed England greedily. As Elizabeth rode into London that autumn she was greeted by cheering crowds. After the bloody turmoil and ultimate failure of Queen Mary's reign, her people wanted and needed success for the flame-haired princess, whose colouring and regal manner may have reminded them comfortingly of her father, Henry VIII.

PRAGMATIC PROTESTANTISM

Religious passions were running high. In the eleven years before Princess Elizabeth's accession, England had been transformed into a militantly Protestant country by her brother Edward VI, then changed back to a staunchly Catholic realm by her sister Mary. In punitive campaigns enforcing first one religious orthodoxy and then another, hundreds of English men and women had gone to their deaths as martyrs. One of Queen Elizabeth's great achievements in the early part of her reign was averting further major religious bloodshed.

Elizabeth herself was a Protestant, although a pragmatic rather than a radical or passionate one. In Mary's reign she had been willing, under pressure, to submit to Catholicism. Once she became queen, she reverted to the Protestantism espoused by her mother Anne Boleyn. At Elizabeth's magnificent coronation in Westminster Abbey on 15 January 1559, she pointedly refused to witness the Catholic ritual of Bishop Oglethorpe elevating the Host (communion bread).

ELIZABETH I, QUEEN OF ENGLAND, 1558–1603

Birth: 7 Sept 1533, Greenwich Palace
Father: Henry VIII
Mother: Anne Boleyn
Accession: 17 Nov 1558
Coronation: 15 Jan 1559, Westminster Abbey
Succeeded by: James VI of Scots, James I of England
Greatest achievement: Defeat of the Spanish Armada, 1588
Feb 1559: House of Commons urges Queen to marry
April 1559: Acts of Supremacy and Uniformity establish Elizabeth as the supreme governor of the Church of England
23 April 1564: William Shakespeare born, Stratford upon Avon
1568: Mary, Queen of Scots imprisoned by Elizabeth
1569: Catholic uprising in northern England
Feb 1570: Elizabeth excommunicated by Pope Pius V
2 June 1572: The Duke of Norfolk executed for plot to depose Elizabeth
26 Sept 1580: Francis Drake completes circumnavigation of world
1584–9: Foundation of England's first overseas colony, 'Virginia'
1585: Sends English army to back Protestant revolts in the Netherlands
8 Feb 1587: Execution of Mary, Queen of Scots
1588: Defeats Spanish Armada
25 Feb 1601: Essex beheaded for treason
Death: 24 March 1603, Richmond Palace, Surrey

Below: Signature of a queen.

A PRINCESS LEARNED AND WITTY

As a child, Elizabeth was unusually serious, with the gravity of 40 when she was only six, according to one sycophantic account. She received an excellent education that made her fluent in Greek, Latin, French and Italian and instructed her in history, Protestant theology, moral philosophy and rhetoric. She had a shrewd mind – later, as queen, she would write her own speeches – and a capacity to inspire devotion.

In the 1550s, her Greek and Latin tutor, Roger Ascham, praised her strength of mind, her perseverance and her memory which, he said, 'Long keeps what it quickly picks up'. He was also captivated by her beautiful handwriting and her musical skills.

Above: Elizabeth's tutor Roger Ascham was a Cambridge fellow and humanist.

Protestantism was officially reintroduced in England under the Acts of Supremacy and Uniformity of April 1559, which recognized the queen as supreme governor of the Church of England and brought Cranmer's 1552 *Book of Common Prayer* back into use.

The religious settlement was not harsh on Catholics. The wording of the Holy Communion sentences did not endorse transubstantiation (the Catholic doctrine that the bread turned into Christ's body), but at least was possibly compatible with the Catholic faith – communicants were encouraged to 'feed on [Christ] in thy heart by faith'. Elizabeth, who declared that she would not open windows into men's souls, was certainly not about to return to the bloody imposition of orthodoxy.

A HUSBAND FOR THE QUEEN

At her accession Elizabeth was aged 25, and the question of when and whom she would marry to provide an heir loomed large. Even as a princess, in her sister Mary's reign, Elizabeth had received many offers – including ones from Duke Emmanuel Philibert of Savoy and Prince Erik of Sweden, which were both declined. She was also the recipient of flirtatious attention from Queen Mary's husband, King Philip of Spain, and after Elizabeth's accession Philip renewed his interest with indecent haste, making a formal offer of marriage on 10 January 1559, less than a month after Mary's burial. Elizabeth declined. The following month the House of Commons issued a 'loyal address' to the young queen, urging her to accept a husband in order to produce an heir to the throne. However, Elizabeth declared that she had no intention of marrying at present and reassured the Commons that if she changed her mind then she would choose a husband who was as committed as she to England's safety.

Left: The Pelican Portrait of Elizabeth I, c.1574, by miniaturist Nicholas Hilliard.

Above: Contemporary accounts suggest that Elizabeth combined her mother's beauty and wit with her father's natural authority.

Meanwhile, court gossips noted that the queen was extremely close to the young and handsome Lord Robert Dudley, later the Earl of Leicester. This was not the first time that Elizabeth had been associated with handsome men at court; she was even reported to have been involved with Lord Thomas Seymour as a teenager.

While Elizabeth was celebrated as 'the Virgin Queen' she remained close to Dudley and later in her reign had similarly intense friendships with elegant noblemen including Sir Christopher Hatton, Robert Devereux, Earl of Essex, and Sir Walter Raleigh.

THE VIRGIN QUEEN
ELIZABETH AND MARRIAGE

On 28 September 1564, in a splendid ceremony at St James's Palace in London, Elizabeth elevated her long-term favourite Robert Dudley to the earldom of Leicester, a position usually reserved for the king or queen's son, which brought many great territories with it. While Elizabeth officially remained the chaste 'Virgin Queen' and was the object of many a marriage proposal from European kings and princes, at court Dudley effectively lived as her consort, with apartments next to the queen in all her main places of residence and acting as her principal host at entertainments.

Above: In 1560 Elizabeth rejected a marriage proposal from Erik of Sweden, acknowledging his 'zeal and love' but adding 'we have never yet conceived a feeling of that... affection towards anyone'.

CULT OF THE VIRGIN QUEEN

Meanwhile, in 1563, after Elizabeth had suffered an attack of smallpox in December 1562, both Houses of Parliament petitioned her to take heed of the potential for a disastrous renewal of dynastic conflicts should she die unexpectedly and without an heir, and the House of Lords urged her to accept a royal husband.

This approach was the second time that the queen had been asked by Parliament to consider the succession, following an earlier 'loyal address' in 1559. In responding the first time, Elizabeth had declared, 'Nothing, no wordly thing under the sun, is so dear to me as the love and goodwill of my subjects', adding, 'in the end this shall be for me sufficient, that a marble stone shall declare that a queen, having reigned such a time, lived and died a virgin'. In her response in 1563, Elizabeth asked for MPs' trust and denied suggestions that she had taken vows of celibacy.

The cult of the Virgin Queen flourished: Elizabeth needed no princely husband, for she was married to her people. The language and behaviour of Arthurian chivalry and courtly love informed life at court, apparently easing the confusion and difficulty caused by the role reversal of a woman lording over the country's most powerful men. The queen could use her 'prerogative' as a mistress to grant and then withdraw favours or defer decisions on difficult matters. The role suited a woman whose characteristic response to challenges was to be defensive and difficult to read.

Historians are divided as to whether Elizabeth's self-proclaimed virginity was a front or was genuine. Some have suggested that the queen was physically incapable of having sexual relations; indeed, this was the report of her private physician, Dr Huick, in the 1560s. Others suggest that the queen would have been highly conscious of the potential political fallout should she become pregnant with an illegitimate child. To counter Dr Huick's evidence,

FAVOURITES OF THE VIRGIN QUEEN

Robert Dudley (1532/3–88) Handsome, ambitious and a long-term intimate of the queen, Robert Dudley was created Earl of Leicester and Baron Denbigh in 1564. Dudley recovered from Elizabeth's displeasure at his secret marriage to Lettice Knollys,the widowed Countess of Essex, to become lieutenant-general of the army raised to counter the feared invasion of 1588.

Sir Christopher Hatton (1540–91) A beautiful dancer and accomplished in the traditions of 'courtly love', Hatton rose from the queen's bodyguard to become privy councillor and later Lord Chancellor 1587–91.

Robert Devereux (1567–1601) Cousin of the queen and her favourite towards the end of the reign, he inherited the earldom of Essex aged nine and was an experienced soldier. He had a fiery relationship with Elizabeth and often went against her wishes, yet retained her favour. However, in 1601 he tried to lead a revolt against her rule that led to his execution for treason.

Left: Sir Christopher Hatton became a royal bodyguard after giving up legal study.

Right: Robert Devereux often provoked the queen, but stayed in favour.

Sir Walter Raleigh (1554?–1618) Writer, soldier and adventurer, he delighted Elizabeth by asking permission to name territory he discovered in the New World after her: it was called 'Virginia' in honour of the Virgin Queen. He was knighted in 1585.

historians cite the reports of two medical committees at different times in the reign that certified Elizabeth to be capable of conceiving and giving birth.

A HATRED OF MARRIAGE

Elizabeth had a very strong dislike of marriage and was enraged when favourites or courtiers were wed. In the summer of 1579, when she found out that her great favourite of the early years, Leicester, had secretly wed Lettice Knollys, Countess of Essex, she claimed she would despatch Leicester to the Tower of London. In 1592 she found out that her later favourite, Sir Walter Raleigh, had not only married but also fathered a son, she went one better and actually jailed Raleigh and his wife Elizabeth. The queen certainly had ample evidence to suggest that marriage was a risky and probably unrewarding enterprise. Her own mother's marriage had been brief and ended with the executioner's sword, and her sister Mary's marriage to Philip of Spain had been a humiliating disaster. Marrying an Englishman would have encouraged factionalism by favouring one noble family above others. By refusing to marry, Elizabeth was able to retain full independence and avoid expectations that a wife – even a queen – should be obedient to her husband.

Right: Robert Dudley, Earl of Leicester. Elizabeth once put down his attempt to insist upon a favour with the words 'I will have here but one mistress and no master'.

As Elizabeth aged, her virginity was presented and understood increasingly as self-sacrifice. Her image shifted from that of the virginal mistress to that of the virginal mother, with connotations of the Virgin Mary. Symbols such as the crescent moon and the pearl – once associated with the Virgin Mary – now became linked to Elizabeth.

Over the years, by staying clear of the international diplomatic unions into which so many of her regal predecessors had been drawn, she maintained the independent standing of her increasingly confident country, sacrificing her dynasty to maintain internal stability.

ELIZABETH AND MARY

COUSINS AND QUEENS

Queen Elizabeth's cousin Mary Stuart posed a potential threat to the English crown from the very start of the reign. Catholics considered the Protestant Elizabeth to be illegitimate, because they did not recognize Henry's divorce of Catherine of Aragon and marriage to Elizabeth's mother, Anne Boleyn, in 1533. The Catholic Mary Stuart – reigning as Mary, Queen of Scots since 1542 – had a viable claim to the English throne as granddaughter of Henry VIII's elder sister Margaret Tudor. Mary's was the second strongest claim after Elizabeth's, and she became a figurehead to Catholics for those wanting a return to the old religion.

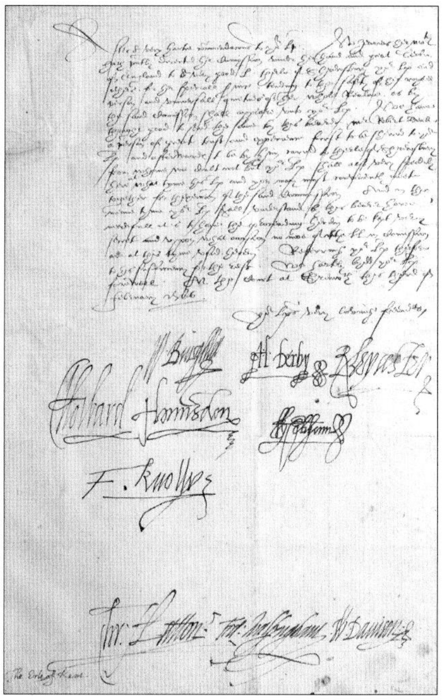

Above: In November 1586, MPs twice asked Elizabeth to order Mary's death. She signed the order on 1 February 1587.

COMPETING QUEENS

In England Elizabeth encountered no opposition to her claim as she was welcomed to London and crowned in Westminster Abbey on 15 January 1559. However, in France, Mary, Queen of Scots and her husband the Dauphin (heir to the French throne) began to quarter the English arms with the French arms in their emblem in a provocative gesture that could only be interpreted as a claim to the English throne either in the present or as Elizabeth's successor. It was a gesture that enraged Elizabeth.

Mary had acceded to the Scottish throne aged just seven days on the death of King James V in 1542, then been exiled to France for her own safety since 1548, early in the reign of Edward

Left: A French portrait of Mary, Queen of Scots. Her execution ended plots to kill Elizabeth and replace her with a Catholic.

VI, while her French mother Mary of Guise (James V's widow) ruled as regent. In July 1559 Mary's husband Francis became King of France on the death of his father King Henry II, but after the former's sudden death aged just 16 in late 1560, negotiations began for Mary's return to claim her throne in Scotland.

The cousins were at loggerheads. Elizabeth initially refused to grant Mary safe passage to England; Mary would not recognize the Treaty of Edinburgh that accepted Elizabeth as Queen of England. Elizabeth would not name Mary as her heir.

Mary arrived in a Scotland that had embraced Protestantism and where government was in the hands of competing groups of fractious nobles. Over the ensuing eight years she tried and failed to win control. In a long and dramatic series of events she married her handsome Tudor cousin Henry Stuart, Earl of Darnley, gave birth to an heir, James, survived Darnley's murder and then unwillingly wed the probable murderer, James Hepburn, 4th Earl of Bothwell. In 1567 she abdicated under threat of death in favour of her one-year-old son, James VI. Then in May 1568, following civil war in Scotland, she fled to England for sanctuary.

LOYALTY TO MARY

Elizabeth refused to see Mary or to provide military or political support, but equally she resisted calls from Parliament and her senior advisors for Mary's execution. She would not consent to do away with Mary, even after a Catholic uprising in late 1569 in northern England. The rebellion was led by the earls of Northumberland and Westmorland in support of a plot to marry Mary to the powerful Duke of Norfolk and depose the queen. A royal army under the Earl of Sussex was victorious and the rebellion melted away, but Elizabeth exacted brutal revenge, ordering the hanging of as many as 900 rebels. She was merciful to Norfolk, who was spared the death penalty, placed in custody and released within six months.

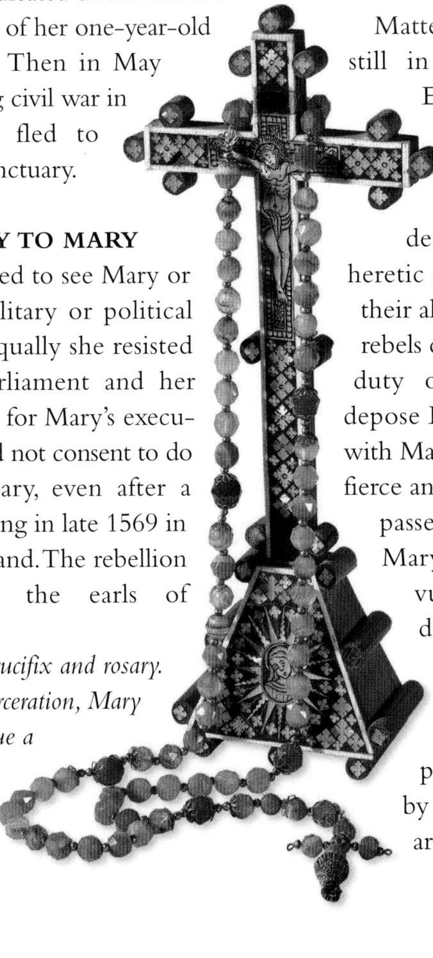

Right: Mary's crucifix and rosary. During her incarceration, Mary had in her retinue a Catholic priest disguised as an almoner.

Matters became more difficult still in February 1570, when Elizabeth was excommunicated by Pope Pius V, whose papal bull *Regnans in Excelsis* denounced the queen as a heretic and freed Catholics from their allegiance to her. After this, rebels could argue that it was the duty of devout Catholics to depose Elizabeth and replace her with Mary. In reponse, increasingly fierce anti-Catholic legislation was passed by Parliament. In 1571 Mary's position became more vulnerable again with the discovery of the 'Ridolfi plot', devised by a Florentine banker named Roberto di Ridolfi. It proposed that a rebellion led by the Duke of Norfolk, arranged to coincide with a Spanish invasion, would depose Elizabeth and crown Mary Queen of England. In the aftermath, Norfolk was found guilty of treason and executed.

Above: Mary pronounced forgiveness on her executioners, declaring sadly 'I hope you will make an end of my troubles'.

AN END TO THE MATTER

Mary remained in captivity for 19 years and on 14 October 1586 she was found guilty of being involved in a plot to assassinate Elizabeth led by Derbyshire nobleman Anthony Babington. Elizabeth prevaricated for as long as she could, hard pressed by her councillors to condemn Mary, but desperate to find a different way of dealing with her cousin. She even tried to arrange Mary's assassination to avoid the need for an execution, but Mary was finally beheaded at Fotheringhay Castle in Northamptonshire on 8 February 1587.

Elizabeth appeared at once to regret what she had done, for she was maddened with grief at the news of the death, claimed she had not meant to send the death warrant and cast Sir William Davison, the secretary of state who supervised the warrant, into the Tower of London.

Mary's death may have caused Elizabeth private grief, but it was met by public rejoicing.

EUROPE IN THE TIME OF ELIZABETH

FRANCE, THE NETHERLANDS AND IRELAND

Elizabeth's foreign policy put defence first. Determined to avoid the large-scale foreign campaigns that devastated royal finances in the reign of Henry VIII, she preferred to use diplomacy and make low-key military interventions in furtherance of Protestant resistance to the might of Catholic France and Spain.

THE CATHOLIC THREAT

At the start of the reign, the main concern of the queen and her advisors was the threat of a Franco-Scottish Catholic alliance. The 16-year-old Mary, Queen of Scots was married to Francis, heir to the French throne; meanwhile, Mary's French mother, Mary of Guise, ruled Scotland as regent. England was officially at peace with France, having signed the treaty of Cateau-Cambrésis in April 1559. In Scotland, Elizabeth provided aid to the Protestant Lords of the Congregation, who deposed Mary of Guise and attempted to drive out the French presence. Under the Treaty of Edinburgh in July 1560, a Protestant Regency Council was established. In France, too, Elizabeth supplied aid to Protestants seeking to undermine a Catholic ruler, and under the 1562 Treaty of Hampton Court she supported the French Huguenots.

Above: The slaughter of Huguenots in the St Bartholomew's Day Massacre of 1572 horrified Protestants across Europe.

Left: Europe in the reign of Elizabeth. The most important military clash was the sea battle of Gravelines against the Armada.

AN ENEMY OF ROME

After Elizabeth's excommunication in 1570 and the discovery of the Ridolfi plot the following year, the queen came under pressure from her Privy Council

Above: Don John, Catholic scourge of the Dutch Protestants, wanted to invade England and marry Mary, Queen of Scots.

not only to execute Mary but also to take a more active role in Continental struggles between Protestants and Catholics. In 1572 the stakes were raised by a series of violent outbursts against French Huguenots (called the 'St Bartholomew's Day Massacre') that resulted in the deaths of approximately 70,000–100,000 Protestants there. Queen Elizabeth quietly sent money and munitions to the Huguenots but publicly remained on friendly terms with the French Catholic regime.

DUTCH COURAGE

Elizabeth also backed Dutch Protestants in their rebellion against Spanish rule. In 1576 when Spain sent Austrian commander Don John to put down the revolt, Elizabeth was offered the sovereignty of the Netherlands if she would provide military force and agree an Anglo-Dutch alliance. She declined, but agreed loans and financial support totalling £120,000 to help the Protestant cause. She entered a formal alliance with the rebels in December 1577 but the following year the rebels were decisively defeated by Don John. In 1585, following the assassination of Dutch leader William of Orange and with war against Spain looming, Elizabeth agreed to send a 7,000-strong army to the Netherlands under the Earl of Leicester and to garrison the ports of Flushing and Brill. Elizabeth's decision to help brought her the title 'Protector of the Netherlands'. In 1589, Elizabeth finally sent English troops into France, to back the claim of the prominent Huguenot, Henry of Navarre, to the French throne.

Above: The Earl of Essex. After failing to impose himself on Irish rebels, Essex was unable to regain the favour of the queen.

ELIZABETH AND IRELAND

Elizabeth's attempt to impose the Protestant religious 'settlement' of 1560 in overwhelmingly Catholic Ireland provoked a series of uprisings. The major disturbances were in the years 1569–73, 1579–83 and 1595–8.

June 1569: Military captain James Fitzmaurice Fitzgerald launches a Catholic revolt by attacking English colonists at Kerrycurihy, County Cork.

1570–2: Sir John Perrot, appointed to the new position of Lord President of Munster, wins the submission of James Fitzmaurice Fitzgerald and stamps out revolt in the province.

1579: Fitzgerald heads a new religious revolt, declaring Elizabeth a heretic, with secret support from both the pope and Philip II of Spain.

1580: English forces defeat the rebels. Lord Grey de Wilton, the queen's newly appointed deputy in Ireland, crushes an Irish garrison at Smerwick, Munster.

Nov 1583: Fitzgerald's cousin, the Earl of Desmond, is captured and killed by English forces under de Wilton.

1594: Hugh O'Neill, Earl of Tyrone, heads a new Catholic revolt, in Ulster.

May 1595: Sir John Norris is despatched to Ireland to put down the revolt, but fails.

14 Aug 1598: Tyrone wins a great victory at Yellow Ford, Ulster, over an English army led by Sir Henry Bagenal. The English commander and 830 English troops die.

April 1599: The Earl of Essex, the newly appointed Lord Lieutenant of Ireland, agrees a truce with Tyrone against Elizabeth's express instructions. However, following accusations that Essex had made a treasonable pact with the Irish earl, he abandons his post and returns to England to explain his conduct to the Queen. He is later arrested, charged with maladministration and finally – on 25 February 1601 – beheaded for treason.

Sept 1601: The continuing Irish revolt is strengthened by the arrival of 3,400 Spanish troops.

24 Dec 1601: Charles Blount, Lord Mountjoy, defeats Irish rebels and their Spanish reinforcements in battle near Kinsale.

March 1603: Tyrone's revolt has not recovered from the 1601 defeat. He submits to Elizabeth and after her death receives a royal pardon from King James I.

THE ARMADA

A FAMOUS VICTORY, 1588

The defeat of the Spanish Armada in 1588 occupies a hallowed place in English history. Elizabeth's navy, commanded by Lord Howard of Effingham, forced the 130-galleon fleet of King Philip II of Spain to abandon plans for an invasion of England and to set sail for home. Around 15,000 Spaniards died in the encounter, compared with English losses of fewer than 100. Lord Howard afterwards declared: 'I do warrant you, all the world never saw such a force as theirs was'.

THE RUN-UP TO INVASION

The Armada invasion came after years of growing tension between England and Spain. King Philip, former husband of Elizabeth's sister Mary and a one-time suitor of Elizabeth herself, was increasingly enraged by Elizabeth's support for Protestant revolt against Spanish rule in the Netherlands and by the activities of English adventurers such as Francis Drake and John Hawkins in harrying Spanish colonial shipping.

AN INVINCIBLE FLEET

The impetus for Philip's military action was Elizabeth's 1585 despatch of an English army to the Netherlands and the 1587 execution of Mary, Queen of Scots. With the death of Mary, Philip saw that he himself could now lay claim to the English crown in the event of the restoration of Catholicism.

Philip had become king of Portugal in 1580 and so had access to the Atlantic port of Lisbon. The Spanish ships –

Above: Elizabeth gave the 'Armada Jewel' to Sir Thomas Heneage, Treasurer of War, to celebrate the triumph of 1588.

THE QUEEN'S SPEECH

In facing the threat of invasion Elizabeth was characteristically fearless, inspirational and defiant. On 9 August, before it was clear at home that the Armada was a spent force, she visited the troops assembled at Tilbury in Essex under the command of the Earl of Leicester. As her army prepared to repel a Spanish force commanded by the Duke of Parma, King Philip's regent in the Netherlands, Elizabeth rode among them, wearing a steel breastplate and seated on a grey gelding, to deliver a stirring speech that lived long in popular memory. Onlooker James Aske likened her to a 'sacred general'.

'My loving people, We have been persuaded by some that are careful of our safety to take heed how we commit ourselves to armed multitudes for fear of treachery, but I assure you I do not desire to live to distrust my faithful and loving people. Let tyrants fear...I have always so behaved myself that, under God, I have placed my chiefest strength and safeguard in the loyal hearts and good will of my subjects, and therefore I am come amongst you as you see at this time, not for my recreation and disport, but being resolved, in the midst and heat of the battle, to live or die amongst you all, to lay down for my God and for my kingdom, and for my people, my honour and my blood, even in the dust. I know I have the body of a weak and feeble woman, but I have the heart and stomach of a king, and of a king of England too, and think it foul scorn that Parma or Spain or any Prince of Europe should dare invade the borders of my realm, to which, rather than any dishonour shall grow by me, I myself will take up arms, I myself will be your general, judge and rewarder of every one of your virtues in the field. I know already for your forwardness you have deserved rewards and crowns; and we do assure you, on the word of a Prince, they shall be duly paid to you....By your valour in the field, we shall shortly have a famous victory over these enemies of my God, of my kingdom and of my people.'

Left: A painted 17th-century panel from St Faith's Church at Gaywood, Norfolk, shows Elizabeth arriving at Tilbury.

Above: Spanish ships flounder in the teeth of a south-west wind. This image of the sea battle off Gravelines is by Nicholas Hilliard.

ironically dubbed *El Armada Invencible* ('The Invincible Fleet') – set sail from there on 30 May 1588 under the command of the Duke of Medina Sidonia.

The plan was to sail to the Netherlands and ferry 16,000 Spanish troops from there to England, where they would support a popular uprising among Catholic sympathizers in the south-west. Philip's ultimate goal was to sweep Elizabeth from the throne and restore freedom of Catholic worship in England. He sent his admiral, the Duke of Medina Sidonia, on what he saw as a sacred mission, with these words ringing in his ears. 'If you fail, you fail; but the cause being the cause of God, you will not fail.'

SPANISH SEA POWER WRECKED

The fleet of some 130 ships had a troubled voyage northwards and was forced by storms into the northern Spanish port of Coruña; it did not reach the Channel for over two months. The English watched and waited and finally sighted the Armada off the Lizard coast of Cornwall on 29 July. As news of the invasion threat was spread across southern England by messengers and hilltop beacons, Francis Drake and Lord Howard put to sea with about 120 ships. They engaged the Spanish fleet three times – off Eddystone, off Portland and near the Isle of Wight – before the Armada anchored out from Calais, the former English possession in France.

Then in a dramatic midnight mission conceived by Lord Howard's vice-admiral, none other than Sir Francis Drake, empty English fireships stocked with wood and explosives were sent in and, helped by strong winds, created a wall of fire among the Spanish ships.

Below: Drake's drum. Over the years since 1588 its ghostly roll has reputedly been heard at times of English deliverance – such as the German navy's surrender in 1918.

The Spanish galleons put to sea in a panic and, in the face of storming south-west winds were unable to regroup before the English ships attacked again off Gravelines. The chief ships of the English fleet, the 20 royal galleons, were faster than the Spanish ships, more manoeuvrable, better armed and bigger.

With his fleet in disarray and having already lost 2,000 men in a week of fighting the superior English fleet, the Duke of Medina Sidonia ordered retreat. The wind forced the Armada to sail not back down the English Channel, but north up the east coast of England and Scotland, hoping to round the Orkneys and the Hebrides and regain the relative safety of the Atlantic Ocean. They were harried by English ships as far as Scottish waters and in the Atlantic were hit by storms. By the time that the fleet arrived back home it had lost at least 63 ships and around half of its 30,000 men.

The defeat was a key event of Elizabeth's reign. As well as safeguarding Elizabeth's religious settlement and preventing a potential bloodbath in England, it boosted the reputation of the English fleet and consolidated the growing self-confidence of the English. The victory also marked a shift in power from Catholic southern Europe to Protestant northern countries.

VOYAGES OF DISCOVERY

GLOBAL EXPLORATION

In the service of the great Queen Elizabeth, English adventurers such as Sir Francis Drake, Sir Martin Frobisher, Sir John Hawkins and Sir Walter Raleigh tamed the high seas as they made voyages of exploration, piracy and colonization around the globe.

Above: This contemporary engraving of the arrival of the English in Virginia was made by Theodore de Bry (1528–98).

LAND OF THE 'VIRGIN QUEEN'

Under Elizabeth, England founded its first short-lived overseas colony, named Virginia in honour of the Virgin Queen, at Roanoke Island, now North Carolina in the years 1584–9. Virginia was established by one of Elizabeth's principal favourites, Sir Walter Raleigh, who in the 1580s was employed at court and in trade in London; he did not visit the New World himself until later years. In 1584, however, he sent two men, Philip Amadas and Arthur Barlowe, to find a site for a colony, and upon their return with promising reports, he despatched 107 settlers under the command of Sir Richard Grenville in 1585. The first group, discouraged by Native American attacks, abandoned the settlement and returned to England, but Raleigh sent a second group of around 150 settlers in 1587. The settlers built houses, but their commander, John White, sailed to England for further supplies and was delayed in returning because of the Spanish Armada's threat. When he did return in 1590 he found the colony had mysteriously vanished – the only clue was the word 'Croatoan' cut in a tree trunk. The attempt to establish the colony was abandoned.

Below: Scourge of Spain. Sir Francis Drake was known as El Draque *('the Dragon') by his Spanish foes.*

Raleigh did later lead a New World voyage: in 1595 he explored what is now Venezuela and sailed the Orinoco river in search of the legendary city of gold, Manoa, which was said to be ruled by a king named 'El Dorado'.

SIR FRANCIS DRAKE

The most celebrated of Elizabeth's roving seafarers, Francis Drake, first made his name and fortune in a voyage to South America and Panama in 1572–3. He set sail from Plymouth on 24 May 1572, with a privateering commission from the queen; essentially the permission to plunder Spanish territories and riches. A militant Protestant, he saw it not only as profitable but as a religious duty to plunder Catholic Spain. In Panama he attacked the Spanish settlement of Nombre de Dios and left with great riches before exploring the Isthmus of Panama on foot and, from a tree on high ground, becoming the first Englishman to see the Pacific Ocean. He captured a Spanish caravan and took large amounts of silver to add to his plunder from attacking Spanish shipping on the high seas and returned to England with the most astonishing haul of New World riches yet seen.

Drake next departed in 1577 on a voyage to explore South America and the South Pacific, where a vast hidden continent was rumoured to exist. Before his departure he had an audience with Queen Elizabeth, who told him she hoped he could win some measure of revenge for various slights against her by

Above: England's first slave trader and a cousin of Sir Francis Drake, Sir John Hawkins explored Guinea and the Spanish West Indies.

the king of Spain. He set sail in the *Golden Hind* in December 1577. Reaching South America, he sailed through the Strait of Magellan and entered the Pacific, then sailed up the western coast of the continent, winning rich pickings from Spanish ships and colonial settlements, before trying and failing to find the Northwest Passage. Anchoring off the area of modern San Francisco, he claimed the land for Queen Elizabeth and dubbed it 'New Albion'. From there he sailed westwards across the Pacific, then home across the Indian Ocean and around the Cape of Good Hope to the Atlantic.

Drake landed at Plymouth on 26 September 1580 to complete his circumnavigation of the world; the first by an Englishman and only the second ever, following that by Portuguese captain Ferdinand Magellan. The *Golden Hind* was weighed down with glittering treasures and exotic spices. On 4 April 1581, Queen Elizabeth – secretly delighted at the damage Drake had done to Spanish interests – came aboard the *Golden Hind* on the Thames at Deptford and knighted Sir Francis. The Spanish ambassador was outraged.

Sir Francis Drake was now a trusted royal servant. In 1587 Elizabeth sent him to attack Spain's empire: on this voyage he plundered Spanish settlements in the Cape Verde Islands, Colombia, Florida and Hispaniola (the Dominican Republic and Haiti).

FROBISHER AND HAWKINS

Another of Queen Elizabeth's free-ranging 'privateers' was Martin Frobisher, who led three voyages to Baffin Island and Labrador in search of gold mines in 1576–8, the second two with the queen's financial investment. He left his name in Frobisher Bay (south-eastern Baffin Island), but failed to find any gold. Like Raleigh, Frobisher also attempted to establish a New World colony, but failed. Subsequently, he sailed with Drake to the West Indies in 1585 and was knighted for his services to the queen in defeating the Armada.

Sir John Hawkins was England's first slave trader. After making a great fortune in a pioneering 1562–3 voyage financed by London merchants in which he sold Africans captured in Guinea as slaves in

Above: Sir Walter Raleigh was a natural philosopher as well as an adventurer. He was fascinated by potential uses of mathematics as a navigational aid.

the Spanish West Indies, he won the queen's backing for a second successful trip in 1564–65. A third trip with his relative, Francis Drake, nearly ended in disaster, however.

Later Hawkins was responsible for supervising the construction of the swift, well-armed ships that outgunned the galleons of the Spanish navy in 1588. He was knighted for his part in England's great victory.

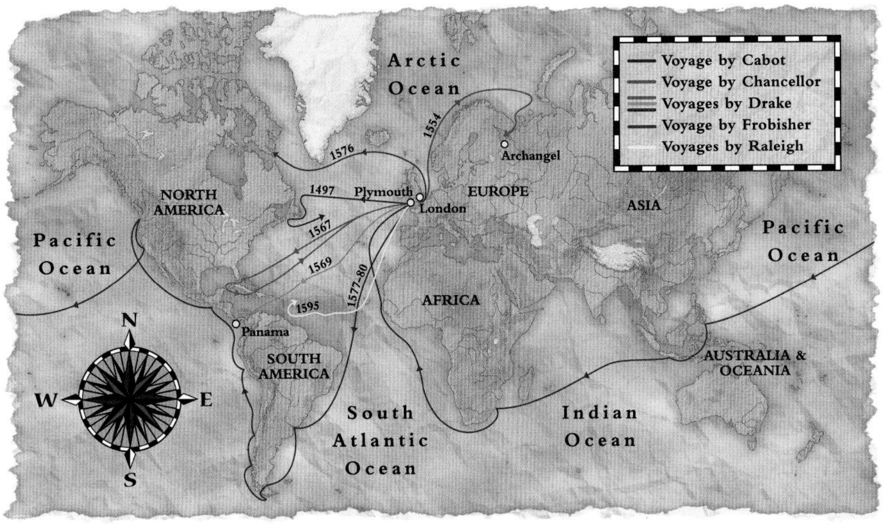

Right: Map of exploration routes to the Americas and the Far East followed by some of Elizabeth's fearless naval pioneers.

ELIZABETH'S COURT

A GLITTERING PRESENCE

In July 1575 the Earl of Leicester laid on lavish celebrations for Elizabeth and her travelling court at Kenilworth Castle, in Warwickshire, which had been a gift from the queen ten years earlier.

Above: The queen's glory. Admirers crowd close as Elizabeth, a shimmering white vision in a sedan chair, is carried past.

AN ARCADIAN FANTASY

At enormous expense, the castle and grounds were transformed into a chivalric and arcadian fantasy. Leicester gave over to Elizabeth an entire, extravagantly decorated wing of the building and flooded a field in front of the castle to make an artificial lake. As she arrived, Elizabeth was greeted by a boy dressed as a nymph on an island in the lake. He declaimed the words, 'The Lake, the Lodge, the Lord are yours for to command.' At the castle gates a scholar disguised as Hercules hailed the queen in blank verse. As she entered, the clocks were stopped – time would stand still while the queen was in residence.

The queen stayed at Kenilworth for 18 days of hunting, dancing, feasting and elaborate pageants. On one evening, a banquet of 300 dishes was provided, on another Elizabeth greatly enjoyed a play, *The Slaughter of the Danes at Hock Tide*, put on by the Men of Coventry.

At every turn, Leicester had laid on surprises and entertainments. When the queen complained that she could not view the castle gardens from the window of her bedchamber, Leicester secretly had a garden laid out in the course of one night so that when she awoke, she might find that her wish had been granted.

Below: Elizabethan noblemen kept alive the traditions of knightly chivalry revived under Edward III and popular in the reign of Elizabeth's father, Henry VIII.

The events at Kenilworth were part of Elizabeth's majestic 'summer progress' in 1575 when, with Leicester as her guide, she made a series of visits to country houses across central England. In these 'progresses', held each year, Elizabeth descended upon her nobles and people to impress all with her glittering magnificence. She travelled with some 300 wagons and 2,000 horses, either riding on horseback or carried in a litter. Country folk lined the roads to watch this vision of regal power pass.

COURTLY FASHIONS

By the 1570s, Elizabeth's court was a place of extravagant display, whose running costs had reached several hundred pounds a week. Elizabeth had a huge abundance of dresses, jewellery and precious stones, since she received vast numbers of jewels as gifts from ambassadors, courtiers and suitors. Each New Year's Day was a time of ceremonial gift-giving, when the Queen received dresses, jewellery, gloves, petticoats and other presents from leading courtiers. On New Year's Day 1588, Sir Christopher Hatton gave Elizabeth a gold necklace and earrings set with rubies and diamonds; the queen's jewellery collection was thought to be the most valuable in Europe.

Elizabeth's devotion to glittering display was, in part, a political decision to project herself as magnificence personified; a goddess on earth.

In 1575, summer progress celebrations were held in Warwick, where a vast firework display over the River Avon was backed up with the booming of cannon from the Tower of London, transported from the capital at the expense of Lord Warwick, Master of the Ordinance. The queen's encounter with town people and officials in Warwick is revealing of both her magnificence in their eyes and of her easy manner. When the town recorder was overcome with nerves at speaking in front of her, she called him forth saying, 'Come hither, little Recorder. It was told me that you would be afraid to look upon me or to speak boldly, but you were not so afraid of me as I was of you and I now thank you for putting me in mind of my duty'. When the firework display started a fire that damaged a house, Elizabeth summoned the elderly couple who owned the dwelling and offered to right the damage.

ENGLAND'S GODDESS

From the 1570s onward, Elizabeth's accession day, 17 November, was celebrated as a national holiday, with bonfires, the ringing of church bells, services of thanksgiving and ceremonial tilts and pageants at Whitehall Palace. It was a day of English Protestant pride that put half-remembered Catholic saints' days deep in the shade. Henry Lee, the Queen's Champion in tilting, initiated and organized the celebrations at Whitehall Palace each year until he retired aged 57 in 1590.

Above: This delicate miniature portrait of the queen by the great Nicholas Hilliard is found within the 'Armada Jewel'.

Above: A celestial presence. This portrait, by Italian Taddeo Zuccari (d. 1566), is one of many from the reign showing the queen lavishly dressed and smothered in jewellery.

GLORIANA
THE REALM OF THE FAERIE QUEEN

Towards the end of the reign, the poet Edmund Spenser dedicated his allegorical chivalric romance, *The Faerie Queen*, to Elizabeth, 'by the Grace of God Queen of England, France and Ireland and of Virginia, Defender of the Faith, &c'. In the work, published in 1590–6, the Queen of Fairie land, named Gloriana, represents glory both in the abstract and in the person of Elizabeth. As Spenser wrote, 'In that Faerie Queen I mean glory in my general intention, but in my particular I conceive the most excellent and glorious person of our sovereign the Queen'. The poet presented the first three manuscript books of the poem to the queen at court in 1589.

Elizabeth was an enthusiastic and discerning patron of the arts, which burst forth in an extraordinary flowering during her reign. In addition to Spenser, whose epic is considered one of the finest poems in English, the period produced dramatists William Shakespeare, Christopher Marlowe and Ben Jonson; musicians Thomas Tallis and William Byrd; and the renowned miniaturist artist Nicholas Hilliard.

Below: A Christian warrior slays a beast in an engraving from the 1590 edition of Edmund Spenser's The Faerie Queene.

Above: William Shakespeare at 34, in 1598. By this time the playwright's work was already a favourite of the queen's.

FLOWERING OF DRAMA

London's first theatre was founded in Holywell Street, Shoreditch, by actor James Burbage in December 1576. At Christmas 1582, five plays were put on at court for the entertainment of Elizabeth and her current suitor, the Duke of Alençon. In 1583 'the Queen's Men' were one of the companies of theatrical players formed in London. Some probably fanciful accounts of William Shakespeare's life claim that he first came to London having joined the Queen's Men as an actor in his native Stratford in 1587.

Shakespeare's plays were first performed in London in the early- to mid-1590s. His early works included the histories *Richard III* and the first part of *Henry VI*, comedies *The Taming of the Shrew* and *Two Gentlemen of Verona* and the tragedy *Romeo and Juliet*.

From 1594, he was one of the Lord Chamberlain's Men, based at the Globe Theatre in Bankside from 1598. Elizabeth so much enjoyed Shakespeare's *The History of Henry IV, with the Humorous Conceits of Sir John Falstaff* in 1597 that she asked for a new play showing Falstaff 'in love'; Shakespeare produced *The Merry Wives of Windsor*, which first played in 1600.

Above: This manuscript poem in praise of Elizabeth was presented to the queen in 1586 by its author, Georges de la Motthe.

ELIZABETH'S PLAYWRIGHTS

Ben Jonson's dramatic genius is considered in some quarters to have been the equal of Shakespeare, but his major works were written after Elizabeth's death, when he was a favourite at the court of King James I.

The playwright Christopher Marlowe is believed also to have been an agent in Elizabeth's secret service, who was sent in 1587 to spy on Catholics in France. He also had a reputation as an atheist and blasphemer and, perhaps for this reason, the Privy Council issued an order for his arrest on 18 May 1593. He was killed in a tavern brawl in Deptford on 30 May 1593, probably over nothing more significant than the bill. His plays, which include *Tamburlaine the Great, The Tragical History of Doctor Faustus* and *The Jew of Malta*, were performed to great acclaim in London by the Admiral's Men and their star Edward Alleyn.

Nicholas Hilliard was the pre-eminent portrait artist of Elizabeth's day. He worked mainly in miniature – an art known to Elizabethans as 'limning'– and was also a jeweller and goldsmith. In 1572 he was appointed the queen's official limner. In 1584 he designed the queen's second great seal.

TALLIS AND BYRD

Queen Elizabeth recognized the musical genius of the great sacred composers Thomas Tallis (right, top) and William Byrd (right, bottom) by granting them, a monopoly licence to print and sell music in England in 1575. In the same year, the two composers published *Cantiones Sacrae* ('Sacred Songs'), containing 16 motets by Tallis and 18 by Byrd. The book was dedicated to Queen Elizabeth. Tallis was by this time a man of 65 and had served as a gentleman of the Chapel Royal, the queen's musical body, since *c*.1542, well before the beginning of Elizabeth's reign. Byrd, Tallis's protégé, had joined the Chapel Royal from a position as organist at Lincoln Cathedral three years earlier.

THE REALITY BEHIND THE MASK
THE LAST DAYS OF ELIZABETH

Queen Elizabeth was very conscious of her public image. As early as 1563, the production of unauthorized portraits of the queen was banned. From the 1570s onwards, the projection of Elizabeth as the Virgin Queen, an earthly goddess or Protestant Madonna, was carefully managed. However, as she aged, the image of magnificence she wished to promote was increasingly at odds with physical reality.

Above: Even the 'Faerie Queene' was subject to the ravages of ageing. This portrait of Elizabeth in old age is by Dutch artist Marcus Gheeraerts the Younger.

THE EFFECTS OF AGE

Some authorities suggest that Elizabeth manufactured a glittering, magnificently costumed, jewel-laden public image to compensate for her waning physical charms. Essayist and philosopher Sir Francis Bacon, Lord Chancellor under King James I, wrote, 'She imagined that the people, who are much influenced by externals, would be diverted by the glitter of her jewels from noticing the decay of her personal attractions'. If this was a deliberate strategy, it largely succeeded, but it became more and more difficult to operate. The effects of ageing could not be avoided, even by the Queen, and beneath the laboriously constructed public face she became an old woman in a red wig, with bad teeth. In 1596, now aged over 60, she ordered the seizure of all paintings in which she looked ill, old or weak. In public, Elizabeth's age was clearly taking its toll: at the opening of the 1601 Parliament she found the velvet and ermine robes were too heavy and stumbled, falling into the arms of a peer alongside her. On a visit to Sir Robert Sidney around this time, she needed a walking stick to climb a staircase and appeared weary and forgetful.

Below: William Cecil, Lord Burghley. Elizabeth was devoted to her great statesman, and in his final illness she sat by his bed and fed him with a spoon.

CHANGE MUST COME

In the 1590s, Elizabeth was worn out and a little of the gloss had come off her reputation and achievements. Unemployment and taxation were both high, harvests failed in 1594–7, hard times led to rising crime rates and

TRUTHS IN THE MIRROR

For years Elizabeth avoided seeing herself in a looking glass, but in 1603 she commanded her courtiers to show her her true reflection, for the first time in two decades. She was devastated by the sight of the sickly, 69-year-old face she saw in the mirror. By this time the ailing queen was close to death, stubbornly refusing food and medicine, resisting sleep, sitting forlornly on a floor cushion at Richmond Palace. She had been ill since late 1602. Her dearest friends and confidants were already dead: Leicester had died long before, in 1588; Sir Christopher Hatton, in 1591; William Cecil, Lord Burghley, in 1598; and she had sent Robert Devereux, Earl of Essex, to a traitor's death in 1601. Her favourite cousin, Kate Carey, Countess of Nottingham, died in late February 1603, and this was perhaps the final blow.

Left: A symbol of death hovers behind the now weary queen in this anonymous panel from Corsham Court, Wiltshire.

record numbers of executions for felons, Spain remained a threat and there was a troubling uncertainty over the succession. Some began to speak out against Elizabeth's rule, and to call for change.

Yet the mythology of the Virgin Queen was sustained to the end. Sir Robert Cecil laid on an entertainment for Elizabeth in December 1602, in which he celebrated her as Astraea, virgin of Roman poet Virgil's *Eclogues*: a just and saintly figure, whose presence on Earth brought a wonderful age of eternal spring and endless peace.

Elizabeth herself maintained her stance of devotion to her people: in her celebrated 'golden speech' to representatives of the 1601 Parliament she declared, 'I do not so much rejoice that God hath made me to be a Queen, as to be a Queen over so thankful a people', adding, 'I have cause to wish nothing more than to content the subject' and, 'It is my desire to live nor reign no longer than my life and reign shall be for your good.' As before, she used the language of love in place of a language of politics, casting herself as the mistress, wife or mother of her country, driven always by care and devotion rather than duty or self-interest.

Elizabeth's own sun was preparing to set, but as the celebrated Virgin Queen she had no child to succeed to her throne. There were as many as a dozen people with at least a potentially viable claim to the English crown, including the Catholic Infanta Isabella Clara Eugenia, daughter of Philip II of Spain and wife of the Governor of Flanders, Archduke Albert; Lord Beauchamp, a descendant of Lady Jane Grey's family; and the Protestant James Stuart, the son of her cousin Mary Queen of Scots, ruling as King James VI of Scots. Yet Elizabeth could not bring herself to name a successor, since this would involve accepting her own end.

THE SETTING OF THE SUN

Queen Elizabeth died at last in the early hours of 24 March 1603. According to some accounts she was unable to the last to name a successor, but did rouse herself on her deathbed to condemn the claim of Lord Beauchamp: 'I will have no rascal's son in my seat, but one worthy to be a king'. In other versions of events she was by now unable to speak and indicated by a movement of her hand that she wished the throne to pass to James Stuart. On her final evening she was visited by John Whitgift, Archbishop of Canterbury, who told the dying queen, 'Though she had been long a great queen here upon earth, yet shortly she was to yield an account of her stewardship to the King of Kings'.

Below: William Cecil's Burghley House. He entertained Elizabeth no fewer than 12 times at his various country houses.

CHAPTER SEVEN

THE UNION OF THE CROWNS AND CIVIL WAR

1603–1660

The royal House of Stewart – or Stuart as it came to be spelled in the late 16th century – had been ruling in Scotland for 232 years by the time King James VI of Scots travelled south from Edinburgh to take possession of the English crown as King James I of England in 1603. The first Stewart king was King Robert II (1371–90), who acceded as the son of Robert I the Bruce's daughter, Marjorie. Robert II's descendants ruled in a direct male line until the death of King James V (1513–42), when James's daughter Mary, Queen of Scots, began her troubled reign at the age of seven days. Mary's son, another James, acceded as James VI on his mother's abdication in July 1567.

On the Scots throne James proved himself an effective ruler, but in England his indulgence of favourites, authoritarian approach and apparent disdain for MPs provoked increasingly severe clashes with Parliament that worsened to the point of breaking during the reign of his son, Charles I. Charles had many opportunities to broker a mutually beneficial deal with Parliament, but his refusal to compromise was a key reason for the slide into civil war in the 1640s, which led to his conviction for treason and subsequent execution on a wooden platform outside the Banqueting House in Whitehall one freezing January day in 1649.

Left: This magnificent triple portrait of Charles I is by Sir Anthony van Dyck. As king, Charles made a series of disastrous political decisions that hastened his own end and the monarchy's temporary abolition, but he proved a discerning patron in the visual arts.

JAMES I AND VI

1603–1625

James VI of Scotland learned of his accession to the throne of England in Edinburgh on 26 March 1603, when a horseman brought news to Holyrood Palace of the death two days earlier of Queen Elizabeth I. After an emotional farewell to his own people, James began a prolonged procession through England, reaching London a month later, on 7 May. Everywhere, vast crowds were eager to see the Stuart king come to claim the throne vacated by the Tudors. James became James I when he and his wife Anne were crowned at Westminster Abbey on 25 July 1603.

THE KING'S DIGNITY

In person and manners King James presented a stark and unwelcome contrast to the regal dignity of his illustrious predecessor. A slovenly man, with over-prominent eyes, a large tongue that tended to make him drool and an unfortunate tendency to drunkenness and laziness, he could scarcely have made a greater contrast to the carefully stage-managed public persona of the Virgin Queen. Leading nobles – already somewhat suspicious of the elevation of a Scottish king to rule over England – resented James's expression of his homosexuality in infatuations with effeminate young men such as Robert Carr and George Villiers, both of whom he raised to high office. The king also had a forthright manner of speaking that was far removed from tact. It is said that when annoyed by the large crowds dogging his every move in London, he exclaimed 'God's wounds, I will pull down my breeches and they shall see my arse'.

Yet James's self-indulgent behaviour was allied to a vast intelligence and a highly educated mind convinced of the king's dignity and his absolute right to demand obedience. He had very difficult relations with Parliament, which he treated with great tactlessness, often lecturing the Commons on their duty of obedience. Despite his appearance and behaviour, he saw himself as a man of regal bearing, dignity and authority.

Above: Scots king on the English throne. James wanted to create, in his words, 'one kingdom...one uniformity of laws'.

JAMES I AND VI, KING OF ENGLAND, SCOTLAND AND IRELAND, 1603–1625

Birth: 19 June 1566, Edinburgh Castle
Father: Henry Stewart, Lord Darnley
Mother: Mary, Queen of Scots
Accession: 24 July 1567 (Scotland); 24 March 1603 (England)
Inauguration/Coronation: 29 July 1567 (Stirling); 25 July 1603 (Westminster)
Queen: Anne of Denmark (m. 23 Nov 1589; d. 2 March 1619)
Succeeded by: His son Charles I
Greatest achievement: Peaceful union of the crowns of England and Scotland
1603: James recognizes Shakespeare's theatre company as 'King's Men'
18 Aug 1604: England is at peace with Spain
20 Oct 1604: James declares himself 'King of Great Britain'
Nov 1604: Shakespeare's great tragedy *Othello* plays at court
5 Nov 1605: Gunpowder Plot fails
13 May 1607: English settlers found 'Jamestown' in Virginia
1611: King James Authorized Version of the Bible is published
1616: Native American princess Pocahontas meet James at court
23 April 1616: William Shakespeare dies
16 Sept 1620: Pilgrim Fathers leave Plymouth aboard the *Mayflower*
26 Dec 1620: *Mayflower* pilgrims found settlement of New Plymouth
1624: Virginia becomes King's Royal Colony
Death: 27 March 1625, at Theobalds, Hertfordshire. Buried in Westminster Abbey

'GREAT BRITAIN'

Early in his reign James attempted to combine England and Scotland in a unified kingdom of 'Great Britain'. This was the policy he presented to his first Parliament, called on 22 March 1604. The Commons was not convinced and resisted the union: one member complained that to combine the (Tudor) rose with the (Scottish) thistle might produce a monstrous result.

James defied them. On 20 October 1604 he proclaimed a new title for himself as 'King of Great Britain'. On 12 April 1606 a new Anglo-Scottish flag was introduced for shipping, combining

THE 'KING JAMES VERSION' OF THE BIBLE

A new English translation of the Holy Bible, 'authorized' by King James, was published in 1611. James had proposed a new easily comprehensible English-language version of the Bible in 1601, before his accession in London, when he was ruling as King James VI of Scots. In January 1604, the idea was brought forward again by Oxford University's John Reynolds at a conference on the church, which was held at Hampton Court under Archbishop of Canterbury John Whitgift. James personally approved 54 scholars to work on the translation, of whom 47 were finally involved, working for seven years with the original texts as well as existing English translations. For more than three centuries the work – known as the 'Authorised version' or the 'King James version' – was the standard Bible in English churches.

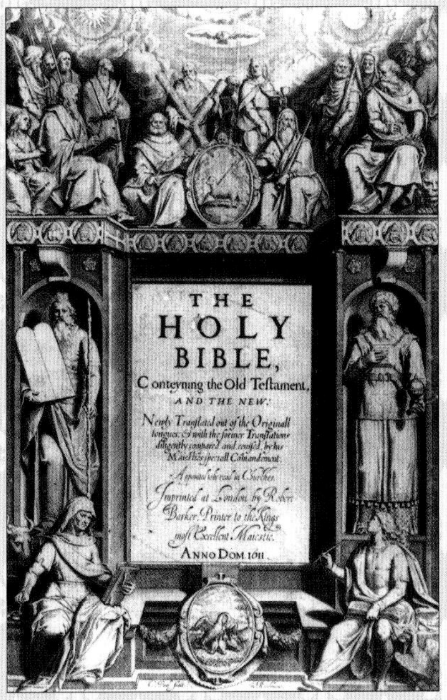

Above: The Authorised Bible, dedicated to James, 'principal mover and author'.

the crosses of St George and St Andrew and called the 'Great Union' – or the 'Union Jack' (from 'Jacques', the French form of the king's name, which he preferred to use). Nevertheless, the instrument seeking to establish the union of the two countries was rejected in both Parliaments in 1607.

Another matter of pressing concern at the start of the reign was the need to bring an end to the ruinously expensive war with Spain. This was achieved with speed and efficiency – to a large extent, because Spain needed peace even more than England did – in a peace treaty signed in London on 18 August 1604.

THE GUNPOWDER PLOT

James's early reign was marked by rebellions against his rule. The first came in the very year of his accession, when Lord Cobham, Sir Walter Raleigh and other lords were arrested and found guilty of planning to depose James in favour of the king's cousin, Lady Arabella Stuart. On 10 December 1603 James spared Cobham at the very moment of execution, thus making a dramatic demonstration of his royal authority. The second and more serious plot aimed to depose the Protestant James

Above: Gunpowder, treason and plot. Victorian artist Sir John Gilbert represents Guy Fawkes kneeling before King James.

and restore Catholicism in England. It followed harsh new laws passed in 1604 against Catholics who refused to worship in Church of England services.

The plot centred on the opening of James's second session of Parliament, scheduled for 5 November 1605. Catholic lords led by Robert Catesby and Guy Fawkes planned to blow up the Palace of Westminster with gunpowder and then foment a Catholic rebellion in the Midlands. Details of the plan came out when one of the gang, Francis Tresham, warned his brother-in-law Lord Mounteagle, who would have been killed in the Lords by the explosion. Lord Mounteagle passed on the information to those in authority and the plot was foiled at the last moment.

Right: There was an outbreak of the plague at the time, but crowds still flocked to see the coronation of King James in 1603.

JAMES AND THE 'NEW WORLD'

THE SETTLEMENT OF AMERICA, 1603–1625

On 10 April 1606, James granted the Virginia companies in London and Bristol a royal charter to explore and settle land on part of the eastern seaboard of North America (roughly corresponding to the territory between northern Maine and Wilmington, North Carolina). Tudor adventurer Sir Walter Raleigh had founded the colony of Virginia, England's first in North America, but settlement there had foundered following the failure of the 'Lost Colony' of Roanoke.

THE JAMESTOWN SETTLEMENT

Three ships under the command of Captain Christopher Newport carrying 120 Virginia Company settlers set sail for North America in December 1606.

When they arrived in Virginia, in April 1607, they named the natural features of the area for the king and princes of the Stuart dynasty – the River James and Capes Henry and Charles – and honoured the king himself in the name of their settlement, Jamestown, which they established on 14 May 1607.

Under the terms of the charter, the land they claimed belonged to the king, with the settlers as sub-tenants of the Charter company. Jamestown had the distinction of becoming the first permanent English settlement in North America. Government was undertaken by a royal council that was appointed by the king in London.

THE PRINCESS POCAHONTAS

Jamestown came under regular attack by local Native American Algonquians. One of the settlement leaders, Captain John Smith, was kidnapped and held by the Algonquian chief Wahunsonacock, or Powhatan, for four weeks, during which he survived a form of life or death trial in which, the story goes, his life was saved by Powhatan's 11-year-daughter, Pocahontas. Smith was released, became president of the Jamestown council and then was injured by a gunpowder burn and returned to England.

Pocahontas became a regular visitor to the Jamestown settlers, even bringing them gifts of food to help them survive. However, in 1613 one settler, Captain Samuel Argall, repaid her generosity by kidnapping her and holding her to ransom. He demanded the return of English prisoners and stolen firearms plus 'payment' of corn.

Pocahontas's father, Powhatan, paid a part of the ransom, but while Pocahontas was in captivity she was baptized a Christian as 'Lady Rebecca'

NOVA BRITANNIA.
OFFRING MOST
Excellent fruites by Planting in
VIRGINIA.
Exciting all ſuch as be well affected
to further the ſame.

LONDON
Printed for SAMVEL MACHAM, and are to be ſold at
his Shop in Pauls Church-yard, at the
Signe of the Bul-head.
1609.

Above: This 1609 advertisement promises 'most Excellent fruites', but the first settlers of Virginia endured very lean times.

and fell in love with a European tobacco planter named John Rolfe. Pocahontas and John Rolfe were subsequently married and in 1616 sailed to England for a visit.

The Native American princess and convert was a great attraction in London society. Pocahontas was presented to King James I at court, and she sat with the king watching a masque written by the leading playwright Ben Jonson.

James was captivated by the young woman, and spoke of his plan to found a school in Virginia to educate young Native American children. Most unfortunately, before she and Rolfe could return to Virginia, Pocahontas contracted a fatal illness. She died in 1617 aged only 22.

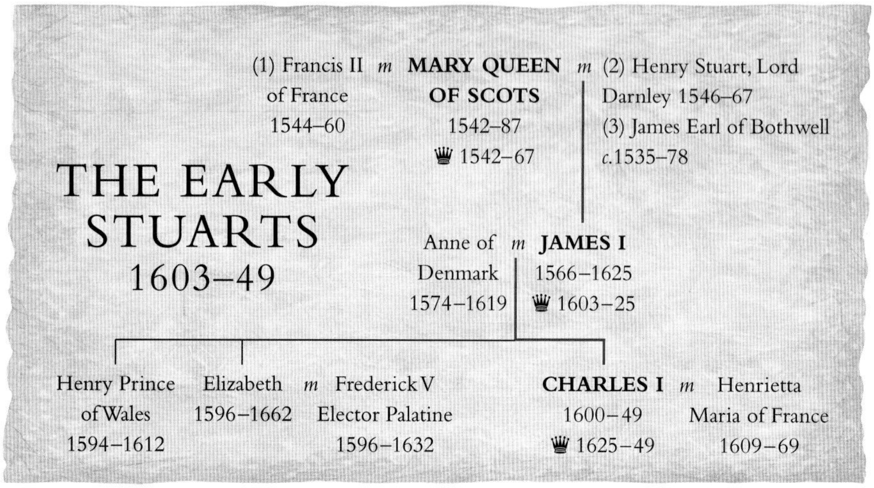

THE KING'S ROYAL COLONY

A new royal charter of 1609 offered financial interests in the city of London the chance to invest in the Virginia colony. Government was in the hands of the Virginia company treasurer and his council in London, as well as that of a governor and advisory council in Jamestown. Profits were poor, because conditions were difficult and many ships were lost in the Atlantic.

Another royal charter, in 1612, widened the colony boundaries to include the Bermuda Islands and introduced a democratic assembly in Jamestown in 1619.

Conditions remained poor in the colony. James ordered an investigation: the result was that in 1624 he dissolved the London company and Virginia became the King's Royal Colony.

JAMES AND THE MAYFLOWER

On 16 September 1620 one of the most celebrated transatlantic voyages in history began under licence from King James. Some 101 Puritans departed from Plymouth on board the *Mayflower* seeking a new life free from the religious persecution they suffered at home.

James and the Church of England authorities had been a major source of persecution for those – like many of the *Mayflower* pilgrims – who refused to accept the religious authority of king and church establishment. The king famously declared, 'I shall make them conform or I will harry them out of the land or else do worse'.

One group on board the *Mayflower* joined other travellers from the Netherlands: they were a congregation of English 'Separatists'. The 'Separatists' had been living in exile from James's persecution in the Low Countries for 12 years, since 1608. It was their declared belief that only Christ had authority over the Church.

Despite the fact that the *Mayflower* travellers had had major difficulties with the king, they sought and received royal backing for their venture before they departed. They won both the support of the Virginia Company and a licence from James after an interview in which the king was reportedly impressed by the adventurers' declaration that they would live by fishing. 'It is certainly an honest trade,' James responded, 'and was indeed the calling of the apostles themselves.'

Storms and high seas prevented the *Mayflower* from landing as intended in Virginia. The ship instead put in at Cape Cod (at the site of modern Provincetown, Massachusetts) on 21 November 1620 before unloading fully on 26 December at a nearby site that the new arrivals christened 'New Plymouth', 37 miles (60 km) south-east of Boston. William Brewster, leader of the Dutch 'Separatists', also became leader of the colony of New Plymouth. In 1621 the settlers in Plymouth gave thanks to God for the first good harvest of the colony with a three-day celebration to which they invited local Native Americans. This is celebrated in the modern 'Thanksgiving' holiday in the United States.

Above: Pocahontas. This portrait is based on an engraving made during her 1616 visit to King James's court in London.

Below: A map of Virginia, with scenes of its early settlement. The engraving was made and published by Thedore de Bry in the first part (1590) of a book on America.

AT THE COURT OF KING JAMES

PLAYERS AND FAVOURITES, 1603–1625

The extraordinary 'English renaissance' of cultural life that began in the London of Queen Elizabeth continued in the reign of King James. In the first year of his reign James honoured William Shakespeare's theatrical company by making them the 'King's Men', and many of Shakespeare's greatest plays were performed at the royal court.

The tragedy *Hamlet*, first performed in 1601, just predated the new reign, but 1603 saw the first performance of *Othello* and the play is known to have been performed at James's court in November 1604. *All's Well that Ends Well* and *Measure for Measure* were first performed in 1604, *King Lear* in 1605, *Macbeth* in 1606 and *Antony and Cleopatra* and *Coriolanus* in 1607. The year 1611 was notable for the first productions of *Cymbeline*, *The Winter's Tale* and *The Tempest*. These later years also saw the publication of Shakespeare's extraordinary *Sonnets*, a collection of 154 poems printed in 1609 by the publisher Thomas Thorpe. The sonnets are mostly in praise of a young nobleman of great beauty, and the published edition was dedicated to 'Mr WH, the onlie begetter of these insuing sonnets'. Rival theories identify WH as William, Lord Herbert, or Henry Wriothesley, Earl of Southampton.

Below: A scene from Ben Jonson's Masque of Queens *in the romantic style by Henry Fuseli (1741–1825).*

BEN JONSON AND THE MASQUE

In the years after 1605, King James, Queen Anne and their family and courtiers developed a great fondness for 'masques': theatrical performances with ornate costumes, choreographed dances and songs, often on classical themes. Rising playwright Ben Jonson forged a reputation as a creator of these entertainments. A clergyman's son and former bricklayer and soldier, Jonson had already made his mark in the late Elizabethan theatre world. His play *Every Man in His Humour* was performed at the Curtain Theatre in 1598 with Shakespeare himself in the cast.

Above: 'Steenie'. This portrait of King James's great favourite George Villiers is by Flemish artist Paul van Somer (d. *1621).*

Under King James, Jonson became a popular and well-rewarded figure at court. His first masque was created to give James's queen, Anne, the chance to make up and play a black woman: *The Masque of Blackness* was first put on to celebrate Twelfth Night in 1605. On the same day in 1610, Jonson's masque *Miles a Deo* ('Soldier of God') starred James's eldest son Henry in a performance to celebrate both the Christmas season and Henry's investiture that day as Prince of Wales. In these years Jonson also produced major plays, including *Volpone* (1605), *The Alchemist* (1610) and *Bartholomew Fair* (1614). In 1616 James granted Jonson a life pension: some scholars regard his court position as a forerunner of the 'poet laureate'.

In the first 12 years of the reign the poet John Donne (who was suffering from poverty after a secret 1601 marriage led to imprisonment and ruined his political prospects) made several attempts to gain employment at court. He was repeatedly rebuffed by King James, who disliked his poetry and once declared, 'Dr. Donne's verses are like the peace of God; they pass all understanding'. James urged Donne to become an Anglican priest. When Donne finally agreed to enter the Church in 1615, James made him a royal chaplain and ordered Cambridge University to make the poet a Doctor of Divinity. Subsequently Donne won the favour of the new court favourite, George Villiers, Marquis of Buckingham, and with his support was made Dean of St Paul's, London. In addition to being a great poet, Donne was one of the greatest preachers of his day.

Also active at James's court was the architect and artist Inigo Jones, remembered as the founder of the English 'classical tradition' in architecture. Beginning in 1605, Jones made his name in London under the patronage of Queen Anne, designing the scenery and costumes for the court masques written by Ben Jonson. Then in 1615 he was appointed James's surveyor of building works. His first major work was the Queen's Palace at Greenwich, which he began in 1616 fresh from a 1613-14 tour of Italy in the company of Thomas Howard, second Earl of Arundel, during which Jones studied classical ruins and the work of modern Italian classical architect Andrea Palladio. Jones next rebuilt the Banqueting House in Whitehall in 1619–22.

Below: Shakespeare and friends. The great cultural figures of King James's London are portrayed by Victorian artist John Faed.

COURT SCANDALS

King James's homosexual interest in and preferential treatment of handsome young men added spice to life at court. Early in the reign, the favourite was the 17-year-old Robert Carr (or Ker), the son of Scottish nobleman Sir Thomas Ker of Ferniehurst, who enjoyed a meteoric rise. The young man fell just as swiftly from favour, however, when he was found guilty of murder in 1616.

Around this time, James became enamoured of a new favourite, George Villiers, son of a Leicestershire squire. First introduced to the king at the age of 22 in August 1614, Villiers was made a gentleman of the bedchamber in April 1615, Master of the Horse in January 1616, a Knight of the Garter in April 1616, Viscount Villiers and Baron Whaddon in August 1616, Earl of Buckingham in 1617, Marquis of Buckingham on 1 January 1618 and Duke of Buckingham in 1623. Villiers was tall and beautifully built with blue eyes and chestnut hair; courtiers reported that the king could scarcely keep his hands off the young man he called 'my Steenie', due to a supposed resemblance to St Stephen, who had 'the face of an angel'.

Buckingham made many enemies at court and among the aristocracy when he exploited his influence to raise his relatives to positions of power. He also succeeded in befriending the heir to the throne, Prince Charles, and travelled with Charles – in disguise – to Madrid on an unsuccessful attempt to negotiate a marriage with the Infanta, daughter of King Philip of Spain. Buckingham's almost entirely negative influence in government and at court lasted beyond the death of King James in 1625.

Above: Shakespeare's fellow actors John Heming and Henry Condell prepared this first collected edition of his works (1623), known to scholars as the First Folio.

THE WISEST FOOL IN CHRISTENDOM

KING JAMES'S LEGACY, 1603–1625

James was dubbed 'the wisest fool in Christendom' by King Henry IV of France and he was certainly a king of contradictions: an intellectual who was a bawdy drunkard, a man who claimed regal dignity while behaving with none, a king who declared his divinely sanctioned authority but then allowed himself and his government to be dominated by incompetent 'favourites'. His reign was marked by repeated clashes with an increasingly troublesome and self-willed Parliament.

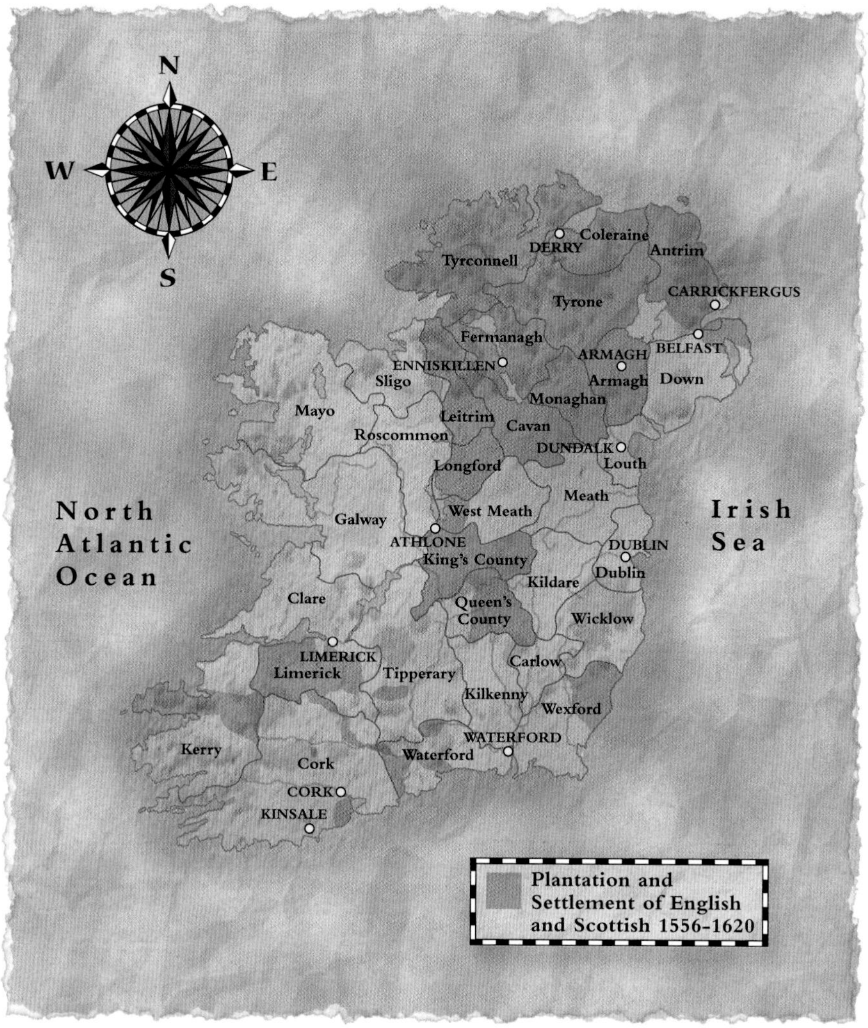

Above: The 'Plantation' of Protestants in 17th-century Ireland occurred mainly in the north, but also in pockets elsewhere.

STRUGGLE WITH PARLIAMENT

As early as 1604 there were disagreements over the extent of the king's self-proclaimed royal prerogatives, and James's extravagance at court led to several angry encounters with Parliament over finance. When MPs refused to place a new series of import duties on merchants, James had the duties declared law by the courts in 1608 as he again sought to undermine Parliament's role as supreme legislative body. This led Robert Cecil, Lord Salisbury, to propose a 'Great Contract' under which the king would abandon his royal prerogative to raise money in this way in return for a guaranteed annual grant of taxation. The contract could not be agreed, however, and in February 1611 James dissolved Parliament, angry at its failure to help him solve his financial problems.

Below: King James left a difficult legacy for Charles I, particularly in the troubled relationship he had with MPs.

The next Parliament of his reign was an unmitigated disaster. James called the Parliament in April 1614 on the advice of Sir Francis Bacon, the attorney general. James wanted the House to vote him money, but MPs were opposed to the king's foreign policy and refused to cooperate. The Parliament lasted only two months and did not pass a single piece of legislation.

James's third Parliament, in 1621, brought about a total breakdown of relations between king and MPs. This dramatic clash was largely fuelled by MPs' distaste for James's plan to forge an alliance with Catholic Spain and to negotiate a diplomatic marriage for his son Charles (the future Charles I) with the Infanta, daughter of the Spanish king. When Parliament demanded that Prince Charles seek a Protestant bride,

Above: England and Scotland. The Tudor arms were quartered with the lion rampant of Scotland in the king's great seal.

that James declare war on Spain and that existing anti-Catholic laws should be imposed with greater force, the king was furious, telling MPs that they had no right to meddle. When MPs then made a protestation of their ancient privileges and declared that every member should enjoy freedom of speech, James dissolved Parliament once more on 30 December 1621. He ripped from the House of Commons journal the pages on which the 'protestation' had been written.

A fourth Parliament, in March 1624, again urged war against Spain and an end to marriage negotiations with the Infanta. Later that year the proposed Spanish marriage – which had been very unlikely since the failure of a diplomatic trip to Spain by Charles and the Duke of Buckingham in 1623 – was replaced with a French match: in November 1624 Charles was betrothed to Henrietta Maria, the 15-year-old sister of King Louis XIII of France. During negotiations James (under pressure from Buckingham, who was determined that the marriage should go through) made secret commitments to the French on improved conditions for Catholics in England.

A KING OF CONTRADICTIONS

By this time King James was unwell, severely troubled by arthritis and swiftly ageing. Government was almost entirely in the hands of his favourite, the Duke of Buckingham. James died on 27 March 1625 at his favourite residence, the country mansion of Theobalds in Hertfordshire, after suffering a stroke. He had been a king for all but one of his 59 years and, given the circumstances of his accession to the throne of Scotland in 1567, it was remarkable that he survived his youth to achieve such a long and largely peaceful reign.

A BLOODY INHERITANCE

James left a tragic legacy in Ireland. He backed the 'Plantation' or settlement of Catholic Ulster by Protestant Scots and Englishmen, which began in 1611. Ulster was one of the most strongly Catholic parts of Ireland and was actively rebellious against English government. Under the scheme, Catholic landowners' estates were confiscated and six new counties of Tyrone, Donegal, Armagh, Fermanagh, Derry and Cavan were created. The land was given to Protestant settlers. The 'Plantation', under plans enthusiastically approved by King James in 1608, added further fuel to flames of religious conflict in the region.

Right: James enjoyed hearing sermons. He patronized John Donne, whom he appointed Dean of St Paul's Cathedral in London.

CHARLES I
1625–1649

Above: *Charles I was 24 when he became king. He remained under the disastrous influence of the Duke of Buckingham.*

Charles I's belief in his right to absolute and divinely sanctioned rule was allied to a haughty manner, a refusal to change his mind and a damaging willingness to do anything to have his way. These characteristics made him profoundly ill-suited for the task history set him, of handling a troublesome Parliament and maintaining peace between religious factions. His failure led to civil war, his own execution, the abolition of the monarchy and Britain's reinvention as a 'commonwealth'.

Born in Dunfermline Palace in 1600, Charles was six years the junior of Prince Henry, heir to the throne. Charles was a sickly child, so feeble that he did not walk until he turned seven in 1607, and at first he was left behind in Scotland when James progressed southwards to claim the throne of England. However, in 1612 he became heir to the throne, when Henry died of typhoid, and thereafter he grew in confidence. He had a lonely childhood, missing Henry and his sister Elizabeth, who left England in 1613 when she married Frederick, the Elector Palatine of the Rhine. As an adult Charles remained short – he grew no taller than 5ft 4in (1.6m) – and was frail and shy, with a minor speech defect that he never conquered.

Left: This medal was struck in 1633 to mark the king's return to London following his Scottish coronation in Edinburgh.

INFLUENCE OF BUCKINGHAM

Life at Charles's court was rather more civilized than it had been under the often boorish King James I. Charles was a believer in the importance of manners, ritual and appearances, and he was a keen patron of the arts with a very fine eye for painting. However, in one important sense, government and court life were unchanged: George Villiers, the Duke of Buckingham was a favourite of Charles, just as he had been of James, and he continued to exert a largely disastrous influence.

MPs were strongly critical of the Duke of Buckingham's disastrous diplomacy and military leadership. The duke's poorly resourced and incompetently led attack on Cadiz was driven back by Spain with humiliating ease in early summer 1626; in June 1626 Charles dissolved the second Parliament

Left: A contemporary woodcut depicts Charles's visit to Spain, before he became king, to negotiate a planned marriage.

Above: Charles married Henrietta Maria in 1625. Their first son, Charles James, was born and died on 13 May 1629.

of his reign after MPs called for the Duke of Buckingham's impeachment. Buckingham, in 1627, led one of two failed attacks to help the Huguenots who were besieged in the French port of La Rochelle; in June 1628 MPs called again for Buckingham to be dismissed from court and government. The sorry saga finally ended with Buckingham's death at the hands of a knife-wielding assassin in 1628. The killer, who stabbed Buckingham at the *Greyhound Inn* in Portsmouth, as the duke prepared for yet another raid on La Rochelle, was found to be John Felton, a disgruntled veteran of the previous La Rochelle campaign. He made himself many new friends by despatching the enemy of the House of Commons.

RELIGIOUS TENSIONS HEAT UP

One of Charles's first acts as king was to welcome his new bride to England. In May 1625, Charles and the princess Henrietta Maria, daughter of France's King Henry IV and Queen Marie de'Medici, were married by proxy, and the following month Henrietta Maria landed at Dover from her homeland. Although the Catholic princess was not the Protestant bride that the English Commons and people had hoped for, she was generally preferred to James and Charles's original choice – the Catholic Infanta, daughter of the Spanish king.

Unfortunately, religious tension interfered with Charles's coronation in February 1626: Henrietta Maria refused to attend because the ceremony was performed by a Protestant bishop. She also grew angry over Charles's failure to honour promises made by his father James in the marriage agreement that conditions for English Catholics would be improved.

Religious differences also led to the dissolution of Charles's first Parliament, in August 1625: Charles took offence at MPs' repeated attacks on a clerical group known as the Arminians, who argued – with Charles's sympathy – for a revival of early Church doctrine. They were viewed by members of the 'reformed religion' as Catholics.

CHARLES I, KING OF ENGLAND, SCOTLAND AND IRELAND, 1625–1649

Birth: 19 Nov 1600, Dunfermline Palace
Father: James VI of Scots (later James I of 'Great Britain')
Mother: Anne of Denmark
Accession: 27 March 1625
Coronation: 2 Feb 1626, Westminster Abbey; 18 June 1633, Holyrood Palace, Edinburgh
Queen: Henrietta Maria (m. 13 June 1625; d. 21/31 August 1669)
Succeeded by: His son Charles II in Scotland; after Charles I was executed in 1649, the monarchy was abolished and England declared a commonwealth
Greatest achievement: Dignity with which he faced trial and execution
23 Aug 1628: Buckingham assassinated
10 March 1629: Dissolves Parliament and declares he will rule alone
April 1630: John Winthrop leads Puritans into exile in Massachussetts
1638–9: Defeated in the First Bishops' War in Scotland
1640: Defeated in the Second Bishops' War in Scotland
12 May 1641: Execution of Sir Thomas Wentworth, Earl of Strafford
22 Nov 1641: Parliament passes Grand Remonstrance against the king
3 Jan 1642: Charles fails to arrest leaders of parliamentary opposition
13 Sept 1642: Civil war: Charles raises royal standard
23 Oct 1642: First skirmish, Battle of Edghill
25 Sept 1643: Solemn League and Covenant allies English Puritans and Scots Presbyterians
2 July 1644: Major royalist defeat at Battle of Marston Moor
14 June 1645: Decisive Parliamentary victory in Battle of Naseby
Jan 1647: After fleeing to Scotland, Charles is handed into the care of Parliament
20–27 Jan 1649: On trial before High Court in London
Death: 30 Jan 1649, executed in Whitehall, buried in St George's Chapel, Windsor

COUNTDOWN TO CIVIL WAR

CHARLES I AND PARLIAMENT, 1625–1641

In the late 1620s Charles continued to be in direct conflict with Parliament over two main issues – revenue and religion.

Following great unrest provoked by his imposition of a 'forced loan' collected under threat of imprisonment, in 1628 Charles was forced to approve a 'petition of right' that guaranteed his subjects freedom from, among other things, arbitrary taxation. Henceforth, no man might be 'Compelled to make or yield any gift, loan, benevolence, tax or such like charge, without common consent by Act of Parliament'.

The same year William Laud, a supporter of the controversial Arminian doctrine became Bishop of London. In a dramatic development on 2 March 1629, MPs outmanoeuvred the king to pass laws condemning attempts to raise taxes without parliamentary backing and attacking efforts to impose Arminianism. Charles had instructed the Speaker of the House, Sir John Finch, to rise when MPs began to debate and so prevent any laws being passed, but two MPs – Denzil Holles and Benjamin Valentine – forcibly held the Speaker in the chair, while others locked the door against the king's messenger, Black Rod, who had been sent to dissolve Parliament. In this way they were able to pass the laws that Charles opposed.

As a result on 10 March 1629 Charles dissolved Parliament, announcing that he would rule without its backing.

Above: Charles I. Anthony van Dyck, court painter from 1632, is celebrated for his sensitivity to the character of his subjects.

Speaking of the Commons, he declared, 'I know there are many there as dutiful subjects as any in the world; it being but some few Vipers amongst them that did cast this Mist of Undutifulness over most of their Eyes'.

DEFICIT IN ROYAL FINANCES

Thereafter, unable to levy taxation with parliamentary backing, Charles had to come up with ingenious schemes of doubtful legality to raise money in order to cover a deficit in the royal finances that was running at £20,000 a year by the mid-1630s. The 'ship tax' was levied on coastal areas – officially to fund the Royal Navy – and afterwards extended to inland areas also. Charles also raised customs duties and revived venerable 'forest laws'. These allowed fines to be imposed on those who encroached on ancient royal forests and were now applied to areas such as Essex, which had been forest in the past but had since been cleared. Having bypassed Parliament, the king was acting with no apparent restraint – a landowner named

RELIGIOUS EXILES

In 1630 John Winthrop led a mass exodus of Puritans to the New World, in flight from what they saw as excessive Catholic influence at court. In 1629 they obtained a charter from King Charles to establish the Massachussetts Bay Company. The king understood it to be a commercial venture, but Winthrop and friends were determined to found a Puritan colony. Winthrop was elected governor of the new colony before departure. He set sail aboard the *Arbella* at the head of a fleet of 11 ships containing 700 people in April 1630. In America, he was re-elected a number of times as governor of the fledgling colony. He wrote a celebrated sermon, 'The City on a Hill', which cast Puritan exiles as parties to a special agreement with God to found a sacred society. Another quite different religious exile founded Maryland, named in honour of Charles's queen, Henrietta Maria. Cecilius Calvert, second Baron Baltimore, was a Roman Catholic who received a grant of territory from Charles to establish Maryland in 1632. Baltimore founded the colony both as a commercial enterprise and as a place of refuge where Catholics could live and worship in freedom.

Right: George, father of Cecilius Calvert. The colony of Maryland was his idea, but he died before it was realized.

John Bankes challenged the legality of the extension of the ship money but lost his case in court, in June 1638, in a decision that served to increase bad feeling against the king.

The fear of Catholic influence at home was heightened by Charles's reissue in 1633 of King James's *Book of Sports*. This specified the sports that were permissible on the Sabbath – and offended Puritans who argued that the Sabbath should be kept free of all sports and recreations, including music. Worse still in Puritan eyes was the 1634 visit to Queen Henrietta Maria of papal legate Gregorio Panzani and the public knowledge that the Catholic Mass was celebrated every day for the queen in the palace in Whitehall.

Above: Van Dyck painted several imposing portraits of Charles, seeking to express the king's belief in his divine right to rule.

LAVISH ARTS SPENDING

Meanwhile at court, despite financial troubles and increasing public ill-feeling at Charles's unusual means of raising money from his people, the king spent lavishly on the arts. He hired the finest artists and put together a collection of Europe's greatest paintings. He commissioned works by leading artists such as Peter Paul Rubens and Anthony van Dyck and in 1632 made van Dyck court painter. He hired Rubens to paint scenes of King James I's apotheosis on the ceiling of the Inigo Jones's Banqueting House in Whitehall. In 1634 van Dyck painted a celebrated equestrian portrait of King Charles and in 1637 the well-known *Charles I in Three Positions*.

The king bought works by Titian, Raphael and Mantegna for the royal art collection. He viewed the collection as an expression of his regal authority and dignity and wanted it to be the equal to that of any European royal house. To this end, he put the collection under the control of Dutch art expert Abraham van der Doort.

Left: John Winthrop, first governor of Massachusetts, believed that God had chosen him for sainthood in his lifetime.

As in his father James's reign, masques were a popular form of entertainment at court, with many designed by the great Inigo Jones. Doubtless Charles enjoyed escaping from the troubling political and religious struggles of his day into a well-ordered world that honoured ruler and courtiers. Inigo Jones and Ben Jonson collaborated on more than 30 masques, but had a disagreement in 1631 after which other playwrights and poets including James Shirley and Thomas Carew authored the masques.

THE ENGLISH CIVIL WAR

1642–1649

Above: *Key figures of the Civil War, including the Earl of Essex (top left) and Cromwell (bottom, second from left).*

The beginning of the long struggle that became the English Civil War can be traced to Charles's 1637 decision to impose on the Scots a Book of Common Prayer almost exactly the same as the one used in England. This provoked strong opposition among Scottish Presbyterians, who saw the move as an Anglo-Catholic assault on the purity of their religion: in 1638 they signed a National Covenant to uphold their faith. Charles first attempted negotiation, at a general assembly of the Church of Scotland, in Glasgow, in November 1638, and when that failed, he found himself faced by a Scottish Covenanter army. He raised a royalist force and marched north, but in the First Bishops' War could not defeat the Covenanters and was forced to agree peace in June 1639.

THE LONG PARLIAMENT

In April 1640, Charles called his first Parliament for 11 years to try to raise money for further military action in Scotland. He encountered concerted opposition in the Commons and so dismissed the Short Parliament after just three weeks. He then went ahead with the planned campaign in Scotland, but the Second Bishops' War ended in another defeat and Charles was forced into both a humiliating peace at Ripon and into recalling Parliament.

This Parliament would sit until 1660 and is known as the Long Parliament. The king's opponents in the Commons had Charles's most able minister, Thomas Wentworth, Earl of Strafford, impeached and then executed under a bill of attainder in May 1641. Charles was forced to concede that 'ship money' and his other financial levies were illegal and that Parliament could not be dissolved without its own agreement. On 22 November 1641 the Commons then passed a 'Grand Remonstrance' listing Charles's many failings since his accession. It called for royal ministers to be approved by Parliament and for the appointment of a Parliament-nominated assembly to oversee church reform.

A Catholic uprising in Ireland led Charles to raise another army, and MPs, fearful that he would use it against them, demanded that he relinquish control of the troops. He angrily refused and, in January 1642, took the bold step

Left: Captive king. This woodcut shows Charles under house arrest at Carisbrooke Castle, Isle of Wight, in late 1647.

of entering the Commons with an armed guard to arrest ringleader MPs for treason. He came too late. The MPs in question had been tipped off and escaped into hiding on a river barge.

Charles now fled London, heading for northern England. Queen Henrietta Maria and Princess Mary left the country to raise financial support for the king in Continental Europe, and England prepared for civil war.

FIRST SKIRMISHES

Charles raised the royal standard at Nottingham on 13 September 1642 and began to move on London as the Parliamentarians gathered an untrained army under the Earl of Essex. The first major clash, at Edghill near Banbury on 23 October 1642, was a victory for the king, although the Parliamentarian army retreated in good order. A second clash at Brentford, west of London, on 11 November was also a royalist victory, but a third, at nearby Turnham Green two days later, saw the 12,000-odd royalist troops defeated by a 25,000-strong Parliamentarian force.

The royalist advance on London was thus turned back, ending Charles's chances of securing a quick victory.

HONOURS EVEN

In 1643 fortunes swung to and fro, with royalist victories in Yorkshire and the south-west followed by a Parliamentarian fight-back that again blocked the king's approach to London. A key event was the signing of the 'Solemn League and Covenant', which pledged alliance between English Puritans and Scottish Presbyterians and provided a Scottish army to support the Parliamentary cause.

The Scottish Covenanters provided crucial support to the Parliamentarian army at the Battle of Marston Moor on 2 July 1644, when the royalists were swept away by a crack cavalry force led by Oliver Cromwell. However, later in the year Charles defeated the Earl of Essex at Lostwithiel, in Cornwall.

Above: Major battles of the English Civil Wars. Parliamentarians won key victories at Marston Moor and Naseby in 1644–5.

THE TIDE TURNS

1645 was the decisive year. Although royalist troops in Scotland under Montrose won a famous victory over Covenanters at Inverlochy in February, in England the Parliamentarians established the highly disciplined 'New Model Army' under the command of Fairfax and Cromwell and won a series of important victories; not least the overwhelming defeat of Charles's army at Naseby, Northants, on 14 June. In November Charles retreated to Oxford.

In spring 1646, as the Parliamentarians prepared to besiege Oxford, the king fled in disguise. He escaped to Scotland, but was handed back to the care of the English Parliament in January 1647. Kept at first under house arrest in Northants, Charles was taken into army custody in June 1647 as a new civil conflict developed between the New Model Army and Parliament. After a final victory over Scottish royalists at Preston in August 1648, the army took control.

On 20 November, General Henry Ireton presented Parliament with the 'Remonstrance of the Army', which demanded that Charles be put on trial for treason. Parliament still hoped to reach a compromise with the king and rejected the document.

On 6 December Colonel Thomas Pride reduced the Commons to a 'rump' that would be obedient to the will of the military. At Christmas 1648 Charles was brought to Windsor Castle. The army hierarchy was determined to achieve its aims: the trial and execution of the king and the abolition of the monarchy.

THE EXECUTION OF CHARLES I

1649

King Charles appeared on trial before a specially created 'high court of justice', consisting of 159 commissioners appointed by the 'Rump' Parliament, in the Painted Chamber at the Palace of Westminster on 20 January 1649. Security was tight: soldiers watched the movements of the crowd, guards perched on the palace roof and the high court president, John Bradshaw, wore a steel-lined hat to protect him from assassins' bullets.

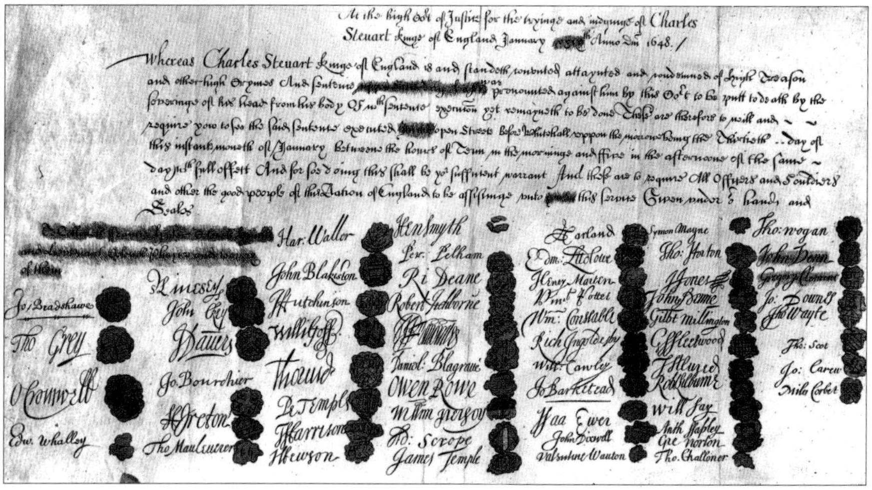

Above: Signatories of Charles's death warrant included army men Oliver Cromwell and Henry Ireton but not Sir Thomas Fairfax, army commander.

CHARGED WITH TREASON

The king was charged with having governed according to his will and not by law, with having waged war 'against the present Parliament and the people there represented' and with having committed treason against his own people – a neat reversal of the usual definition of treason. Charles refused to defend himself, or enter a plea in response to the charge, as he denied that the court had any authority over him. He declared, 'I would know by what power I am called hither…by what authority' and warned the court, 'Remember I am your king, your lawful king', adding, 'I have a trust committed to me by God, by old and lawful descent, [and] I will not betray it, to answer a new unlawful authority'.

Below: Charles tried to project an aura of authority despite losing control of his destiny. This portrait by Edward Bower (fl. 1635–67) shows the king at trial.

'TYRANT AND PUBLIC ENEMY'

The trial lasted eight days. Witnesses described the king's physical involvement in the battles of the civil war, while alleging that he approved atrocities against the people and that he tried his utmost while in captivity to stir up and prolong the wars.

Sentence was passed on 27 January. The high court found the king guilty as a 'Tyrant, traitor, murderer and public enemy to the Commonwealth of England' and sentenced him to be 'Put to death by the severing of his head from his body'.

John Bradshaw, president of the court, addressed Charles for 40 minutes, declaring that when a king entered battle against his own people he lost his claim to their allegiance, and arguing that even a monarch was subject to the law as it issued from Parliament. Charles was shocked and upset to discover that he was not allowed to reply. Instead, with the death sentence ringing in his ears, he was taken to St James's Palace to await his end. Just 59 commissioners of the 159 appointed signed the king's death warrant.

Below: The king faces his accusers in the High Court of Justice on 27 January.

'MARTYR OF THE PEOPLE'

The execution was planned for early in the morning of the following day, 30 January 1649. It was a bitterly cold day: Charles wore two shirts from fear that he would be cold and shiver, giving onlookers the impression that he was trembling with fear. He gave instructions for sharing out his intimate possessions among his children, including his gold watch and his Bible, and he received Holy Communion.

However, the execution was delayed because Cromwell was told that under current law a king's successor must be declared at the moment of a royal death. The king was forced to wait while Parliament drafted and hurried through three readings of a bill declaring it illegal to make a proclamation of succession. It was not until 2 p.m. that Charles came out from the Banqueting House in Whitehall on to the platform specially raised against its side, where a large crowd had gathered.

Charles walked forth confident and fearless and made a final statement, declaring his loyalty to the Church of England and arguing that the people should have no part in government, saying, 'A subject and a sovereign are clean different things'. He then proclaimed, 'I am the martyr of the people' and forgave those who were responsible for his death. His last words were, 'I go from a corruptible to an incorruptible crown, where no disturbance can be'.

Because the executioner's block was very low, Charles had to lie down rather than kneel. When he was ready he made a pre-arranged signal with his hands and his head was cut off with one blow. The assistant to the executioner held the decapitated head aloft and a moan – perhaps of grief, perhaps of horror at the killing of a king – was heard from the watching crowd.

Pandemonium broke out among the crowd as hundreds of people struggled to dip scraps of cloth in the royal blood.

THE CULT OF THE KING

Mindful that Charles could indeed become a martyr in death, the authorities arranged for his burial in St George's Chapel, Windsor Castle, well away from the London crowds, rather than in Westminster Abbey. His embalmed body – with the head sewn back in place – was moved to Windsor by water and he was buried in the castle on 8 February 1649. The authorities outlawed public mourning and declared that there would be no state funeral for the king.

But they were unable to stop the tide of emotion that made a bestseller of a book of the king's supposed meditations and prayers in his final days. The book – *Eikon Basilike, the Pourtraiture of His Sacred Majestie in his Solitude and Sufferings*, ghostwritten by John Gauden, chaplain to the earl of Warwick – went through 40 English-language editions in 1649 alone, and was translated into many languages including French, Latin, Dutch and Danish.

Subsequently, with the Restoration of the monarchy, the 'cult' of King Charles I was encouraged and in 1660 Parliament declared the king to be a martyr and made him a saint of the Anglican Church.

Below: Charles was defiant unto death. Dutch artist Weesop painted this Eyewitness Representation of the Execution of King Charles I.

COMMONWEALTH AND PROTECTORATE

1649–1660

On 17 March 1649 the MPs in the 'Rump Parliament' finished the job begun with King Charles I's execution when they passed an act abolishing the monarchy and making England a 'Commonwealth and free state'. The act also abolished the House of Lords and proclaimed Parliament 'supreme authority of this nation'.

There was still powerful opposition to be faced, however. In September 1649, Cromwell was despatched to Ireland to put down a royalist uprising among Irish royalists. He won devastating victories at Wexford and Drogheda. Then in June 1650, having been made Commander-in-Chief of the Commonwealth forces, Cromwell marched north to Scotland, where the Covenanters were promoting the cause of Charles I's son, Charles.

Cromwell won a resounding victory over a Covenanter army at Dunbar on 3 September 1650, but royalist opposition

Below: Army commander, England's Protector. True to his convictions, Cromwell twice turned down the offer of the throne.

Above: Cromwell's crown. This gold five-shilling coin was minted in London in 1658.

persisted, and on 1 January 1651 Charles Stuart was crowned King Charles II of England, Scotland, Ireland and France (the last title traditional), at Scone in Scotland.

In August that year Charles led an army of Scots and royalist sympathisers across the border and marched on London. However, Cromwell inflicted a devastating defeat on him at Worcester on 3 September, forcing him to flee in disguise and go into hiding.

GOVERNING WITHOUT A KING

Although Oliver Cromwell had made the Commonwealth safe, the execution of the king had created a power vacuum and the search for a stable form of government proved a difficult one. As Commander-in-Chief of the army, Cromwell was the dominant figure. He eventually became frustrated at delays in the Rump Parliament, which was supposed to be planning for the election of a new assembly.

On 20 April 1653 Cromwell declared the Rump Parliament dissolved, angrily telling the House, 'You have sat here too long for the good you do. In the name of God, go!' He did not act in order to bolster his own position, but his behaviour was painfully reminiscent of the acts of Stuart 'tyranny' that had provoked the Civil War and led to the execution of a king.

KING OR LORD PROTECTOR?

A new Parliament was appointed, made up of 140 officially approved Puritans. The first parliament to represent the whole of the British Isles, it was nicknamed the 'Barebones Parliament' from the name of one of its members, the Anabaptist Praisegod Barebones. It was short-lived, for in December 1653 it voted itself out of existence and put power into the hands of Cromwell. He thus became the first man to rule a unitary state of Great Britain and Ireland.

A SUCCESSION OF PARLIAMENTS

13 April–6 May 1640: 'Short Parliament' dissolved by King Charles I after three weeks
3 Nov 1640: Charles I calls 'Long Parliament'; not formally dissolved until 16 March 1660
7 Dec 1648: Col Thomas Pride 'purges' the Long Parliament to create the compliant 'Rump Parliament'
20 April 1653: Cromwell dissolves the Rump Parliament;
4 July 1653: New 'Barebones Parliament' assembles
12 Dec 1653: Barebones Parliament dissolved; Cromwell becomes Lord Protector
16 May 1659: Army leaders recall the Rump Parliament
Feb 1660: Members excluded in Pride's Purge are recalled to reconstitute the Long Parliament
16 March 1660: The Long Parliament votes to dissolve ahead of new elections
25 April 1660: The Pro-Royalist 'Convention Parliament' meets

Above: 'In the name of God, go!' Like the Stuart kings before him, Cromwell dismissed troublesome MPs – including members of the Rump Parliament in 1653.

Major-General John Lambert was behind this development – essentially a coup – and he tried to persuade Cromwell to become king. Cromwell refused, however, providing proof of his religious sincerity and rectitude of character: he was convinced that it had been God's will for the monarchy to be abolished and he would not countenance its reintroduction. Instead he agreed to become 'Lord Protector'.

This change was introduced under England's first written constitution, the 'Instrument of Government', which made the country a Protectorate. Government was to be by the Lord Protector through a council of state and the House of Commons. Religious toleration was to be guaranteed for all, except Catholics.

When the new Parliament met in 1654 its attempts to alter the constitution and notably to restrict religious toleration led Cromwell to dissolve it once more. In July 1655 he introduced a new system of government under which 12 major-generals were appointed, with each ruling one of 12 English regions. However, this system also proved unpopular and ineffective. Another House of Commons was elected in 1656.

In April-May 1657, the Commons again urged Cromwell to take the crown and become King Oliver, but after agonizing over the decision and, according to some accounts coming very close to accepting, Cromwell refused again. He declared, 'I would not seek to set up that that providence hath destroyed and laid in the dust'.

On 3 September 1658, Cromwell died aged 59. The extent to which he had become king in all but name, and in contradiction of his dearly held beliefs, was marked by the fact that he named his son, Richard, to be Lord Protector in his stead.

THE RETURN TO MONARCHY

Richard Cromwell's rule lasted only eight months. He resigned as Lord Protector when army leaders recalled the 'Rump Parliament' of 1648. The Rump Parliament could not impose its authority, however, and MPs and army still fought for supremacy.

In early 1660 General Monck, commander of the army in Scotland, marched to London and won the agreement of the Rump assembly to dissolve itself and recall the Long Parliament originally formed in 1640. This opened the way for a new election and another new Parliament and the prospect of a return of the monarchy.

A KING ON THE RUN

After the destruction of his hopes of regaining the crown at the Battle of Worcester on 3 September 1651, Charles II fled the battlefield in a charge of cavalry down Worcester High Street. He was on the run.

Changing into some old clothes and applying blacking to his face as disguise, he cut across country towards the sea. He attempted to take the ferry over the river Severn but, finding it guarded, he turned back to seek cover in woodland. By good fortune he met a Catholic royalist, William Carlis, who warned him that Cromwell's men were searching the woods. The pair decided to hide in the branches of a lone oak tree in an open field, reasoning that it was so prominent a spot that it would not be searched. Later Charles travelled in disguise as the servant of Miss Jane Lane, sister of a royalist colonel, and finally – some six weeks after Worcester – made it to Shoreham, west Sussex, from where he fled to safety in France aboard a coal brig, the *Surprise*.

Below: Before his failed invasion of England, Charles II was crowned at Scone in 1651.

CHAPTER EIGHT

THE RESTORATION OF THE STUARTS

1660–1714

The execution of King Charles I on 30 January 1649 appeared to be the end for the royal house of Stuart. Indeed, when Parliament abolished the monarchy on 17 March 1649, it seemed to mark the point of no return for all of England's royal rulers. However, after the death of Oliver Cromwell in 1658 and the apparent failure of the Commonwealth and Protectorate, Charles I's son Charles Stuart was recalled from exile in the Low Countries. He returned to London amid public rejoicing on 29 May 1660. Diarist John Evelyn recorded, 'This day came in his Majesty Charles the 2nd to London after a sad and long exile ... with a triumph of above 20,000 horse and foot, brandishing their swords and shouting with unexpressable joy: the ways strewn with flowers, the bells ringing, the streets hung with tapestry ... the windows and balconies all set with ladys, trumpets, music, and ... people flocking the streets.' Charles II was crowned on 23 April 1661.

Stuart monarchs reigned for a further 54 years. Even when Charles II's Catholic brother, James II, was overthrown and replaced according to the will of Parliament by the Protestant William III, Stuarts remained on the throne, for William was Charles II's nephew and William's wife and joint sovereign, Mary II, was James II's daughter. The Stuart line is said to have ended with the death of Mary's sister, Queen Anne, and the accession under the Act of Settlement of King George, first ruler of the House of Hanover. However, even George had a blood connection to the Stuarts, for he was the son of Sophia, Electress of Hanover, who was King James I's granddaughter.

Left: Monarchy restored, in an imposing figure. Charles II was powerfully built, standing 6ft 2in (1.88m) tall. He had black hair, an olive complexion and dark brown eyes.

CHARLES II

1660–1685

Charles Stuart, son of the executed King Charles I, arrived in London to claim the English throne on 29 May 1660, his 30th birthday. Cheering crowds lined the streets, flowers were cast in the roadway and the bells rang out in the City of London to acclaim the restoration of the English monarchy following the harsh years of the English Commonwealth and Protectorate.

Some three and a half months earlier, on 16 March, the reconstituted Long Parliament of 1640 had voted to dissolve ahead of elections. The newly elected Convention Parliament that assembled on 25 April was strongly pro-royalist and on 1 May declared that the government should be by a restored king, House of Lords and House of Commons. MPs approved Charles's restoration on the basis of the king's Declaration of Breda, in the Low Countries, which he issued on 4 April. He promised a general pardon; liberty of conscience in religion; to pay the army and take soldiers into his own service on the same conditions they presently enjoyed; and to entrust Parliament with settling disputes over land ownership arising from the troubles of the previous 20 years. On this basis, the Lords and Commons proclaimed Charles king on 8 May.

CHARLES II, KING OF ENGLAND, SCOTLAND AND IRELAND, 1660–1685

Birth: 29 May 1630, St James's Palace, London
Father: Charles I
Mother: Henrietta Maria
Accession: 30 Jan 1649
Coronation: 1 Jan 1651, Scone (Scotland); 23 April 1661 (Westminster Abbey)
Queen: Catherine of Braganza (m. 21 May 1662; d. 1705)
Succeeded by: His brother, James II
Greatest achievement: Regaining and retaining the crown
4 April 1660: Charles Stuart issues Declaration of Breda
8 May 1660: Parliament proclaims him King Charles II
29 May 1660: Charles enters London
24 March 1663: Grants North American lands of 'Carolina' to eight wealthy noblemen
8 July 1663: Grants royal charter to Rhode Island colony
2–6 Sept 1666: Great Fire of London
1678: Former priest Titus Oates alleges Catholic plot to kill Charles
1681: Grants lands of Pennsylvania to Quaker William Penn
1683: Rye House Plot foiled
Death: 6 Feb 1685. Buried in King Henry VIII Chapel, Westminster Abbey

A FINE CORONATION

Colour, spectacle and glamour were emphasized in Charles's coronation on 23 April 1661. Wearing robes of crimson velvet and cloth of gold, riding a horse fitted with a gold- and pearl-encrusted saddle, he rode through the city in a magnificent procession past splendid theatrical tableaux, from Tower Hill to Westminster Abbey.

London diarist Samuel Pepys attended the Coronation ceremony in the Abbey. It was so crowded, he reported, that he had to take his place some seven hours before the service began. He saw, 'The king in his robes, bare headed, which was very fine ... in the Quire at the high altar he passed all the ceremonies of the Coronacion ... the crowne being put upon his head, a great shout begun ... and three times the King-at-armes ... proclaimed that if any one could show any reason why Ch.Steward should not be King of

Below: King Charles II's coronation procession. New crowns and regalia were made at a cost of £12,000.

Above: On the night of the Great Fire of London, flames illuminate Ludgate and old St Paul's. This anonymous oil painting of the disaster was made c.1670.

England, that he should come and speak'. Afterwards silver medals were thrown into the congregation, but Pepys was unable to get hold of one. A splendid coronation feast followed, then as the day ended a great thunderstorm burst over Whitehall – which Pepys interpreted as a good omen for the new king's reign.

A LOVER OF PLEASURE

While he was astute in his handling of parliamentary, military and religious factions, and a convinced believer in the sacredness of absolute monarchy, Charles was not a pious or particularly serious man. He was charismatic and charming and a passionate collector of mistresses, even after his 1662 wedding to the Portuguese Infanta, Catherine of Braganza. He once declared that he did not believe God would 'Make a man miserable only for taking a little pleasure out of the way'.

PLAGUE AND FIRE

There were many among the new king's population who looked with horror at his court's devotion to pleasure. When two disasters struck England within years of the Restoration, Puritan critics could claim that the events were evidence of God's displeasure at the hasty abandonment of England's great republican experiment.

Bubonic plague was a regular threat to London's crowded streets from the start of the 17th century onwards, but it hit with particular virulence following a heat wave in June 1665. Charles, his court and Parliament fled to Oxford, while the exchequer was moved to Surrey. In London, fires burned in the streets in an attempt to cleanse the air. As many as 70,000 people died.

Then on 2–6 September 1666 the Great Fire of London ravaged the capital. Beginning in the early hours of 2 September at the king's bakery in Pudding Lane, close to London Bridge, the fire was whipped by a strong east wind and spread quickly through London's narrow streets of tightly packed wooden houses. Pepys wrote, 'We saw the fire as only one entire arch of fire…it made me weep to see it. The churches, houses, and all on fire and flaming at once, and horrid noise the flames made, and the cracking of houses at their ruin'.

The Great Fire made 100,000 people homeless and destroyed 13,000 houses and 87 parish churches as well as St Paul's Cathedral. On 4 September King Charles did his reputation no harm by turning out to fight the fire with his people in the streets. He could be seen, clothes sodden and face blackened with smoke, working side by side with the desperate Londoners. He also sent food to the poverty-stricken and money to boost fire control efforts. Afterwards he promised the devastated people of London that he would build a splendid new city of stone and brick.

Above: The plague was a recurrent threat. Charles was happy to revive the traditional practice of royal cure by laying on hands.

OAK APPLE DAY

After Charles's triumphant entry into London on 29 May 1660, Parliament voted that this day should be kept as a national holiday; in the words of diarist Samuel Pepys, 'As a day of thanksgiving for our redemption from tyranny and the king's return to his Government'. It was named Oak Apple Day, a reference to Charles's escape from the troops of the Parliamentary army when he hid in an oak tree near Boscobel House, Shropshire, following the Battle of Worcester, in 1651.

Above: Protective species that sheltered a king, the oak tree is celebrated as a symbol of endurance and of Englishness.

THE MERRY MONARCH

RESTORATION LIFE

On 21 May 1662 Charles II married the pious Catholic princess Catherine of Braganza, daughter of the King of Portugal. Under the marriage treaty, which cemented an English-Portuguese-French alliance against Spain, Catherine would maintain her allegiance to the Catholic Church while agreeing that any children of the marriage should be raised as Protestants. On the wedding day, the royal couple went through two ceremonies. The first, conducted in private, was a Catholic one. The second, conducted in public, was the official Church of England rite.

MANY MISTRESSES

Queen Catherine brought a vast dowry to the marriage, which included £360,000 and the Portuguese overseas possessions of Bombay and Tangier. Charles, for his part, promised that he intended to be a good husband. However, marriage vows did not prevent the promiscuous king from continuing to pursue his favourite sport of collecting mistresses. One of these, Lady Castlemaine, was a long-standing lover whom Charles had met before the Restoration, at Breda. At his wedding she was appointed among Queen Catherine's ladies of the bedchamber, despite the fact that she had borne Charles a son the previous year. Subsequently, Charles recognized several children of this liaison as his own, and according to royal convention gave them the name 'Fitzroy'.

Another mistress of the early years was Lucy Walter, the daughter of a prominent Welsh family and 'Brown, beautiful and bold' according to diarist John Evelyn. She was intimate with the king in 1648–51, and her son of 1649, initially known as 'James Fitzroy', later became James Scott, Duke of Monmouth, who was championed as a possible Protestant successor to King Charles in his latter years.

Another mistress was Italian duchess Hortense Mancini, to whom Charles gave rooms in St James's Palace, where he visited her nightly. According to court gossips, he was drawn as much by her expertise in the arts of love as by her alluring dark beauty.

Among Charles's most celebrated lovers was actress Nell Gwynn, who became the king's mistress in 1670. She reportedly called him Charles the Third on the grounds that he was 'The third Charley' she had accepted into her bed. The following year the king also took up with a French Catholic noblewoman, Louise de Kéroualle. When the outspoken Nell Gwynn had her carriage jostled by a crowd who had mistaken her for her unpopular Catholic rival, she exclaimed, 'Pray good people be civil, I am the Protestant whore'.

Above: Restoration gallant. The king's roguish love of pleasure is suggested in this portrait by Peter Lely (1618–80).

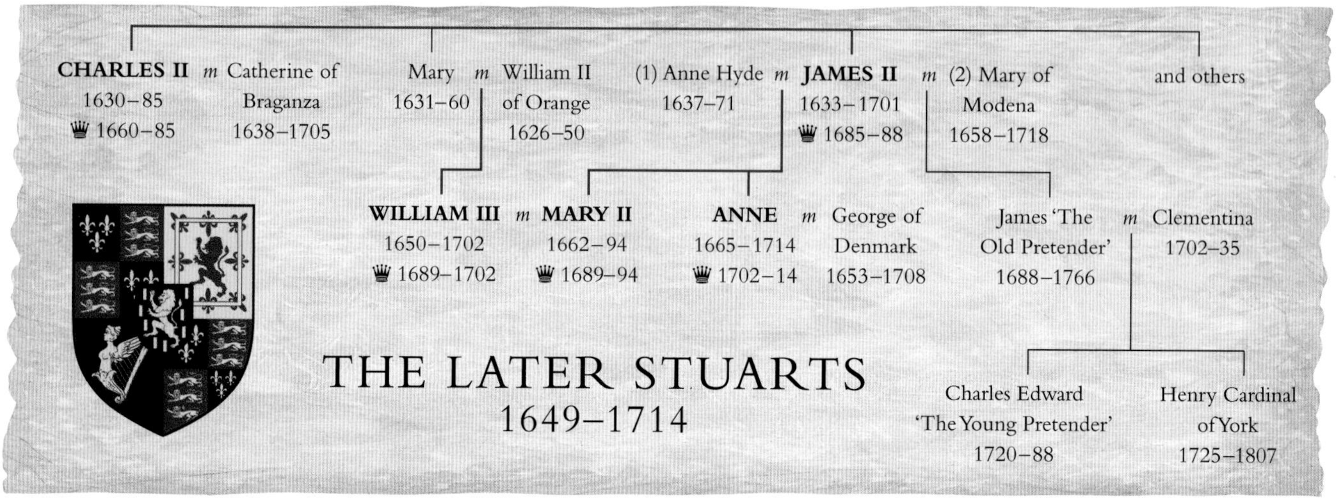

Above: Barbara Villiers, Lady Castlemaine. Charles II reputedly spent his first night as king in her company. Samuel Pepys reported her exceptional beauty.

Above: 'Pretty, witty Nell'. Nell Gwynn was the only one of Charles's mistresses to be popular with the public. She was widely liked for her impudence and indiscretions.

SPORT AND GAMES

Charles was also a lover of sports. Before the English Restoration, when he was crowned King by the Scots at Scone in 1651, he rounded off the celebrations that followed a vast banquet by playing a round of golf. He also pioneered yachting in England. His first taste of the sport came when he received a small racing yacht, the *Mary*, from the City of Amsterdam as a present to mark the Restoration. He himself then designed a larger version that was christened the *Jamie*. On 1 October 1661 he raced the *Jamie* against his brother, the Duke of York, sailing a Dutch yacht called the *Bezan* from Greenwich to Gravesend and back again. Charles's *Jamie* won by a distance of 3 miles (5km).

At Newmarket in Suffolk the king was a frequent visitor to the racecourse, and rode his own stallion, 'Old Rowley', in races on the heath. On 14 October 1671 the king won a race over 4 miles (6.5km) on the Newmarket course. He built a summer house, afterwards called 'the King's Chair', from which he could watch the races – and began his own racing establishment, the Palace House Stables. His love of entertainment, coupled with his easy-going manner and enjoyment of pleasure, won him the nickname the 'Merry Monarch'.

RESTORATION THEATRE

Charles II was a keen and appreciative patron of the arts and sciences. London's theatres had been closed by the Puritan establishment in the years of the Commonwealth and the Protectorate. In 1662, Charles granted patents to Thomas Killigrew and Sir William Davenant to open theatres. Thomas Killigrew inaugurated the *Theatre Royal* in Covent Garden on 7 May 1663 with a performance of *The Humorous Lieutenant* by John Fletcher and Francis Beaumont.

After the years of repression, London's theatres burst forth once more in the vibrant stage scene of 'Restoration theatre'. The works of playwrights John Dryden (appointed Poet Laureate in 1668), Beaumont and Fletcher, and William Wycherley were widely performed and praised to the skies. Henry Purcell was appointed court composer in 1677.

Below: Londoners rejoiced at the reopening of the city's theatres at the Restoration. This engraving shows the Duke's Theatre, Lincoln's Inn Fields, in Charles II's time.

A ROYAL SOCIETY OF SCIENTISTS

The reign of Charles saw a powerful surge of scientific achievement. Robert Boyle, Robert Hooke, Isaac Newton, Edmond Halley and John Flamsteed were all at work during this period. This achievement was encouraged by the king, who granted a charter to a group of scientists to found the Royal Society on 22 April 1662.

In 1675 Charles appointed Flamsteed the first 'Astronomer Royal' and in 1675–76 built the Greenwich Royal Observatory. Boyle published his *The Sceptical Chemist* in 1661; Newton demonstrated his theories on the laws of gravity at the Royal Society in 1683–4, and in 1687 he published his masterwork, the *Philosophiae Naturalis Principia Mathematica* ('Mathematical Principles of Natural Philosophy' – generally known as the Principia).

Hooke experimented with early reflecting microscopes and published his *Micrographia* ('Small Drawings') in 1665. He was one of the earliest pioneers of the theory of evolution.

CHARLES II AND THE 'NEW WORLD'

THE GROWTH OF NORTH AMERICA

Above: A European treaty with major consequences for America. The Dutch ceded the future 'New York' to England under the Treaty of Breda, 31 July 1667.

The England of Charles II was in fierce competition with the Netherlands for control of maritime trade around the globe and in particular the sea transport of West African slaves to North America.

'NEW AMSTERDAM'

In 1664 an English privateering fleet took possession of the Dutch fur-trading post at 'New Amsterdam' on the Hudson River in North America. This settlement, at the foot of Manhattan Island, had been established for almost 40 years, since 1625. In 1664 its Dutch director-general, Peter Stuyvesant, offered no resistance to the English occupiers.

However, the following year, in the wake of this attack and English raids on Dutch slave-trading posts in West Africa, the Dutch declared war on England.

Below: James, Duke of York, ruled the territory of 'New York' with absolute authority under the 'duke's laws'.

The war lasted just two years. It began with a great English victory, as James, the Duke of York, sunk 16 Dutch vessels and captured nine more in the Battle of Lowestoft. However, in June and August 1666 ferocious sea battles caused vast losses of men and ships on both sides. England's position was further weakened by the effects of the 1665 Great Plague and the 1666 Great Fire of London. Then in 1667, with the English navy staying in port to conserve resources, the Dutch struck a humiliating blow: sailing brazenly up the Thames estuary, they burst into Chatham harbour, sunk four warships and left with no less a prize than the *Royal Charles*, the Duke of York's flagship. Both England and the Netherlands were by now keen to broker peace, and the Treaty of Breda ending the war was signed on 31 July 1667.

Under the treaty, the Dutch gave England 'New Amsterdam' and the surrounding area, while in return they gained possession of Surinam in South America. The English renamed the Manhattan Island settlement 'New York' in honour of the king's brother James, the Duke of York. The two principal boroughs were King's (for King Charles) and Queen's (for Queen Catherine); the first is now called Brooklyn but the second has retained its original name.

The wider surrounding area was the former Dutch colony of New Netherland, established by the Dutch West India Company in 1624 at Fort Orange (modern Albany, New York state) to provide access to the lucrative trade in furs from the Great Lakes. Charles gave this land to the Duke of York in return for an annual 'rent' of 40 beaver skins.

The Duke of York granted control of land between the Hudson and Delaware rivers to John, Lord Berkeley and Sir George Carteret. They named the land 'New Jersey' after the island of Jersey in the English Channel where Carteret was born and where he had served as Lieutenant Governor. The territory later passed into the hands of Quaker entrepreneurs, one of whom was William Penn, founder of Pennsylvania.

THE COLONY OF CAROLINA

Shortly after the Restoration, on 24 March 1663, Charles granted a wide tract of North America to a group of eight nobles, including Lord Ashley, the Duke of Albemarle, the Earl of Clarendon and the New Jersey founders Lord Berkeley and Sir George Carteret. These men founded the colony of Carolina (from the Latin form of their monarch's name). Lord Ashley's secretary, the philosopher John Locke, wrote the constitution for the new colony.

Two years later, the area of the colony, which already ran from the Atlantic to the Pacific, was further extended. In this form the vast landholding included all the following US states: North and South Carolina, Alabama, Arkansas, Arizona, Georgia, Louisiana, Mississippi, New Mexico, Oklahoma and Tennessee, as well as parts of southern California, Nevada, Florida, Missouri and of Mexico.

A RELIGIOUS HAVEN

In 1663 Charles granted a royal charter to Baptist clergyman John Clarke for the colony of Rhode Island. The colony had been founded in 1636, by Roger Williams, a religious émigré. Charles's charter guaranteed the Rhode Island colonists freedom of religious conscience: 'No person within the said colony, at any time hereafter shall be any wise molested, punished, disquieted, or called in question, for any differences in opinion in matters of religion'.

In 1679 Charles declared the land of New Hampshire a separate royal province. The colony had been founded under King Charles I in the 1620s, and named New Hampshire in 1629. For almost 40 years prior to the 1679 declaration, New Hampshire was governed as part of Massachussetts Bay Colony. English colonization of North America was therefore well advanced by the end of Charles II's reign.

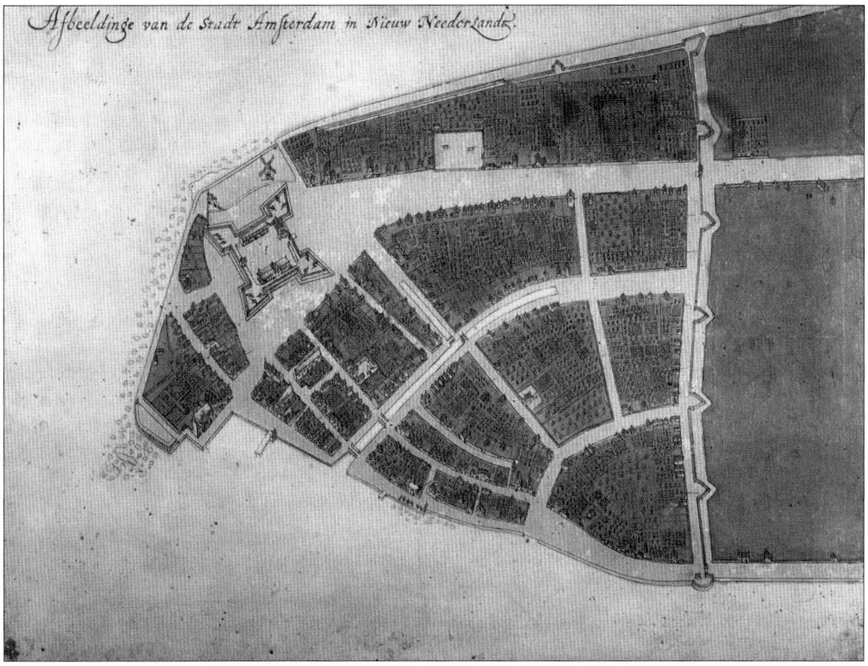

Above: Manhattan as it was. This view of New Amsterdam is from 1660, before the settlement passed into English hands.

A CHRISTIAN COMMONWEALTH: PENNSYLVANIA

In 1681 King Charles made a large grant of land west of the Delaware river to his friend William Penn, a leading Quaker. The grant was by way of cancelling a large debt Charles owed to Penn's father, Admiral Sir William Penn.

On the land so given, William Penn founded the American Commonwealth of Pennsylvania (named in honour of his father). It was intended to be a refuge for Quakers and other religious groups exiled by European persecution, and an explicit attempt to create a perfect Christian commonwealth.

In the same year, Penn also received the 'lower counties' (the lands that became the modern US state of Delaware) as a grant from the Duke of York. The city of Philadelphia was laid out on a grid pattern according to Penn's instructions.

Above: At court in London, a soberly dressed William Penn (right) receives the charter for Pennsylvania from the king.

THE REBUILDING OF LONDON
AFTER THE GREAT FIRE OF 1666

The Great Fire of London broke out in a baker's shop in Pudding Lane on the night of 2 September 1666 and destroyed most of the City.

Above: Sir Christopher Wren, with St Paul's behind. Wren was a Mason, and full Masonic rites attended the laying of the St Paul's foundation stone in June 1675.

A NEW CITY

Just days after the fire, Charles II was presented with three separate plans for reconstruction. One was drawn up by chemist and architect Robert Hooke, one by diarist and courtier John Evelyn, who had already served on pre-fire commissions for improving London's streets (1662), and one by Christopher Wren, Savilian Professor of Astronomy at Oxford University (from 1661), who had already designed the Sheldonian Theatre in Oxford (1662).

All three plans recommended regularizing the street layout, but in the event none was adopted, principally because London's landlords were unwilling to countenance changes that would lead to drops in rent, and there was a shortage of money to offer them compensation. In 1667 a Rebuilding Act provided for certain streets to be made wider, set improved standards for house-building and imposed a tax on coal imports to raise funds for rebuilding. This tax was increased in another act of 1670. Charles also gave a boost to redevelopment by repealing the tax on hearthstones. Hooke and Wren both played central roles in the reconstruction of the city. Hooke was appointed city surveyor for the building of houses, while Wren was made surveyor-general of the king's works in 1669.

In this capacity Wren supervised the rebuilding of St Paul's Cathedral and of London's parish churches. Although 87 churches had been destroyed, only 52 were rebuilt because smaller parishes were amalgamated. Wren personally designed or approved each one.

Below: Wren's masterpiece. The section, elevation and half-plan of the architect's third and final design for St Paul's.

'RESURGAM'

Wren's new St Paul's Cathedral was built to the third design he produced: his second and favourite design was approved by King Charles but had to be dropped because of opposition to it among the canons of St Paul's. Building began in 1675 following the issue of a royal warrant that gave Wren liberty 'To make some variations rather ornamental than essential, as from time to time he should see proper'. For the foundation stone, Wren asked a workman to find a flat piece from the remains of the first cathedral. The stone, which Wren laid himself, was a fragment of a grave headstone bearing the Latin inscription

Resurgam ('I will rise again'). St Paul's Cathedral was not finished until 1710 – although the structure was complete enough for the first service to be held there in 1697. Its magnificent dome became a London landmark.

Above: Whitehall Palace and St James's Park in the 17th century. In 1678, Titus Oates claimed that 'Popish plotters' intended to kidnap the king in the park.

THE SUCCESSION QUESTION

In the 1670s, after Queen Catherine had had several miscarriages, Charles's subjects began to suspect that he would not produce a legitimate heir, despite the fact that he had maintained a regular and generous output of illegitimate offspring with his many mistresses. The likelihood that the throne would pass to Charles's brother James, Duke of York, began to seem a potential calamity after James married the Catholic Mary of Modena in 1673 and word spread that the duke had himself secretly converted to Catholicism.

The staunchly Protestant Whig party in the Commons repeatedly sought to bar the Duke of York from the accession, but although bills were voted through in the Commons, Charles outmanoeuvred the Whigs to prevent them becoming law. However, the king was unable to prevent the passing of severe laws that barred Catholics from Parliament and even from residing in London, and the Catholic Duke of York was sent into exile in 1679–80.

An assassination plan was uncovered in 1683. The Rye House Plot took its name from a house used by Charles and the Duke of York when they travelled from London to Newmarket in Suffolk to attend horse-racing meetings. The plan was to seize the royal pair and place Charles's illegitimate son, the Protestant Duke of Monmouth, on the throne. When the plot was uncovered, Monmouth, Charles's son by his mistress Lucy Walter, fled into exile.

A CATHOLIC AT THE LAST

King Charles II died on 6 February 1685. On his deathbed he secretly converted to the Catholicism espoused by his wife and feared by his subjects. He was severely unwell for four days after suffering a stroke, but maintained his good humour and before he died made his peace with his queen and many illegitimate offspring. Queen Catherine, who had loved him powerfully throughout his years of philandering, sat patiently with him during the illness, but was absent at the end because she grieved so fiercely. When she sent an apology for not being present, the king exclaimed, 'Alas, poor woman. She beg my pardon? I beg hers with all my heart!'

Above: In his final hours, Charles found peace and listened to his conscience.

Meanwhile in 1670, 1678 and 1681 Charles made secret deals allying himself with the French king Louis XIV in return for substantial payments. The first agreement contained an explosive clause in which Charles promised to announce his conversion to Catholicism and to accept military and financial aid from the French if – as it surely would – this provoked unrest among his subjects. Historians are divided over whether Charles was committed to these agreements or whether he played Louis along for the financial benefit, which was significant enough to make him independent of Parliament for the last four years of his reign, 1681–5.

'A PRETTY, WITTY KING'

Charles was remembered indulgently by his subjects as the 'Merry Monarch', celebrated in the Earl of Rochester's lines, 'We have a pretty witty king, Whose word no man relies on; Who never said a foolish thing, nor ever did a wise one.' Although he has been criticised for lacking seriousness of mind and application to the affairs of government, he did succeed in stabilizing the monarchy after the troubled years of the Commonwealth and Protectorate.

JAMES II AND VII
1685–1688

The Catholic succession to King Charles II's throne that had been so feared and agitated against by the Whigs in Parliament became reality on 6 February 1685. The king's avowedly Catholic brother, James, was crowned in Westminster Abbey on 23 April and almost at once had to deal with a Protestant challenge to his authority.

PROTESTANT REBELLION

Charles's illegitimate son, the Duke of Monmouth, landed at Lyme Regis on 11 June with a mere 82 supporters to stake his claim as the Protestant heir to the throne. Although he managed to gather a force of 4,000-odd soldiers, his army was routed by royalists at the Battle of Sedgemoor on 6 July.

Meanwhile the Presbyterian Earl of Argyll returned from exile in the Low Countries to try to provoke a Scottish uprising. He did raise an army of around 1,500 – largely from his own Clan Campbell – but, faced with royalist troops, Argyll was captured and the rebellion melted away.

Above: James II's three years on the throne were a brief interlude between life as a prince, before, and a long exile, afterwards.

JAMES II AND VII, KING OF ENGLAND, SCOTLAND AND IRELAND, 1685–1688

Birth: 14 Oct 1633
Father: Charles I
Mother: Henrietta Maria
Accession: 6 Feb 1685
Coronation: 23 April 1685, Westminster Abbey
Wives: (1) before accession married to Anne Hyde (m. 3 Sept 1660; d. 31 March 1671); (2) Mary of Modena (m. 30 Sept 1673; d. 7 May 1718)
Succeeded by: His daughter Mary II and his son-in-law Prince William of Orange
Greatest achievement: Putting down anti-Catholic revolts in 1685
6 July 1685: Battle of Sedgemoor: defeat of Duke of Monmouth
15 July 1685: Monmouth executed
4 April 1687: James issues Declaration of Indulgence
10 June 1688: Birth of King James's son, Prince James Francis Edward
30 June 1688: Nobles call on William of Orange to invade
5 Nov 1688: William of Orange lands at Torbay
23 Dec 1688: Formally deposed as king by Parliament
Death: 6 Sept 1701, in exile at St Germain, France

King James was triumphant – and secure. Argyll was beheaded in Edinburgh on 30 June. Monmouth begged for his life but was despatched in a horribly bungled execution on 15 July in which six strokes of the axe were required to kill the duke.

In the wake of these revolts James greatly expanded the army and granted command of new regiments to Catholic officers, especially in Ireland. This latter issue provoked a row with Parliament, which the king prorogued in November 1685. It did not meet again during his brief reign.

PRINCE OR FOUNDLING?

Protestant opponents of the Catholic King James II drew comfort from the fact that his only feasible heirs were Protestant. None of the 10 children of James and his queen Mary of Modena survived infancy, and his two surviving daughters from his previous marriage to Anne Hyde, Mary and Anne, had both made marriages to important Protestant royals; Mary to Prince William of Orange and Anne to Prince George of Denmark.

On 10 June 1688 all that changed as Queen Mary gave birth to a healthy boy, later given a Catholic christening as James Francis Edward and a powerful godfather in Pope Innocent XI. A Catholic succession was again a possibility. Some Protestants refused to accept this unwelcome development: they argued that the infant was not Mary's own, but was a foundling child who had been smuggled into the palace in a warming pan. Mary and Anne's representatives were absent from the birth and so they could not vouch for the child.

RELIGIOUS TOLERATION

James then tried to take on the Anglican establishment. On 4 April 1687 he issued a Declaration of Indulgence that suspended all laws punishing Catholic or Protestant dissenters against the Church of England. He began to promote Catholics to positions of authority in the Privy Council, courts and universities. Some of his public statements suggested that he acted out a desire for religious toleration, others that he was truly – as his opponents feared – seeking to re-establish Catholicism as the English state religion.

Matters came to a head in 1688 when Queen Mary gave birth to a healthy son after a long succession of miscarriages and infant deaths, suddenly and unexpectedly raising the prospect of a Catholic succession to the throne.

Above: The Duke of Monmouth begs for his life before the king. Victorian artist John Pettie painted this dramatic canvas.

Earlier James had ordered his Declaration of Indulgence to be reissued and read in churches, and when the Archbishop of Canterbury and six bishops wrote a petition asking him to withdraw the order, he had them cast into the Tower of London and prosecuted for seditious libel.

On 30 June all seven churchmen were acquitted of the charge. It became clear that public opinion had swung decisively against the king, for crowds on the London streets cheered the release of the bishops and bonfires were lit to celebrate their freedom. On the very same day, seven leading Protestant noblemen wrote to Prince William of Orange – husband of Princess Mary, the king's eldest daughter by his first marriage to Anne Hyde – asking him to invade and so secure Protestantism against the Catholic threat.

Prince William landed at Torbay with 15,000 troops on 5 November. The men of the West Country rose in support. A royalist army marched as far as Salisbury but was decimated by senior desertions. James fled back to London. On 11 December, after William had marched into the capital and begun negotiations, James took flight again. As he crossed the Thames at Vauxhall, he let the Great Seal fall into the water. He got as far as Faversham and took ship for France, but was arrested and returned to London. Finally, William ordered him to leave and he escaped to France on 23 December 1688.

Below: In 1688 the Archbishop of Canterbury and six bishops were sent to the Tower of London on charges of seditious libel.

THE 'GLORIOUS REVOLUTION'

1688

When William of Orange and Princess Mary, daughter of King James II, jointly acceded to the throne on 13 February 1689, it marked the first time in English history that a royal succession had been settled not by hereditary right, military might or possession of the crown and treasury, but by the will of the two Houses of Parliament.

CONSORT OR KING?

On 23 December 1688 – the day that King James II succeeded in escaping to France – the peers and bishops of the House of Lords asked William to assume the duties of government. William summoned all the surviving MPs from the reign of Charles II to sit in the Commons. William turned down a suggestion that he should claim the throne himself by right of conquest.

On 28 January 1689 the Commons declared that James II's flight to France was an abdication of the government and that the throne was therefore vacant. The Protestant Whigs in the House of Commons were largely in favour of the throne passing to William and Mary, but in the Lords the Tory supporters of absolute monarchy were concerned to safeguard the principle of hereditary succession. Tory suggestions that Mary should rule alone (having inherited the throne as King James II's daughter), or that William and Mary should govern as regents until James II died, came to nothing. On 3 February 1689 William declared that he would not agree to rule as regent or as Mary's consort. He demanded the full power and sovereignty of a monarch, jointly held with his wife.

Below: An allegory of the 'Glorious Revolution'. The pope (right) is offended, but Magna Carta and Liberty approve.

CONSTITUTIONAL MONARCHY

On 12 February 1689 Princess Mary arrived in London after travelling from the Netherlands, and both houses of Parliament agreed a 'Declaration of Rights'. When on the following day William and Mary accepted the terms of this declaration and were elevated to the throne as joint rulers, a new kind of royal government was brought into being: constitutional monarchy.

The Declaration of Rights, which was made formal in a Bill of Rights passed on 16 December 1689, made a number of ground-breaking changes to the relationship between monarch and Parliament. The monarch was barred from keeping a standing army, and Parliament had final authority in declaring war, raising taxes and passing laws. Free elections to Parliament would be held every three years, and MPs would be guaranteed freedom of speech. Subjects also had the right to petition the monarch on matters of concern. All Protestants had the right to carry arms for self-defence, to enjoy freedom from cruel and unusual punishments and excessive bail, and to live free from fines imposed without trial.

Above: A detail from James Thornhill's Painted Hall at Greenwich shows William and Mary enthroned in regal splendour.

The new settlement also safeguarded the Protestant faith and made explicit a connection between Protestantism and the liberty of Englishmen. The Bill of Rights declared that, 'It hath pleased

THE CIVIL LIST

Under the Civil List Act 1697 Parliament granted William III annual funds of £700,000 for the rest of his life. These were to cover the king's royal and civil expenses.

The Civil List grant replaced an earlier parliamentary voting of funds, made on William's accession with Mary in 1689, of £600,000 annually. The custom of the Civil List was new: previous monarchs were expected to find money for these expenses from hereditary revenues and taxes. However, many earlier kings and queens had had far greater freedom to raise tax income without needing parliamentary approval.

Almighty God to make [William] the glorious instrument of delivering this kingdom from popery and arbitrary power'. Under the bill, all Catholics – including James II and his offspring – and all those married to Catholics were barred from the succession. The document declared, 'It hath been found be experience that it is inconsistent with the safety and welfare of this Protestant Kingdom to be governed by a popish prince'. When William and Mary were

Below: Queen and king. A beadwork bag made by Mary for William celebrates their loving relationship and their joint rule.

Above: A new relationship between monarch and subjects. The Bill of Rights is presented to William and Mary.

crowned on 11 April in Westminster Abbey, they swore new oaths that required them to uphold 'The Protestant reformed religion established by law' and to govern in accordance with the 'Statutes of Parliament'.

The Bill also specified the future Protestant succession: first, through the heirs of Queen Mary II, then through Mary's sister Princess Anne and her heirs and then through any heirs of William III by a later marriage.

SCOTTISH RIGHTS

In Scotland a Convention of Scottish Estates drew up a similar document to the declaration, called a Claim of Right, and passed it on 11 April 1689.

The document declared that James had 'Forfeited the right to the crown' since as a 'Professed papist' he had 'Assumed regal power without ever taking the oath required by law'; that is, 'To swear to maintain the Protestant religion'. He had also, the Claim declared, 'Invaded the fundamental constitution of the Kingdom, and altered it from a legal limited monarchy to an arbitrary despotic power'. Therefore, the Estates said, the throne was vacant.

The Claim, like its English counterpart, barred Catholics from the throne; it also declared the printing of 'popish books' to be illegal and outlawed the practice of sending children abroad for a Catholic education.

William and Mary accepted the Scottish crown on 11 May 1689 in Whitehall. However, they faced considerable opposition to their rule there, particularly in the Highlands, where allegiance to Catholicism and the House of Stuart was strong.

WILLIAM III AND MARY II

1689–1694

On 13 February 1689 William and Mary were jointly offered the throne under a Bill of Rights agreed in both Lords and Commons that made the monarchy subject to Parliament. On 11 April 1689 they were crowned England's joint rulers King William III and Queen Mary II. Almost at once they faced opposition in Scotland from those loyal to King James II. These opponents were called 'Jacobites' from the Latin form, *Jacobus*, of 'James'.

Above: Protestants ride to triumph. American artist Benjamin West painted this view of William's victory at the Boyne.

BONNIE DUNDEE

James II was in exile at the Versailles court of the French king, Louis XIV. He gave his backing to Scots nobleman John Graham, Viscount Dundee, to be his military commander in Scotland. Just two days after William and Mary's coronation, Dundee raised the Jacobite standard in Scotland. Rebels loyal to the ousted king began to muster under the command of this charismatic figure known as 'Bonnie Dundee', a veteran of 1679 struggles against Presbyterians in the cause of Charles II. On 27 July 1689 Dundee led a force of highlanders in a famous victory over a royalist army commanded by General Hugh Mackay at Killiecrankie. This could have proved a turning point, but after the battle Dundee died from a musket shot he received in conflict, and without his leadership the Jacobite cause foundered. The royalist forces regrouped and on 21 August at Dunkeld inflicted a major defeat on the Jacobites that was decisive in the short term.

William demanded oaths of loyalty from the leaders of the Highland clans. When the MacDonald clan chief Alastair MacIain failed to make the oath by the required deadline, troops of the Argyll regiment inflicted a terrible massacre on the MacDonalds at Glencoe on 13 February 1692. Public outrage at this incident combined with the fact that William did not try to punish those responsible for the massacre, undermined his popularity.

IRISH WAR

In Ireland the struggle to secure the Protestant succession provoked a two-year war. James II landed at Kinsale, County Cork, on 12 March 1689 to reclaim his throne. His 20,000-strong

WILLIAM III, KING OF ENGLAND, SCOTLAND AND IRELAND AND PRINCE OF ORANGE, 1689–1702

Birth: 4 Nov 1650, Binnenhof Palace, The Hague
Father: William II, Prince of Orange
Mother: Princess Mary, daughter of Charles I
Accession: 13 Feb 1689
Coronation: 11 April 1689, Westminster Abbey
Queen: Mary (m. 4 Nov 1677; d. 28 Dec 1694)
Succeeded by: His sister-in-law Anne
Greatest achievement: Battle of the Boyne
27 July 1689: Jacobites clash with royalists at Killiecrankie
21 Aug 1689: Royalists victorious at the Battle of Dunkeld
1689–90: Bloody siege of Londonderry
1 July 1690: Defeats James II at the Battle of the Boyne
3 Oct 1691: Irish 'Williamite War' ends with Treaty of Limerick
13 Feb 1692: Glencoe Massacre of MacDonald clansmen
31 Dec 1694: A griefstricken King William breaks down before Parliament
Feb 1695: William acknowledges Princess Anne as his heir
30 July 1700: Anne's only son, William Duke of Gloucester, dies aged 11
6 Sept 1701: Death of exiled King James II at St Germain
Death: 8 March 1702. Buried in Westminster Abbey

MARY II, QUEEN OF ENGLAND, SCOTLAND AND IRELAND, 1689–1694

Birth: 30 April 1662, St James's Palace, London
Father: James, Duke of York (afterwards King James II of England)
Mother: Anne Hyde, daughter of Edward Hyde, 1st Earl of Clarendon
Accession: 13 Feb 1689
Coronation: 11 April 1689, Westminster Abbey
Husband: William (m. 4 Nov 1677; d. 8 March 1702)
Succeeded by: Her husband William, who ruled alone 1694–1702
Greatest achievement: Making the rule of William and Mary popular, despite English dislike of her husband
Death: 28 Dec 1694, dies at Kensington Palace and is buried in Westminster Abbey

French army was boosted by vast numbers of Irish Catholics loyal to his rule. On 4 May 1689 the Irish parliament in Dublin declared the country to be behind James. At first James swept Protestant opposition aside, but at Londonderry (Derry), Ulster, he found the gates closed against him. In December he embarked on a siege of around 105 days. Thousands of lives were lost and the enduring Irish Protestant slogan of 'No Surrender' was born as the city endured the siege until it was lifted by a relief ship.

William landed at Carrickfergus on 24 June 1690. On 1 July, at the head of a vast army of 36,000 soldiers that included Dutch, Germans, French Huguenots and Ulster Protestants as well as Englishmen, he inflicted a decisive defeat on James's army at the Battle of the Boyne, near Drogheda. James fled to France; William returned to England, summoning John Churchill, the Duke of Marlborough, to command royalist forces in Ireland. The war continued for a further 15 months until the Peace of Limerick was signed on 3 October 1691.

A UNITED COUPLE

Although he was celebrated as the upholder of England's Protestant destiny, William was never really popular with his people. He was doubtless distrusted as a foreigner and, in sharp contrast to the flamboyant Charles II, he had an unattractive appearance and manner – short and stooped with severe asthma and a withdrawn character. Queen Mary, by contrast, had an elegant figure and charming manners and at 5ft 11in (1.8m) was a full 5in (12cm) taller than her husband. She was widely acclaimed and proved a dutiful wife. In the normal run of affairs, she left affairs of state and government to William, but when he was abroad at war she demonstrated fine judgement. Mary died aged just 32 from smallpox in 1694. Her devastated husband was left to rule alone.

Above: After defeat at the Battle of the Boyne, the former James II escapes from Ireland by boat, bound for France.

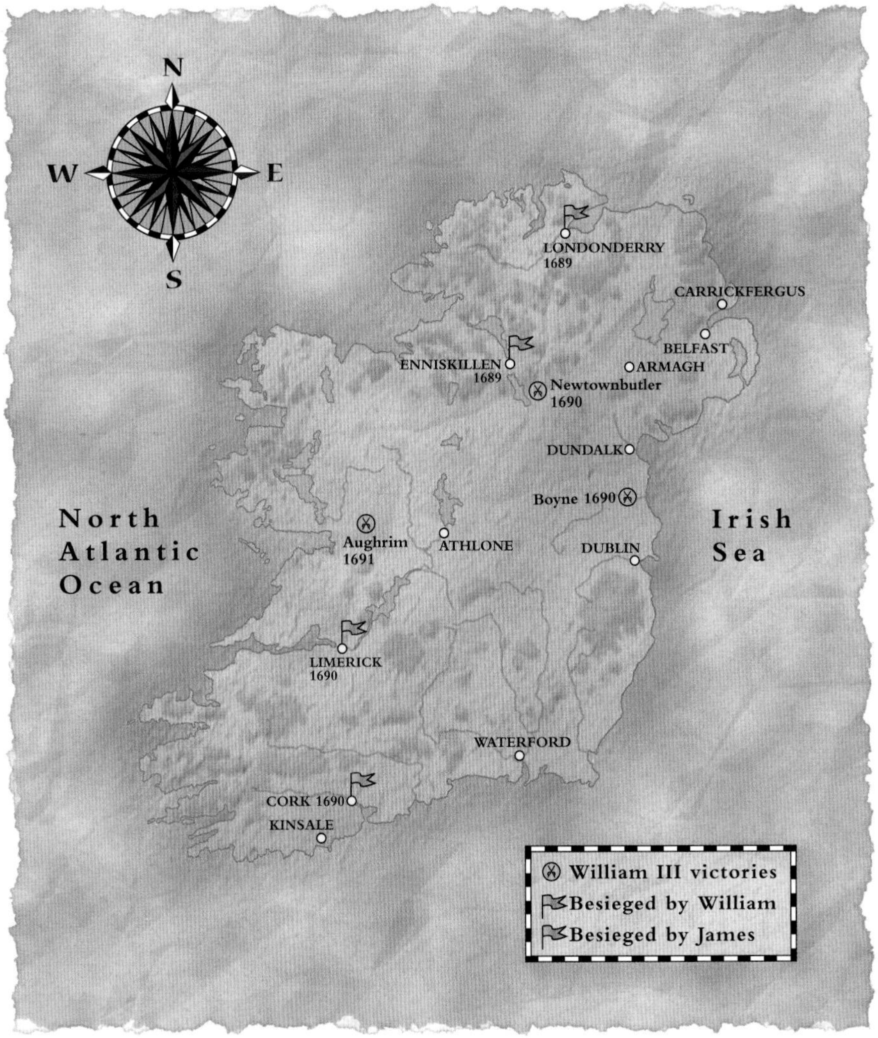

Right: Major battles of the 'Williamite war'. After victory at the Boyne, William's army swept across southern Ireland.

WILLIAM III RULES ALONE

1694–1702

William was so devastated by the death of Queen Mary in 1694 that he was overcome by his emotions in Parliament and could not make a reply when offered the condolences of MPs.

He apparently saw the queen's untimely death as God's judgment on him for his sins. He withdrew from his long-standing affair with Elizabeth Villiers, the eldest daughter of Richmond gentleman Sir Edward Villiers. It seems that it was as a parting gift that he made over to Elizabeth Villiers all King James II's landholdings in Ireland in January 1695.

To escape his grief, William threw himself into the Continental war that had been running since the creation of a Protestant 'Grand Coalition' in 1689, and in September 1695 he led the army to victory over the French at Namur. In the absence of the heirs he had hoped to produce with Queen Mary, he also formally recognized his sister-in-law, the increasingly overweight 30-year-old Princess Anne, as his successor.

JACOBITE PLOTS

In 1696 a failed Jacobite assassination plot had the effect of rallying public opinion in William's favour. The

Above: Sir Godfrey Kneller's portrait masks William's physical failings. In reality the king had a short, stooping figure.

plan, developed at the French court, was for Sir George Barclay – a former associate of 'Bonnie Dundee' – to kidnap and kill the king at Turnham Green as he returned to London from Richmond. However, the details were leaked to the royal party and the attempt was never made; Barclay escaped back to France. Afterwards Parliament passed the Act of Association, laying a requirement on all holders of public office to swear that William was 'rightful and lawful king'; and, because Jacobites made trips to the court of the French king, Louis XIV, to hatch their plans, it was declared high treason to travel from France to England without official authority.

Left: Namur. Despite troublesome swelling of his legs, William himself commanded the English army in France in 1695.

Above: William dies amidst courtiers in the royal bedroom. The crying figure (right) is probably the future Queen Anne.

The Continental war came to an end in 1697 with the Treaty of Ryswick (on the outskirts of the Hague), signed on 20 September between William III, Louis XIV of France and Spain's Charles II. For the first time Louis – who had previously viewed James II as the rightful English king – accepted William as king of England. Other terms of the treaty saw Louis restore most of the conquests he had made since the start of the war in 1689 and recognize the independence of Savoy.

Following the death of James II on 6 September 1701 at St Germain, Louis recognized James's 13-year-old son, James Francis Edward, as the rightful king of England – in direct contravention of the treaty. In England opinion swelled in favour of war with the French. The Commons had voted in April to back the Dutch against the French and in June to ally with Austria and the United Provinces – and on 7 September in the Hague William agreed to ally Britain with the Netherlands and the Holy Roman Empire.

A NEW SUCCESSION CRISIS

At home, the death of the 11-year-old Duke William of Gloucester, only son of William's recognized successor, Princess Anne, put the Protestant succession in jeopardy. On 12 June 1701 Parliament passed the Act of Settlement, which nominated a new and unexpected Protestant heir to follow Anne. The heir was to be Sophia, Electress of Hanover, the daughter of Charles I's sister Elizabeth and her husband Frederick V the Elector Palatinate. The act made it abundantly clear where final authority now resided: in Parliament, which had the gift of the crown among its powers.

Parliament's decision was that it was better to pass the crown to a foreign royal family than to risk it falling into Catholic hands. The Act of Settlement excluded from succession any Catholics who married princesses of the Stuart line. It also tried to limit potential problems arising from giving royal power to the Hanoverian royal line by stating that future monarchs would not be permitted to launch a war 'for the defence of dominions or territories which do not belong to the Crown of England, without the consent of Parliament'. It also stated that future monarchs would not be permitted to depart Britain without parliamentary consent. Additionally, monarchs would be prevented from appointing foreign courtiers to high position under a clause that declared that those born outside Britain might not serve on the privy council.

King William did not live to see the war with France towards which he was manoeuvring the country. On 21 February 1702 he fell from his horse and broke his collarbone after the animal stumbled over a molehill in Richmond Park. The fall plunged him into a terminal decline; he developed pulmonary fever and died on 8 March. In France gleeful Jacobites toasted the mole assassin, 'the little gentleman in his black velvet jacket'.

Right: A king in waiting? This French portrait depicts James II's son, James Edward Stuart, in his early teens.

ANNE
1702–1714

Princess Anne, aged 37, plain of face and prematurely troubled by rheumatism and gout, did not make an inspiring queen when she was crowned in Westminster Abbey on 23 April 1702. She could not offer an heir: the veteran of six miscarriages and eleven stillbirths or infant mortalities, she was childless following the death of her only healthy child, Duke William of Gloucester, in 1700. Moreover, she was inexperienced in government and in affairs of state.

Nevertheless, she presided over a great period for her country, in which English armies won stunning victories over the French and re-established England as a significant European force with growing imperial possessions. The kingdoms of England and Scotland were formally joined in the Kingdom of Great Britain, and in decorative arts Britain reached a new height of elegance with the development of the Queen Anne style.

THE ACT OF UNION

The 1701 Act of Settlement that named the Protestant Hanoverian royal family as Anne's successors had provoked anger in Scotland. The Act of Security of the Kingdom, passed by the Scottish Parliament, in Edinburgh, in August 1703, declared the Scots' willingness to bar the Hanoverian accession and raised the possibility that a Stuart king could be installed in Scotland and join forces with France against England as in the days of the 'Auld Alliance'.

Right: Queen Anne. The suddenness of her death seems to have caught pro-Jacobite Tories unprepared and so helped to secure the Protestant succession to the crown.

To rectify this situation, negotiations for the legal union of England and Scotland formally began in 1706 and on 22 July of that year a draft treaty was agreed by the 62 appointed commissioners, providing for a united kingdom with a single Parliament in Westminster, a single currency, a common union flag and, crucially, a guaranteed Protestant succession to the Hanoverian royal line. In addition, the treaty provided for the Scottish church, education and legal systems to be independent of those in England. With a few minor amendments, and thanks to the sweetening effect of a £400,000 one-off English payment to Scotland and numerous behind-the-scenes bribes – and despite Scottish public opposition strong enough to fuel riots in Edinburgh and Glasgow – the Act of Union was passed by the Scottish Parliament on 16 January 1707. The Act received royal assent in Westminster on 6 March 1707. At a special service of thanksgiving in Sir Christopher Wren's recently completed St Paul's Cathedral on 1 May 1707,

Below: Queen of Great Britain. The articles of Anglo-Scottish union are presented to Anne in 1706.

ANNE, QUEEN OF GREAT BRITAIN AND IRELAND, 1702–1714

Birth: 6 February 1665, St James's Palace
Father: James, Duke of York (afterwards James II)
Mother: Anne Hyde
Accession: 8 March 1702
Coronation: 23 April 1702, Westminster Abbey
Husband: Prince George of Denmark (m. 28 July 1683; d. 28 Oct 1708)
Succeeded by: Her second cousin George I
Greatest achievement: Her government's creation of the Kingdom of Great Britain
1702: England at war with France
August 1704: The Battle of Blenheim
16 January 1707: Scottish Parliament approves Act of Union
6 March 1707: Royal assent to Act of Union
Death: 1 August 1714, Kensington Palace. Buried at Westminster Abbey on 24 August

Right: John Churchill, Duke of Marlborough, signs the despatch at the Battle of Blenheim in August 1704.

Queen Anne wore the insignia of the combined Order of the Garter and Order of the Thistle.

WAR WITH FRANCE

Queen Anne proved a more able and astute ruler than anyone had imagined. Her three principal ministers were all exceptionally able: John Churchill, Duke of Marlborough, who was commander-in-chief and in charge of diplomatic and military affairs; Sidney, Baron Godolphin, Lord Treasurer; and Sir Robert Harley, Secretary of State. The Continental war that was suspended following the 1697 Treaty of Ryswick reignited in 1702, largely in response to Louis XIV's backing of James' II's exiled son, James Francis Edward Stuart, in his claim for the English throne. In this conflict the English army and navy won a series of battles, most famously over Louis's army at the Battle of Blenheim (a village in south-central Germany) in August 1704, which was hailed by contemporaries as a new Agincourt or Crécy. For this great victory Churchill was rewarded with a victory parade in London on 3 January 1705 and the gift of the formerly royal manor of Woodstock, Oxfordshire, later that year. The war continued until 1713 – and one of its enduring consequences was British possession of Gibraltar in southern Spain.

QUEEN ANNE'S FAVOURITES

Before her accession Anne was very close to Sarah, wife of John Churchill, who was made Duke of Marlborough in 1702 and went on to military glory. However, after 1703, Anne's relationship with Sarah became increasingly troubled. The queen appeared to have a new favourite, Abigail Hill. Ironically she was Sarah's relation and had first gained employment as lady of the queen's bedchamber thanks to Sarah's influence. The dispute became very bitter: in 1708 Sarah even accused Anne of being a lesbian, declaring that she had 'no liking for anyone but only her own sex' and quoting a ribald poem that suggested that Abigail and Anne were involved in 'dark Deeds at night'. Anne's friendship with Sarah was cut off finally in 1710. Abigail Masham, as she became on her marriage in 1707, remained close to the queen and was created Lady Masham in 1711.

Right: This portrait of Sarah was made by Robert White (d.1703) during the period in which she dominated Anne.

THE AILING MONARCH

Even at her accession, Queen Anne was visibly unwell, so troubled by rheumatism, weight and gout that she could walk for only a short way with the support of a stick. From at least 1707, she was virtually incapacitated by her poor health, although she continued to play her role in affairs of state. The loss of her devoted husband, Prince George of Denmark, who died in 1708, was a great blow to her. He was a dull but sensible man and she had relied greatly on his advice and support. She had a serious fever in 1713 and the following summer died on 1 August 1714, after falling into a coma. The Stuart line was ended. After some debate in cabinet, the government – in line with the Succession Act – invited Elector George of Hanover to take the throne.

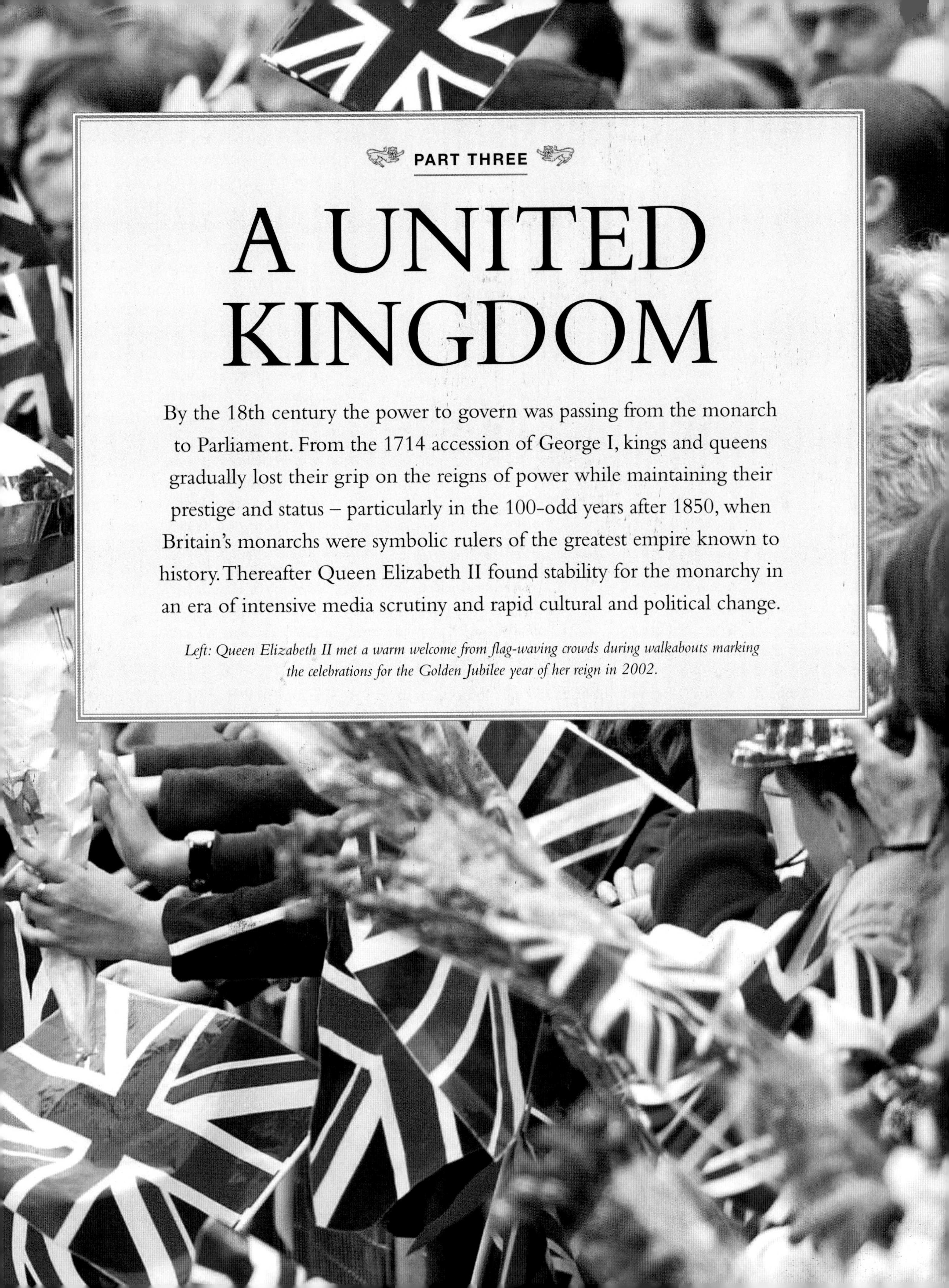

PART THREE

A UNITED KINGDOM

By the 18th century the power to govern was passing from the monarch to Parliament. From the 1714 accession of George I, kings and queens gradually lost their grip on the reigns of power while maintaining their prestige and status – particularly in the 100-odd years after 1850, when Britain's monarchs were symbolic rulers of the greatest empire known to history. Thereafter Queen Elizabeth II found stability for the monarchy in an era of intensive media scrutiny and rapid cultural and political change.

Left: Queen Elizabeth II met a warm welcome from flag-waving crowds during walkabouts marking the celebrations for the Golden Jubilee year of her reign in 2002.

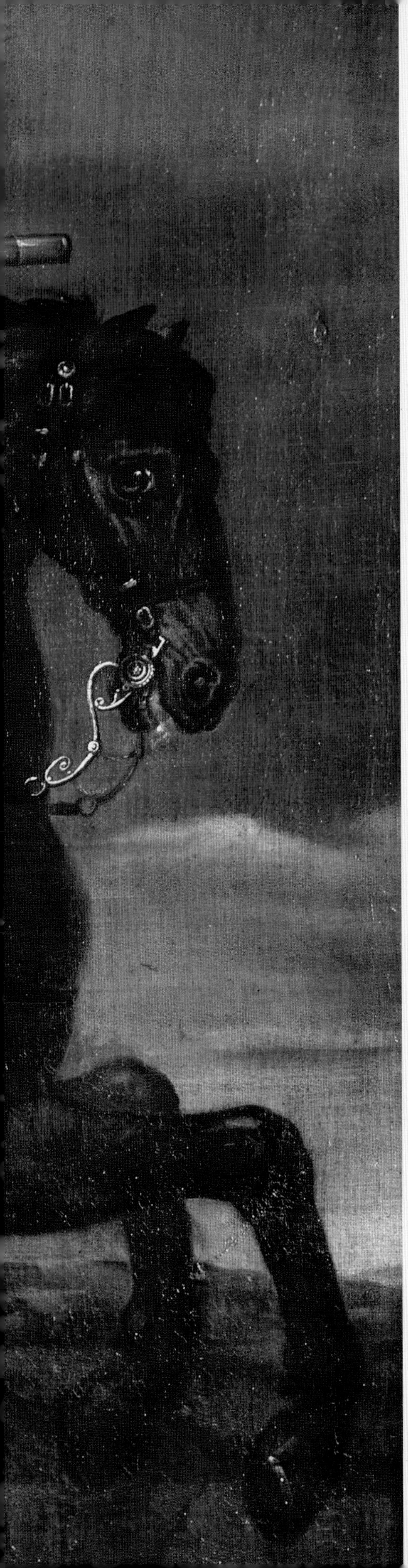

CHAPTER NINE

THE HOUSE OF HANOVER

1714–1760

The 1701 Act of Settlement appeared to establish beyond doubt that on the death of Queen Anne the crown would pass to the Protestant Sophia, Electress of Hanover. However, in the summer of 1714 as Queen Anne was nearing death, the succession remained in the balance, with senior government figures, including Henry St John, Viscount Bolingbroke, supporting the accession of Anne's Stuart half-brother, James Francis Edward, Catholic son of James II. On the very day of Anne's death, 1 August 1714, Viscount Bolingbroke and senior Tories considered declaring James Stuart as King James III. In the end, however, they realized that James's refusal to abandon his Catholicism would make him an unworkable choice, and they acquiesced in the decision of their Whig parliamentary opponents to follow the Act of Settlement. Because the 84-year-old Electress Sophia had died two months earlier, the crown passed to her son, Prince George Louis of Brunswick-Lüneburg, who was declared 'George, by the Grace of God King of Great Britain, France and Ireland'. So the royal House of Stuart, founded in 1371 by Robert II of Scots and ruling in England since the accession of James VI of Scots as James I of England in 1603, came to its end. Its successor was the royal House of Hanover, which was destined to survive a series of attacks by 'Jacobite' supporters of the deposed Stuarts and to endure – through a change of family name to 'Windsor' in the reign of King George V in 1917 – right through to the 21st century.

Left: Hanoverian majesty. Sir Godfrey Kneller, an established Stuart court painter, added lustre to the newly established royal house when he painted this portrait of King George I.

GEORGE I

1714–1727

Prince George Louis, Elector of Brunswick-Lüneburg, was declared King George I outside St James's Palace, London on 1 August 1714, less than nine hours after Queen Anne had died in bed in Kensington. At the age of 54, he set a record as the oldest monarch on accession in British history.

George was in Hanover when he became king. As a monarch, he remained strongly attached to his German roots and throughout his reign as king of Britain was fonder of his birth country than he was of his new domains. He spent as much time as his duties permitted in Hanover and never learned to speak English more than haltingly. He did not gain the affection of his British subjects. From the start he was distrusted as a foreigner, and he took little interest in British customs. He was short, overweight, bad-tempered and lacking in both manners and charm. He was dismissed as 'An honest blockhead' by Lady Mary Wortley Montagu and as 'An honest, dull German gentleman, as unfit as unwilling to act the part of a king' by Lord Chesterfield.

GEORGE I, KING OF GREAT BRITAIN AND IRELAND AND ELECTOR OF HANOVER, 1714–1727

Birth: 28 May 1660, Hanover
Father: Ernst August of Brunswick-Lüneburg
Mother: Sophia, Electress of Hanover
Accession: 1 Aug 1714
Coronation: 20 Oct 1714, Westminster Abbey
Married: Princess Sophia Dorothea of Celle (m. 22 Nov 1682; divorced Dec 1694; d. 13 Nov 1726)
Succeeded by: His son George II
Greatest achievement: Establishing Hanoverian royal rule in Britain
1715: Jacobite rebellion led by Earl of Mar
1717: Handel's *Water Music* performed
1719: Jacobites defeated at Glenshiel, near Inverness
1720: South Sea Bubble scandal
1722: Jacobite 'Atterbury Plot' foiled
1726: King George's divorced wife, Sophia Dorothea, dies
May 1727: George I becomes patron of the Royal Society
Death: 11 June 1727, Osnabrück. Buried in the Leineschloss Church, Hanover

George's claim to the throne lay chiefly as a Protestant with a viable – if distant – blood relationship to the English ruling line. He acceded under the 1701 Act of Settlement, which in order to secure a Protestant succession, had raised George's mother Sophia, Electress of Hanover, above more than 50 Stuart relations with better claims. George's own relationship to the Stuart line was through his maternal grandmother, Princess Elizabeth, the daughter of James I, who had married Frederick, Elector Palatine of the Rhine in 1620.

Left: A detail from James Thornhill's epic decoration in the Painted Hall at Greenwich presents a regal George I.

THE OLD PRETENDER

George's potentially troublesome accession initially passed off peacefully. On 6 August, Parliament proclaimed George was to be crowned at Westminster Abbey on 20 October and, although there were demonstrations in favour of the Jacobite claim of James Stuart, the 'Old Pretender', the occasion went well.

In 1715 the new king faced a large-scale rebellion of Highlanders and northern English Jacobites in support of the 'Old Pretender'. The Stuart standard was raised at Braemar on 6 September by the Earl of Mar, a Tory landowner snubbed by King George, who gave open expression to his support for the staunchly Protestant Whig party at Westminster. Mar attracted some support. A minority of Scots favoured the Jacobite cause for several reasons: one pressing factor was resentment at the Act of Union; another was affection for the House of Stuart, originally a Scottish royal family; a third was loyalty to the Catholic cause, which remained strong among the Highland clans although it had little appeal to most Presbyterian Lowland Scots.

However, Mar was not a great general and was unable to turn numerical superiority over the Hanoverian army into victory. The Battle of Sheriffmuir, near Stirling, on 13 November ended inconclusively and the English Jacobites were crushingly defeated the next day at Preston. The Old Pretender landed at Peterhead just before Christmas, but the uprising dwindled to nothing and on 4 February 1716 he returned to France, having achieved nothing.

Above: At St Germain-en-Laye, France's King Louis XIV threw a party in honour of James Stuart, whom the French court recognized as the rightful king of England.

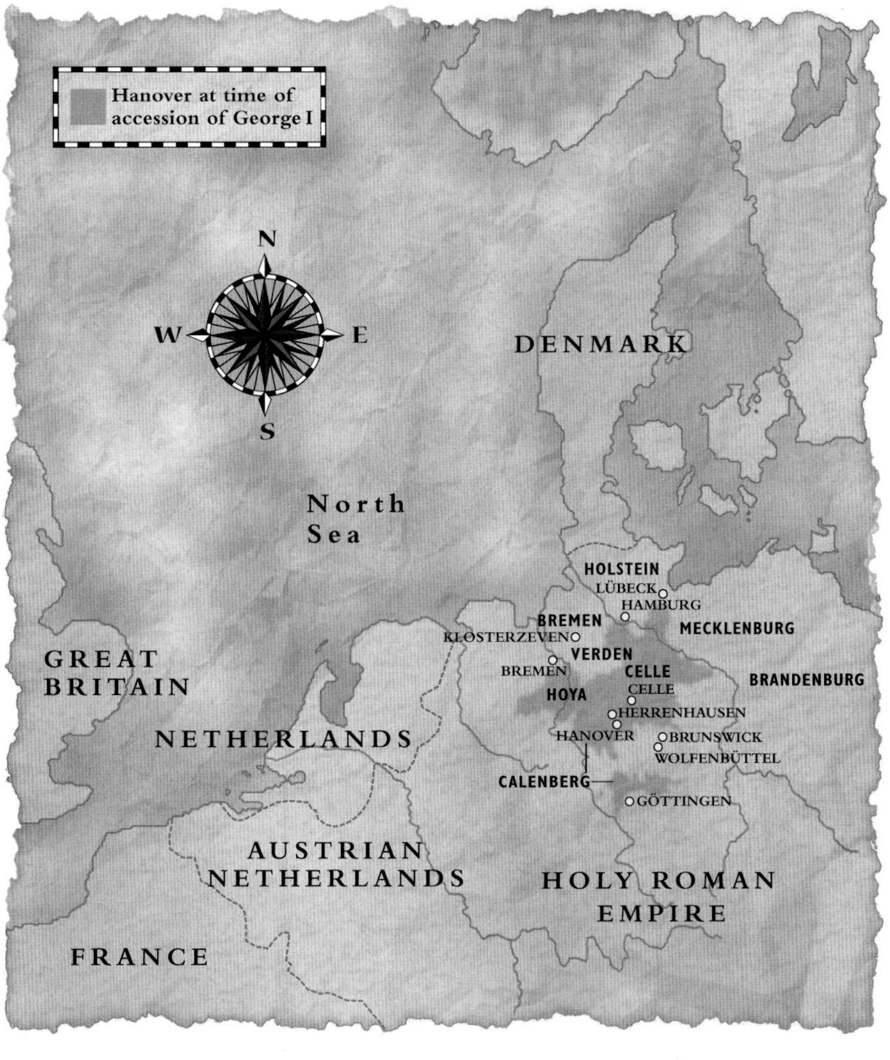

Left: Before he became king of Britain and Ireland, George I became Elector of Brunswick-Lüneburg in January 1698.

A GERMAN KING

THE FIRST JACOBITES AND OTHER TROUBLES, 1714–1727

The suspicion with which many Englishmen viewed their stout Hanoverian monarch was certainly not eased by the king's prolonged and spiteful falling out with his son, George, the Prince of Wales. This had its roots in King George's treatment of his divorced wife – and Prince George's mother – Sophia Dorothea. George punished her for a love affair by keeping her imprisoned in Germany and barring her from seeing her son or his sister (another Sophia Dorothea, who subsequently became Queen of Prussia as wife of Frederick William I) until her death.

THE EARLY HANOVERIANS 1714–1760

GEORGE I *m* Sophia Dorothea of Celle
1660–1727 | 1666–1726
♛ 1714–1727

GEORGE II *m* Caroline of Brandenburg-Ansbach
1683–1760 | 1683–1737
♛ 1727–1760

Frederick Louis Prince of Wales 1707–51 *m* Augusta of Saxe-Gotha 1719–72

William Duke of Cumberland 1721–65

and others

Below: 'German George'. The first Hanoverian king did not manage to win the affection of his British subjects.

Early in King George's reign, the Prince of Wales's growing popularity in London contrasted sharply with king's own public profile, exacerbating the difficulties. Tension erupted in an open quarrel in 1717 when, following the birth of the Prince of Wales's second son, George William, King George imperiously insisted on making the Duke of Newcastle the child's godfather. The Prince of Wales was angry and argued with Newcastle, who misunderstood what had happened and believed that the prince had challenged him to a duel. When the king discovered these events, he briefly imprisoned the Prince of Wales, then barred prince and princess from the royal palace. To further demonstrate his disapproval, he kept the Prince's children in his own care, took charge of their education and refused to allow the parents to see their offspring more than once a week.

JACOBITE TROUBLES

The collapse of the Jacobite uprising in Scotland in 1715 was by no means the end of efforts by supporters of James II's son, James Stuart, to undo the Hanoverian succession and put a Catholic Stuart monarch on the English throne. James – the self-declared King James III of England and King James VIII of Scots – could count on the intermittent backing of France and

Spain, for both countries wanted to destabilize an increasingly powerful Great Britain and also in principle supported the idea of a Catholic monarchy in London. In 1719 a planned Spanish invasion of Scotland went awry when the main fleet was forced back by storms and a tiny Spanish force of no more than 300 soldiers, supplemented by a small group of Jacobite Highlanders, was defeated by Hanoverians in a skirmish at Glenshiel.

Then in 1722 a Jacobite plot to take control in London was uncovered. The plan was for armed supporters of James Stuart to seize the Tower of London and St James's Palace while King George was visiting Hanover. The unlikely leader was Francis Atterbury, Bishop of Rochester, a secret supporter of the Jacobite cause. However, details of the 'Atterbury plot' were leaked to the King's mistress, Melusine von Schulenberg, and the uprising did not occur. Atterbury was exiled and only one plotter – a London barrister named Christopher Layer – was convicted of treason and executed.

Above: Sir Robert Walpole is generally remembered as Britain's first prime minister. His capable response to the Atterbury plot consolidated his position.

Above: James II's son, James Edward Stuart, in 1716. He was the focus of the Jacobite uprising of 1715 and became known as the Old Pretender or Chevalier de St George.

THE SOUTH SEA BUBBLE

The sudden collapse of stock in the South Sea Company in September 1720 came closer than the Jacobites ever did to destroying the House of Hanover. The bursting of the 'South Sea Bubble' following a period of frenzied financial speculation left a huge hole in the monarch's finances, while the king and royal family's role in the affair left them looking very stupid if not corrupt.

The South Sea Company was formed in 1711 to trade with South America, primarily in slaves. When George became a governor of the company, stock sold very fast and was paying 100 per cent interest. There was a tremendous boom in shares and the king invested £60,000 of civil list funds. When the collapse came, it was very painful for all but a few canny investors. The royal court came under severe attack but survived thanks to Robert Walpole, appointed Chancellor of the Exchequer after the bubble burst. Walpole succeeded in stabilizing the situation and diverting blame from the king and the directors of the company.

Left: 'The Bubblers bubbl'd or The Devil take the hindmost'. James Cole's 1720 engraving satirizes the South Sea Bubble.

GEORGE'S FAILING HEALTH

From around 1724, King George, by now severely obese, was in failing health. He was regularly struck down by gout and often lost consciousness in fits of fainting. The king increasingly withdrew from public life, leaving control of government in the hands of the immensely capable Sir Robert Walpole, and went to Hanover whenever he could.

It was in Hanover that George I died, on 11 June 1727, in bed. While travelling to Hanover via the Netherlands from Greenwich, he had been struck down with severe diarrhoea, after consuming a very large quantity of fruit for dinner, and fainted more than once. The final fit was permanent: his courtiers could not revive him. He died aged 67 after a reign of 12 years. George was buried in the Leineschloss Church, Hanover. His son George Augustus, with whom he had had many disagreements, succeeded him as King George II.

GEORGE I, PATRON OF THE ARTS

MUSIC, ART AND ARCHITECTURE, 1714–1727

On 17 July 1717, King George, his mistress Sophia Charlotte von Kielmannsegge and an elite gathering of the nobility enjoyed a musical entertainment on the river Thames. In the early evening the party boarded barges at Whitehall and then sailed upriver as far as Chelsea, where they disembarked and took supper in a secluded garden. After the meal, which did not finish until 3 a.m, they climbed back into the barges and returned to Whitehall, where they arrived at St James's Palace at 4.30 a.m.

On both journeys the royal party was entertained by a group of 50 musicians sailing alongside them in their own barge playing a suite – later known as the *Water Music* – by the German-born composer George Frideric Handel. King George enjoyed the music – played on strings, trumpets, flutes, recorders, horns, oboes and bassoons – so much that he had the musicians play the one-hour suite three times over.

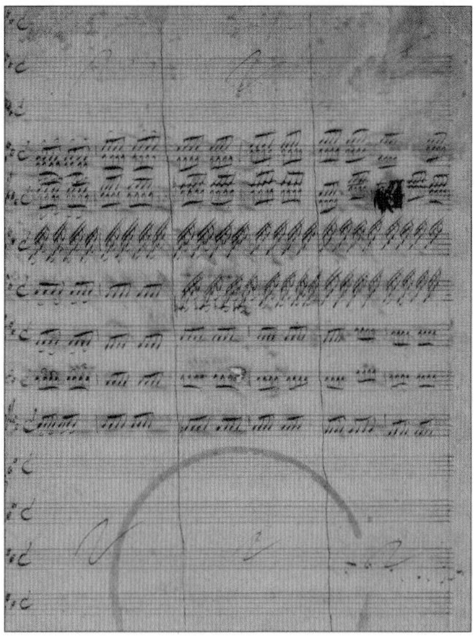

Above: Working life of a great composer. Handel's setting of the Coronation Anthem Zadok the Priest, *first used in 1727, is stained with the mark of a coffee cup.*

The triumphantly successful evening was arranged and paid for by Sophia Charlotte and her husband Baron von Kielmannsegge.

HANDEL'S PATRON

George had become a patron of the composer Handel before acceding to the throne: he appointed him Kapellmeister to the Hanover court in 1710. That same year Handel had made his first impact in England and over the next four years so pleased Queen Anne – with an *Ode for the Queen's Birthday* and a *Te Deum* to celebrate the Peace of Utrecht (both 1713) – that she awarded him a pension of £200 a year for life. As king, George appointed Handel music teacher to his granddaughters, regularly attended performances of Handel's operas – such as *Rinaldo* and *Amadigi* – and granted the composer a further £200 annual pension. In 1726 Handel became a British subject and was appointed composer of the Chapel Royal. George also demonstrated his love of music by signing up for a £1,000 subscription to help establish the Royal Academy of Music.

Left: Sir Godfrey Kneller, who painted this portrait of King George, was the first painter to be made a baronet, in 1715.

Above: Handel's career as a royal musician extended from the success of his Water Music *in 1717 to his* Music for the Royal Fireworks *in 1749.*

George I was also a patron of the visual arts, a supporter of British-born artist James Thornhill, who painted allegories of the Protestant succession in the Painted Hall, Greenwich (1708–27) and eight scenes on the inner dome of St Paul's Cathedral (1715–19). George appointed Thornhill royal history painter in 1718 and knighted him in 1720.

GEORGIAN ARCHITECTURE

Many fine churches and residential buildings were raised or completed in George's reign. Hanover Square in London's West End (just to the south of modern Oxford Street) was named in honour of the new royal house when it was laid out in 1717–19. More tributes

Right: Vanbrugh had a theatrical triumph with The Provok'd Wife *in 1697. With Castle Howard (1702) and his work on Blenheim, he had also established himself as a leading architect by George I's reign.*

included the naming of its church (St George's) and of its southerly approach (George Street). At the end of Queen Anne's reign, architect Nicholas Hawksmoor, who had worked with his professional patron Sir Christopher Wren on St Paul's Cathedral, was appointed one of two surveyors to commission or design 50 new churches. Four of his celebrated designs were built largely within King George's reign, mainly in London's East End: St Anne, Limehouse, St Mary, Woolnoth, St George in the east, Wapping and Christ Church, Spitalfields.

In the year of his accession King George appointed leading architect John Vanbrugh comptroller of royal works. Vanbrugh's Blenheim Palace, in Oxfordshire, originally commissioned by Queen Anne in 1705 and designed and built with the help of Hawksmoor, was completed in 1719 for the Duke of Marlborough, hero of the Battle of Blenheim, after which the magnificent country house was named. Vanbrugh was the first man to be knighted by the King George in 1714. He worked for the king on Kensington Palace, where three state rooms and a series of courtyards were added. Vanbrugh also won acclaim as a playwright, celebrated for plays such as *The Provok'd Wife* and *The Relapse or Virtue in Danger.*

Below: Blenheim Palace. Architects Vanbrugh and Hawksmoor, carver Grinling Gibbons and painters Thornhill and Laguerre all contributed to its grandeur.

King George was far less interested in the world of literature and theatre than in that of music and opera. French philosopher and poet François Voltaire, exiled in London from 1726 to 1729, dedicated his epic poem *La Henriade* (1723–28) to King George, but scholars believe that the king's support for the Frenchman – whom he received and gave £200 in January 1727 – was probably politically motivated, in the interest of promoting an Anglo-French alliance.

Many leading writers made or consolidated reputations during George's reign. These included Alexander Pope, Jonathan Swift (whose *Gulliver's Travels* was published in 1726) and Daniel Defoe, who published *Robinson Crusoe* (1719) and *Moll Flanders* (1722). However, the king's very poor grasp of English inevitably limited his contact with writing in that language.

THE ROYAL SOCIETY

Like his predecessor Charles II, George showed a keen interest in scientific developments. He received a number of prominent scientists at court, including the Italian mathematician Schinella-Conti, although language difficulties caused problems. He became patron of the Royal Society – the scientific body founded in 1660 – in May 1727.

Below: St George's, Hanover Square. The king and ruling house were both honoured, but the plan to place a statue of George on the pediment was not carried through.

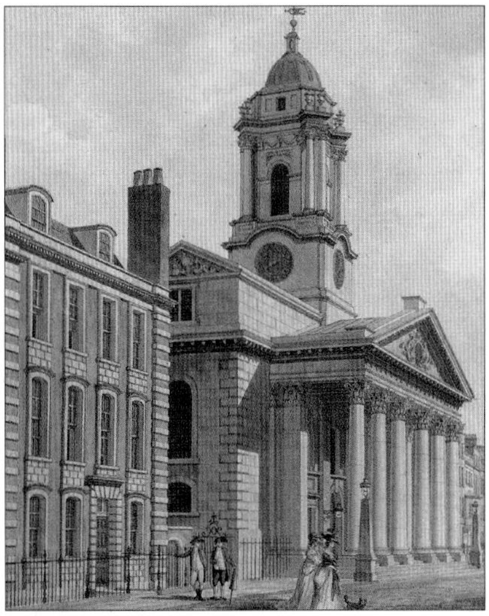

GEORGE II
1727–1760

George Augustus, Prince of Wales, was proclaimed King George II – the second ruler of the House of Hanover – on 15 June 1727. This was just four days after his father's George I's death in Osnabrück, Hanover.

On 27 June George II opened the first Parliament of his reign, and in its very first sitting it voted a generous rise in the king's civil list financial settlement. George was granted £800,000 a year – an increase of £100,000 on his father's entitlement – plus a further £100,000 entitlement for the king's popular consort, Queen Caroline.

WALPOLE RETAINED

The vote was a triumph for Sir Robert Walpole, who thereby consolidated his position as chief government minister. King George had intended to replace Walpole, so powerful in George I's reign, with Sir Spencer Compton. However, Walpole's generosity with the civil list settlement, combined with the influence of Queen Caroline, who was a close friend of Sir Robert, convinced the king to keep the minister on.

Below: House of a royal mistress. Henrietta Howard built the splendid Palladian villa of Marble Hill House in Twickenham.

GEORGE II, KING OF GREAT BRITAIN AND IRELAND AND ELECTOR OF HANOVER, 1727–1760

Birth: 30 Oct 1683, Hanover
Father: Prince George Louis, Elector of Brunswick-Lüneburg – later King George I
Mother: Princess Sophia Dorothea of Celle
Accession: 11 June 1727
Coronation: 11 Oct 1727, Westminster Abbey
Married: Caroline of Brandenburg-Ansbach (m. 22 Aug 1705; d. 20 Nov 1737)
Succeeded by: His grandson George III
Greatest achievement: Last British king personally to lead his troops in battle
1732: King signs royal charter for North American colony of 'Georgia'
1737: Queen Caroline dies
1742: Resignation of Sir Robert Walpole
27 June 1743: Leads troops to victory in Battle of Dettingen
21 Sept 1745: 'Bonnie Prince Charlie', the 'Young Pretender', defeats royal army at the Battle of Prestonpans
16 April 1746: Jacobites defeated at Battle of Culloden
20 March 1751: Frederick, Prince of Wales, dies
2 Jan 1757: Robert Clive retakes Calcutta from viceroy of Bengal, India
23 June 1757: Clive's victory at the Battle of Plassey
1 Aug 1759: British victory at Battle of Minden, Germany
18 Sept 1759: British troops capture Quebec
8 Sept 1760: British troops capture Montreal and have total control in Canada
Death: 25 Oct 1760, Kensington Palace. Buried at Westminster Abbey

The following month, July 1727, brought more good news for King George when Sir Robert Walpole's brother, Horatio Walpole, who was the English ambassador to Paris, arrived in London with the news that Louis XV of France was to back George II as England's king rather than support the claim of the Catholic claimant James Stuart.

A STATELY CORONATION

King George and Queen Caroline were crowned with great ceremony in Westminster Abbey on 11 October 1727. They approached the Abbey from Westminster Hall along a blue carpet strewn with herbs. The moment at which King George took the coronation oath was marked by the firing of guns at the Tower of London and in Hyde Park. Handel wrote four new anthems for the service, including the majestic *Zadok the Priest*, which so impressed king and court that it became standard fare for coronation services, and has been used at every British crowning from 1727 to the present day. Another of the Handel anthems, the beautiful *My Heart is Inditing*, was composed especially for the moment at which Queen Caroline was crowned. Other musical splendours of the service included *O Lord, Grant the King a Long Life* by William Child and a magnificent *Te Deum* by Orlando Gibbons.

ROYAL LIFESTYLE

King George settled into court life at St James's Palace, where he openly kept two mistresses: Henrietta Howard, the Countess of Suffolk and Mary Scott, the Countess of Deloraine. In company

Above: George II made Irish artist Charles Jervas, who painted this portrait, his principal court painter in 1723.

Above: Queen Caroline. She put up with George's long-term infidelities; he had a deep and lasting reliance on her.

he could be ill-mannered and, like his father, he was short-tempered. He spoke English with a heavy German accent and, according to contemporary accounts, was obsessively attentive to court etiquette. His main interest was in military uniforms and he had little time for painting or poetry, although he did enjoy music. In general, as in this particular, he considered things Hanoverian superior to things British.

Each night George would visit his mistress the Countess of Suffolk in her court apartments at 7 p.m. He would never go early: he could be seen pacing up and down looking at his watch for a full quarter of an hour before the time came. He was rude both about his mistresses and about the queen, but it was plain to all that behind the façade he was devoted to Queen Caroline, who had great influence over him. The queen, by contrast with King George, was quick-witted and interested in ideas. She read widely, enjoyed theological and philosophical discussions and was a friend of Sir Robert Walpole. It was common knowledge at court that the way to promote a project was via Walpole and the queen. If a person convinced Walpole, Walpole would secretly convince Queen Caroline, who would convince King George and the king would ask Walpole to look into the matter. Writing of the queen's influence on the king, Walpole noted, 'She can make him propose the thing which one week earlier he had rejected'.

King George was a keen hunter and rode frequently in pursuit of stags in Windsor Great Park. However, in line with Hanoverian opinion, he was dismissive of British fox hunting. In an exchange with the Duke of Grafton, George declared that the fox, 'Was generally a much better beast than any of those that pursued him'.

Right: Sir Robert Walpole. He has been called 'the queen's minister' because he owed his influence to her hidden support.

THE UNPOPULARITY OF GEORGE II

THE ROYAL COURT, 1727–1743

King George and Queen Caroline shared a very low opinion of their first-born son, Frederick Lewis. Caroline appears unaccountably to have taken against the baby almost as soon as he was born, in 1707. George dismissed him as 'The greatest ass…in the whole world'. Some people unkindly suggested he was not the royal couple's offspring at all, but a foundling. In December 1728, Frederick, as heir to the British throne, now honoured as Prince of Wales, arrived in London for the first time from Hanover at the aged of 20.

King George made every effort to ostracize his son from society, limiting him to an annual income of £24,000 – significantly less than the £100,000 a year his own father had allowed him. Nonetheless, he became increasingly popular in London, effectively keeping a rival court, which became the focus of political opposition to George's favoured minister, Sir Robert Walpole.

Above: Royal warrior George II in the saddle at the Battle of Dettingen on 27 June 1743. George was the last British king to lead soldiers into conflict.

Left: Frederick, Prince of Wales. This portrait, by Charles Phillips (d.1747), shows the prince in 1732 aged 25.

ROYAL FAMILY SQUABBLES

On 25 April 1736 Prince Frederick married a 17-year-old German princess, Augusta of Saxe-Gotha, in London. In August the following year, when Princess Augusta was at the point of giving birth at King George's Hampton Court, Prince Frederick swept her off in a carriage to give birth away from his parents in St James's Palace. Enraged by this slight, the king split publicly with the prince in September 1737, declaring that any who attended the prince's rival establishment at Kew would not be welcome at Hampton Court.

The prince was kept away even when his mother, Queen Caroline, fell seriously ill in November 1737; indeed, as she approached death the queen declared that she was at least consoled by the thought that she would never again have to see 'that monster' her son. She died on 20 November 1737. The following year, on 4 June 1738, Princess Augusta gave birth to a second child, a boy named George William Frederick. He was a sickly infant and many expected him to die in infancy; he was christened on the day of his birth in case the worst happened. However, he proved the doubters wrong and grew into a healthy boy.

A KING MOCKED AND ABUSED

In the mid-1730s King George's popularity in Britain was at a very low ebb. His frequent absences in Hanover, where he had taken up with a new mistress named Amelia Sophia von Walmoden, were resented and mocked. One critic made a public display of his

THE BIRTH OF 'GEORGIA'

On 9 June 1732, King George granted a royal charter for the formation of a new English colony in North America, to be called 'Georgia' in his honour. The holder of the charter, James Oglethorpe, planned to allow imprisoned debtors and other people in severe poverty to make a new life in the colony. A group of 114 colonists departed from Gravesend on a frigate named the *Anne* and commanded by Captain John Thomas. After transferring to a group of small boats in South Carolina, some of these settlers landed at Yamacraw Bluff on the Savannah river on 12 February 1733 and founded the settlement of Savannah. Local Yamacraw Indians helped the first Georgians, and after a difficult beginning the colony soon began to thrive and prosper.

Above: James Oglethorpe (d. 1785) meets Yamacraw Indians after landing in the future colony of Georgia in 1733.

contempt by setting an old nag loose on the streets of London with the following words pinned to a broken saddle: 'Do not stop me, for I am the King of Hanover's horse galloping to fetch his majesty and his whore to London'. In December 1736 news circulated in London that the king had been drowned in a Channel storm as he tried to return from Hanover to London. This news provoked brief celebration – and the arrival of the Prince of Wales's supporters at his palace to hail a new king – until it emerged that King George II was safe and well.

GEORGE'S MILITARY TRIUMPH

The Prince of Wales's supporters opposed Walpole's efforts to keep Britain out of Continental wars and pressed for England to assert its military might, particularly against France. Walpole dismissed them as the 'Patriot Boys'. However, the king was also inclined to favour war, since he was fascinated by military matters and was himself a soldier of proven ability who had covered himself in glory when fighting under John Churchill, the Duke of Marlborough, at the Battle of Oudenarde in 1708.

THE AUSTRIAN SUCCESSION

Following Walpole's resignation from government in February 1742, Britain plunged into the Continental 'War of the Austrian Succession' in 1743. This conflict arose from the inheritance and succession disputes that followed the death of Holy Roman Emperor Charles VI in 1740.

On 27 June 1743, King George II led British troops to victory over a French army commanded by Marshal Noailles at Dettingen, in Germany, boldly declaring, 'Now boys, fight for England's honour – shoot and be brave and the French will not stand their ground!' In fact the victory brought few if any benefits because the king did not press home his advantage. Yet, when he returned to London in November, he was greeted like the victor of Agincourt by rapturous crowds, the pealing of church bells and the burning of huge victory bonfires.

Below: Musicians in the bandstand (right) entertain Georgian society. This 1751 engraving shows the tree-lined Grand Walk in Vauxhall pleasure gardens.

CHARLES EDWARD STUART

BONNIE PRINCE CHARLIE AND THE 1745 RISING

In 1745 Prince Charles Edward Stuart, grandson of the ousted King James II of England, launched the last attempt by Jacobite supporters of the Stuart claim to regain the British crown. The charismatic 24-year-old was the elder son of James Stuart, the man derided as the 'Old Pretender', who had been the figurehead of failed Jacobite revolts in 1708, 1715 and 1722. Charles sailed from France to Scotland to claim the throne for his father.

On 23 July 1745, Charles Stuart landed in the Outer Hebrides and declared, 'I am come home'. He was supported by just 12 men and had lost a large part of his military supplies when the Royal Navy drove back a French support ship. However, after travelling on to the mainland he was able to raise the support of the largely pro-Stuart and virulently anti-English Highland clans. On 17 September 1745 he entered Edinburgh at the head of a force of 2,400 men. His Scots supporters acclaimed him as 'Bonnie Prince Charlie' while the Hanoverians mocked him as the 'Young Pretender'. In Edinburgh he proclaimed his father King James VIII of Scots.

Above: 17 September 1745. On entering Edinburgh in triumph, the 'Bonnie Prince' proclaimed his father King James VIII.

BATTLE OF PRESTONPANS

On 21 September the Jacobites surprised and defeated a government force of around 2,500 at Prestonpans, 10 miles (16km) to the east of Edinburgh. The government commander in Scotland, Sir John Cope, had encamped beside a marsh at Prestonpans, thinking that the Jacobites would not be able to cross it without giving themselves away. However, a local guide led the Jacobite troops safely through by night and at first light they overwhelmed the unprepared government troops. Three hundred Hanoverian soldiers were killed and the rest of Cope's army fled.

'GOD SAVE THE KING'

In London King George and the Hanoverian establishment began to fear that, after so many failed attempts, the Jacobites might finally succeed. A popular song began to do the rounds, lauding King George and begging God for help. It was first played in public after a performance of Ben Jonson's play *The Alchemist* at the Theatre Royal, Drury Lane, on 28 September – just one week after the Jacobite victory at Prestonpans. Three days later, the words were printed in *The Gentleman's Magazine*.

At this stage, the song consisted of the first three verses, but a fourth, virulently anti-Jacobite verse was later added. The words were by an unknown author while the tune may have been

Left: The Jacobites' hopes of a Stuart restoration were undone at Culloden.

based on a Tudor galliard or a tune by French composer Jean-Baptiste Lully. By 1819 it was established as the national anthem.

MARCH ON LONDON

Buoyed by his success at Prestonpans, Charles wanted to march on London. His Jacobite generals advised him to consolidate in Scotland and wait – for French support or perhaps a rising against the Hanoverians in England. However, Charles was both impatient and impetuous. He held a ballot of his advisors and won a majority of just one in favour of pressing on. He marched into England, capturing Carlisle in passing on 15 November. The 5,000-strong Jacobite army got as far as Derby, where on 5 December it was faced by a government force six times its size.

Charles wanted to make a dash for London, since he thought resistance would collapse if he took the capital quickly, but he was persuaded by his council and generals to retreat.

Under the skilful command of Lord George Murray, his army extricated itself from a difficult situation and retreated safely to Scotland. On 17 January, after gathering reinforcements from Glasgow, the Jacobite army defeated a government force commanded by General Hawley at Falkirk before retreating to Inverness to regroup and reconsider its position.

Above: Flora MacDonald became a heroine to Scottish Jacobites for her role in facilitating Bonnie Prince Charlie's escape.

Above: The tall prince was unconvincing as a woman. An onlooker called him 'a very odd, muckle, ill-shapen up wife'.

GOD SAVE THE KING

This patriotic song of 1745 became Britain's national anthem in 1790 – without the final verse about Wade.

God save great George our king,
Long live our noble king,
God save the king.
Send him victorious,
Happy and glorious,
Long to reign over us,
God save the king!

O Lord our God arise,
Scatter his enemies,
And make them fall;
Confound their politics,
Frustrate their knavish tricks,
On him our hopes we fix;
God save us all!

Thy choicest gifts in store,
On George be pleased to pour,
Long may he reign;
May he defend our laws,
And ever give us cause
With heart and voice to sing
God save the king!

God grant that Marshal Wade
May by Thy mighty aid
Victory bring!
May he sedition hush
And like a torrent rush
Rebellious Scots to crush
God save the king!

Some accounts suggest the words, including the final verse about the royalist Wade, were written in 1740 by Henry Carey.

SLAUGHTER AT CULLODEN

The Jacobites were pursued northwards by the Duke of Cumberland at the head of a large Hanoverian army. Charles insisted on facing the pursuing Hanoverians in a pitched battle, despite the urging of Lord Murray to hold back and fight a guerrilla war in the difficult northern country. Moreover, Charles's supplies began to dwindle, so his 5,000-strong force was ill equipped when on the morning of 16 April 1746 they went into battle against the 9,000-odd troops of Cumberland's army on Culloden Moor, near Nairn.

Cumberland's army overwhelmed Charles's bedraggled force and brutally slaughtered the wounded and prisoners. Few escaped the massacre, but Prince Charles was one of them. He eluded his pursuers – despite the offer of a £30,000 reward for his capture and many near misses – for five months. The most dramatic moment was, without doubt, when he escaped from South Uist in female disguise as the Irish maid of local woman Flora MacDonald. On 20 September 1746 at Loch na Uamh he boarded a French frigate, *L'Heureux*, and escaped into exile forever.

GEORGIAN BRITAIN

A VIBRANT COUNTRY, 1745–1760

In the latter years of King George II's reign, a vibrant Britain greatly expanded its colonial holdings. This took place in the course of the French and Indian War (1754–63), which was the North American phase of the Seven Years War fought with France in Europe (usually dated 1756–63). The military triumphs of James Wolfe in North America settled Anglo-French colonial rivalry in Britain's favour and further established the foundations of Britain's overseas empire.

IMPERIAL TRIUMPHS

In North America, British and American colonial forces came into conflict with the better-equipped armies of New France, the French colonial holding in the region. Fighting began in 1754 in the upper valley of the Ohio River and for four years resulted in uninterrupted French victories.

Below: The king in ripe old age. This portrait shows him at the age of 76 in 1759, the year before his death.

Above: Italian artist Antonio Canaletto lived in London 1746–56 and painted several masterful views of the city. This is of the Thames on Lord Mayor's Day 1747.

However, in 1758–9, thanks to a British naval blockade that prevented French supplies getting through, the British won a series of astonishing victories. These culminated in the Battle of Quebec on 13 September 1759, which forced the surrender of Quebec. In October 1760, the month of King George II's death, the British also captured the city of Montreal.

These triumphs reflected well on King George II, who was a strong supporter of the hero of the North American campaign, General James Wolfe, (unfortunately killed in the Battle of Quebec). Other victories came in India, where Robert Clive defended British interests and chipped away at French holdings and on Continental Europe, where British troops crushed a French army under Marshal de Contades at the Battle of Minden on 1 August 1759. Horace Walpole commented that in 1759, 'The church bells are worn threadbare with the ringing-in of victories', while Lord Temple, commented with satisfaction that, 'The closing years of the king's reign are distinguished by lustre of every kind'.

A RICH CULTURE

Meanwhile, at home, a king who declared his lack of interest in books and learning presided over and made a major contribution to the foundation of the British Museum, as well as a culture of glittering musical, artistic and literary achievement.

The British Museum was established by an Act of Parliament on 7 June 1753. Its principal collection consisted of 71,000 objects and 50,000 books left to King George for the nation in a will that year by physicist Sir Hans Sloane. In 1757 King George then donated the 'Old Royal Library' belonging to the monarchs of England, a rich and venerable collection of 10,000 books and 1800 manuscripts. The new collection was housed in Montagu House in Bloomsbury and opened to the public on 15 January 1759.

At this time London had a thriving literary culture: Dr Samuel Johnson's *Dictionary of the English Language* was published in 1755, while the novels *Clarissa* by Samuel Richardson and *Tom Jones* by Henry Fielding had recently been published. In the visual arts William Hogarth was at the height of his powers. He was named painter to the court of King George in June 1757.

In music, George Frideric Handel remained an active composer for his royal patrons throughout the reign, producing the *Funeral Anthem for Queen Caroline* (1737), the *Dettingen Te Deum* (1743) to celebrate the king's triumph at the Battle of Dettingen and the *Music for the Royal Fireworks* in 1749 for a celebration planned to mark the Peace of Aix-la-Chapelle that ended the War of the Austrian Succession. German-born, but a British citizen since 1726, by the time of his death on 14 April 1759, Handel was established as a British institution. He was buried in Poets' Corner, Westminster Abbey.

Above: Triumph in North America. A Victorian engraving celebrates General James Wolfe's victory in Quebec in 1759.

Below: William Hogarth's engraving Gin Lane. *Hogarth won a wide reputation for what he called 'modern moral subjects'.*

DEATH OF THE KING

King George II died an undignified death at Kensington Palace on 25 October 1760 shortly before his 77th birthday. He suffered a fatal heart attack while seated on the lavatory. His 33-year reign had seen a consolidation of the arrangements of constitutional monarchy, under which the king reigned but scarcely ruled. In his latter years, he was involved less and less in government as power became concentrated in the hands of ministers such as William Pitt.

The threat presented by the Jacobites in 1745 and the string of military victories in the late 1750s had repaired the king's formerly antagonistic relationship with his people. He may have preferred Hanover to Britain, but on his death he left an increasingly secure and successful nation, with British naval and military might bringing rapid expansion in overseas possessions. He would be remembered as the last British monarch to lead his army into battle. Following the death of his hated son Frederick in 1751, George's heir was his grandson George William Frederick, who succeeded as King George III.

Below: Handel. Although he was German-born, his music was seen as an embodiment of England's national character.

CHAPTER TEN

BRITISH HANOVERIANS

1760–1837

George III, third king of the Hanoverian line, acceded to the throne, aged 22, on 25 October 1760. He was the first of the Hanoverian kings to have been born in England and to speak English without a German accent. At his coronation in Westminster Abbey on 22 September 1761, he declared, 'I glory in the name of Briton'.

King George III saw it as his duty to maintain the authority and power of the British monarchy, but failed in his struggle to do so. The king, remembered as the ruler who lost Britain's North American colonies, who saw the rise to independence of the United States of America, was increasingly sidelined at home, as powers of government passed to ministers in Parliament. The monarch became a figurehead, who reigned more than he ruled. In his final years, Parliament appointed the Prince of Wales to serve as Regent during his father's mental illness. The Prince Regent oversaw a great flowering of architecture and the arts in Britain. The architect John Nash reshaped the face of London with developments in and around Regent's Park and Buckingham Palace and extravagantly transformed the Royal Pavilion in Brighton. George III (1760–1820) and his successors George IV (1820–30) and William IV (1830–7) occupied the throne at a time in which Britain defied Napoleon Bonaparte and restored its reputation as a great military power. It won feted victories such as those under Nelson at Trafalgar in 1805 and under Wellington at Waterloo in 1815. In this period, Britain gained widespread overseas territories that formed the basis for the great worldwide empire of the Victorian era.

Left: His Majesty enthroned. On 19 July 1821, in Westminster Abbey, the former Prince Regent was finally crowned King George IV, at the age of 58.

GEORGE III

1760–1820

George III was proclaimed King of Great Britain and Ireland on 25 October 1760. He was told of his elevation as he rode across Kew Bridge and asked for the announcement to be delayed until he could inform his mentor John Stuart, Earl of Bute, whom he called his 'dearest friend'.

Aware of the need to produce an heir to the throne, King George almost at once set about the task of finding a suitable bride. He was reliant in this, as in all matters at this time, on the advice and help of Bute. Within a year, even before the coronation took place, George married Princess Charlotte of Mecklenburg-Strelitz on 8 September 1761 in St James's Palace, London. The couple's first child, a boy, was born on 12 August 1762 and christened George Augustus Frederick.

Above: George III was admired for his upright character and humility. At the coronation, he removed his crown when receiving Holy Communion.

THE KING'S CHARACTER

George III was moral, devout and hard-working, usually kind-hearted although sometimes uncharitable, viewing others' failings with a certain censorious superiority. Before he established such a close relationship with the Earl of Bute, he had been through a number of tutors, many of whom complained of his 'indolence' and 'inattention', and highlighted a certain melancholy in his character that could cause him to become withdrawn, 'sullen and silent'.

Under Bute's tutelage George gradually overcame his shyness and self-doubt, although early in his reign he

GEORGE III, KING OF GREAT BRITAIN AND IRELAND AND ELECTOR OF HANOVER, 1760–1820

Birth: 24 May 1738, Duke of Norfolk's house, St James's Square, London
Father: Frederick Lewis, Prince of Wales
Mother: Princess Augusta of Saxe-Gotha
Accession: 25 Oct 1760
Coronation: 22 Sept 1761, Westminster Abbey
Queen: Princess Charlotte of Mecklenburg-Strelitz (m. 8 Sept 1761; d. 17 Nov 1818)
Succeeded by: His son George Augustus Frederick, who rules as Prince Regent 1811–20 and as George IV 1820–30
Greatest achievement: Despite loss of North American colonies, his reign saw the gain of overseas territories that formed the basis of Britain's 19th-century empire
1762: George suffers from mystery illness
1768: George founds Royal Academy of Arts
16 Dec 1773: Boston Tea Party
1775: Parliament gives Buckingham House to Queen Charlotte
19 April 1775: War of the American Revolution begins with the Battle of Lexington and Concord, Massachusetts
4 July 1776: Americans denounce George as a tyrant in the Declaration of Independence
June 1780: Anti-Catholic 'Gordon riots' kill 850 in London
19 Oct 1781: American war effectively ends with surrender of British General Cornwallis to American troops at Yorktown
3 Sept 1783: Treaty of Versailles recognizes an independent United States of America
1788–9: Madness strikes the king as illness recurs
1793–1802: Britain at war with France
1 Aug 1798: Horatio Nelson destroys a French fleet in the Battle of the Nile
1 Jan 1801: Act of Union creates the United Kingdom of Great Britain and Ireland
1803: Britain is at war with France (until 1815)
1801, 1804: The king's madness recurs
21 Oct 1805: Nelson victorious over French and Spanish in Battle of Trafalgar
25 Oct 1810: King George's Golden Jubilee is celebrated
2 Nov 1810: George devastated by the death of Princess Amelia
3 Nov 1810: George confined in a straitjacket
6 Feb 1811: King George declared unfit to rule; Prince of Wales becomes regent
18 June 1815: Generals Wellington and Blucher defeat Napoleon Bonaparte at the Battle of Waterloo
Death: 29 Jan 1820 dies at Windsor Castle. Buried in St George's Chapel, Windsor, on 15 Feb 1820

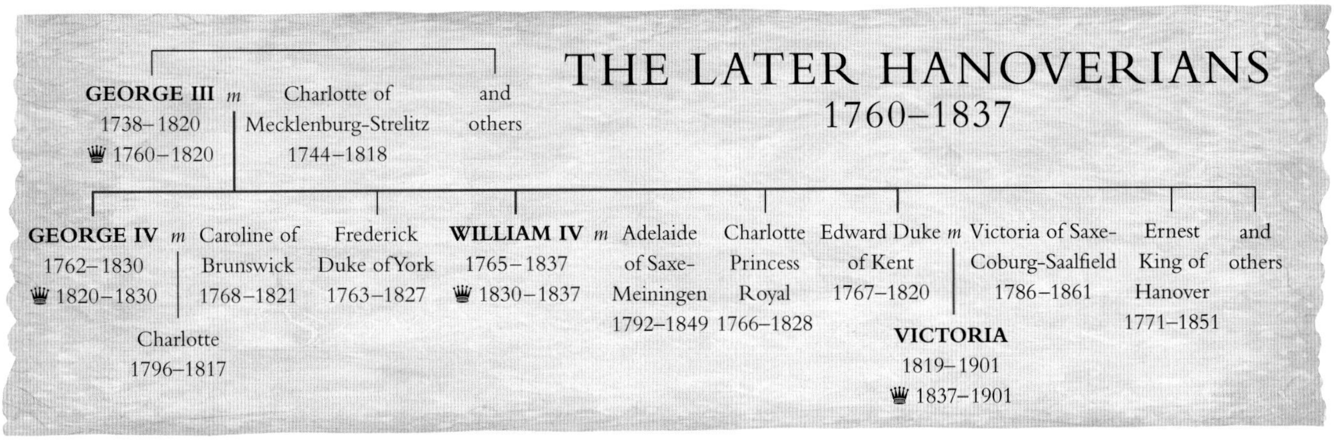

found making speeches and granting audiences something of an ordeal. In 1766 the young king began a letter to his son, then only five years old, in which he offered a statement of his own character and aims. 'I do not pretend to any superior abilities, but will give place to no-one in meaning to preserve the freedom, happiness and glory of my dominions, and all their inhabitants, and to fulfil the duty to my God and my neighbours in the most extended sense.'

His mind and character, however, would be quite unbalanced by repeated attacks from the late 1780s onwards of a mysterious illness that made him unfit to govern by 1811, when the 48-year-old Prince of Wales became 'Prince Regent'.

VICE AND ROYAL EXAMPLE

George's moral nature, together with a strongly developed sense of the dignity of the monarchy, found expression in his attempts to place limits on the amorous exploits of members of the royal family. His own marriage was happy and he was the first king since Charles I not to keep a royal mistress. However, the behaviour of many of his close relatives fell far below his own standards.

In 1770 an affair between his brother Henry, the Duke of Cumberland, and Lady Grosvenor led to a divorce case in which costs and damages of £13,000 were awarded against the duke. George himself had to cover the bill.

Two years later the king broke off relations with Henry after learning that the duke had secretly married a commoner named Ann Horton. Then, in 1772, George discovered that another brother – William Henry, Duke of Gloucester – had secretly wed Maria, Lady Waldegrave, and kept the marriage secret for no less than six years.

Although George was gratified by the passing, on 24 March 1772, of the Royal Marriages Act – which provided that, almost without exception, royal marriages required the king's permission before they could go ahead – he remained concerned that the royal family set a poor example to their subjects at a time of increasing vice. In 1780 he had to pay off an actress who had demanded a bribe in order to return compromising letters that she had received from the Prince of Wales. He wrote to his son, exhorting him to remember his position: 'In the exalted station you are placed in, every step is of consequence'.

Left: The king's brother Henry, Duke of Cumberland, secretly wed commoner Ann Horton. George was furious.

On 1 June 1787 came the embarrassment of the revelation of the Prince of Wales's secret 1785 marriage to a Catholic widow named Maria Fitzherbert. In response, King George issued a royal proclamation against immorality and vice that was sent to mayors and sheriffs across the country.

Below: Princess Charlotte of Mecklenburg-Strelitz became Queen Charlotte on 8 September 1761 at the age of 17.

WAR WITH AMERICA

REVOLUTION, 1773–1783

King George III's reign saw Britain at war with its American colonies and the issue – in Philadelphia on 4 July 1776 – of the American Declaration of Independence. This document declared George 'Unfit to be the Ruler of a free People' and stated that 'The History of the present King of Great-Britain is a History of repeated Injuries and Usurpations, all having in direct Object the Establishment of an absolute Tyranny over these States'.

ROAD TO INDEPENDENCE

Conflict began around a decade earlier over the Stamp Act, imposed in March 1765 on legal documents, newspapers, pamphlets and many other paper items, including playing cards, as a way of raising revenue to help cover the costs of the Seven Years War (1756–63). Americans resisted, declaring that Parliament in London could not impose an internal tax in this way in distant colonies; the Stamp Act was repealed in 1766. However, further taxes on tea, glass, lead, paper and paint were introduced under the 1767 Townshend Act (named after the Chancellor of the Exchequer, Charles Townshend). In Boston, Massachusetts, they provoked a boycott of British goods and rioting. British regiments were called in to try to uphold the law and impose a peace, resulting in the 'Boston Massacre' of 5 March 1770, when British soldiers fired on a group of Americans at the custom house, killing five people. In the same month in Westminster all the taxes were repealed, save that on tea.

Then, in October 1773, Parliament passed the Tea Act, which attempted to establish for the East India Company a monopoly on importing tea to North America. This provoked further unrest in Boston, including the 'Boston Tea Party' of 16 December 1773, when American colonists armed with axes and dressed as Native Americans attacked and boarded three British ships in the harbour, casting overboard hundreds of tea chests containing 90,000lb (41,000kg) of tea.

The disagreement escalated. In 1774 Parliament passed the Coercive Acts, containing punitive measures against the colonists and, in February 1775, Massachusetts was declared to be in a state of rebellion.

Below: Tea overboard. Americans angry at the duties imposed by the Tea Act hurl a precious cargo into Boston Harbour.

Above: American triumph. Britain's Charles Cornwallis surrenders to George Washington at Yorktown in October 1781.

CONFLICT BREAKS OUT

The American War of Independence began on 19 April 1775. In clashes between British troops and colonial soldiers at Lexington and Concord, Massachusetts, the British were foiled in their efforts to destroy arms and supplies.

The next principal event was the besieging of Boston by 15,000-odd colonial troops gathered from Rhode Island, New Hampshire, Connecticut and Massachusetts. The Battle of Bunker Hill, fought nearby on 17 June 1775, was boosted American confidence and self-belief because British casualties were so high: around 1,000 troops were killed or injured, between one quarter and one fifth of the total force. The colonial army, under General George Washington, drove the British out of Boston on 17 March 1776.

King George was not greatly interested in the American colonies until the revolts there called for an official response. Then it became apparent that he was in favour of strong action, to defend the dignity and authority of both monarch and Parliament.

In November 1774 he wrote, 'The New England governments are in a state of rebellion. Blows must decide whether they are to be subject to this country or be independent'.

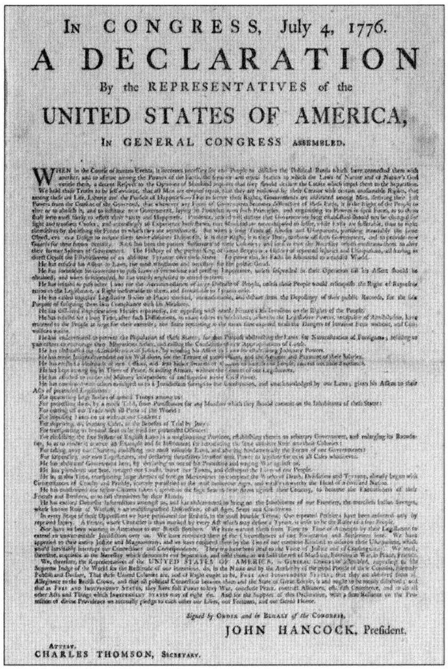
In CONGRESS, July 4, 1776.

A DECLARATION

By the REPRESENTATIVES of the

UNITED STATES OF AMERICA,

In GENERAL CONGRESS assembled.

JOHN HANCOCK, President.

Attest.
CHARLES THOMSON, Secretary.

Above: The American Declaration of Independence of 4 July 1776 was a ringing statement of human equality.

Above: In 1776, after a public reading of the Declaration of Independence, New Yorkers tore down a statue of the king.

The conflict in North America was prolonged and expensive. Britain found itself in the hugely expensive and strategically difficult position of being at war with France, Spain and the Netherlands as well as General George Washington's colonial armies. British troops won a few major victories, but could not build on them, not least because their supply lines were being almost constantly attacked by American guerrilla forces.

After Britain lost control of the seas to the French in the five-day Battle of the Capes, 5–9 September 1781, final defeat in America was only a matter of time. General Cornwallis surrendered to American forces at Yorktown on 19 October 1781.

AMERICANS DENOUNCE GEORGE'S RULE

The Declaration of Independence contained a list of George's despotic acts, including the following.

• He has refused his Assent to Laws, the most wholesome and necessary for the public good.

• He has dissolved Representative Houses repeatedly, for opposing with manly firmness his invasions on the rights of the people.

• He has erected a multitude of New Offices, and sent hither swarms of Officers to harass our people and eat out their substance.

• For cutting off our Trade with all parts of the world:

• For imposing Taxes on us without our Consent:

• He has kept among us, in times of peace, Standing Armies, without the Consent of our legislature.

• He has combined with others to subject us to a jurisdiction foreign to our constitution, and unacknowledged by our laws; giving his Assent to their Acts of pretended Legislation:

• For depriving us in many cases, of the benefit of Trial by Jury:

• For transporting us beyond Seas to be tried for pretended offences.

• He has abdicated Government here, by declaring us out of his Protection and waging War against us.

• He has plundered our seas, ravaged our Coasts, burnt our Towns, and destroyed the Lives of our People.

INDEPENDENCE RECOGNIZED

Back in London, King George refused to accept that the conflict was over. However, the House of Commons voted against continuing the struggle and the Prime Minister, Lord North, who had wanted to scale down rather than conclude the conflict, resigned on 20 March 1782. King George contemplated abdication and drafted a message explaining his decision, but stayed on and accepted a Whig ministry led by the Marquis of Rockingham.

British naval victories in 1782 – notably Admiral Rodney's defeat of the French in the Battle of the Saints, off Dominica, on 12 April – meant that the peace agreed in the Treaty of Versailles, on 3 September 1783, was far more favourable to Britain that it might have otherwise have been.

The United States of America gained its independence; France took Tobago and Senegal; Spain had Minorca and Florida; Britain retained possession of Gibraltar, India, Canada and the West Indies. King George had by this time reconciled himself with some sadness to the loss of Britain's American colonies.

THE GOVERNMENT OF GEORGE III

CONFLICT AT HOME, 1760–1780

King George III's attempts to maintain the power of the monarchy both at home and in the American colonies were attacked as tyranny or attempts at absolutism. However, George did not want to turn the clock back to the Stuart era of absolute royal rule. Devout and conscientious, he saw it as his God-given duty to rule with authority and expected the willing consent of Parliament. Right from the start of the reign he struggled to maintain this authority in the face of an ever-stronger and more independent Parliament and public criticism of his actions.

GEORGE III IN GOVERNMENT

The first ten years of the reign, 1760–70, saw a succession of ministries come and go. George had expected to enjoy a lengthy rule alongside his former tutor the Earl of Bute when he appointed him Prime Minister in May 1762, but Bute resigned in April 1763 after a short and extremely ineffective spell in government. His successor, George Grenville, lasted only until 16 July 1765, when he was replaced by the Marquis of Rockingham. He in turn was replaced on 4 August 1766 by William Pitt, Earl of Chatham, who resigned due to ill health on 19 October 1768 and was replaced by the Duke of Grafton. Only with the government of Lord North, Prime Minister from 28 January 1770, was some measure of stability achieved. Nonetheless, North's 12-year tenure saw the escalation of troubles in North America and the loss of the American colonies.

'THAT DEVIL WILKES'

The reign's first decade was also marred for King George by the activities of politician and journalist John Wilkes. MP for Aylesbury from 1757, Wilkes was also editor of the *North Briton* newspaper, in which he made raucous attacks on King George and the Earl of Bute's government.

The man dismissed by the king as 'that devil Wilkes' was initially thrown in the Tower of London, provoking a public outcry under the slogan 'Wilkes and Liberty!' He was released after less than a week on the grounds that his detention violated parliamentary privilege. However, following the discovery of an obscene poem at his printing press he was expelled from the Commons and found guilty of seditious libel and

Above: Hogarth's engraving shows John Wilkes in 1763, the year in which the radical published issue 45 of the North Briton*, which attacked the king.*

Below: This Protestant demonstration against the 1778 Catholic Repeal Act sparked the week-long Gordon Riots.

END OF AN ERA

James Stuart, son of King James II and figurehead for the Jacobite revolts of 1715, 1719 and 1745, died in Rome on 1 January 1766 at the age of 77. He was buried in St Peter's after a truly splendid memorial ceremony – in which his body, dressed in robes of crimson velvet and wearing a crown, was laid beneath a banner proclaiming him *Jacobus Tertius Magnae Britannia Rex* ('King James III of Great Britain'). His son, 'Bonnie Prince Charlie', survived him. But he, too, died on 30 January 1788 in Rome. The deaths of the men known as the 'Old Pretender' and the 'Young Pretender' marked the end of the Stuart era in European royal life.

Above: The future Buckingham Palace was built to William Talman's designs in 1702. It belonged to the Duke of Buckingham before becoming a royal possession in 1762.

obscenity on 21 February 1764. He was by now in French exile, having travelled to Paris at Christmas 1763.

In a general election of March 1768 he was elected MP for Middlesex and the following month returned to London, where he gave himself up for imprisonment. He remained in jail until April 1770, despite being re-elected MP and expelled from the Commons no fewer than three times in the period. He was a persistent problem for king and government. Always popular with Londoners, in October-November 1774 he was elected Mayor of London and returned again as MP for Middlesex.

THE KING DENOUNCED

Criticism of the king and his role in government remained strong. In April 1780, MPs in the House of Commons voted by 233 to 215 to pass the motion that, 'The influence of the crown has increased, is increasing and ought to be diminished'. As the war in North America ran down to a humiliating defeat, the king and Lord North's government were cast as incompetent.

In Parliament, Charles James Fox, the MP for Westminster, was a committed opponent of George and of royal power. He declared that, 'The influence of the crown', which he called 'one grand evil', was the primary cause of Britain's troubles at home and abroad.

The year 1780 saw violent London riots, sparked by an atmosphere of anti-Catholic hysteria that had developed in the wake of the passing of the 1778 Catholic Relief Act, which lifted some anti-Catholic laws. This troubling atmosphere exploded in June 1780, when Wiltshire MP Lord George Gordon incited a five-day London riot in which Catholic churches and houses were burned and around 850 people were killed. In the face of this unrest King George acted with calm authority. Indeed, although he endured criticism in Parliament and from radicals such as Wilkes and Fox, among the people George III maintained a significant level of popularity – even after the loss of the American colonies.

KING GEORGE AND THE ARTS

George III was a keen musician and an able performer on harpsichord and flute. He liked chess, was an amateur painter and also enjoyed collecting books. He took an interest in mechanics and science, investigating the workings of clocks as well as studying astronomy.

George was also a significant patron of the arts. In 1768 he founded the Royal Academy, 'For the purpose of cultivating the arts of painting, sculpture and architecture'. Its first president was portrait painter Sir Joshua Reynolds.

King George and Queen Charlotte received the eight-year-old boy genius Wolfgang Amadeus Mozart in 1764. Later in the reign the Austrian composer Joseph Haydn became a favourite.

Right: Wolfgang Amadeus Mozart performed twice for the king and Queen Charlotte during his 1764 visit.

George also bought Buckingham House, the future Buckingham Palace, in 1762 and had Dr Johnson create a library there in 1767. Robert Adam was appointed to the post of royal architect 1761–9 and Josiah Wedgwood served as the Queen's potter from 1765.

THE MADNESS OF GEORGE III

INSANITY AND THE KING, 1810–1820

On 3 November 1810 King George was confined in a straitjacket. The death on the previous day of his beloved youngest child, Princess Amelia, at the age of 27, brought on a recurrence of the mysterious illness that robbed him of his mental faculties. He had recovered from previous attacks but this time, despite initial intervals of mental clarity, he descended beyond the reach of his doctors into a decade-long darkness that lasted until his death in January 1820.

A MYSTERY ILLNESS

The king was struck down with serious illness very early in the reign. In 1762 and 1765 he suffered attacks of serious chest pains, hoarseness, a racing pulse and violent coughing. Following an official visit during the second bout, the Prime Minister George Grenville reported that George's '...countenance and manner were a good deal estranged'. George himself was brought to an awareness of his own mortality and was sufficiently alarmed to propose that plans should be made to establish a regency should he die suddenly.

The first attack of madness came in the autumn of 1788. The illness affected the king's eyesight – he complained of a mist clouding his vision and his eyes appeared bloodshot – and also made him talk in a rambling, incoherent and sometimes lewd manner. He also behaved violently on occasion. During a walk in Windsor Great Park at this time he was discovered talking to an oak tree, which he had apparently mistaken for the king of Prussia. At another point during this bout he attacked his son, the Prince of Wales.

King George's doctors were at a loss. In 1788, Queen Charlotte lost faith in them and entrusted her husband to the care of the Reverend Francis Willis, owner of an asylum for the mentally unbalanced in Wiltshire but not a qualified doctor. Willis promised a cure. The first attack ended after three months in the spring of 1789, and the recovery was celebrated in a service of thanksgiving in St Paul's Cathedral on 23 April 1789. Afterwards he and Queen Charlotte spent the summer of 1789 recuperating at a house belonging to the Duke of Gloucester in Weymouth, Dorset.

A second attack, with identical symptoms to the first, including the profound mental confusion so alarming to the

Above: Princesses Mary, Sophia and Amelia. The death of George's beloved Amelia precipitated his final madness.

BRITAIN ABROAD

In King George III's long reign the foundations were laid for Britain's great global empire of the 19th and early 20th centuries. At the close of the Seven Years War, the 1763 Treaty of Paris brought Britain widespread territories. Many of these were retained, following the loss of the North American colonies, in the 1783 Treaty of Versailles, when Britain remained in control of the West Indies, India, Canada and Gibraltar. Captain James Cook also claimed Australia and New Zealand for Britain in the early 1770s; the penal colony of Botany Bay was established near the 'new town' of Sydney in January 1788. The 1801 Act of Union eased British anxieties that following the creation of the USA and the French Revolution of 1789, Ireland would achieve independence.

Below: By George III's reign, Britain's overseas empire took in parts of Africa and India as well as North America.

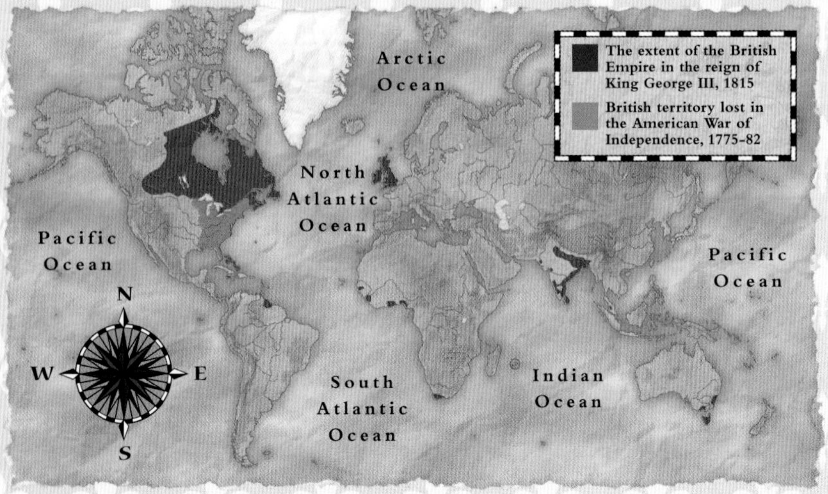

WHAT WAS THE KING'S ILLNESS?

Historians once thought that the king's sickness was largely psychosomatic, brought on by the enormous stresses of political upheaval, the loss of Britain's North American colonies, and family tragedy, including the death in 1810 of his youngest and favourite daughter Amelia.

However, we now know that George III probably suffered from acute intermittent porphyria, a hereditary condition in which, from time to time, the body cannot manufacture the blood pigment haemoglobin and as a result porphyrins (substances normally used to make haemoglobin) accumulate in the blood stream and damage the nervous system. Attacks normally come and go because the body's failure to make haemoglobin is triggered by other illness or profound emotional stress.

Right: In his pathetic final years, George often wore nothing more formal than a dressing gown and was bullied by doctors.

government, struck on 13 February 1801 and lasted around four weeks. George's recovery was, however, assured on 11 March 1801.

Another attack in February 1804 led to the appointment of Dr Simons, from St Luke's Hospital for Lunatics, a great believer in the use of the straitjacket to confine disturbed individuals. George had fully recovered by the summer when he visited Weymouth once more to recuperate.

KING GEORGE'S LAST YEARS

After 1811 the king was a truly pathetic figure, completely blind and increasingly deaf, with long straggling white hair and beard. He did not recognize Queen Charlotte when she visited him and he could not sleep, even after taking laudanum. He took comfort in a harpsichord that had once belonged to Handel, but could not play it as he once had because of his deteriorating hearing. He was detached from his former self and the glorious life he had once lived. He reportedly told a courtier that the harpsichord in question had once been a favourite of the late King George, when that monarch was alive. He conducted conversations with Lord North, who had been dead since 1792, and inspected invisible military parades.

THE KING'S REPUTATION

History has not been kind to King George III. He is remembered as a pathetic figure in his madness. As a sane man, he is generally remembered as something of a fool; a hopeless king who rode roughshod over American sensibilities, provoking a war that brought about the loss of the North American colonies – a catastrophic event for Britain if a proud one for the nascent United States of America. He is made the source of foolish quotes: his diary entry for 4 July 1776, the day of the American Declaration of Independence, read, 'Nothing of importance happened today'; but of course events in America were not known in Europe for weeks.

King George is viewed as a faintly ridiculous figure in his guise as 'Farmer George'. The epithet refers to the interest he took in modern agricultural methods, which he applied with some success in farms at Windsor and Richmond. In the years before madness carried him off, George was a devout and highly conscientious ruler, with a developed sense of his destiny that was somewhat at odds with his achievements. He endeavoured to follow his appointed duty.

As he said to the US ambassador John Adam at their first meeting, in reference to the American War of Independence, 'I have done nothing in the late contest, but what I thought myself indispensably bound to do by the Duty which I owed to my people.'

Below: A cartoon by William Charles shows Charles James Fox, a persistent enemy of George III, with fellow radicals.

THE PRINCE REGENT

1811–1821

Parliament passed the Regency Act on 5 February 1811, under which the Prince of Wales, 'by reason of the severe Indisposition with which it hath pleased God to afflict the King's Most Excellent Majesty', took 'Full power and authority, in the name and on behalf of His Majesty, and under the stile and title of Regent of the United Kingdom of Great Britain and Ireland, to exercise and administer the royal power'. The 'Prince Regent' swore oaths of office on 6 February 1811.

Initially both the prince and the government hoped that the Regency would be short-lived, for the king had previously recovered from his bouts of illness after a few weeks or months and the regency provision were set to expire after a year. However, by February 1812 it was becoming increasingly apparent

Above: Heroics described. The Duke of Wellington (left) shows the battlefield at Waterloo to the Prince Regent.

that the king would not recover and accordingly the Prince of Wales's regency was made permanent.

HANOVERIAN CENTENARY

On 1 August 1814 the Prince Regent hosted lavish celebrations in the parks of central London to mark the 100th anniversary of the Hanoverian accession. The celebrations included the erection of a spectacular seven-storey Chinese pagoda in St James's Park and of arcades and roundabouts in Hyde Park; meanwhile, a 'sea battle' was enacted on the waters of the Serpentine. After dark, fireworks lit the sky above Green Park, where a gothic castle had been temporarily built.

Earlier that summer, Prince George had helped King Louis XVIII celebrate the restoration to the French throne of the House of Bourbon. This followed the abdication of the French emperor, Napoleon, on 6 April and his subsequent exile to the island of Elba. The prince processed through central London in a state carriage with the restored king and, after a short London

Left: Prince regal. This imposing portrait by royal painter Sir Thomas Lawrence shows George in his Garter robes in 1816.

stay, Louis was escorted by the Royal Navy on his return to France. Prince George also threw a gala at Carlton House to celebrate the military triumphs of the Duke of Wellington.

Above: James Gillray's cartoon shows the voluptuary Prince Regent hard at work digesting his latest epic dinner.

THE DEPARTURE OF CAROLINE

On 8 August 1814 Caroline, Princess of Wales, left the Prince Regent and returned to her native Duchy of Brunswick (northern Germany). This followed many years of open marital difficulties exacerbated by the fact that the Princess was far more popular than the dissolute Prince with the British public. The Prince of Wales was not only openly unfaithful with a string of mistresses but also tried to exclude the princess from public life.

VICTORY AT WATERLOO

The Duke of Wellington's defeat of the French emperor Napoleon at the Battle of Waterloo on 18 June 1815 was one of the great events of the prince's regency. The prince learned the news on the very evening of the battle, when the society party he was attending was interrupted by the arrival of Major Henry Percy, who had ridden directly from the battlefield in Belgium. Major Percy, dirty and bloodspattered, dropped to one knee as he laid the captured battle insignia of the French army on the floor at the Prince Regent's feet and Lord Liverpool read aloud the battle despatch from Wellington. On the spot the Prince Regent promoted Major Percy to Colonel. A little later, Prince George commented, 'It is a glorious victory and we must rejoice at it. But the loss of life has been fearful.'

Left: The prince's only child, Princess Charlotte. Her death sparked a royal scramble to produce a suitable heir.

A NEW SUCCESSION CRISIS

The Prince Regent's only child, Princess Charlotte, died on 6 November 1817 after a stillbirth. The succession was suddenly plunged into doubt and later in the month Parliament recommended that all unmarried royals of suitable age should be wed. On 24 May 1819 the Duke of Kent's wife, Princess Victoria of Saxe-Coburg, who had travelled all the way from Germany to England in a coach to ensure that her child was born in England, gave birth to the future Queen Victoria.

With the death of the 82-year-old King George III on 29 January 1820, the Prince Regent acceded to the throne as King George IV.

REGENCY ARTS AND ARCHITECTURE

A CLASSICAL REVIVAL, 1811–1821

Above: The Prince's lavish London home, Carlton House. Novelist Jane Austen visited, at George's invitation, in 1815.

First as Prince of Wales, then Prince Regent and finally King George IV, George Augustus Frederick was forcibly criticized for self-indulgence and extravagance. However, in one important area his free spending left an enduring and positive legacy, for he was an enthusiastic and discerning patron of the arts, particularly in the field of architecture. He indisputably enriched his realm through his association with architect John Nash, designer of Regent's Park and Regent Street in London and extravagant remodeller of the Royal Pavilion in Brighton.

NASH'S GREAT PROJECTS

After an unsuccessful period in 1780s London, Nash made his name as an architect of country houses in Wales before returning to London and entering the employment of the Prince of Wales in 1798. In 1806, as Prince Regent, George engineered Nash's appointment as Architect in the Office of Woods and Forests, which allowed Nash to make his mark in the design of the 'New Street' proposed to link the Regent's palace, Carlton House, to planned new developments in Marylebone Park (now Regent's Park). The twin projects came under the aegis of this office because they involved building on Marylebone Park, where large areas were due to revert to the crown on the expiry of leases in 1811. In the event, Nash was architect both of the 'New Street' and of the Marylebone Park developments.

Below: East meets West. John Nash's 'Hindu-Gothic' designs transformed George's Marine Pavilion in Brighton.

Work began on the street under the New Street Act of 1813 and was completed around 1825. Nash's design included the development of partly residential Lower Regent Street, Piccadilly Circus, a curved shopping section (the Quadrant) between Piccadilly Circus and Oxford Circus, and north of Oxford Circus an upper residential stretch running as far as Portland Place. The grandest section was the Quadrant, laid out with rows of cast-iron colonnades, creating covered walkways that allowed shoppers to carry on their business despite London rain. Nash's original and highly stylish plans for the park, which created an elegant layout with grand terraces, scattered villas, a

Left: Regency elegance. This is 'New Street' (later 'Regent's Street') in London as it appeared in the early 19th century.

lake and a wooded area, attracted considerable criticism, but the Prince Regent strenuously defended them and ensured they came to fruition. Building work began in 1817 and was largely complete by 1828.

In the years 1815–23 Nash remodelled George's Royal Pavilion in Brighton in an extravagant 'Hindu-Gothic' style that combined classical architecture with elements derived from Indian temples and palaces. Originally a farmhouse, the building had been rebuilt for George as a 'Marine Pavilion' by architect Henry Holland in 1787.

Other Nash projects included the redesign of St James's Park (1827–29) and the redevelopment of Buckingham House as a palace. On the death of King George IV in 1830, however, Nash was removed from the Buckingham Palace job because of escalating costs and doubts about the building's structural soundness.

ART, MUSIC AND LITERATURE

In the field of the visual arts, George commissioned works from John Constable, George Stubbs, Thomas Gainsborough, Thomas Lawrence and Joshua Reynolds, while also buying art by masters such as Rubens and Rembrandt for his Carlton House collection. He showed his appreciation of Italian neoclassical sculptor Antonio Canova by welcoming him on his visit to London in 1815 and commissioning the life-size group sculpture 'Venus and Mars'. He opened his collection to the public, and he played an important role in the 1824 establishment of the National Gallery.

In music George was a keen patron of the Austrian composer Joseph Haydn, whom he first met in the course of the composer's 1791–2 visit to London. On this and a second visit to London in 1794, Haydn wrote 12 symphonies, which were ecstatically received by the royal family and the London public. They included *The Surprise* (Number 94), *The Drumroll* (Number 103) and the *London Symphonies* (Numbers 99–104).

In 1820 George was a founding member of the Royal Society of Literature. He was a friend of Sir Walter Scott and reportedly a keen reader of the novels of Jane Austen.

George invited Austen to Carlton House in 1815 and she is known to have attended, although it does not appear that she actually met the prince, rather spending her time with George's librarian, a Mr Clarke. She was informed that George kept a set of her novels in each of his houses. She returned the compliment by putting this dedication at the start of her next novel, *Emma* (1816): 'To His Royal Highness, The Prince Regent, this work is, by his Royal Highness's permission, most respectfully dedicated, by His Royal Highness's dutiful and obedient humble servant, the Author'.

Below: John Nash set about adding regal grandeur to Buckingham Palace. This view of the imposing Saloon appeared in W.H. Pyne's Royal Residences *(1818).*

GEORGE IV

1820–1830

Two days after the death of George III, his son the Prince Regent was proclaimed King George IV on 29 January 1820. The portly, self-indulgent prince had pursued a hard-drinking, womanizing lifestyle since at least 1779 when, at the age of 17, he began a love affair with a married actress. His behaviour made him unpopular, and this was exacerbated by his refusal to mend his ways following his marriage to Princess Caroline of Brunswick-Wolfenbüttel in 1795. The royal couple lived together for only one out of the 19 years from that date until 1814, when the princess abandoned her husband and returned to Brunswick.

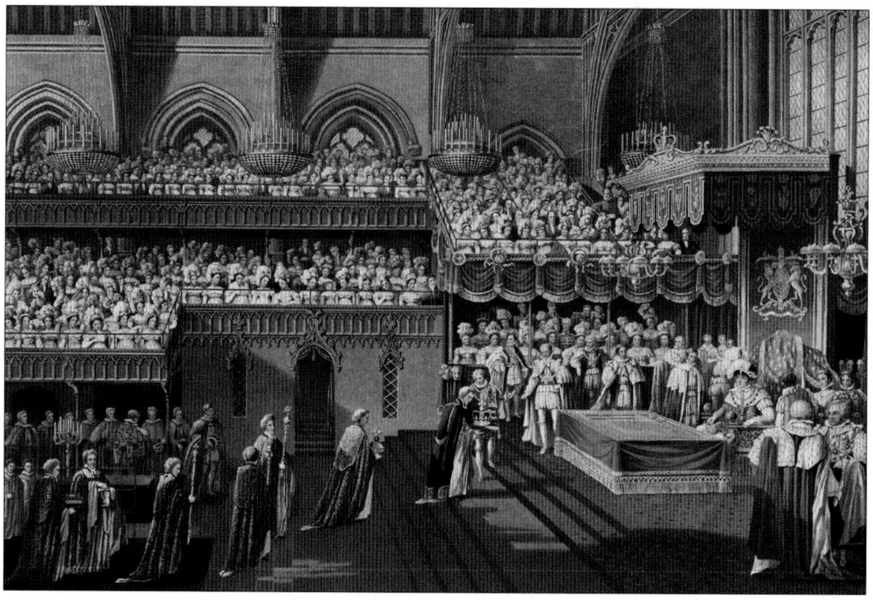

Above: In his coronation sermon, the Archbishop of York urged the king to deliver Britain from the 'contagion of vice'.

THE INJURED QUEEN

Within six months of George's accession, the former Princess of Wales returned from the Continent in June 1820 to claim her rightful position as Queen of England. A bill was introduced in the House of Lords to dissolve the marriage on the grounds of the queen's alleged adultery and so exclude her from the monarchy. Public feeling was aroused by the king's ill-treatment of his wife and, when the bill failed to pass in November 1820, the news sparked wholly remarkable scenes of public rejoicing: bonfires were lit, processions and dances were laid on and Londoners celebrated in the streets.

The following year, when King George IV was crowned in the utmost splendour at Westminster Abbey, his queen tried several times without success to gain admission to the abbey.

George's coronation was as extravagant as the rest of his life: he wore a crimson velvet train some 27ft (8.2m) long and processed from Westminster Hall to the abbey beneath a canopy of cloth of gold. The celebrations, which included a five-hour service, a vast banquet and fireworks in Hyde Park, cost around £240,000.

Queen Caroline did not live long to trouble her royal husband. She was taken ill on the very night of the coronation, and died from an inflammation

GEORGE IV, KING OF THE UNITED KINGDOM OF GREAT BRITAIN AND IRELAND AND ELECTOR OF HANOVER, 1820–1830

Birth: 12 Aug 1762, St James's Palace, London
Father: George III
Mother: Charlotte of Mecklenburg-Strelitz
Accession: As Prince Regent, 6 Feb 1811; as King: 29 Jan 1820
Coronation: 19 July 1821
Queen: Princess Caroline of Brunswick-Wolfenbüttel (m. 8 April 1795; d. 7 Aug 1821)
Succeeded by: His brother William IV
Greatest achievement: Artistic patronage, especially the creation of Regent's Park and Regent Street
6 Feb 1811: Becomes Prince Regent due to King George III's illness
8 Aug 1814: Princess of Wales abandons George and returns to Brunswick
6 Nov 1817: George's only daughter, Princess Charlotte, dies
29 Jan 1820: Accedes to throne on death of King George III
23 Feb 1820: 'Conspirators of Cato Street', plotting murder of the cabinet, are arrested
29 Nov 1820: Inquiry clears Queen Caroline of adultery
7 Aug 1821: Queen Caroline dies
Aug–Sept 1821: George makes triumphant visit to Ireland
Aug 1822: George visits Edinburgh and dons a kilt
16 April 1829: Catholic Emancipation Act lifts restrictions on Catholics holding public office
Death: 26 June 1830 at Windsor. Buried in St George's Chapel, Windsor

Above: Queen Caroline appears to loom out of George's mirror in an anonymous cartoon published on his accession.

or blockage of the bowels on 7 August 1821 in Hammersmith, west of London. One of her final requests was that she be interred not in England but in Brunswick. Her coffin was carried on a funeral procession to Harwich, where those sympathetic to her memory placed on it the inscription 'Caroline, the injured Queen of England'.

THE KING KILTED

King George IV made a royal visit to Edinburgh in August 1822, as part of a post-coronation 'royal progress' through his kingdom. Arrangements were placed in the hands of the king's friend, the novelist Sir Walter Scott, who had been a guest at the coronation the previous year. Keen to stress the independence and richness of Scots culture, Scott arranged for Highland clan chiefs, bagpipes and kilts to play a prominent part in the proceedings.

George sailed to Scotland on board his yacht, the *Royal George*, and disembarked at the port of Leith. As he processed through the streets of Edinburgh he was greeted by banners emphasizing Scottish links to the royal line. One read, 'Descendant of the immortal Bruce, thrice welcome', another, 'Welcome to the land of your ancestors'. He attended a levée at Holyrood Palace dressed in a kilt, much to the delight of his hosts, and processed alongside MacGregor, Drummond and MacDonnell clansmen from Holyrood to Edinburgh Castle. From the castle, he looked down on the city and exclaimed, 'What a fine sight...the people are as beautiful and extraordinary as the scene.' He also attended several balls and a dramatization at the Theatre Royal of Scott's novel *Rob Roy*. The popularity of Scott's novels and also of King George's visit to Scotland was to spark a revival of interest in the history and traditions of the Highland clans – not least in the wearing of clan tartan in the late Victorian period.

THE KING'S ILLNESS

From 1823 George increasingly kept away from London, living in his extravagant Brighton Pavilion and at Windsor Castle with his latest mistress, Marchioness Conyngham. Years of debauchery had ruined his physique, which was severely bloated by dropsy and wracked with pain from rheumatism. He continued in his bad habits, drinking very heavily, while also complaining of his afflictions. The Duke of Wellington, who visited him in Windsor, declared that there was nothing wrong with the king save the troubles caused by 'Strong liquors taken too frequently and in too large quantities', adding that George 'Drinks spirits morning, noon and night'.

The king also took laudanum – often as much as 250 drops per day – to counter bladder inflammation; he may also, like his father, have suffered from porphyria. He had attacks of severe breathlessness in which he would have to struggle so hard to draw breath that his fingertips tuned black. He died at Windsor on 26 June 1830. His last words, delivered to his doctor Sir Wathen Waller in a paroxysm of pain, were, 'My dear boy! This is death!'

There was little sadness at his passing. *The Times* declared that there had never been 'An individual less regretted by his fellow creatures than this deceased king'. George was succeeded by his brother William, Duke of Clarence, who reigned as King William IV.

Below: Caroline. She accepted a payment of £50,000 per annum to go abroad, but died within a fortnight of the coronation.

Below: King of Scots. George's visit to Scotland in 1822 was the first by a ruling monarch since that of Charles II.

WILLIAM IV
1830–1837

William, Duke of Clarence, was woken at 6 a.m. on 26 June 1830 to be told that he was king because his older brother, George IV, had died in the small hours. William reportedly shook the messengers by the hand and retired to bed with the joke that it had long been his ambition to sleep with a queen. Later that morning he rode from his home, Bushy House, Teddington, to Windsor, cheerfully receiving the acclamations of the people he passed and exhibiting no signs of grief at his brother's death.

WILLIAM IV, KING OF THE UNITED KINGDOM OF GREAT BRITAIN AND IRELAND AND ELECTOR OF HANOVER, 1830–1837

Birth: 21 Aug 1765 at Buckingham House, London
Father: George III
Mother: Charlotte of Mecklenburg-Strelitz
Accession: 26 June 1830
Coronation: 8 Sept 1831, Westminster Abbey
Queen: Princess Adelaide of Saxe-Meiningen (m. 11 July 1818; d. 2 Dec 1849)
Succeeded by: His niece, Victoria
Greatest achievement: Intervening in the passage of the first Reform Act, which marked Britain's progress towards full democracy
7 June 1832: Reform Act passed
Nov 1834: Fire destroys the Houses of Parliament
24 May 1837: Princess Victoria, heir to the throne, celebrates her 18th birthday; she can now inherit the throne in her own right
20 June 1837: Dies at Windsor and is buried in St George's Chapel, Windsor

A VERY DIFFERENT BROTHER

The 64-year-old duke had been heir to the throne for only three years following the death in January 1827 of Frederick, Duke of York. He had a bluff, easy-going manner, perhaps explained by the fact that he joined the navy aged 13. He had risen to the rank of lieutenant and taken command of a frigate of 28 guns before he was recalled to civilian life by the Prince of Wales in 1788 at a time when their father was incapacitated by physical illness and mental confusion.

Below: The king's name is forever linked to the 1832 Reform Act, which moved Britain towards fuller democracy.

William lived from 1791 to 1811 with the celebrated actress Mrs Dorothy Jordan, with whom he had ten illegitimate children (five daughters and five sons). In 1818, when the death of Princess Charlotte sparked a mini succession crisis, he married Princess Adelaide of Saxe-Meiningen in a double ceremony on 11 July with his brother Edward, Duke of Kent (who married Princess Victoria of Saxe-Coburg). However, all the children of William's marriage died, so on his accession he was unable to offer a succession through legitimate heirs.

A POPULAR KING

William was immediately popular with his people. In Windsor he opened the East Terrace and various parts of the Great Park to the public and threw an open-air banquet for 3,000 impoverished locals to mark his birthday on 21 August 1830. The king sat with his people to eat from a menu of veal, ham, beef and plum pudding.

He regularly walked the streets of Windsor, London and Brighton rather than ride in a carriage and had the facility of talking easily to strangers. Acutely aware of the resentment that had been caused by the extravagance of his self-indulgent brother George IV, he took care to have a relatively frugal, low-key coronation in Westminster Abbey on 8 September 1831.

The ceremony cost around £30,000, one-eighth of the £240,000 lavished by George IV on his coronation. One wag called King William's event the 'half-crownation', a reference to the low-denomination half-crown coin.

Below: J.M.W. Turner's painting of Parliament ablaze. The king's household troops were unable to stop the 1834 fire.

Above: Dorothy Jordan was a working actress both before and after embarking on her long relationship with William.

'REFORM BILLY'

The king's actions in April 1831 earned him the nickname 'Reform Billy'. The Tory-dominated House of Lords was attempting to block the Reform Bill introduced by Prime Minister Lord Grey and already passed by the Whig-dominated House of Commons. The Bill extended the franchise and made much-needed changes in seat distribution. On 21 April 1831 King William went personally to the Lords and used his power to dissolve Parliament, thus forcing an election in which the Whigs won a greater majority.

The following year, after a prolonged Parliamentary struggle and street riots to protest against the Lords' continuing efforts to block the bill, William created sufficient Whig peers to pass the bill and for the Act to become law.

PARLIAMENT DESTROYED

A terrible fire in November 1834 reduced the Palace of Westminster, location of the House of Commons and the House of Lords, to a ruin. The fire began when two workmen overstocked a stove in which they were burning elm-wood tally-sticks that had been discarded by the Exchequer. The stove, situated beneath the chamber of the House of Lords, overheated and began a vast conflagration.

In the aftermath, King William offered Buckingham Palace, which he did not like because he associated it with the over-indulgence of his brother's reign, as a replacement home for the two houses of Parliament. His offer was declined.

VICTORIA COMES OF AGE

King William had a long-running feud with his sister-in-law Victoria, Duchess of Kent who, in the event of his death, was set to become regent for her daughter Victoria. He publicly declared that he would live at least as long as Victoria's 18th birthday – 24 May 1837 – to thwart the Duchess of Kent.

In the event, William fell ill just before that day, in April 1837: the death of his daughter Sophia, Lady de L'Isle, in childbirth appeared to deprive him of much of the will to go on. He nonetheless survived until 20 June 1837, so that on his death aged 71 the 18-year-old princess acceded to the throne as Queen Victoria.

Below: Like George III before him, William fell into an irreversible decline after hearing of a beloved daughter's death.

CHAPTER ELEVEN

THE AGE OF VICTORIA

1837–1901

When the 18-year-old Princess Victoria came to the throne on 20 June 1837, the reputation of the monarchy had been considerably damaged by the excesses of the first four kings of the House of Hanover – from George I (1714–27) to George IV (1820–30) – and its reputation was only partially restored by the more restrained William IV (1830–37). However, by the time Queen Victoria died on 22 January 1901, after a reign of sixty-three-and-a-half years, the monarchy was a well-respected and essential British institution: the queen had become a proud symbol of the stability and power of Britain, a country that now possessed 20 per cent of global territory in the greatest empire known to history. The presence of representatives from across the British Empire at the celebrations that marked the Queen's Golden and Diamond Jubilees in 1887 and 1897, marked the establishment of Britain as a worldwide empire.

Largely as a result of this imperial expansion, Queen Victoria's reign saw a tremendous rise in the prestige of the British monarchy. After 1877, when she became Empress of India, the queen was proud to sign herself *Victoria Regina et Imperatrix* ('Victoria, Queen and Empress'). Yet the reign also saw a steady decline in the monarch's real power in government in a continuation of the transformation of the British monarch from ruler to figurehead that was set in motion by the 'Glorious Revolution' of 1689.

Left: The domestic calm of the royal family is presented in a group portrait of Queen Victoria and Prince Albert in 1847 with the eldest five of their offspring – Princess Victoria, Prince Edward, Princess Alice, Prince Alfred and Princess Helena. Victoria would eventually have nine children and 31 surviving grandchildren.

VICTORIA
1837–1901

Like her predecessor King William IV, Victoria was woken in the night to be told the momentous news that the previous occupant of the throne had died. At around 6 a.m. on 20 June 1837 the Archbishop of Canterbury, William Howley, and the Lord Chamberlain, Marquis Conyngham, informed the 18-year-old princess that she was now queen. Within three hours the young queen held a meeting with the Prime Minister Lord Melbourne and informed him that she wanted him to remain in government.

VICTORIA, QUEEN OF THE UNITED KINGDOM OF GREAT BRITAIN AND IRELAND AND EMPRESS OF INDIA, 1837–1901

Birth: 24 May 1819, Kensington Palace, London
Father: Edward Augustus, Duke of Kent
Mother: Victoria of Saxe-Coburg-Saalfeld
Accession: 20 June 1837
Coronation: 28 June 1838
Married: Albert Augustus Charles Emmanuel of Saxe-Coburg-Gotha (m. 10 Feb 1840; d. 14 Dec 1861)
Succeeded by: Her son, Edward VII
Greatest achievement: Figurehead as Empress of the British Empire
10 Feb 1840: Marries Prince Albert of Saxe-Coburg and Gotha
21 Nov 1840: Birth of Victoria's first child, Princess Victoria Adelaide
9 Nov 1841: Birth of Prince Albert Edward, future King Edward VII
1 May 1851: Victoria and Albert open the Great Exhibition
25 June 1857: Albert is 'Prince Consort'
10 March 1863: Prince of Wales marries Princess Alexandra of Denmark
14 Dec 1861: Prince Albert dies
8 April 1871: Queen Victoria opens the Royal Albert Hall as a memorial
1 Jan 1877: Queen Victoria becomes Empress of India
29 March 1883: Death of John Brown, Victoria's 'Highland servant'
20 June 1887: Victoria's Golden Jubilee
20 June 1897: Victoria's Diamond Jubilee
Death: 22 Jan 1901, Osborne House, Isle of Wight. Buried at Frogmore

DESTINED TO BE QUEEN?

Victoria came to the throne as the only legitimate child of Edward Augustus, Duke of Kent, the fourth son of King George III. In 1818, Edward married Princess Victoria of Saxe-Coburg-Saalfeld, and their daughter Alexandrina Victoria was born in Kensington Palace on 24 May 1819. The duke was extremely proud of his baby daughter, and would tell people she was destined to be queen. Unfortunately, within months of the princess's birth he died of pneumonia.

Below: Princess Victoria aged four. Her upbringing was lonely, in the hands of strict German governess Baroness Lehzen.

WILLING TO LEARN

Victoria grew up into a serious-minded young woman. On her accession she noted in her diary, 'Since it has pleased Providence to place me in this station, I shall do my utmost to fulfil my duty towards my country; I am very young, and perhaps in many, though not all things, inexperienced, but I am sure that very few have more real good will and more real desire to do what is fit and right than I have'. She was crowned in great splendour in Westminster Abbey on 28 June 1838.

The young queen was just 4ft 11in (1.5m) tall. Despite rather large blue eyes and a small mouth, she could not be described as beautiful, but she was engaging and charming and observers often described her as 'lovely'.

Left: Victoria had a thorough education. By the age of ten, she was having formal lessons five hours a day, six days a week.

Above: Royal newlyweds and leaders of musical fashion. A piece of sheet music shows the queen dancing with Albert.

'LORD M'

The young queen was aware that she lacked experience in the ways of government and became devoted to her Prime Minister Lord Melbourne, whom she called 'Lord M'. Melbourne was a Whig and Victoria supported the Whigs over the Conservatives, in part because she believed her late father to have been a Whig himself.

However, having lost the support of the House of the Commons, Melbourne was forced to resign on 7 May 1839. Victoria was distressed and wrote in her diary, 'All my happiness gone!…dearest kind Lord Melbourne no more my minister!'

Victoria was obstructive to Melbourne's Conservative successor, Sir Robert Peel. When Peel sought to replace Whig-supporting ladies of the bedchamber with Conservative-supporting ladies, the queen refused to accept the new appointments. After a standoff, Peel declined to form a government and Melbourne returned. Some interpreted this crisis as an attempt by the queen to reassert the monarch's authority over ministers, while many others have seen it as an inappropriately emotional outburst.

PRINCE ALBERT

Victoria announced her engagement to Prince Albert of Saxe-Coburg-Gotha on 23 November 1839. Victoria's uncle, King Leopold of the Belgians, had long envisaged Albert as a suitable match for his niece and had arranged a visit to Britain in May 1836 for Albert and his brother Ernest.

Victoria met Albert then and found him to have 'Every quality that could be desired' but subsequently, and even as late as June 1839, she was convinced that she would prefer to remain single for several years. However, on 10 October, when Albert arrived at Windsor at the start of a prearranged visit, Victoria fell swiftly in love. She afterwards recalled, 'It was with some emotion that I beheld Albert, who is *beautiful*'. Five days later she proposed to him declaring, as she later recalled, that, 'It would make me too happy if he would consent to what I wished (to marry me)'.

ROYAL WEDDING

Victoria and Albert were married at St James's Palace on 10 February 1840. After a magnificent wedding breakfast at Buckingham Palace, they travelled to Windsor for their honeymoon. Their first child, Victoria Adelaide, was born on 21 November 1840. When the doctor announced that the baby was a daughter, a princess, Victoria replied, 'Never mind, the next one will be a prince'. Sure enough, a boy – Albert Edward, the future King Edward VII – was born on 9 November 1841.

Below: Young queen with a great future. In her coronation robes in 1838, Victoria appears to look heavenwards for guidance.

THE CROWN UNDER THREAT

1840–1850

In the 1840s the youthful Queen Victoria survived a number of botched assassination attempts, at a time of growing republican sentiment among radical groups. The first attack came on 10 June 1840, when an 18-year-old named Edward Oxford fired pistols twice at Victoria and Prince Albert as they rode up Constitution Hill in London. The royal couple calmly continued their drive after the attack, as the assailant was captured by a bystander, Mr Millais, and his art student son.

Oxford was tried for high treason, but claimed insanity and was acquitted. Some contemporaries suggested that he was part of a conspiracy by 'Chartists' (working-class supporters of parliamentary reform, in particular of universal suffrage for all males over 21).

Above: On 18 May 1856 the queen presented the Victoria Cross to crippled Crimean war veteran Sir Thomas Troubridge.

THE 'VICTORIA CROSS' AND THE CRIMEAN WAR

Victoria took great pride in the valorous achievements of the British Army in the Crimean War of 1854–6. On 29 January 1856 she introduced a new decoration for bravery called the Victoria Cross and inscribed 'for valour': it brought with it a pension of £10 a year.

Britain had declared war on Russia on 28 February 1854 to defend Turkey against Russian expansion in the regions of the Balkans and the Mediterranean. When Britain's French allies stormed Russian-held Sebastopol in September 1855, Victoria and Albert celebrated by dancing wildly around a bonfire on Craig Gowan near Balmoral. Albert reported it 'A veritable witches' dance supported by whisky'.

At other times Victoria played out her part in the conflict by knitting socks and mittens for the soldiers and writing letters of condolence to be sent to relatives of those killed in the fighting. When the troops returned she reviewed them with great pride at Aldershot on 30 July 1856.

Right: An 1856 engraving celebrates the new honour and various acts of bravery.

Two more attacks followed in summer 1842. The first was made on 30 May, when John Francis attempted to shoot the queen from a distance of only five paces as she and Albert drove down the Mall; the man's pistol was unloaded and he was easily overpowered. The second was made on 3 July, when a youth named John William Bean succeeded in firing a pistol at the queen, but did not hurt her as the weapon was not correctly loaded. Francis was convicted of high treason, but the sentence was commuted to transportation; Bean was sentenced to 18 months' imprisonment.

The more lenient sentence came under a new act passed by Parliament under which hitting the queen or producing a weapon in her presence was no longer considered treason but was made subject to a seven-year prison term and a flogging; in this case, Bean

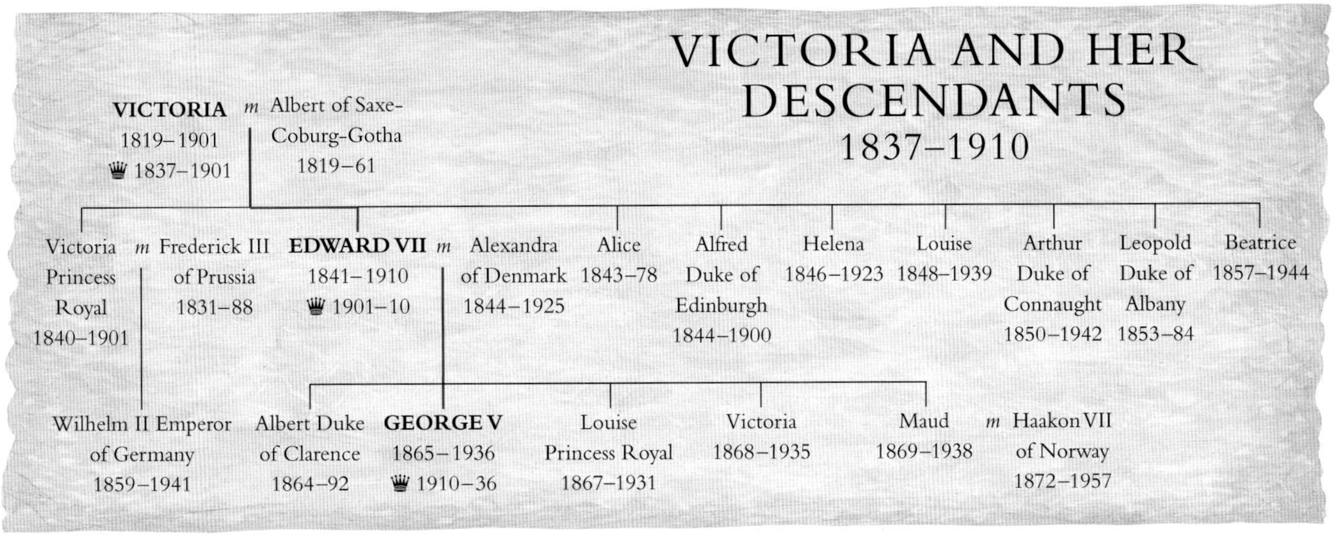

escaped the flogging. Prince Albert supported the introduction of the act. He felt that if attacks were treated as treason and subject to a death penalty they often ended with acquittal, whereas if a less draconian punishment were made available it would be more likely to be imposed – and so act as a deterrent.

FEAR OF REVOLUTION

The year 1848 saw an explosion of revolutionary activity in Europe. In February, King Louis Philippe of France was deposed and took refuge with Queen Victoria. This was followed a month later by revolutionary outbursts in Italy, Germany, Hungary and Austria. Marx and Engels' *Communist Manifesto* was also published in German and French. Given this climate, the British government, royal family and aristocracy were understandably nervous.

On 8 April 1848, two days ahead of a planned Chartist rally in London, Victoria, Albert and their six children left the capital for the safety of their house on the Isle of Wight. They left London in the hands of the Duke of Wellington, who was commanding yeoman regiments with guns arranged to defend the bridges across the Thames. In the event the feared uprising did not take place.

The queen's everyday movements around London nonetheless left her very vulnerable to attack and by the start of the 1850s she had been attacked twice more on the streets of the capital.

On 19 May 1849 an Irishman named William Hamilton shot at her from almost point-blank range as she drove in her carriage down Constitution Hill towards Buckingham Palace following her official birthday celebrations. Once again, and most fortunately, the pistol had not been properly loaded.

On 27 July 1850 she was actually struck by a man named Robert Pate who attacked her with a stick as she travelled in an open carriage through Piccadilly. The queen was left with facial bruises and a very bad headache.

Below: Assassination attempts continued throughout the reign. This one, by Roderick MacLean in Windsor, was in March 1882.

Below: Victoria and Albert had been married only four months when they were attacked by Edward Oxford in June 1840.

THE GREAT EXHIBITION

CRYSTAL PALACE, 1851

On 1 May 1851, Queen Victoria and Prince Albert rode in a fleet of nine state carriages from Buckingham Palace to Hyde Park to open an 'Exhibition of the Works of Industry of all Nations'. The 'Great Exhibition' had been organized principally by Prince Albert and civil servant Henry Cole to celebrate the achievements of modern industry, to 'Combine engineering, utility and beauty in one staggering whole'.

More than 100,000 items were put on display by 14,000 exhibitors from around the world: more than half were from Britain and the British empire. There were 560 exhibits from the United States, including a Colt pistol, Goodyear India rubber products and false teeth.

British exhibits included automated spinning machines, steam engines and pumps. Other magnificent display items included the world's largest pearl and the Koh-i-Noor ('Mountain of brightness') diamond, a Mughal Indian stone that had been acquired by Britain in the 1849 annexation of the Punjab and since placed among Victoria's crown jewels.

Above: This picture of the Italian Court was taken after the Palace and Exhibition were moved to Sydenham, south London.

THE CRYSTAL PALACE

The exhibition was housed in the magnificent Crystal Palace, made of glass and cast-iron. It was designed by Joseph Paxton and based on the design of the conservatory of Chatsworth House, where he worked for the Duke of Devonshire as garden superintendant. The palace stood 1848ft (563m) long and 408ft (124m) across. It covered 18 acres (7 hectares) of parkland, while the exhibition floorspace was 23 acres (9 hectares). It contained almost 300,000 panes of glass and 4000 tons of iron. William Thackeray wrote of the palace, 'A blazing arch of lucid glass/Leaps like a Fountain from the grass'.

At its tallest point, the Crystal Palace was 108ft (33m) tall; its roof rose above the tops of the ancient elms that stood in the part of Hyde Park chosen to erect the building. Initially the developers had problems with sparrows, which flew in and out of the vast building and spattered exhibits with their droppings, but the problem was solved by the Duke of Wellington, who had the idea of deterring the sparrows by introducing sparrowhawks to hunt them.

The sun shone brilliantly through the glass roof as Victoria, Albert and their eldest offspring, 'Vicky' and 'Bertie', took their place on a dais in the centre of the building. A 600-strong choir sang the National Anthem, before the Archbishop of Canterbury read a prayer and the choir performed Handel's 'Hallelujah' Chorus. The Marquis of Breadalbane declared, 'Her Majesty commands me to declare the Exhibition opened'. Victoria was overwhelmed by the triumph. As she afterwards reported, the occasion was 'The greatest day in our history...the triumph of my beloved

Left: On 1 May 1851, the royal party arrives at the Crystal Palace in Hyde Park to open the fêted Great Exhibition.

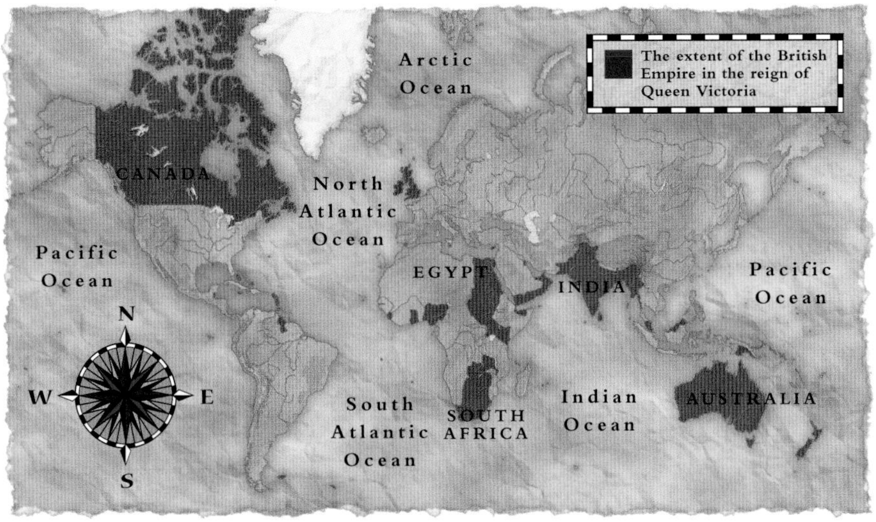

Above: The Exhibition celebrated the pride of queen and people in the achievements of industry and the spread of the empire.

Above: Victoria reported that the opening was 'The most beautiful and imposing and touching spectacle ever seen'.

Albert...It was the happiest, proudest day in my life, and I can think of nothing else, Albert's dearest name immortalized with this great conception...The triumph is immense.'

The project was closely associated with Prince Albert, who at a meeting of the Royal Society of Arts in 1849 had promoted an earlier suggestion by Henry Cole to put on such an exhibition. Albert chaired a Royal Commission, established in 1850 and containing many members of the great and the good, including Gladstone, Peel and the Duke of Devonshire, to raise funds and make practical preparations.

At a meeting at the Mansion House on 21 March 1850 to launch preparations for the exhibition, Albert declared that it would promote 'Achievements of modern invention' and be a 'Living picture of the point of development at which mankind has arrived, and a new starting point from which all nations will be able to direct their future exertions'. For three months after the opening, Victoria came as often as every other day to the exhibition: she even visited the Crystal Palace on her 32nd birthday, 24 May.

Right: A writer in The Times *likened the crowds gathered around Victoria at the opening to the heavenly host: 'Some were reminded of that day when all...should be gathered round the Throne of their maker'.*

SYMBOL OF AN AGE

The Great Exhibition was open from 1 May to 15 October 1851. It attracted six million visitors from around the world and made a profit of £186,000, which was used to build the Natural History Museum, the Victoria and Albert Museum and the Science Museum in the second half of the 19th century; the area of South Kensington in which the museums were built was nicknamed 'Albertopolis' in the Victorian age. The Crystal Palace was dismantled and rebuilt in Sydenham Hill, south London where, such was the quality of its construction, it survived intact until 1936, when it burnt down.

The Great Exhibition and the Crystal Palace are generally seen as symbols of the Victorian age. The exhibition contained many modern industrial items and exhibits. The world was changing: in the 1851 population census, for the first time in British history, town-dwellers outnumbered people living in the country. At the centre was the queen, a reassuring source of stability.

ALBERT AND THE ROYAL FAMILY

1840–1861

In the first years after Victoria's marriage to Prince Albert in 1840, the queen was determined that the responsibilities of government should not be shared by her husband, but she very quickly became dependent on his advice and – particularly during her pregnancies – he played an increasingly central role in affairs of state and meetings with ministers.

As early as 1845, Charles Greville commented, 'It is obvious that while she has the title, he is really discharging the functions of the Sovereign. He is the King to all intents and purposes.'

When Prince Albert died in 1861, Victoria reflected that she had 'Leant on him for all and everything – without whom I did nothing, moved not a finger, arranged not a print or photograph, didn't put on a gown or bonnet if he didn't approve it'.

A MODEL FOR DOMESTIC LIFE

Victoria and Albert's marriage, stable life and large family did much to restore the dignity and standing of the monarchy after the excesses and public disgraces of the early Hanoverian kings.

The royal couple had no fewer than nine children, all of whom survived to adulthood, which was highly unusual even among the wealthy at the time. In addition to Princess Victoria and Prince Edward, the queen gave birth to seven other children: Princess Alice (born 25 April 1843), Prince Alfred ('Affie', born 6 August 1844), Princess Helena (born 25 May 1846), Princess Louise (born 18 March 1848), Prince Arthur (born 1 May 1850), Prince Leopold (born 7 April 1853) and Princess Beatrice (born 14 April 1857). In 1853 Victoria did much to popularize the use of anaesthesia during childbirth when she took chloroform while in labour prior to the birth of Prince Leopold. She later reported that it was 'Soothing, quieting and delightful beyond measure'.

Many of Victoria's children married into other European royal families, weaving a complex web of dynastic relationships that led her to become known as the 'matriarch of Europe'. When she died, she had 31 surviving grandchildren and 40 great-grandchildren. Her granddaughters included the queens of Sweden, Norway, Greece, Romania and Spain, and the Tsarina of Russia. One of her grandsons became Kaiser Wilhelm II of Germany.

In their life together at Windsor, Balmoral and the family home of Osborne House on the Isle of Wight, the royal family was held up to the nation as the perfect exemplar of

Above: Prince Consort. This celebrated portrait by Franz Winterhalter shows Prince Albert in 1859, at the age of 40.

GATHERED AROUND THE CHRISTMAS TREE

Prince Albert is generally credited with introducing to Britain the German custom of decorating a tree as part of a family's Christmas celebrations. The custom became popular following its use by Victoria and Albert and particularly after the publication in the December 1848 *Illustrated London News* of a picture of the royal family gathered around the Christmas tree. However, the true royal pioneer of the tradition in Britain was Queen Charlotte, wife of King George III. She first had a Christmas tree in 1800. Victoria, indeed, had been enchanted by the custom in her own childhood and reported enjoying Christmas trees in 1832, when she was 13. Prince Albert's first Christmas tree, in Windsor Castle, in December 1841, was hung with German glass ornaments, candles, gingerbread, sweets and fruit. That Christmas, Victoria and Albert had two infant children – Victoria and Edward – to entertain. Albert noted that his children were 'full of happy wonder' on Christmas Eve.

Left: This Illustrated London News *engraving, of royal children around the tree in 1848, popularized the custom.*

Above: At Osborne, 26 May 1857. Left to right: Alfred, Albert, Helena, Alice, Arthur, Victoria holding Beatrice, Vicky, Louise, Leopold and Albert Edward.

domestic life. However, the reality of family life, even for a king and queen, was somewhat different. Victoria had a fierce temper and would sometimes throw tantrums when her will was crossed. Albert became distant and withdrew in the face of sharp words, but usually managed to bring the queen around to a mood of repentance and deference. Victoria also feared childbirth, which she called the 'Shadow-side of marriage'. She wrote to Vicky, the Princess Royal in 1858, that giving birth made her feel 'Like a cow or a dog'. Our poor nature becomes so very animal and unecstatic'.

DEATH AND MOURNING

Prince Albert's death from typhoid fever aged just 42 was unexpected until a few days before he died at Windsor on 14 December 1861. He had been unwell for years – modern doctors believe he may have suffered from bowel or stomach cancer – and the fatal attack was initially seen by the queen as another in a series of episodes. It was only in the last three days that she was aware that he was dying. At the last she knelt by his bedside and held his hand.

Albert's death came at the end of a truly terrible year for the queen, in which she lost her mother, the Duchess of Kent (d. 16 March 1861) and may herself have suffered from a mental breakdown. She also learned that the Prince of Wales had been conducting an affair with the Irish courtesan Nellie Clifden while official negotiations were being conducted for his marriage to Denmark's Princess Alexandra.

Below: The Albert Memorial (1872) in Kensington Gardens, London. The golden statue of the Prince was added in 1876.

The loss of the man she described as 'The purest and best of human beings' devastated Victoria. 'He was my life', she wrote. She later recalled the deep desolation she felt, 'Those paroxysms of despair and yearning and longing and of daily, nightly longing to die…for the first three years never left me'. She withdrew to the Isle of Wight and was represented at her husband's funeral, in Windsor on 23 December 1861, by the Prince of Wales.

Victoria's withdrawal from public life was almost total and lasted at least ten years. She was effectively invisible as queen until the early 1870s. The public was initially respectful and sympathetic, but as time passed and the queen did not re-emerge to play her public role, the national mood became impatient. In 1871, however, Victoria was able to open a lasting memorial to her husband in the form of the magnificent Royal Albert Hall in Kensington, London, and that same year she began to re-emerge.

QUEEN VICTORIA'S SCOTLAND

1843–1901

In 1843 Queen Victoria and Prince Albert began a long love affair with Scotland when they visited Lord Breadalbane in Taymouth Castle. The royal couple were keen readers of the novels of Sir Walter Scott, with their taste for romances of the Highlands and for the traditional tartans worn by the clans. Prince Albert wrote, 'Scotland has made a most favourable impression on us both'. He praised the beautiful countryside, the many opportunities for sport and the 'Remarkably light and pure' air.

Above: Balmoral Castle. Albert's design made the Scottish baronial style popular.

BALMORAL

The couple leased the manor house of Balmoral – which Victoria described as 'A pretty little castle in the old Scotch style' – in September 1848. In 1852 they bought the castle and its estate of 20,000 acres on the bank of the river Dee in Grampian for 300,000 guineas.

The 15th-century building stood on the site of an earlier hunting lodge belonging to King Robert II (1371–90). It was demolished and a significantly larger castle was built following Prince Albert's own designs in the 'Scottish baronial style', using grey granite from the nearby quarries of Glen Gelder. It was finished in 1855.

The queen was enchanted by the finished building, and the royal couple made repeated visits. She wrote in her journal, 'Every year my heart becomes more fixed in this dear paradise and so much more so now that all has become my dearest Albert's own creation'.

The queen was particularly appreciative of the service of John Brown, Prince Albert's hunting guide or *ghillie* and later her own personal attendant, whom she praised as 'Really the perfection of a servant.'

Victoria continued to visit Balmoral after Albert's death in 1861, often staying in its secluded surroundings for as much as four months at a time while she pined for her late husband. She ordered a large statue of Albert to be raised on the estate. She was greatly helped in her mourning by the loyalty and devotion of John Brown. In 1868 she published a book, based on her journal, detailing her stays there with Albert and family. *Leaves from the Journal of Our Life in the Highlands 1848–61* was an instant bestseller. Such was its success that Victoria produced a follow-up, *More Leaves*, in 1883, based on journal entries for the years 1862–63, immediately after Albert's death. The queen's books and interest in Balmoral helped restore the link between the monarchy and Scotland, which had been lacking since the Act of Union.

Below: The romance of Scotland. This image of Balmoral is from sheet music entitled 'The Highland Home'.

Below: After Albert's death, Victoria was so close to former Balmoral guide John Brown that she was nicknamed 'Mrs Brown'.

VICTORIAN PALACES

1844–1901

Victoria and Albert found a pleasant retreat from the formal surroundings of Buckingham Palace on the Isle of Wight, where they bought Osborne House and around 1,000 acres (400 hectares) in 1844.

OSBORNE HOUSE

The house was demolished and a new villa in the Italian renaissance style built to the designs of Prince Albert and architect Thomas Cubitt. The very large villa contained a 'pavilion wing' for the royal family and another, less grand, wing for the household servants. A grand corridor between the two wings was used to display classical statues.

The royal family moved in in September 1846. Osborne House was subsequently the setting for many family holidays. It was at Osborne House on 26 May 1857 that the queen's family posed for the first official royal group photograph in British history.

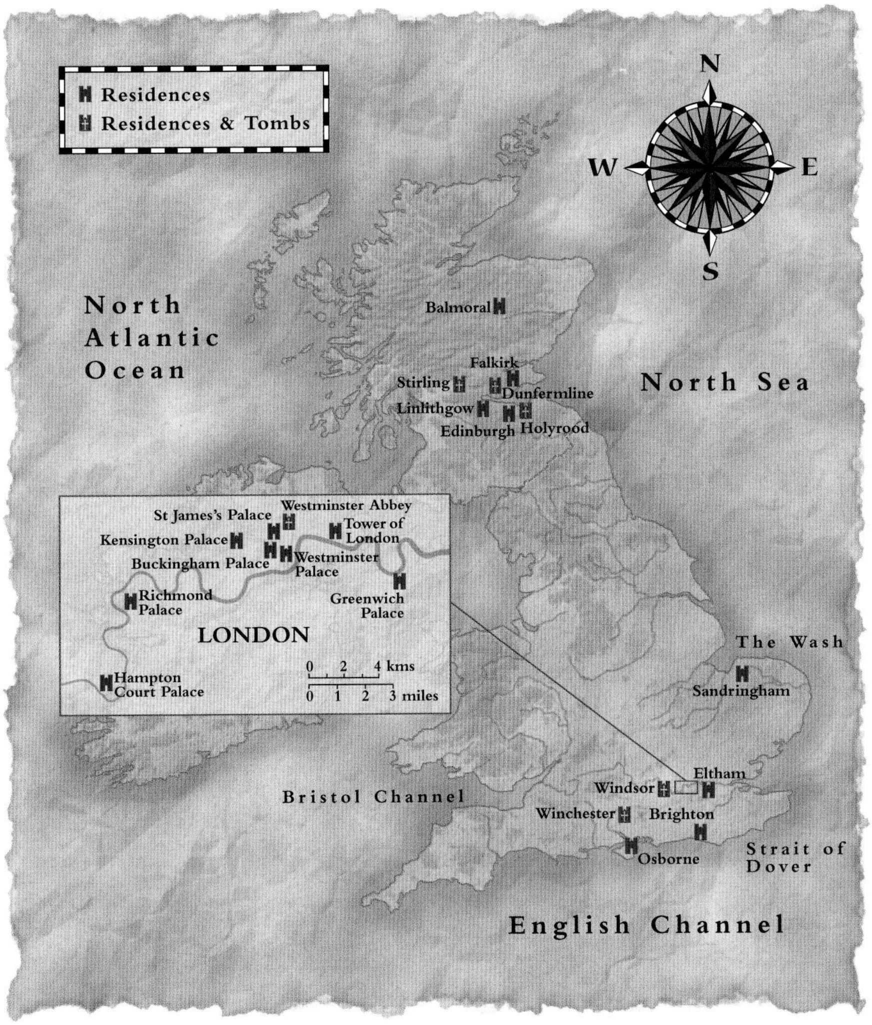

Above: Royal palaces, residences and tombs range from Anglo-Saxon Winchester to Victorian Balmoral and Sandringham.

BUCKINGHAM PALACE

At the start of Victoria's reign Buckingham Palace was made the monarch's official state residence in London, and the period of her rule saw significant work on the palace. Earlier, in the reign of George IV (1820–30), John Nash had raised a large three-sided courtyard that gave on to the Mall through a grandiose arch. In 1847 Edmund Blore completed a fourth wing that enclosed the courtyard: this is the side of the palace currently visible from the Mall. In 1851, Nash's archway was moved to the former Tyburn execution ground at the northeast corner of Hyde Park – the spot now known as 'Marble Arch'. In 1851–5, James Pennethorne built a ballroom and supper-room in Buckingham Palace.

Left: The Victoria Memorial (1911) stands in front of Buckingham Palace today.

Right: The Italianate terrace at Osborne House gives onto an ornate courtyard.

EDWARD, PRINCE OF WALES
1841–1901

Queen Victoria and Prince Albert tried hard to raise their offspring with a highly developed sense of duty, an industrious attitude and respect for others. Right from the start the royal parents took a close, controlling interest in their children's education and most particularly in that of their eldest son, 'Bertie', the Prince of Wales and heir to the throne. However, from an early age he disappointed his mother and father by exhibiting a wilful attitude and a lack of commitment to his studies.

BERTIE'S 'FALL'

In 1861 the Prince of Wales caused great distress to his parents by losing his virginity in an all-too-public affair with a Dublin courtesan named Nellie Clifden. Prince Albert was horrified by the potential impact of this unwelcome news upon the hard-won moral image of the royal family and within months succumbed to an attack of typhoid fever. Victoria afterwards blamed Bertie for causing his father's death. She refused to grant her son a public role and found his mere presence a provocation. 'It quite irritates me to see him in the room', she told Lord Clarendon, while she wrote to her eldest daughter, Vicky, 'Much as I pity him, I never can or shall look at him without a shudder'.

Above: In the company of Lt-Col Baker, the Prince of Wales reviews the 10th Hussars at Aldershot on 8 September 1871.

Below: By 1863, when Bertie married Princess Alexandra, Queen Victoria was 44 and in the 26th year of her reign.

A FAMILY LIFE?

On 10 March 1863, with his mother's full blessing, Prince Bertie married Princess Alexandra of Denmark. The royal couple made their London home in Marlborough House, in Pall Mall, while their country residence was Sandringham. On 8 January 1864 Bertie became a father when Princess Alexandra gave birth to a son two months prematurely. He was christened Albert Victor. A second son, George Frederick, (the future George V) was born on 3 June 1865.

The queen remained determined to exclude the Prince of Wales from an active life as a royal. Although he took a seat in the House of Lords, where he occasionally made speeches, and served

Below: The 'Jersey Lily'. Lillie Langtry, Bertie's mistress after 1877, was the first society lady to work as an actress.

in positions such as President of the Society of Arts, he gave most of his energy to a wild social life, gambling at whist, attending music halls, visiting pleasure gardens, enjoying himself on the Riviera and in Paris, attending meetings of horse racing at Goodwood and yachting at Cowes; and hosting lavish house parties at Sandringham.

THE PRINCE AS WITNESS

In 1869–70 the prince became embroiled in a scandalous divorce case involving Lady Harriet Mordaunt, the mentally unhinged wife of Sir Charles Mordaunt, Conservative MP for South Warwickshire. Sir Charles brought a divorce case against Lady Mordaunt on the grounds of adultery with two of the prince's friends; there was press and public outcry after it emerged that Lady Mordaunt had also named the prince as her lover. On 21 February 1870 the prince appeared in court as a witness and was openly asked whether he had been drawn into 'improper familiarity' with Lady Harriet; his simple negative reply was not enough to calm the storm of public feeling, and he was hissed when out and about in London.

Below: Prince 'Bertie' married the beautiful Princess Alexandra of Denmark in St George's Chapel, Windsor, in March 1863.

Above: Four princes. Bertie and his brothers, Alfred Duke of Edinburgh, Arthur Duke of Connaught and Leopold Duke of Albany.

Then in 1871 two of the Prince of Wales's indiscretions came back to haunt him. A former mistress, Lady Susan Vane Tempest, was left badly off on the death of her husband and repeatedly pressed the prince for money, which he was forced to provide. In addition, the prince was blackmailed over indiscreet letters he had written to Giulia Baruci, a renowned Italian prostitute. In the end he had to pay £240 to retrieve the letters from Giulia's brother, Pirro Benini.

These problems could not have come at a worse time. In 1870, France proclaimed a republic, and republican feeling was running high in Britain too, where Liberal MP Sir Charles Dilke was a figurehead for a movement calling for an English republic. Dilke declared that the monarchy was politically corrupt and accused the mourning queen of 'dereliction of duty'.

However, potential disaster was averted. In December 1871 the Prince of Wales fell very seriously ill with typhoid and it was feared he would die. The public mood swung immediately and firmly behind the royal family. On 27 February 1872, when a Service of Thanksgiving for the prince's recovery was held in St Paul's Cathedral, crowds lined the streets to cheer Victoria and the Prince of Wales.

This was far from the end of the Prince of Wales's scandals and indiscretions, but the republican crisis of 1870–2 was over and, as Queen Victoria emerged from her period of mourning for Prince Albert, the popularity of the monarchy reached new heights.

VICTORIA, QUEEN AND EMPRESS

YEARS OF JUBILEE, 1877–1901

On 22 June 1897 Queen Victoria paraded for 6 miles (10km) through London past vast, cheering crowds to celebrate her Diamond Jubilee – the 60th anniversary of her accession to the throne. The Jubilee procession included representatives from far and wide across the vast British empire – from Australia, Borneo, India, Canada and British parts of Africa.

In a landau carriage pulled by a splendidly attired team of eight horses, she paraded to St Paul's Cathedral, where a service of thanksgiving was held, then on across London Bridge and through the poorer parts of London south of the river Thames. Everywhere she went, she was cheered to the skies and was several times reduced to tears. She wrote in her diary, 'A never to be forgotten day. No one ever, I believe, has met with such an ovation as was given me...The crowds were quite indescribable...The cheering was quite deafening, and every face seemed to be filled with real joy.'

Right: This combination of family portraits and views of royal residences was published in Victoria's Golden Jubilee Book.

Below: This rare picture of Victoria smiling was taken on the occasion of her Golden Jubilee celebrations in June 1887.

THE VICTORIAN EMPIRE

Since 1877, Queen Victoria had been Empress of India – *Victoria Regina et Imperatrix* ('Victoria, Queen and Empress'). She was ruler of history's greatest empire and revered in many far-flung parts of the world. No fewer than eleven colonial prime ministers travelled to London for the Diamond Jubilee and afterwards held an imperial conference. From Buckingham Palace Victoria sent greetings to the empire: 'From my heart, I thank my beloved people. May God bless them!'

On 23 September 1896 Victoria had become the longest-reigning monarch in British history, when she passed the previous record, set by George III, of 59

Above: The privileged few received this invitation to Queen Victoria's Diamond Jubilee Reception and Ball in 1897.

Right: On 'A never to be forgotten day', crowds lined the streets to watch the queen's Diamond Jubilee procession.

years and 96 days. George III, of course, was a forgotten man for the final ten years of his reign, reduced by the madness that accompanied his undiagnosed porphyria to a shadow of his former self. However, Victoria remained active and had never been more popular.

THE GOLDEN JUBILEE

At the close of the previous decade, equally lavish ceremonies had been held in July 1887 to mark the Golden Jubilee – the 50th anniversary of Victoria's accession. In 1887, London's streets were packed by thousands of well-wishers, who cheered Victoria as she rode in procession to Westminster Abbey. At a party in Hyde Park 30,000 children were treated to buns and milk in special Jubilee mugs. She received telegrams of congratulation from across the empire including one from India which read, 'Empress of Hindoostan, Head of all Kings and Rulers, and King of all Kings, who is one in a hundred, is Her Majesty Queen Victoria'.

THE LAST MONTHS

In 1900 Victoria's health began to give way. In the year that she turned 81, she was plagued by indigestion, loss of appetite, insomnia and exhaustion. She was badly shaken by reverses for British troops fighting Boer irregulars in Cape Colony (southern Africa) and by the death in July 1900 of her third child and second son, Prince Alfred, of cancer of the throat, aged 55.

Queen Victoria slipped into a terminal decline. She spent her final weeks at Osborne House on the Isle of Wight. She suffered a stroke on 17 January and died on 22 January 1901 at 6.30 p.m. in the company of her children and grandchildren. At the last she was reconciled with her eldest son and heir to the throne, with whom she had had so many difficulties and endured so many estrangements: her final act was to breathe his name 'Bertie!' and stretch out her arms to him.

Victoria's death was truly the end of an era. From the 1850s, the adjective 'Victorian' had been given to the reign and the historical age in Britain, in the United States and across Europe. When she died, none of her subjects below the age of 64 years knew what it was like to live under any other monarch.

The 63 years of her reign saw sweeping changes, with widespread industrialization and the advent of trains, photography and moving pictures, the telephone, electric lighting and the motor car. However, on 22 January 1901 the 'Victorian age' ended.

VICTORIA'S EMPIRE

By 1900 Britain's empire included the dominions of Canada and Australia and colonies in the Honduras, the Bahamas, the West Indies, Guyana, southern, western and eastern Africa, Kuwait, India and Burma, Hong Kong, Malaya, North Borneo and the South Solomon islands. The empire contained 20 per cent of the world's territory and 23 per cent of the global population.

Right: Queen Victoria was hailed as the 'mother of the Empire'. Her reign saw the consolidation of a vast trading empire.

CHAPTER TWELVE

THE HOUSE OF WINDSOR

1901–

Victoria reigned for over 60 years and celebrated her Diamond Jubilee in 1897. Her death on 22 January 1901 marked the end of British rule by the House of Hanover, which had reigned since the accession of George I in 1714. Victoria's son, Edward VII, was the first king of the House of Saxe-Coburg and Gotha: its name came from that of Victoria's husband, Prince Albert of Saxe-Coburg and Gotha. Edward VII and his son George V ruled as kings of the House of Saxe-Coburg and Gotha. However, on 17 July 1917, in the midst of the First World War against Germany, George V decreed that henceforth he and his descendants would be known as 'Windsor'. The name was that of one of his principal palaces, Windsor Castle, and was thought to have a reassuringly British resonance. George V's descendants have ruled under this name to the present day. The children of Elizabeth II would normally be expected to take the surname Mountbatten, that of Elizabeth's husband Prince Philip (and an Anglicized form of the German 'Battenberg'). However, in the first year of her reign, 1952, Elizabeth II declared that her descendants would be called Windsor. Thus her successor – for instance, her son, ruling as King Charles III, or his son, ruling as King William V – will maintain the rule of the House of Windsor. The enthusiasm with which the British people celebrated Prince William's wedding and the Diamond and Platinum Jubilees show the long-lasting appeal of the British monarchy in the 21st century, and Queen Elizabeth reached a major milestone in 2015, becoming Britain's longest-reigning monarch.

Left: For over seventy years, Queen Elizabeth II has attended the State Opening of Parliament, shown here in 2004 accompanied by Prince Philip and her ladies-in-waiting.

EDWARD VII

1901–1910

Edward VII lived a large part of his life as Prince of Wales, prevented by his mother Queen Victoria from taking a role in government affairs. On his accession in 1901, he was 59 years old and keen to make his mark.

Above: Regal grandeur. Edward combined the dignity proper to his position with a modern outlook and charming manner.

FROM PRINCE TO KING

The new king, who had been christened Edward Albert, made clear his desire to put some distance between his rule and that of his mother when he declared that he would be known as Edward VII and not – as Victoria had wanted in honour of his father – as Albert I. He was proclaimed King Edward VII on 23 January 1901.

In his long period as Prince of Wales, Edward had become associated with a riotous social life in which he indulged his taste for 'fast' living, with gambling, and horse racing. However, he had also proved, during trips to Canada and the United States in 1860 and to India in 1876, that he made a very effective overseas ambassador for his country. Both his personality and his achievements as ambassador would play a notable part during his reign as king.

EDWARD VII, KING OF THE UNITED KINGDOM OF GREAT BRITAIN AND IRELAND AND EMPEROR OF INDIA, 1901–1910

Birth: 9 Nov 1841, Buckingham Palace
Father: Prince Albert
Mother: Victoria
Accession: 22 Jan 1901
Coronation: 9 Aug 1902
Queen: Princess Alexandra of Denmark (m. 10 March 1863; d. 20 Nov 1925)
Succeeded by: His son George V
Greatest achievement: The Entente Cordiale with France
1 Jan 1901: Australia becomes a British dominion
1 Jan 1903: Edward VII created Emperor of India
29 April 1903: Edward visits Rome and has audience with Pope Leo XIII
8 April 1904: Entente Cordiale signed with France
1907: New Zealand becomes a British dominion
9 June 1908: Edward makes state visit to Tsar Nicholas II in Russia
Death: 6 May 1910, dies at Buckingham Palace. Buried in the vault beneath St George's Chapel, Windsor

A NEW AGE

Edward VII's relatively brief nine-year reign matched his mother's 63-year rule by giving a name to an age and culture: 'the Edwardian era'. Edward embodied this new culture in the way he modernized the monarchy and brought new life and a sense of fun to a royal court that had become staid and rather gloomy over the long years of Queen Victoria's reign. He lived principally in London, redecorating Buckingham Palace, where he held balls and sessions of court. He

Above: Before he was king. A family shot shows 'Bertie' with wife Alexandra and offspring Albert, George and Louise.

THE SPORT OF KINGS

Both as Prince of Wales and as king, Edward had a passionate interest in horse racing. He achieved great successes as a horse owner in the last years of Victoria's reign. In 1896 his horse Persimmon won the Derby, while in 1900 he was the most successful horse owner in the country. His horse Diamond Jubilee won no fewer than five major races (including the Derby, the St Leger and the '2000 Guineas') and another horse, Ambush II, won the Grand National steeplechase. He won a third victory at the Derby in 1909 with his horse Minoru. As he was dying from bronchitis in 1910, Edward was cheered in his last moments by the news that another of his horses, Witch of Air, had won a race at Kempton Park. In fact, his last words were a reference to this fact. 'Yes I have heard of it', he replied to a question. 'I am very glad.'

Right: This image of Edward in the grandstand at Epsom was published in the Illustrated London News *(1902).*

enthusiastically took to the motor car, which his mother had hated, and owned both a Renault and a Mercedes-Benz.

THE 'ENTENTE CORDIALE'

Edward fell in love with France as a teenager in 1854. He spoke perfect French and made visits to Paris and the southern resorts of Biarritz and Cannes throughout his years as Prince of Wales. He came up with the phrase 'Entente Cordiale ('Friendly Understanding') as early as 1870, but the impetus for the signing of the agreement known by that name came from his visit as king in 1903, when he proved a skilled diplomat. The Entente of 8 April 1904 established a mutual agreement that Britain could pursue its interest in Egypt, and France could do likewise in Morocco, and settled various colonial disagreements in Africa and Asia. In June 1908 Edward also made a state visit to his nephew-in-law Tsar Nicholas II of Russia, cementing an alliance established in a diplomatic agreement the previous year. The king's active diplomacy helped his country to establish itself in a new alignment of European countries: Britain would have the backing of France and Russia in any conflict with Germany, Austria or Italy.

BRONCHITIS AND DEATH

King Edward VII suffered from bronchitis for many years, but in 1910, after catching a chill, he had a very serious attack and died on 6 May. At the last, Queen Alexandra behaved with the greatest dignity in allowing her husband's long-term mistress, Mrs Keppel, to visit him as he prepared for death. He was succeeded by his son, the Prince of Wales, who became King George V.

Left: Royal hospitality. Edward VII receives maharajahs and other dignitaries from around the empire before his Coronation.

GEORGE V
1910–1936

George V was not raised to be king. He was recalled from naval duty in January 1892, when the death from pneumonia of his older brother Albert, Duke of Clarence, made George heir to his father, then still Prince of Wales.

On 6 July 1893, George married his late brother's fiancé, Princess Mary of Teck. A genuinely devoted family man, he produced six children with Princess Mary, including the future King Edward VIII and the future King George VI.

MYSTIQUE OF MONARCHY

As king, George V maintained the mystique of the monarchy, projecting a regal grandeur through elaborate ceremonial. He led the mourning for his father in a very grand funeral attended by leading members of all the European royal houses on 20 May 1910. His coronation in Westminster Abbey in 1911 was attended by rulers and government figures from across the empire. Later that year, on 12 December in Delhi, George was hailed as Emperor of India in a lavish enthronement ceremony in which he wore a new crown worth £60,000.

Above: The man who did not expect to become king enjoyed a sumptuous coronation ceremony in June 1911.

GEORGE V, KING OF THE UNITED KINGDOM OF GREAT BRITAIN AND IRELAND AND EMPEROR OF INDIA, 1910–1936

Birth: 3 June 1865, Marlborough House, London
Father: Edward Albert, Prince of Wales (later Edward VII)
Mother: Princess Alexandra of Denmark
Accession: 6 May 1910
Coronation: 22 June 1911
Queen: Princess Mary of Teck (m. 6 July 1893; d. 24 March 1953)
Succeeded by: His son Edward VIII
Greatest achievement: Preserving the monarchy in a time of great change
Dec 1911: George enthroned as Emperor of India in Delhi
4 Aug 1914: Start of World War I – Britain declares war on Germany
26 May 1917: George decrees that Britain's ruling royal house will be known as 'Windsor' rather than 'Saxe-Coburg-Gotha'
15 Nov 1918: George parades through London on 'Victory Day', celebrating end of World War I
Jan 1919: George's youngest son, John, dies at Sandringham aged 13
23 April 1924: George opens British Empire Exhibition at Wembley
Oct 1931: George receives Gandhi at Buckingham Palace
11 Dec 1931: Statute of Westminster establishes the British Commonwealth of Nations
6 May 1935: King and people celebrate the Silver Jubilee of his reign
Death: 20 Jan 1936 at Sandringham. Buried in St George's Chapel, Windsor

FROM CRISIS TO CRISIS

George V's reign saw the years of the First World War, which erupted in 1914. The royal family came out of the war with great credit, largely because George displayed good sense in acting as a national figurehead while leaving the politicians to manage the war. Another difficult development in a period of rapid and profound change was the break-up of the British empire. An Imperial Conference of October–November 1926 agreed the autonomy

Above: George V saw himself as a family man and took seriously the responsibility of training his children to take up royal duties.

in domestic and foreign policy of the British 'dominions over the seas' (Australia, Canada, New Zealand and South Africa). The Statute of Westminster of 11 December 1931 established the British Commonwealth of Nations. In India, Mohandas Gandhi led a peaceful campaign for independence. In October 1931, while in London for an India Round Table Conference, Gandhi was received at Buckingham Palace. India finally achieved independence in August 1947, in the reign of George VI.

At home, George faced the formation of the first Labour government in 1924, the General Strike of 1926 and the economic crisis of 1930–31. He was a force for common sense and decency, urging moderation and national unity.

SILVER JUBILEE

King George celebrated the Silver Jubilee of his reign in May 1935, riding through cheering crowds of Londoners to a service of celebration in St Paul's Cathedral, while, across the country, hill-top beacons were lit and church bells rang out. The king was serenaded at Buckingham Palace by a crowd singing 'For He's a Jolly Good Fellow'. King George V died aged 70 at Sandringham from chest and heart problems probably brought on by his long-term cigarette-smoking habit. His eldest son, Edward, succeeded at the age of 41 as King Edward VIII.

Above: In 1915, during a visit to the front line, George accompanied French dignitaries to inspect troops at Blincourt.

THE HOUSE OF WINDSOR 1910–

GEORGE V *m* Mary of Teck
1865–1936, ♛ 1910–36 | 1867–1953

- **EDWARD VIII** *m* Wallis Simpson
  1894–1972, ♛ 1936 | 1896–1986
- **GEORGE VI** *m* Elizabeth Bowes-Lyon
  1895–1952, ♛ 1936–52 | 1900–2002
  - **ELIZABETH II** *m* Philip Mountbatten Duke of Edinburgh
    1926–, ♛ 1952– | 1921–
    - Charles Prince of Wales 1948– *m* (1) Lady Diana Spencer 1961–97 (2) Camilla Parker Bowles 1947–
      - William Duke of Cambridge 1982– *m* Catherine Middleton 1982–
        - George 2013–
        - Charlotte 2015–
        - Louis 2018-
      - Henry 1984– *m* Meghan Markle 1981-
        - Archie 2019–
        - Lilibet 2021–
    - Anne Princess Royal 1950– *m* (1) Mark Phillips 1948– (2) Timothy Laurence 1955–
      - Peter 1977– *m* Autumn Kelly 1978–
        - Savannah 2010–
        - Isla 2012–
      - Zara 1981– *m* Michael Tindall 1981–
        - Mia 2014–
        - Lena 2818–
        - Lucas 2021–
    - Andrew Duke of York 1960– *m* Sarah Ferguson 1959–
      - Beatrice 1988– *m* Edoardo Mapelli Monzo 1983–
        - Sienna 2021–
      - Eugenie 1990– *m* Jack Brooksbank 1986–
        - August 2021–
    - Edward Earl of Wessex 1964– *m* Sophie Rhys-Jones 1965–
      - Louise 2003–
      - James 2007–
  - Margaret Rose 1930–2002 *m* Antony Armstrong-Jones Earl of Snowdon 1930–
- Mary Princess Royal 1897–1965 *m* Henry Earl of Harewood 1882–1947
- Henry Duke of Gloucester 1900–74
- George Duke of Kent 1902–42 *m* Princess Marina of Greece 1906–68
- John 1905–19

EDWARD VIII

1936

The reign of King Edward VIII lasted less than 11 months. After acceding to the throne on the death of his father King George V on 20 January 1936, he abdicated in a storm of controversy on 10 December the same year in order to marry American divorcée Wallis Simpson. Edward is generally remembered without fondness as the king who put private pleasure before public duty.

UNFIT TO BE KING?

The memory of Edward VIII is further tarnished by evidence that he was sympathetic to the Nazi regime in Germany. He made a visit to Germany with Wallis Simpson in October 1937 and was photographed smiling broadly as he was introduced to Nazi *Führer* Adolf Hitler at Berchtesgaden. On this occasion he made a modified Nazi salute and on two other occasions was seen making full forms of the salute.

There is, furthermore, evidence in the form of official German papers discovered after the Second World War that the Germans intended to restore Edward to the throne at the head of a British fascist state allied to Germany. Many historians argue that it was a blessing for the British monarchy and the House of Windsor that Edward's reign was truncated.

As Prince of Wales, Edward won admirers in the army during the First World War, on trips to working-class areas of Britain in 1919 and on tours of Canada, the United States and Australia in 1919–20. However, long before his accession, he was exhibiting troubling signs of boredom with official duties. He evidently did not have his father's strong character and sense of duty. The

Above: On 13 July 1911, aged 17, Edward was invested at Caernarfon as Prince of Wales.

Below: Edward inspects troops in 1921. He won the Military Cross for army service in France in the First World War.

EDWARD VIII, KING OF THE UNITED KINGDOM OF GREAT BRITAIN AND IRELAND AND EMPEROR OF INDIA, 1936

Birth: 23 June 1894, White Lodge, Richmond Park
Father: George, Duke of York (later King George V)
Mother: Mary, Duchess of York (later Queen Mary)
Accession: 21 Jan 1936
Abdication: 10 Dec 1936; becomes the Duke of Windsor
Married: Mrs Wallis Simpson (m. 3 June 1937; d. 24 April 1986)
Succeeded by: His brother, George VI
Greatest achievement: Tours as Prince of Wales
21 Jan 1936: Edward takes oath of accession
22 Jan 1936: Edward is proclaimed King Edward VIII
28 Jan 1936: Edward leads national mourning at Windsor funeral of King George V
14 Sept 1936: Edward returns from a summer holiday with Mrs Simpson, that is widely covered in the international press
27 Oct 1936: Mrs Simpson wins *decree nisi* from her second husband, Ernest
16 Nov 1936: Edward informs Prime Minister Stanley Baldwin that he is determined to marry Wallis Simpson, even if it results in his abdication
2 Dec 1936: First British press reports of abdication crisis
10 Dec 1936: Edward signs instrument of abdication
11 Dec 1936: Edward makes abdication broadcast on radio from Windsor
3 June 1937: Edward, now Duke of Windsor, marries Wallis Simpson in France
Death: 28 May 1972, Edward dies in Paris and is buried at Frogmore

Above: The common touch? At a time of great economic hardship, Edward made successful visits to British mining towns.

likelihood is that he would have made a disastrous king in the long term. George V certainly feared the worst, saying with remarkable prescience of his eldest son, 'After I am dead, the boy will ruin himself in 12 months'.

AN ADVISABLE SUCCESSION

Edward suggested, in a book he published in 1951 entitled *A King's Story*, that he was constitutionally ill-equipped to rule. 'The fault', he wrote, 'lay not in my stars but in my genes'.

Some writers propose that Edward was happy to escape the life of a king and that he used the circumstance of his romance with the divorcée Wallis Simpson as a way out of an intolerable situation. Others argue that, while Edward wished to remain king, his obvious unsuitability meant that leading religious and political figures in the drama – such as Cosmo Gordon Lang, the Archbishop of Canterbury, and Prime Minister Stanley Baldwin – were happy to see him depart. It is argued that they preferred to see the throne pass to his brother Prince Albert (subsequently George VI) and later to George VI's daughter Elizabeth (the future Elizabeth II) who, it was already clear, were better equipped to reign.

Such, indeed, was the will of the late King George V, who had declared, 'I pray to God that my eldest son Edward will never marry and have children and that nothing will come between Bertie and Lilibet and the throne'. ('Lilibet' was the family name for Princess Elizabeth.)

Yet while Edward's departure may have been convenient, the act of abdication set a troubling precedent and undermined the constitutional monarchy. Under generally accepted rules, monarch and subject were bound by duty: the one to rule, the other to serve with loyalty. If a king could set aside duty and choose not to rule when it pleased him, surely subjects could set aside loyalty and unseat an unpopular king or queen?

As part of his abdication negotiations, Edward thrashed out a settlement covering his finances and royal status with his younger brother and successor, George VI. Under this agreement, Edward would receive £25,000 a year and the title His Royal Highness the Duke of Windsor. The title HRH was denied to Wallis, who was to be known simply as the Duchess of Windsor.

Edward reportedly was unable to forgive George for this rebuff. Some sources suggest that King George did not expect the marriage to last and therefore did not want to confer a title that is traditionally permanent.

'SOMETHING MUST BE DONE'

Edward more than once suggested that he had sympathy with the plight of the working man.

On 19 November 1936 Edward made a well-publicized visit to economically devastated areas of South Wales. At the Bessemer Steel Works, at Dowlais, a group of unemployed and largely destitute men serenaded him with an ancient Welsh hymn. He declared 'Something must be done to find them work'.

He established a connection with servicemen during the First World War and in 1919 was well received when touring mining areas of South Wales. Later, as Governor of Bahamas, he achieved a number of improvements for unemployed black workers there.

Below: A nation's hopes. This poster for Edward VIII's accession offers prayers for a bright future under the new king.

THE ABDICATION

YEAR OF CRISIS, 1936

Edward VIII first met Wallis Simpson, the American woman for whom he gave up the British throne, on 10 January 1931, when he was still Prince of Wales. The prince's close friend and then lover, Thelma, Lady Furness, introduced him to Pennsylvania-born Wallis and her Anglo-American husband Ernest Simpson in Lady Furness's house at Melton Mowbray. Edward soon became a close associate of the Simpsons, with whom he frequently dined in London.

Above: Edward broadcasts. After breaking the news of his abdication and his brother's accession he declared, 'God save the king'.

THE AMERICAN BELLE

Wallis was born Bessie Wallis Warfield in Blue Ridge Summit, Pennsylvania, on 19 June 1896, the only child of American businessman Teackle Wallis Warfield and Alice Montague. After her father's death when she was five months old and throughout her childhood, 'Bessie Wallis' and her mother were extremely poor.

In 1916, aged 19, she married Earl Winfield Spencer, but divorced him in 1927. On 2 July 1928 she married her second husband, Ernest Simpson. They came to London, where Ernest managed an office of his father's shipping company. By mid-1934 the prince had cut contacts with Lady Furness and his other long-term female intimate, Freda Dudley Ward, and concentrated all his attentions on Wallis – although to the end of his life he denied that they had become lovers before they were married in 1937.

Below: After abdication, Edward and Wallis visited Nazi Germany and had a friendly meeting with Adolf Hitler.

Edward appears to have convinced himself that he could not live without Wallis and must marry her at all costs. Many writers comment on the bullying and aggressive nature of her interaction with the prince and speculate that the relationship may have had a sado-masochistic element.

Prince Edward's intimacy with Wallis was a matter of increasing public comment and scandal on the international scene. In Britain the press kept silent, but American and European newspapers followed the developing drama in lurid detail. In 1934–5 Wallis spent three holidays with the prince, first in the Mediterranean, then skiing in Austria and third, cruising the Mediterranean and visiting Budapest and Vienna. Meanwhile, her husband stayed home.

Edward's accession to the throne only strengthened his desire to make Wallis Simpson his wife. In summer 1936 they holidayed as a couple more openly than ever before on a chartered yacht, the *Nahlin*, in the eastern Mediterranean. International pressmen followed their every move and a crowd was heard to shout, '*Vive l'amour!*' ('The wonders of love!') when the couple came ashore.

On 27 October 1936 Wallis won a *decree nisi* divorce from Ernest at a court in Ipswich, adding further weight to international speculation that Edward planned to marry her. Prime Minister Stanley Baldwin asked Edward his intentions. The prince confirmed, on 16 November 1936, that he was determined to marry the woman he loved.

Above: In the summer of 1936, the king and Wallis Simpson were clearly travelling as a romantic couple on holiday in Yugoslavia.

POSSIBLE SOLUTIONS

Edward's abdication was by no means inevitable. The difficulty was that Wallis had been married twice and was in the throes of gaining her second divorce. As Supreme Governor of the Church of England, which did not allow church marriage for divorced people, Edward would undermine his coronation oath to uphold the Church if he married her and made her his queen. A possible solution was a 'morganatic marriage', in which Edward would marry Mrs Simpson but she would not become queen and their children would not inherit the throne. Edward apparently backed this option, but Baldwin opposed it. Such a development would have required an Act of Parliament, and Baldwin did not believe that he could win a debate on the issue. As the crisis came to breaking point, events developed quickly.

On 3 December Mrs Simpson fled London for Paris. Four days later she issued a statement declaring her willingness to withdraw from the relationship. However, Edward would not give up. On 10 December he signed an instrument of abdication. 'I Edward the Eighth, of Great Britain, Ireland, and the British Dominions beyond the Seas, King, Emperor of India, do hereby declare my irrevocable determination to renounce the throne for Myself and for My descendants, and My desire that effect should be given to this Instrument of Abdication immediately'.

On 11 December he made an abdication broadcast from Windsor Castle declaring, 'I have for 25 years tried to serve...But you must believe me when I tell you that I have found it impossible to carry the heavy burden of responsibility and to discharge my duties as king as I would wish to do without the help and support of the woman I love...And now we have a new King. I wish him, and you, his people, happiness and prosperity with all my heart.'

LIFE AFTER ABDICATION

The former King Edward VIII departed Portsmouth on board HMS *Fury* on 12 December 1936, headed for Paris, where he set up home with Wallis. The couple were married at the Château de Condé, near Tours, on 3 June 1937. An Anglican clergyman married them using the Church of England service despite official opposition to church marriage of divorced people. No members of the royal family attended, and thereafter the Duke and Duchess of Windsor were effectively excluded from royal life.

In the Second World War, Edward initially served as a member of the British military mission to France. With the fall of France in June 1940, he and Wallis fled to Madrid and then Lisbon. They left Lisbon to enable Edward take up the governorship of the Bahamas, safely out of the war.

After the war they returned to Paris, where they largely lived for the rest of their lives. Edward died from throat cancer aged 77 in his Paris home on 28 May 1972. His body was flown back to Windsor, where 60,000 mourners viewed it as it lay in state in St George's Chapel. He was buried in the Frogmore Mausoleum following his funeral on 5 June. Wallis died on 24 April 1986 and was buried beside Edward.

Right: Edward and Wallis at a film premiere in 1967. In Parisian exile, the former king and his wife lived in style.

GEORGE VI

1936–1952

George VI was crowned in Westminster Abbey on 12 May 1937, the day originally set for the coronation of his older brother, Edward VIII. The new king's elevation to the throne had been swift and unexpected.

Albert Frederick Arthur George, Duke of York, learned that he was to be king on 8 December 1936, two days before Edward VIII's abdication. As a shy man with a stammer that made public speaking a trial and who had had an undistinguished naval education, he would not have wished for the role of king – he told Lord Louis Mountbatten, 'I'm quite unprepared for it...I've never even seen a state paper. I'm only a Naval Officer, it's the only thing I know'.

Above: 'Long to reign over us'? After the abdication crisis, George's subjects looked for stability and propriety in the new king.

A DUTIFUL MAN

The new king had a strong sense of duty and set out to restore the good name and dignity of the royal family, which he felt had been blemished by the abdication crisis. To this end, the man known before his accession as Prince Albert – and in the royal family as 'Bertie' – chose the name George VI to reassert the qualities of decency and dutiful service embodied by his father.

In his unlooked-for role as king, George VI was greatly supported by his elegant and charming wife Elizabeth,

GEORGE VI, KING OF THE UNITED KINGDOM OF GREAT BRITAIN AND NORTHERN IRELAND AND EMPEROR OF INDIA, 1936–1952

Birth: 14 Dec 1895, York Cottage, Sandringham
Father: George, Duke of York (later George V)
Mother: Mary, Duchess of York (later Queen Mary)
Accession: 11 Dec 1936
Coronation: 12 May 1937
Married: Lady Elizabeth Bowes-Lyon (m. 26 April 1923; d. 30 March 2002)
Succeeded by: His daughter Elizabeth II
Greatest achievement: Restoring dignity to the monarchy after the abdication crisis
July 1938: George and Queen Elizabeth make triumphant state visit to Paris
May–June 1939: George and Queen Elizabeth tour Canada and the US
Dec 1939: George visits British troops in France
9 Sept 1940: Buckingham Palace hit by German bombs
June 1943: George inspects British troops in Africa
8 May 1945: Royal family lead London celebrations of the end of the war in Europe
15 Aug 1947: Under the India Independence Act, the British monarch loses his title of Imperator (Emperor) of India
30 April 1948: George and Queen Elizabeth celebrate their silver wedding anniversary
Death: 6 Feb 1952 at Sandringham. Buried in St George's Chapel, Windsor

Below: Royal wed commoner when the future George VI (then Albert, Duke of York) married Elizabeth Bowes-Lyon.

Left: On Coronation Day, George and the royal family greet adoring crowds from the balcony at Buckingham Palace.

of Canada and the USA. The visit, the first by a reigning British king and queen to North America, had the added purpose of countering 'isolationism' in the USA and reasserting links with the Dominion of Canada, in the hope that both countries would give Britain much-needed backing in the war against Germany. The trip was a triumph. A total of 15 million people flocked to see the couple during their 10,000-mile (16,000-km) journey.

and by the tranquil home life he enjoyed with her and their two daughters Elizabeth (the future Elizabeth II) and Margaret Rose. The happiness and intimacy of his immediate 'royal family' was a genuine help to the king, but it was also publicly promoted as a means of establishing common ground with George's subjects. The image of domestic calm also helped to distance the new king and his heir Elizabeth from the raffish 'bachelor' lifestyle adopted by Edward VIII as Prince of Wales and, briefly, as king.

The public emphasis on King George's sense of duty was another key part of the monarchy's attempt to repair the damage done by Edward VIII's abdication. Edward's decision to stand down seemed to imply that the obligations of kingship could be taken up or set aside at will, but George's dutiful acceptance of a role he did not apparently desire restored gravity to the monarchy.

DUTY'S REWARD

Within three years of George's accession, Britain was plunged into the Second World War. In summer 1939, as war loomed over Europe, George and Queen Elizabeth made a six-week tour

Right: George VI and Elizabeth provided a calm domestic setting for the childhood of Princesses Margaret and Elizabeth.

GEORGE AND ELIZABETH

A ROYAL PARTNERSHIP, 1939–1952

After the beginning of the Second World War on 3 September 1939, George and the royal family played a major role in rallying the spirits of British servicemen and public. They visited bombed-out areas of the East End of London as well as other cities, including Coventry, Bristol and Southampton. On 9 September 1940 Buckingham Palace itself was hit by two bombs, prompting Queen Elizabeth to observe, 'I'm glad we have been bombed. We can now look the East End in the face'.

The royals set out to share in the hardships of the British people, enduring food and clothes rationing, and turning off the central heating in

VICTORY IN EUROPE

On 8 May 1945 Buckingham Palace was a focus for victory celebrations. At one point the princesses left the palace and mingled *incognito* with the crowd.

Above: King George and Queen Elizabeth appeared on the palace balcony eight times. George declared, 'We give thanks for a great deliverance'.

Left: In 1940, as Britain endured the German bombing of the Blitz, George VI and Queen Elizabeth inspected air-raid damage at Buckingham Palace.

Below: An informal portrait of the royal family in 1936 shows the king and queen relaxing with their daughters Elizabeth and Margaret Rose.

Left: This official photograph celebrates the union of the future Elizabeth II and Lt Philip Mountbatten of the Royal Navy.

Buckingham Palace. To help counter food shortages, the king authorized the ploughing of 1,500 acres (600 hectares) of Windsor Great Park to plant cereal crops. Towards the end of the war, in March 1945, Princess Elizabeth joined the ATS (Auxiliary Transport Service).

A ROYAL WEDDING

The post-war years brought marriage celebrations, as well as declining health for King George. On 10 July 1947 the king announced the engagement of Princess Elizabeth, heir to the throne, and Lt Philip Mountbatten of the Royal Navy. Prince Philip was the son of Prince Andrew of Greece and Denmark. Before his engagement, he renounced his Greek nationality and became a British citizen, adopting the surname Mountbatten. The couple were married in Westminster Abbey, amid post-war austerity, on 20 November 1947. The king gave Elizabeth's husband the title of Prince Philip, Duke of Edinburgh.

On 14 November 1948, Elizabeth gave birth at Buckingham Palace to a boy, later christened Charles Philip Arthur George, and on 15 August 1950 at Clarence House she produced a daughter, Anne Elizabeth Alice Louise. The domestic tranquillity of the royal family was again celebrated on 30 April 1948, when King George and Queen Elizabeth marked their silver wedding anniversary with much of the pomp used by previous monarchs for jubilees of their rule. In a thanksgiving service in St Paul's Cathedral, the Archbishop of Canterbury gave thanks to God 'That He has set such a family at the seat of our royalty'. Later both king and queen made radio broadcasts to mark the occasion.

Right: Three queens in black. Elizabeth II, Mary and Elizabeth the Queen Mother attend George VI's funeral.

LAST MONTHS

King George developed lung cancer and in autumn 1951 had an operation to remove his right lung. He died from a heart attack during his convalescence at Sandringham on 6 February 1952, aged 56, and was buried in St George's Chapel, Windsor.

His memory was honoured: the man who had not expected or wanted to be king rose to the daunting challenge presented by Edward VIII's abdication. He re-established the public standing of the monarchy, led the country with dignity through the traumas of the Blitz and the Second World War, and produced an heir, Princess Elizabeth, who was herself devoted to preserving the standing of the monarchy in rapidly changing times.

ELIZABETH II
FROM 1952

Princess Elizabeth learned of her father's death and her elevation to the British throne on 6 February 1952 while on safari in Kenya. A local newspaperman brought the news that King George had died to the lodge where Elizabeth and Philip were staying. It was Prince Philip who broke the news to Elizabeth, who reportedly received it 'Bravely, like a queen'. Her accession as Queen Elizabeth II was proclaimed on 8 February 1952. At the age of 25, she was the youngest British monarch on accession since Queen Victoria came to the throne at 18 in 1837.

The young queen stood just 5ft 4in (1.62m) tall. While she did not possess the large-eyed beauty of her sister Margaret, she cut an elegant and attractive figure and was flattered by the styles of the 1950s. Moreover, from the start of her reign Elizabeth impressed all with the calm and dignity she displayed in taking on large responsibilities at a young age. Not least among her difficulties was that of coming to terms with a new level of press and television scrutiny of her doings and those of her family.

Above: A formal portrait of the Queen in robes of the Order of the Thistle, 1956, one of Sir William Hutchison's finest works.

Below: Elizabeth's coronation, on 2 June 1953, was the first to be shown live on TV.

ELIZABETH II, QUEEN OF THE UNITED KINGDOM OF GREAT BRITAIN AND NORTHERN IRELAND, 1952–

Birth: 21 April 1926, 17 Bruton St, London
Father: Prince Albert, Duke of York (later George VI)
Mother: Elizabeth, Duchess of York (later Queen Elizabeth and Queen Elizabeth, the Queen Mother)
Accession: 6 Feb 1952
Coronation: 2 June 1953
Married: Philip Mountbatten (Prince Philip, Duke of Edinburgh; m. 20 Nov 1947)
Dec 1953–April 1954: First visit by monarch to Australia and New Zealand
25 Dec 1957: Elizabeth makes first televised Christmas broadcast
7 June 1977: National holiday celebrates Elizabeth II's Silver Jubilee
1–4 June 2002: Elizabeth II's Golden Jubilee
2–5 June 2012: Diamond Jubilee Weekend celebrating 60 years
10–12 June 2016: Series of events marking the Queen's 90th birthday.
9 April 2021: Prince Philip, Duke of Edinburgh dies at Windsor Castle
2–5 June 2022: Platinum Jubilee Weekend celebrating 70 years

Above: Elizabeth has had a good relationship with several US Presidents. John and Jackie Kennedy visited the UK in 1961 and met the Queen and Prince Philip.

THE COMMONWEALTH

In the early years of her reign Elizabeth made several tours to visit her subjects, the peoples of the Commonwealth and the USA. In 1953 she made an extensive coronation tour to various parts of the United Kingdom, including Scotland and Northern Ireland. In 1953–4, she became the first ruling monarch to visit Australia and New Zealand, in a three-month tour during which she made the first Christmas broadcast ever given from outside Britain. In this broadcast, made from New Zealand, she declared, 'The Crown is not merely an abstract symbol of our unity, but a personal and living bond between you and me'.

Africa was next on the agenda. In January–February 1956 Elizabeth and Philip received a wildly enthusiastic welcome on a visit to Nigeria, which at that stage was still a British colony. During the tour, the royal couple made a visit to a leper colony situated on the river Oji and agreed to sponsor a leper child. Their visit was praised by the colony manager for its positive effect in diluting public fear of and hostility towards lepers.

The following year Elizabeth and Philip toured North America. In Canada, Elizabeth became the first ruling monarch to open the Canadian parliament, in Ottawa.

Later Elizabeth travelled south to the USA, where she visited Jamestown, Virginia, to mark the 350th anniversary of the establishment of England's first permanent overseas colony, before being received at the White House by President and Mrs Eisenhower. Elizabeth also gave an address to the United Nations general assembly in New York City.

Above: On 1 July 1969, Elizabeth's eldest son, Charles, became the 21st Prince of Wales on his inauguration at Caernarfon.

THE COMMONWEALTH AND ELIZABETH II

The Commonwealth grew out of the British empire. It began as a collection of former British colonies that had been transformed into self-governing 'dominions' and which maintained ties with Britain to promote cooperation and friendship. A 1931 British parliamentary act, the Statute of Westminster, referred to a number of dominions – principally Australia, Canada, the Irish Free State, New Zealand and South Africa – as the 'British Commonwealth of Nations'. The word British was dropped in 1946.

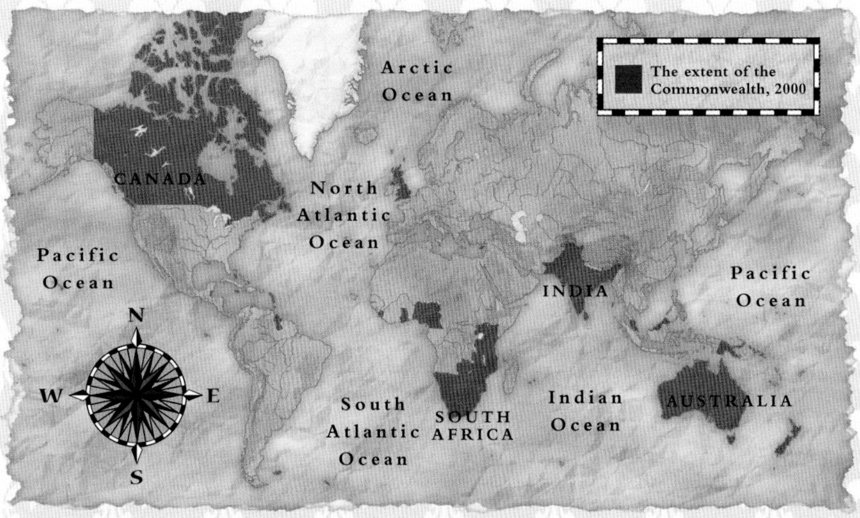

The monarch has an important symbolic role as head of the Commonwealth, and Elizabeth II has always taken this very seriously. On 21 April 1947, when she was still Princess Elizabeth and a subject of King George VI, she turned 21 in South Africa. In a radio broadcast, she declared: 'my whole life, whether it be short or long, shall be devoted to your service, and the service of our great Imperial Commonwealth to which we all belong'. In the 21st century the Commonwealth consists of 54 countries, and has a total population of 2.6 billion.

CROWN AND COMMONWEALTH

THE NEW ELIZABETHANS, 1952–1977

In 1977, Queen Elizabeth II, her British subjects and millions of people around the world celebrated the 25th anniversary of her reign. 'Jubilee Day', 7 June 1977, was a national holiday at Elizabeth's decree.

Above: *Elizabeth 'at home' in 1969. This was the year of the first TV documentary to show scenes of the royals' private lives.*

A YEAR-LONG CELEBRATION

Across the country people threw street parties in an explosion of communal goodwill and royalist fervour. A string of beacons on hilltops from the Shetlands to Land's End included one at Windsor lit by the Queen herself.

In London, Elizabeth processed with Prince Philip in the golden state coach from Buckingham Palace to St Paul's Cathedral for a service of thanksgiving. Afterwards she attended lunch at the Guildhall and then, watched by around 500 million people worldwide on television, she processed down the Mall to Buckingham Palace, where a crowd of a million people had gathered to acclaim her appearance on the balcony.

The year-long celebration began on 6 February, the 25th anniversary of Elizabeth's accession in 1952. The Queen, who had declared that she wanted to mark the Jubilee by meeting as many of her people as possible, made official visits with Prince Philip to Western Samoa, Australia, New Zealand, Tonga, Fiji, Tasmania, Papua New Guinea, Canada and the West Indies in a series of globetrotting tours that totalled 56,000 miles (90,000km) in the year. At home she made six Jubilee tours in the UK and Northern Ireland. Again with Prince Philip, she visited no fewer than 36 counties, beginning in Glasgow on 17 May.

CHARLIE'S ANGELS

In 1977 Prince Charles was 29 and touted in the press as the world's most eligible bachelor. He was linked to a string of beautiful women, dubbed 'Charlie's Angels' after the popular 1970s TV show.

The prince's close friends included Lady Sarah Spencer (elder sister of his eventual first wife, Lady Diana Spencer), Lady Jane Wellesley, Sabrina Guinness, Lucia Santa Cruz, Davina Sheffield and Princess Marie Astrid. Earlier, in 1970–1, he had been very close to Camilla Shand (subsequently Camilla Parker Bowles and now his second wife).

Above: Charles and Camilla at a polo match in Cirencester Park in 1975. Their paths continued to cross after their initial romance foundered.

Above: In 1979 the Queen's cousin, Earl Mountbatten of Burma, congratulates Prince Charles after a polo success.

THE ROYAL FAMILY'S IMAGE

In the first 25 years of her reign Elizabeth II presided over an expanding family, with the births of Prince Andrew (1960) and Prince Edward (1964) and the growth to adulthood of her two older children, Charles and Anne. Charles passed through private school and attended Cambridge University, where he enjoyed taking part in student theatrical revues. Anne began official duties, married Captain Mark Phillips on 14 November 1973, survived a bungled kidnap attempt on 20 March 1974 outside Buckingham Palace and rose to become a prominent horsewoman.

Elizabeth steered the monarchy through the choppy waters of increasingly egalitarian times. She came face to face with symbols of change rather than avoiding them. In June 1965 she met the Beatles and awarded them the MBE. In 1976 she accepted that her sister's marriage to Lord Snowdon (Antony Armstong-Jones) was over and that the couple were to separate.

She also coped with many television-led 'modernizations' in the image and role of the royal family. These included the first televised Christmas broadcast (1957), the first TV documentary showing scenes of the private apartments in royal palaces (1966) and the first TV documentary showing scenes of the royal family's private life (1969). In the course of her reign, the monarch and the royal family had to accept more intrusive scrutiny than ever before.

THE END OF EMPIRE

Meanwhile the remaining British empire had been almost entirely broken up, with the grant of independence to former British colonies in Africa and south-east Asia. However, Elizabeth worked hard to maintain the importance of the Commonwealth. After 1949 it was no longer a requirement for Commonwealth countries to pledge 'an allegiance to the crown' (in the words of the 1926 Balfour report), which opened the way for republics such as India to join, but the British monarch still held an important role as symbolic figurehead. Ghana, which Elizabeth visited in 1961, was one of many former African and Caribbean colonies to join the Commonwealth, which increasingly gained the multiracial character that it has in the early 21st century.

Above: The Queen addresses a Silver Jubilee reception in Canberra, Australia, during a 'world tour' of official visits in 1977.

Right: Queen Elizabeth pioneered the 'royal walkabout', a new and informal way of meeting her subjects, in the 1970s.

CHARLES AND DIANA

A FAIRY TALE SOURED, 1977–1992

Prince Charles met his first wife, Lady Diana Frances Spencer, in November 1977 when he visited the country estate of Althorp, Northamptonshire, which belonged to her father John, 8th Earl Spencer. That year the prince had been romantically connected to Lady Diana's older sister, Lady Sarah Spencer, and Lady Diana was still a schoolgirl, at West Heath school, Sevenoaks, Kent.

BACKGROUND TO ROMANCE

The Spencer family were from the 'top drawer' of the British aristocracy and could trace their lineage back to Henry VII. Lady Diana did not excel academically at school, but she had the attributes expected of a young lady of her class, not least beauty and charm.

At the close of 1977 Lady Diana moved on to finishing school in Switzerland, before settling in London. She lived in Kensington on an inheritance from her great-grandmother, Lady Fermoy, and took a string of part-time jobs as a nanny. She met the Prince again in July 1980, at a party in Sussex. He proposed to her on 6 February 1981, and their engagement was made public on 24 February 1981.

Above: Lady Diana wore a £28,500 diamond and sapphire engagement ring as her engagement was announced.

THE WEDDING DAY

Prince Charles married Lady Diana Spencer in St Paul's Cathedral, London on 29 July 1981. The Archbishop of Canterbury, Robert Runcie, declared, 'This is the stuff of which fairy tales are made'. Diana's ivory silk crinoline wedding dress had a 'train' 25ft (7.5m) in length. The wedding was televised live in 74 countries, producing a global TV audience of 750 million people.

Below: After their wedding, Charles and Diana greeted the crowds from the balcony of Buckingham Palace.

The newlyweds spent their honeymoon on the royal yacht *Britannia* and then visited Balmoral. Almost at once the press began to suggest that all was not as it should be in the marriage. Diana appears to have been less than stimulated by the country pursuits favoured by the royal family and by the Prince's established group of friends. She quickly became pregnant, however, and their first child, a boy, was born on 21 June 1982 at St Mary's Hospital, Paddington). The baby prince, later christened William Arthur Philip Louis and known as Prince William, was third in line to the throne. A second son, Henry Charles Albert David, was born on 15 September 1984.

MARRIAGE AND THE MEDIA

As early as December 1981 the Queen appealed to British newspaper editors to give the Prince and Princess more privacy, but her efforts had little effect: the Waleses were a fatally fascinating couple for the media. Most early press coverage was supportive of Diana and far more critical of her husband, but rumours that she suffered from the eating disorder anorexia nervosa could not be silenced.

The Princess of Wales appears to have entered her marriage believing in the fairy-tale imagery of her romance and wedding, which had been so heavily publicized in the press. The royal marriage was conducted in the full glare of global press and television attention. By 1986–7, the marriage was in serious trouble. Both, by now, had probably taken lovers.

SCANDAL UPON SCANDAL

By the early 1990s the Waleses were in open conflict. Information was leaked to the press about the prince's extramarital affair with Camilla Parker Bowles and from the Prince's camp

Right: Prince Charles, Diana's brother Earl Spencer and Princes William and Harry were united in grief at the funeral.

came indications that Diana was driven by jealousy. The Prince of Wales asked the Queen for a formal separation on 25 November 1992, and this was made public in a House of Commons announcement on 9 December 1992.

Charles and Diana's public agony at the hands of the media continued after their formal separation in 1992. A transcript of a taped conversation between the prince and Camilla Parker Bowles, recorded in 1989, was published in January 1993 and proved publicly once and for all that Charles had been unfaithful to Diana. In 1994 Anna Pasternak's book *Princess in Love* revealed details of Diana's long love affair with Captain James Hewitt.

A ROYAL DIVORCE

The Queen saw that matters had to be brought to a head and proposed a swift divorce. Charles and Diana received their *decree nisi* on 15 July 1996 and their *decree absolute* on 28 August 1996. After the divorce, Diana lost her royal title and became Diana, Princess of Wales.

Following her divorce, Diana remained in the public eye with her high-profile charitable work. Her jet-setting holidays remained a draw for the press. On a Mediterranean cruise in July 1997, she met Dodi Al Fayed, eldest son of the hugely wealthy Egyptian businessman Mohamed Al Fayed, and spent much time with him over the summer.

On the night of Saturday 30 August 1997 Diana dined with Dodi at the Ritz Hotel in Paris. They left in her armoured Mercedes car, chased by a waiting pack of photographers. The ensuing car chase ended in tragedy when Diana's Mercedes crashed in an underpass beneath the Pont d'Alma. The driver and Dodi were killed instantaneously. Diana was taken to La Pitié-Salpêtrière Hospital where she was declared dead on Sunday 31 August.

THE PEOPLE'S PRINCESS

Diana's death provoked an extraordinary outpouring of public emotion in Britain. Crowds flocked to her London home, Kensington Palace, creating an ocean of around one million bouquets. Prime Minister Tony Blair declared her, 'The people's princess'. On Friday 5 September, the eve of the Princess's funeral, Queen Elizabeth made a television broadcast in which she paid glowing tribute to her former daughter-in-law as 'an exceptional and gifted human being'.

On Saturday, 6 September 1997 the princess's coffin was transported from Kensington Palace to Westminster Abbey. The carriage was followed on foot for the final mile with three million people lining the route.

The funeral was televised live in 187 countries around the world. Afterwards Diana's coffin was driven to the Spencer family estate of Althorp, where she was buried on an island in a lake.

A CITIZEN OF THE WORLD

In November 1997 South African President Nelson Mandela praised her work with the poor and sick, and hailed her as, 'One who became a citizen of the world through her care for people everywhere'. Diana's charitable work was an important part of her legacy. From the mid-1980s until her death, she represented a wide range of charities, including those supporting victims of AIDS and leprosy, the Red Cross, hospices, the marriage guidance body RELATE and refuges for abused women. In 1987 she visited the first British ward for AIDS victims. In 1997, Diana served as an International Red Cross VIP volunteer in the organization's campaign against landmines, helping lead the way for the signing of the Ottawa Treaty in December 1997.

Below: Prince Andrew's marriage to Sarah Ferguson, which began with high hopes in 1986, lasted only until March 1992.

GOLDEN AND DIAMOND JUBILEES

2002 AND 2012

In the months leading up to the celebrations planned for Elizabeth II's Golden Jubilee in 2002, the Queen lost both her mother, who died at the age of 101, and her sister Margaret. Criticism of the royal family's response to Diana's death had led to some anxiety in royal circles about public response to the Jubilee. In the event, the Queen's enduring popularity was triumphantly demonstrated in the nationwide celebrations of the 50th anniversary of her acccession.

Above: Walkabout 2002 style. The Queen was greeted by crowds wherever she went during the Golden Jubilee celebrations.

GOLDEN JUBILEE 2002

The celebrations climaxed in a four-day 'Jubilee Weekend' of festivities in London, beginning on Saturday 1 June, with a classical music concert at Buckingham Palace. The event, known as the 'Prom at the Palace', was attended by 12,000 people from across the UK who had been chosen by a ballot the previous March. On 2 June, a Sunday, the Queen and Prince Philip attended a service of thanksgiving at St George's Chapel, Windsor, while other members of the royal family attended Jubilee church services across the country.

On 3 June, another Buckingham Palace concert, this time of pop music and known as the 'Party at the Palace', was held. The Queen and all the members of her immediate family attended the concert. A crowd of 12,000 people within the grounds was supplemented by more than a million more gathered outside in the Mall, and the event was broadcast live on TV. On this day street parties were held in honour of the Jubilee, and in the evening of 3 June, Queen Elizabeth lit a beacon at the Queen Victoria Memorial in front of Buckingham Palace, the last in a worldwide line of beacons in an echo of the previous royal Golden Jubilee celebrated by Queen Victoria in 1887.

Below: Prince Charles declared the Queen Mother to be 'the most magical grandmother you could possibly have'.

PRIDE AND GRATITUDE

On 4 June the Queen processed with the Duke of Edinburgh in the golden state coach from Buckingham Palace via Temple Bar to a service of thanksgiving in St Paul's Cathedral and then, as in 1977, attended lunch at the Guildhall.

She declared herself 'Deeply moved' by the public acclamation of her reign, adding, 'Gratitude, respect and pride, these words sum up how I feel about the people of this country and the Commonwealth and what this Golden Jubilee means to me'. She also said,

Above: On 4 June 2002, the supersonic airliner Concorde led the Red Arrows display team in a celebratory Jubilee fly-past over the Mall and Buckingham Palace.

'I think we can all look back with measured pride on the achievements of the last 50 years'.

A Jubilee festival procession in the Mall was designed to celebrate the many changes in British life during the 50 years of Elizabeth II's reign. It also celebrated the great diversity of life and peoples in the Commonwealth.

AMERICAN TRIBUTE

New York City joined in the Queen's 50th anniversary celebrations when, on the evening of 4 June 2002, the Empire State Building was illuminated in her Golden Jubilee colours of purple and gold for several hours. It was the first time the building had been illuminated in tribute to a non-American since the visit of Nelson Mandela shortly after his release from prison in 1990. The tribute was in part a gesture of thanks to Queen Elizabeth for having ordered the playing of the American national anthem at Buckingham Palace two days after the terrorist attacks of 11 September 2001.

At its climax, 4,000 people from 54 Commonwealth countries paraded in national costume. The Anglo-French supersonic airliner, Concorde, led a celebratory fly-past, accompanied by the Red Arrows aerobatic display team.

Throughout the year the Queen made a series of celebratory trips throughout the Commonweath. These included visits to Jamaica, New Zealand, Australia and Canada.

DIAMOND JUBILEE 2012

Ten years on, Elizabeth II celebrated the Diamond Jubilee of her reign in 2012, becoming only the second British monarch – after Queen Victoria – to mark 60 years on the throne. Celebratory Big Jubilee lunches were held in more than 70 countries worldwide including Nigeria, Afghanistan, India, Nigeria, Nepal and South Africa; an estimated 8.5 million people in the UK took part. Other events included a Diamond Jubilee Pageant celebrating the Queen's State Visits and the Commonwealth at Windsor Castle in May, followed by celebrations on 2–5 June, including the lighting of 4,200 beacons in the UK, Channel Islands, Isle of Man, Overseas Territories and the Commonwealth. For the first time beacons were lit atop the highest mountains in England (Scafell Pike), Scotland (Ben Nevis), Wales (Mount Snowden) and Northern Ireland (Slieve Donard).

Above: The Spirit of Chartwell, *carrying Queen Elizabeth II and Prince Philip, leads the 2012 parade along the Thames to the delight of thousands of visitors.*

In the Thames Diamond Jubilee Pageant on 3 June 670 boats from the UK, the Commonwealth and around the world followed the royal barge the *Spirit of Chartwell*, along the River Thames from Chelsea to Tower Bridge. A floating belfry carrying eight Royal Jubilee Bells went before the flotilla; an estimated 1.2 million people watched from the riverbank. The following day a Diamond Jubilee Concert was held in front of Buckingham Palace. On 5 June a National Service of Thanksgiving was held in St Paul's Cathedral. The Queen rode in the 1902 State Landau from the Palace of Westminster to Buckingham Palace, then later appeared on the Palace balcony for an RAF flypast and a feu de joie – a rifle-fire salute given by the Queen's Guard.

In her Diamond Jubilee Message, Queen Elizabeth II said, "In this special year, as I dedicate myself anew to your service, I hope we will all be reminded of the power of togetherness and the convening strength of family, friendship and good neighbourliness."

THE ROYAL FAMILY TODAY

ACHIEVEMENTS AND PUBLIC DUTIES

On 6 February 2022 Queen Elizabeth II celebrated her Platinum Jubilee, marking a remarkable 70 years on the throne. She is the longest-reigning monarch in British history and the second-longest reigning monarch worldwide. Her eldest son, Charles, has served as Prince of Wales for half a century – a ceremony at Buckingham Palace on 7 March 2019, marked the 50th anniversary of Charles's investiture in Caernarfon in 1969. Moreover, following a series of royal marriages and births among the younger members of the family, the Queen is now a great-grandmother – a status achieved by few reigning monarchs.

Above: Charles, Harry and William on a skiing holiday in Switzerland in 2005.

ROYAL WEDDINGS

On 10 February 2005, Prince Charles announced that he was to marry Camilla Parker Bowles. The wedding was held in Windsor Guildhall on 9 April 2005. The civil marriage was followed by a service of prayer and blessing in St George's Chapel, led by the Archbishop of Canterbury, Rowan Williams, and attended by the Queen and Prince Philip, leading royals and 750 guests.

London was the setting for royal pageantry and celebrations in 2011 when the Queen's grandson Prince William, the new Duke of Cambridge, married Catherine (Kate) Middleton on 29 April at Westminster Abbey. William – second in line of succession to the throne after his father Charles – met Kate in 2001 when both were students at St Andrew's University, Scotland; they announced their engagement on 16 November 2010, when William gave Kate the sapphire and diamond ring given to his late mother Diana, Princess of Wales in 1981.

Two years later, the Duke and Duchess of Cambridge became parents, welcoming George Alexander Louis (born 22 July 2013), who became third in line to the throne. A daughter,

Below: Throughout her reign, the Queen has been renowned for the grace and good humour she brings to her public duties.

Below: Princess Anne, who competed in the 1976 Olympics, helped secure the 2012 games for London, in which her daughter Zara successfully competed.

Charlotte Elizabeth Diana, was born on 2 May 2015, and a second son, Louis Arthur Charles, on 23 April 2018.

Also in 2018, Prince William's younger brother Harry, the new Duke of Sussex, married the American actor Ms Meghan Markle in St George's Chapel, Windsor, on 19 May. The couple met in July 2016 and had announced their engagement on 27 November 2017.

The Los Angeles-born Ms. Markle, daughter of an African American mother and a white American father, described herself in an *Elle* magazine article as 'a strong, confident mixed-race woman'. As an actor she was best known for her long-running role in the TV show *Suits* in 2011–18 as a paralegal who became an attorney.

The following year the Duke and Duchess of Sussex celebrated the birth of their son, Archie Harrison (born 6 May 2019), who became seventh in the line to the throne. A daughter, Lilibet Diana, was born on 4 June 2021.

PRINCESSES MARRIED

On 29 July 2011 Zara Phillips (daughter of Anne, the Princess Royal and Captain Mark Phillips) married Mike Tindall, at the time captain of the England rugby team, at Canongate Kirk, Edinburgh. Zara, a successful equestrian athlete, gave birth to a daughter, Mia Grace Tindall, on 17 January 2014. A second daughter, Lena Elizabeth, was born on 18 June 2018. A son, Lucas Philip, was born on 21 March 2021.

Another of the Queen's granddaughters, Princess Eugenie of York – the daughter of Prince Andrew, Duke of York and Sarah, Duchess of York – married British wine merchant Jack Brooksbank in St George's Chapel, Windsor, on 12 October 2018. Their son, August Philip Hawke, was born on 9 February 2021.

Princess Eugenie's sister, Princess Beatrice – the elder daughter of Prince Andrew and the Duchess of York – married Italian nobleman and property developer Edoardo Mapelli Mozzo on 17 July 2020 at the Royal Chapel of All Saints, Royal Lodge, Windsor. (The wedding had been delayed from 29 May the same year as a result of the COVID-19 pandemic.) A daughter, Sienna Elizabeth, was born on 18 September 2021. Sienna is 11th in line to the throne and the Queen's 12th great-grandchild.

Above: Prince William and Kate exchange a kiss on the balcony at Buckingham Palace, after their wedding in April 2011.

'STEPPING BACK'

On 8 January 2020, the Duke and Duchess of Sussex announced that they were 'to step back as "senior" members of the royal family and work to become financially independent, while continuing to fully support Her Majesty the Queen.' They intended to split their time between Britain and North

Right: Prince Harry and Meghan Markle married at Windsor Castle in May 2018.

Right: Prince Charles poses with singer Laura Mvula and Prince's Trust Ambassadors during the Prince's Trust 'Invest in Futures' reception, London 2019.

America. Their statement said: 'After many months of reflection and internal discussions, we have chosen to make a transition this year in starting to carve out a progressive new role within this institution.'

A 12-month period of review was agreed with Buckingham Palace and the Queen issued a statement on 19 February 2021 confirming that the Duke and Duchess would not be returning to royal duties and were to relinquish honorary military appointments and royal patronages. The statement concluded, 'While all are saddened by their decision, The Duke and Duchess remain much-loved members of the family.'

ENVIRONMENTAL AND SOCIAL CONCERNS

Prince Charles has attempted to develop solutions for environmental and social problems. In 1976, he founded the Prince's Trust to help disadvantaged young people through practical support and training. Charles began to convert his Highgrove estate and Duchy Home Farm to organic methods in 1986. His Duchy Originals brand of organic foods was launched with an oat biscuit in early 1992.

Anne, the Princess Royal, is involved with more than 200 charities. After competing for the British equestrian team in the 1976 Olympics, she became a British representative in the International Olympic Committee and helped present London's campaign to host the 2012 Olympic Games.

Diana, Princess of Wales won many admirers for her campaigning and charitable work, and Princes William and Harry were keen to follow their mother's lead. In 2005, William became patron of the Tusk Trust, a non-profit

Below: Prince Harry and the Duchess of Sussex with their newborn son, Archie Harrison, during a photocall in May 2019.

Below: The Queen hosted a state banquet for President Obama and his wife Michelle in May 2011.

Above: Prince Harry spoke at the closing of the Invictus Games for injured army veterans in Orlando, Florida, in May 2016.

organization established to protect African wildlife. He has also been concerned to combat homelessness in the UK and to support the young. In early 2016, he established a working group, led by industry, to combat online bullying. Harry – who, like his brother, served in the UK armed forces – was inspired to support former service personnel. He founded the Invictus Games, a sporting contest for injured, sick or wounded former service personnel, and the first Games took place in London in 2014. These were followed by Games in Orlando, Florida in 2016, in Toronto in 2017, in Sydney in 2018 and the Hague in 2022, after twice being postponed due to the COVID-19 pandemic. Harry also built on his mother's work for AIDS sufferers when he co-founded the charity Sentebale (a name derived from local words meaning 'Don't forget me') in 2006 to support African children orphaned by the disease in Lesotho.

Mental health has been a major focus of the princes' work. In 2017, William and Harry, together with the Duchess of Cambridge, spearheaded the Heads Together mental health campaign with eight mental health charities to boost awareness and reduce the stigma of talking about mental health difficulties. On 15 May 2019, the Duke of Cambridge announced the Heads-Up mental health campaign with the Football Association, aiming to use the popular appeal of football to encourage men to start to talk about their mental health.

Prince William also became increasingly involved with the environmental concerns particularly associated with his father. In October 2020, he launched the Earthshot Prize, intended to drive development of environmental solutions over the following ten years. The same month he gave an online TED talk on environmental protections and conservation and appeared in an ITV programme focused on environmental protection, *Prince William: A Planet for Us All.* On 11 June 2021, William and the Duchess of Cambridge attended the Summit of the G7 – the intergovernmental group for leading industrial

PRINCES GIVE WAY TO THEIR OLDER SISTERS

The laws of succession to the throne were changed on 28 October 2011. Under existing laws, which dated back to the late 17th century, a male child outranked his older sisters in the line of succession, but under new provisions, which would have become effective if the first child of Prince William and the Duchess of Cambridge had been a girl, the first-born – boy or girl – will be next in line. All 16 of the Commonwealth countries that recognize the Queen as head of state (including Australia, New Zealand and Canada) granted their assent when the change was agreed at the Commonwealth Heads of Government Meeting in Perth, Australia. Rule changes will also allow a monarch to marry a Roman Catholic, although the monarch cannot be a Catholic, since as head of the Church of England the king or queen must be in communion with that church.

Right: Prince William, the Duchess of Cambridge and their three children gather on the balcony of Buckingham Palace after the Trooping of the Colour in June 2019.

Right: Princes Charles, William and Harry meet environmentalist David Attenborough at the world premiere of the BBC nature series Our Planet, *2019.*

nations – for the first time. Afterwards Prince William and the Duchess attended a reception at the Eden Project hosted by the Queen to discuss solutions to environmental problems.

Prince William, Prince Charles and Queen Elizabeth all addressed the COP26 Climate change Summit in Glasgow in October 2021. In a video message, Queen Elizabeth said the environment was a subject close to the heart of her late husband Prince Philip and added, 'It is a source of great pride to me that the leading role my husband played in encouraging people to protect our fragile planet lives on through the work of our eldest son Charles and his eldest son William.'

OFFICIAL VISITS

In May 2011, the Queen and Prince Philip made a state visit to the Republic of Ireland, the first by a British monarch since 1911. Their official trip to Australia in October 2011, the Queen's 16th since 1954, was described as her 'farewell tour' by some journalists on account of her age. However, in April 2014, she visited the Vatican and she made state visits to France in June 2014, and Germany in June 2015.

Meanwhile other members of the royal family have represented the UK around the world: in 2015, William visited Beijing and other cities in the first royal trip to mainland China since 1986 and, in April 2016, he and the Duchess of Cambridge made an official visit to India and Bhutan. In June 2018, William visited Israel and Palestine, the first royal to visit since the expiring of the British Mandate for Palestine in 1948. He and the Duchess of Cambridge visited Pakistan in October 2019, and then, as part of a tour marking the Queen's Platinum Jubilee visited Belize, Jamaica and the Bahamas, in March 2022.

The Duke and Duchess of Cornwall visited Ghana in November 2018 and became the first members of the royal family to visit Cuba when they made an official tour in March 2019. In March 2021, they visited Greece and, as part of the Queen's Platinum Jubilee celebrations, visited the Republic of Ireland in 24–25 March 2022 and undertook a three-day tour of Canada on 17–19 May 2022.

PRINCE PHILIP'S DEATH

Prince Philip, the Duke of Edinburgh, who had retired from royal duties on 2 August 2017 at the age of 96, died peacefully on 9 April 2021. Public commemorative events could not take place because of the COVID-19 pandemic. His funeral was on 17 April 2021 at St George's Chapel, Windsor Castle, and he was buried in the royal vault within the chapel. A Service of Thanksgiving was held at Westminster Abbey on 29 March 2022. Married to Queen Elizabeth from 6 February 1952 onwards, he was the longest-serving consort in British history.

Left: Due to COVID restrictions at the time of the funeral, Queen Elizabeth sits isolated from her family at St George's Chapel.

Above: In 2022, Parliament was opened by Prince Charles and the Duke of Cambridge as Counsellors of State.

SENIOR ROYAL ROLE

The Prince of Wales took on some of the most senior royal duties on behalf of his mother. Most notably, on 10 May 2022, Charles attended the State Opening of Parliament and delivered the Queen's Speech, outlining the government's legislative plans, on behalf of Queen Elizabeth. He was accompanied by Prince William in their role as Counsellors of State, and also by the Duchess of Cornwall. The Queen had missed the State Opening only twice before in her reign – in 1959 and 1963, when she was pregnant with first Prince Andrew and then Prince Edward. A statement indicated that she missed it in 2022 because of 'episodic mobility problems'.

Earlier in 2018, Commonwealth leaders chose Prince Charles to succeed the Queen in due course as head of the Commonwealth. And in November 2021, as the future head of the Commonwealth, Charles attended an official event marking the transition of Barbados from a constitutional monarchy to a parliamentary republic. He was the first royal ever to attend a ceremony marking such a transition.

CAMILLA, QUEEN CONSORT

Some saw these developments as part of preparations for Charles's eventual accession to the throne. In addition, the position of Camilla, Duchess of Cornwall, as future queen appeared to be strengthened. Following their wedding in 2005, it was understood that when Charles became king, Camilla would be known as Princess Consort. However, in her 2022 royal message issued as part of the Platinum Jubilee celebrations, Queen Elizabeth stated that it was her 'sincere wish' that Camilla be known as 'Queen Consort' when Charles acceded to the throne.

Earlier, on 9 June 2016, Queen Elizabeth appointed Camilla to the Privy Council. Prince William was appointed to the Council at the same time and commentators suggested that the Queen had taken the step because she was keen to ensure that both Camilla and William would be on the Accession Council that would meet to formally mark Charles's accession to the throne when the time came.

PLATINUM JUBILEE CELEBRATIONS 2022

Celebrations of Queen Elizabeth II's Platinum Jubilee were held throughout 2022, culminating in a weekend of events on 2–5 June. On 2 June, the Queen's Birthday Parade featured the traditional Trooping of the Colour and a military pageant on Horseguard's Parade in central London together with the firing of a Royal Gun Salute. The following days saw a Service of Thanksgiving at St Paul's Cathedral on 3 June, and on 4 June the Platinum Party at the Palace, a three-hour musical extravaganza before a crowd of 22,000 spectators, including 10,000 with tickets allocated by ballot and 7,500 reserved for key workers such as nurses. It was broadcast live on BBC television. On 5 June, Big Jubilee Lunches were held in the UK, the Commonwealth and beyond, and the Platinum Jubilee Pageant procession led by the Gold State Carriage and the Sovereign's Escort took place, culminating in the singing of the National Anthem, 'God Save the Queen'.

Right: Queen Elizabeth waves to the crowds from the balcony of Buckingham Palace, marking the end of the Platinum Jubilee Pageant procession.

INDEX

Page numbers in *italic* refer to information in captions